A Spirit of
Dialogue

A Spirit of

Dialogue

Incarnations of Ọgbańje,
the Born-to-Die,
in African American Literature

Christopher N. Okonkwo

The University of Tennessee Press
Knoxville

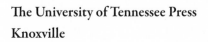

Copyright © 2008 by The University of Tennessee Press / Knoxville.
All Rights Reserved. Manufactured in the United States of America.
First Edition.

Quotations from *Wild Seed* © 1980 by Octavia E. Butler. Reprinted with
permission from the Estate of Octavia E. Butler.

Quotations from *Things Fall Apart* by Chinua Achebe are reprinted by
permission of Harcourt Education.

This book is printed on acid-free paper.

Library of Congress Cataloging-in-Publication Data

Okonkwo, Christopher N.
A spirit of dialogue : incarnations of Ogbanje, the born-to-die, in
African American literature / Christopher N. Okonkwo. — 1st ed.
    p. cm.
Includes bibliographical references and index.
ISBN-13: 978-1-57233-615-5 (hardcover)
ISBN-10: 1-57233-615-3 (hardcover)
1. American literature—African American authors—History and criticism.
2. English literature—20th century—History and criticism. 3. Myth in litera-
ture. 4. Mourning customs in literature. 5. African Americans—Intellectual life.
6. African Americans in literature. 7. Death in literature. I. Title.

PS153.N5O38 2008
813'.540915   2007038322

To my infant son,

Ogochukwu,

in whom I daily witness
God's infinite goodness

Contents

Acknowledgments

In some respects, it has taken almost twenty years to write this book, dating back to my undergraduate days at the University of Nigeria, Nsukka. It was at UNN that, as the editor of the silver-anniversary volume (no. 18, November 1988) of *The Muse: The Literary Journal of the English Association at Nsukka*, I wrote an opinion in which appears a statement that in hindsight marks the beginnings of my cultural, theoretic, critical, and philosophic interest in the spirit child. I recall asserting in that piece how, in the article he sent *The Muse,* Bernth Lindfors observed that small magazines published on the continent at the time were generally short-lived. They suffered, the editorial assented, from the spirit child syndrome. Ọgbañje and àbíkú—appearing and disappearing, shape-changing, surviving, returning and yearning for (more) life, this time in African American literature.

In the many years that it has taken for that editorial remark to evolve into this book, I have benefited immensely from the support, encouragement and wisdom of various people: teachers, colleagues, students, friends and family members too many to mention in full here. I owe them all a hefty debt of gratitude. The University of Missouri–Columbia (UMC) Research Board granted my application for research leave in 2003–4. I thank Elaine Lawless and the UMC's Center for Arts and Humanities (CAH) for travel and other grants. I cannot compliment enough the staff of Ellis library's interlibrary loan office, especially Rebekah Wilson, who processed my numerous requests and also expeditiously tracked down both scarce and new titles. Many thanks go also to the staff of the Research Library, Institute of African Studies, University of Nigeria, Nsukka, for their assistance during my 2004 fieldwork in Nigeria. I am grateful to Maxine Lavon Montgomery, Jerrilyn McGregory, Hunt Hawkins, Darryl Dickson-Carr, Chanta Haywood and Maxine Jones, who encountered this project in its infancy but might now be surprised, pleasantly I hope, at the radically different direction and dimensions the study has taken. Thank you, particularly, Darryl and Jerrilyn, for taking time to critique some draft chapters. My gratitude goes equally to my current and former colleagues at the University of Missouri–Columbia—Anand Prahlad,

Karen Piper, Geta LeSeur, Tom Quirk, Devoney Looser, April Langley, the late Julius Thompson, Flore Zephir, K. C. Morrison, Tola Pearce, Pat Okker, Jeffrey R. Williams, Maureen Konkle, Jeffrey J. Williams, Howard Hinkel, Robert Weems, and JoAnne Banks-Wallace—who either appraised working portions of the study or were supportive. I recognize also the students in my course "The Mystical as Theme and Mode in Africana Literature," especially Christina Williams, for their invigorating enthusiasm and cultural insight.

I acknowledge, with deep gratitude, The Rev. Dr. Anthony Ekwunife, John Edgar Wideman, and Tananarive Due for kindly obliging my requests for interviews. I thank these scholars, academic colleagues and friends at other institutions for their generosity with valuable insights and leads: Ernest Emenyonu, Anthonia Kalu, Okey Ndibe, Emmanuel Obiechina, Gay Wilentz, Chika Okeke-Agulu, Abiola Irele, Dolan Hubbard, Obiwu Iwuanyanwu, Rolland Murray, Ossie Enekwe, Lisa Godfrey, Stanley Ogbonna, Johnston Njoku, G. Ugo Nwokeji, Sabine Jell-Bahlsen, Chris Aniedobe, Douglas McCabe, Lisa Lakes, Nadia Johnson, Olu Oguibe, and Olayinka Oyegbile. Thank you, too, Chante Baker, Lily Mabura, and NaImah Ford for your research and other assistance.

This book has become a reality because of Scot Danforth, the University of Tennessee Press's Acquisitions Editor, whose immediate and unwavering interest in the study boosted my own faith in it and energized me to the finish line. Thank you, the press's external and in-house readers, for strongly recommending publication. I thank also the press's managing editor, Stan Ivester, for his expertise and guidance, and its freelance copyeditor Evelyn Schlatter for helping sharpen my argument and prose. And last though hardly the least, in writing this book I have been sustained by the prayers and support of my parents, my father Maazi Jacob Okonkwo (Ochetere Ochie) and my mother Agnes Okonkwo (Ezi-Agbo, Ezi Nne), my brothers, sisters, other relatives, and close friends. Deserving a most special recognition is my wife, Ijeoma (Ijay), whose love, patience, understanding, and sacrifices strengthened and calmed me even at those moments of uncertainty.

Parts of chapters 1 and 6 have appeared in different versions in my essay, "A Critical Divination: Reading Sula as Ogbanje-Abiku" *African American Review* 38.4 (Winter 2004). I thank the journal for permission to reprint material.

# Note on Orthography

I tone-marked the key words "ogbanje" and "abiku." I have, however, refrained from putting diacritics on "ogbanje" and "abiku" where both words appear originally without stress marks in the titles of books, short stories, poems, and essays, and in character names, within a sentence, or passages quoted verbatim. In addition, when quoting directly I have retained the spellings of other Igbo and Yoruba words if unstressed originally. I italicized any Igbo phrases or sentences to which I added subscript dots. And unless they appear differently in original texts, I also have intentionally left "ogbanje" and "abiku" unitalicized in their various syntactic structures in this book simply to underscore that the terms have now been so sufficiently employed in titles and scholarship as to warrant regular orthography. Words such as "dibia" and "babaláwo" are italicized only the first time used. The consistent uppercase O in the spelling of Ọgbañje adheres to the press's house style.

Introduction An Aesthetic (Re)Mark
on the Spirit Child

[T]he whole of us in this town are burglers [*sic*] and we have burgled uncountable earthly women in every town, country and village. . . . we are [the] "born and die."

Amos Tutuola
My Life in the Bush of Ghosts

[Ekwefi] had borne ten children and nine of them had died in infancy, usually before the age of three. As she buried one child after another her sorrow gave way to despair and then to grim resignation. The birth of her children, which should be a woman's crowning glory, became for Ekwefi mere physical agony devoid of promise. The naming ceremony after seven market weeks became an empty ritual. Her deepening despair found expression in the names she gave her children. One of them was a pathetic cry, Onwumbiko—"Death, I implore you." But Death took no notice; Onwumbiko died in his fifteenth month. The next child was a girl, Ozoemena—"May it not happen again." She died in her eleventh month, and two others after her. Ekwefi then became defiant and called her next child Onwuma—"Death may please himself."

After the death of Ekwefi's second child, Okonkwo had gone to a medicine man, who was also a diviner of the Afa Oracle, to inquire what was amiss. This man told him the child was an *ogbanje*. . . .

Chinua Achebe
Things Fall Apart

Professor, she said, I really think Tupac is an ogbanje.

A former student

A few days after watching the documentary *Tupac: Resurrection* (2003), a former student in my course on West African cosmological precepts in African diaspora literature called at my office. She asked—or, rather, she could not wait to ask—if I had seen the documentary film featuring [the "living dead" rapper] Tupac Shakur.[1] No, I responded, not yet. "Professor," she urged, "you've got to see it! I really think Tupac is an ogbanje. He's got to be an abiku. I'm serious."

In their simplified and conflated meanings, the Igbo word ogbanje (pronounced "Ọgbañje") and the Yoruba term abiku (àbíkú) are culturally specific yet ideologically related names by which the Igbo and Yoruba of Nigeria denominate and grapple with experiences associated with a special category of children. These children are part-human and part-spirit beings. They are also believed to go through a pattern of repeated births, deaths and rebirths to and through the same mother. An aspect of Igbo and Yoruba material existence, metaphysics, and mythic consciousness, the Ọgbañje and àbíkú are assumed to engage in this scheme of transitory and transitive earthly returns with sinister motives, including torturing the mother into believing that she has conceived "normal" children who have come to *stay* in the human world.

When a gnostic diviner—a *dibia* in Igboland or a *babaláwo* in the Yoruba case—determines that a child is such an entity, as Achebe depicts above, parents generally undertake prescribed ritual interventions. They might name the child symbolically, inflict punitive marks on its cadaver, and/or deny it proper burial rites. These measures are designed to make the child *stay* if it reincarnates. In juxtaposing Tupac and the spirit child, my student and I were eliciting the two taxonomies to illuminate Tupac's complicated yet intriguing ontology: his energy, tattoo-*marked* body, rebelliousness, zest for life, obsession with (premature) death and dying, and his insinuations that he would return, postmortem.[2] More crucially, however, we were alluding to the concepts' trans-Atlantic migration, their crosscultural applicability and enormous, aesthetic allure which a number of African American writers of neo-slave narratives have long recognized. In their novels—which repeat, revise, echo, and/or extend adaptations of the beliefs in postcolonial African fiction, namely, *Things Fall Apart* (1958) and Ben Okri's *The Famished Road* (1991)—the spirit child has incarnated. It has taken some New World shapes and performances.

This study investigates those explicit literary re-adaptations, the tropological resonances, as well as the mediative power of the idea of spirit child in and for works of contemporary African American literature. Using the designations Ọgbañje-àbíkú, spirit child, child spirit, born-and-die, born-to-die, and particularly Ọgbañje/born-to-die intentionally and interchangeably to refer to the same mythic concept,[3] I read closely Octavia Butler, Tananarive Due, and John Edgar Wideman's novels in which the idea is consciously reconstructed and resounded as title, character, theme, plot device, and epistemology. I also discuss two of Toni Morrison's novels. Although the characters in the Morrison texts are seemingly less deliberately constructed and specifically identified in terms of "ogbanje" myth, as in Butler's and Wideman's texts, or "born-to-die," as in Due's, an assessment of her works is nevertheless a vital aspect of this study because the two novels interrogated evince the belief's cultural, conceptual and philosophic extensions. Later, I invoke the literal and cryptogrammic status of the spirit child as an intersectionist, a blues-like unifier of superficially incompatible epistemes, to further relate the focal African American novels and novelists in a shared continuum of African diaspora cosmology, culture and experience.

Butler, Due, Wideman and Morrison have found in the spirit-child fount, indeed in "[the] human drama"[4] that is the experience of born-to-die, what Houston A. Baker Jr., describing the blues matrix, appropriately calls "the symbolically anthropological."[5] They have mobilized aspects of this mythic spectacle of spirits-versus-humans as cultural mnemonics. They re-channel its epistemic frequencies also to frame their characters, design narrative interiors, and negotiate inextricably racial, historical, gendered, maternal, political, philosophic, and artistic questions related to the lives of Africans and their descendants enslaved in a hostile New World and still unjustly treated in both life and totalizing white-master narratives. As Jacqueline de Weever writes, in concurrence with such literary appropriation, "The experiences of black people in the New World, into which they have been forcibly thrust against their will, cannot be told or treated in realistic or naturalistic traditions in which much of American literature has been cast—the pain of the results of three centuries of oppression is too great to be faced and confronted in a realistic mode. Such an experience demands another mode for which mythic narrative is more appropriate." Walter Mosley could not agree more. He believes that those racial plights of which de Weever speaks account for black writers' attraction to science fiction. "The genre speaks most clearly to those who are dissatisfied with the way things are," Mosley asserts, " . . . those who have been made to feel powerless. . . . Black people have been cut off from their African ancestry by the scythe of slavery and from an American heritage by being excluded from history. For us, science [and mythic] fiction offers an alternative where that which deviates from the norm is the norm."[6]

The authors under study seek then an (ab)normal metaphor capable of coalescing form and content, and re-interpreting in fiction the complexities of the African, African American, and indeed African diaspora experience. They know that literature's affectivity—its ability to move us so profoundly—is tied to its mythic character and, significantly, that myth encapsulates a culture's ways of being, seeing, remembering, and doing in the world.[7] To the authors, therefore, the idea of Ọgbañje/born-to-die is "an optimum," a rubric that resolves the discrepancies of discourse,[8] the patterns and paradoxes of life.

If dated from the appearance of the Ọgbañje character and the patternist-precursor Doro in Butler's *Mind of My Mind* (1977), one could say that the "Ọgbañje" rubric has had a thirty-year presence in African American literature. Its advent and permutations in African American texts can be attributed to a convergence of factors. They include but are not limited to: the impact of Achebe's *Things Fall Apart;* the 1960s emergence of the contemporary neo-slave narrative; the 1960s and 1970s black consciousness/Black Power movement and the cultural agenda, gendered politics, and centripetal philosophy of the Black Arts movement's nationalist aesthetic; African American identity questions of the post–civil rights and the multicultural eras; and the thematic shifts, as well as the African diaspora orientation of African American fiction of the post-nationalist aesthetic period. We shall get to those in more detail. Suffice it to say for now that, were it the case that "Ọgbañje" has had a three-decade narrative existence in the African American novel, then that long presence should have some bearing on how we study, teach, and critique Butler, Due, and Wideman's neo-slave texts. It ought to inform our "source" study and our instruction of African American literature in general, especially given the interconnections of these authors and African American literature to African literary and other cultural productions.

African American writers' interest in born-to-die theme, along with the theme's facility to deepen our appreciation of two of Morrison's most celebrated stories *Sula* (1973) and the Pulitzer Prize–winning *Beloved* (1987), has yet to receive a contextualized and complicative treatment in studies of contemporary African American fiction. Cultural anthropologists, folklorists, linguists, literary theorists, semioticians, and critics have already helped prime that treatment by unraveling North American Africanisms, their provenances, and continued expression in African American culture, art, and literature. Unfortunately, and perhaps understandably, the words "Ọgbañje" and "àbíkú" or any of their numerous West/ African synonyms are scarcely two of those cultural and philosophic retentions invoked repeatedly and in their specificities. Other than, say, Bonnie Barthold's allusion to the *"ogbanje* cycle" in *Black Time: Fiction of Africa, the Caribbean, and the United States* (1981),[9] it would take the appearance of *Beloved* six years later for criticism to start exploring the concepts relative to the African American novel. Nevertheless, except for Chikwenye Okonjo Ogunyemi's engaging discussion of

Ọgbañje-àbíkú's evocations of mother-child relationship in *Beloved* in "An Abiku-Ogbanje Atlas" (2002),[10] other critical commentaries on Beloved's Ọgbañje/born-to-die linkages are cursory at best. This is because the remarks in question focus predominantly either on other issues and novels or on different matters raised in *Beloved*.[11] Also, although much of the scholarship on Butler's and Wideman's works under study has been culturally sensitive, politically informed, and theoretically enlightening, the discussions often read as though the morpheme Ọgbañje has little or no expandable hermeneutical import in the novels. As for Due, who has emerged recently as one of the most prolific and widely recognized new names in contemporary African American fiction, there is little attention to her fast growing canon. Nor is there much on, specifically, the cultural origins, thematic trajectory, and formal implications of the "born-to-die" principle/characters in her first and cornerstone debut *The Between*.[12]

Regardless of how one views this critical lacuna, a problem remains. The risk is that, as in situations in which African American or African diaspora novels with definite or decipherable impresses of African religious, spiritual, and/or philosophical principles are evaluated either using imposed Eurocentric theoretical and critical apparatuses or without due regard to context, readers might have been under-appraising Butler's *Wild Seed* (1980) and *Mind of My Mind* and Wideman's *The Cattle Killing* (1996). Teachers, students, and critics might have been studying them all these years without the benefit of at least a culturally grounded understanding of the idea of Ọgbañje, the influencing treatment of the experience in *Things Fall Apart,* as well as other specificities of Igbo world, history, and thought that both Butler and Wideman (trans)planted in their works.

For instance, Anyanwu is the name of the powerful, mythic female protagonist in Butler's patternist series that begins chronologically with *Wild* and *Mind*. However, many might be unfamiliar with exactly who or what "Anyanwu" is in Igbo world. Other than noting that in Igboland Anyanwu means literally "sun," we do not always build upon Butler's interview statement that her prototype for Anyanwu is the Onitsha/Igbo mythic shape-shifter Atagbusi. And perhaps not many readers are aware also that Anyanwu's authority in the novels heightens when seen in light of the Igbo sun-deity after which Anyanwu is named. Nor is it widely disseminated that, as a survivor, a healer *and* mother toughened after losing several of her children, Anyanwu relates to and collapses the powerful Agbala priestess Chielo and Okonkwo's resilient wife Ekwefi, who lost most of her offspring in infancy in *Things Fall Apart*—the novel whose portrayal of Ọgbañje mentors Butler's framing of Doro's character traits. By making the enslaved and rebellious Igbo woman Anyanwu a mythic racial foremother, Butler negotiates discussions of slavery. More important, she tables as one of her thematic agendas the under-appreciated Igbo heritage of black America and the African diaspora.

Moreover, Wideman scholars note consistently that *The Cattle Killing* is a demanding postmodern novel. They generally implicate the amorphousness of postmodernism in the novel's structural and linguistic ploys. But as earlier hinted, one might not immediately suspect that it is also the cosmologic, mythic, and met-aphoric grammars of Ọgbañje that Wideman calligraphed and skillfully maneu-vered into the novel to complicate its characterization, narration, self-reflexivity, and semantic difficulty. It is also in comprehending the idea of "àbíkú," which articulates death as an existential certainty (as in born-to-die), that Hilton James's dilemmas achieve greater clarity and coherence in Due's *The Between* (1995), a work that echoes Okri's *Famished Road*. In short, several studies have scrutinized science, mythic and historical black fiction, neo-slave narratives, and African and African American cultural, experiential, and literary ties. They have yet to stress, however, the fascinating indentations of the paradigm of Ọgbañje/born-to-die and especially *Things Fall Apart* on African American literary production since the 1960s. And for that, the need for a rigorous explication grows.

This book's objective throughout is to help shrink that lingering gap. I do that by tracing the West African cultural and formal impresses. I furnish the anthropo-logical, socio-historical, political, and philosophic context against which the Afri-can American writers' (re)constructions of the born-to-die premise should also be understood. And then I explore the conjunctive possibilities of the spirit child idiom for the writers and works under study. I elaborate these constitutive goals in three contiguous discussions that organize this book. I aim, first, to offer that afore-stated backdrop and then examine to what "new" concerns Butler, Due and Wideman have consciously (re)visioned "Ọgbañje" and "born-to-die" mythic themes in that black discursive praxis of repetition-with-a-difference. I call their novels—*Wild Seed* and its genealogical continuation *Mind of My Mind, The Between* and *The Cattle Killing*—"Ọgbañje/born-to-die *imprinted* neo-slave nar-ratives" or simply *imprinted* novels, texts. The phrase emphasizes that the cultural definitions and epistemological convictions that the ideas "Ọgbañje" and "born-to-die" encode are retained purposely in the narratives. It conveys also that the beliefs' nominal presence in the novels is identifiable and "in print." Furthermore, the classification authorizes a differentiation of the imprinted narratives from the numerous other African American and African diaspora texts related to the focal novels in having obvious and/or concealed themes of the ancestor, the supernatu-ral, rebirth, reincarnation, and predestination. This classification also distinguishes the primary works from other stories that feature children whose (para)normal powers recall Ọgbañje and àbíkú as belief, entity, experience, and allegory.

Sula and its posited "sequel" *Beloved* best illustrate such related texts. As earlier hinted, the two works are discussed on the basis of figural and ideological equivalencies for which I designate both novels "spirit child *imbricated* neo-slave narratives." In other words, *Sula* and *Beloved* exemplify the *imbricated* tier because, although neither the word "Ọgbañje" nor its Anglicization "born-to-die" or "born-and-die" is mentioned anywhere in either text, Morrison's portraitures of the novels' title children Sula and Beloved are so nuanced they evoke Achebe. More specifically, they mirror the ontology and the experiences of *Things Fall Apart*'s Ọgbañje figure Ezinma, against who Sula and Beloved are read. Not only that, dilating African American texts such as *Sula* and *Beloved* as imbricated fiction contributes substantially to our appreciation of the extent to which the cosmologic and ideologic tributaries of born-to-die can help us interpret other African diaspora novels' corresponding interests in character, theme, form, and philosophy.

Moreover, if the spirit child's conceptual elasticity helps shape and also augments a better grasp of the imprinted and imbricated novels, then the belief can be viewed, *mutatis mutandis,* as a "ground plan."[13] As foundation, it functions as an infrastructure on which character profiles are sketched, as well as a language that consolidates the African American novels' conscious and incidental interplays with African fiction and with each other. I propose, then, that we imagine the works' numerous intersections in the context of conversation, one that ultimately affirms not Death but Life itself, particularly black life in its blues-like ups, downs, triumphs, and sublimities in a New World that delimits black racial humanity. The United States in this case is a nation where, like the beleaguered parents of an Ọgbañje, African-descended people persevere, believing that better days are ahead, for this, too, shall pass.

For many Igbo and Yoruba people, the words Ọgbañje and àbíkú would not conjure up the blues or the sublime. The terms most likely would not emanate positive pictures or memories, even in casual conversation. In fact, some of the names grieving parents give their spirit children and the postmortem scarring or "marks" they inflict on them are seen in the public imagination, and often lopsidedly, as semiotics of negativity. Therefore, for the spirit child to serve as the platform of the dialogue envisioned in this book, I am *re-marking* (on) it aesthetically in the manner of what Kimberly W. Benston phrases as the black regenerative act of (un)naming. In "I yam what I yam: the topos of (un)naming in Afro-American literature," Benston notes how black people have historically had to engage in what might be called experiential and semantic deconstruction.[14]

This is their willed tendency to disempower pejoratives and daily turn "death" into life. They have had to purge the stench from those socio-linguistic toxins directed at them in a hostile environment by retrofitting the foulness in a more self-enabling light. Mikhail Bakhtin subscribes also to this enactment of linguistic de-otherization. Bakhtin reminds us that in its dynamism and relationality, language—indeed the socially originated, targeted and unstable word—occupies no fixed boundaries and significations. It would not assume agency without contextualization and pollination with each speaker's or each user's intonation and purpose.[15]

Accordingly then, I want to give the largely semantically negativized *spirit* child a rather positive, constructivist job. Instead of denoting singularly or predominantly that disembodied succubus that causes mothers a lot of pain by robbing them of children, the idea connotes also in this study a spirit of dialogue. That is, it is (1) a "spirit," a principle, a force, that animates characters and texts and also (2) creates the occasions of comparability and discursive cooperation among them in meaning-production. In other words, it signifies in the Epilogue, particularly, but also for the entire study the ascribed state of mind of the authors and works under examination. The spirit child arbitrates, in this case, a congress of mutually slavery- and racism-incited and thus thematically congruent African diaspora texts that academic and market forces make us territorialize as "postcolonial," "science," "speculative," "fantasy," "horror," "supernatural," "futurism," "postmodern," and "magical realism."

In its new and expanded charge, the idea of the spirit child has ample conceptual room for "difference." It has space enough for the diversity of the imprinted and imbricated narratives, regardless of their racial and gendered politics, technical choices, canonical standings, and commercial designations. Following comparativist reviews of the West African and African American novels, the texts and authors are brought together in the Epilogue in an analyst-involved conversation, in *a spirit of dialogue.* Contributing their voices, as communicative and rhetorical social texts,[16] to the grand discourse of African American and African diaspora experience—the illumination of which has been the prime business of the African American novel since its inception[17]—the focal New World texts are "talking."[18] They are sharing visions and, more important, making persuasive statements about the continuum of black life, from its beginnings in Africa, hinted in Butler's histo-mythic and narrative return to pre-colonial Igbo world, through the contemporary period of neo-slave narratives and postmodern black subjectivity and text.

As the centered works show, if the postmodern black text seems to disengage with socioliterary realism and instead indulge in "anomalous" formal experimentation, it is not for art's sake alone. Nor is it also to playfully abandon narrative comprehensibility, "attack or assault reality," adopt a Western "vertical, domination-subordination, dualistic, and dialectical logic,"[19] kill the despotic author,[20] or simply to rupture naturalizing notions of being and identity. Rather, even as they help express authorial distrust of sweeping narratives of history, knowledge, and truth, the black text's stylistic deviations also draw attention, ironically, to *the* reality, the known historical fact of slavery, as well as the continued significance of race, racism, culture, and difference.[21]

Likewise, if Butler, Due, Wideman, and Morrison's cross-mappings of the spirit child theme seem to be effortless, knowing and profound, it is not solely because of the existence and illuminative examples of Achebe's and Okri's works. It is more so because the notion of spirit children or, more precisely, constituent properties of the belief in Ọgbañje/born-to-die are apparently syncretized and thus have empirical as well as epistemological counterparts and continuities in African American folk culture and thought dating back to the antebellum years. For example, as research has shown, enslaved Africans in the New World, in Virginia, South Carolina and beyond, dealt with the malaria-implicated and life-threatening hemoglobin disorder Sickle Cell Disease (SCD). The various complications of this devastating condition were manifested in numerous miscarriages and unexplained, repeated infant deaths among bondswomen. The complications were evident also as slave sicknesses that planters mislabeled simply as rheumatic pains and chronic leg ulcers. The sickle cell disorder survives not just in Africa but also in contemporary black America,[22] as many African Americans today are coping with the ailment. Due partly to interracial blood mixing, aggressive modern medical intervention, social programs, and health education, however, the spread and terminality of SCD have considerably declined in the United States.

That SCD is suspected in the evolution of the belief in born-to-die children, particularly on the West coast of Africa, is significant. In addition, African American folk and spiritual convictions on maternity, abnormal births, children with special powers, maternal child care, infant mortality, conjuration, divination, the-seventh-son-of-a-seventh-son, magic, double-sightedness, cosmic signs, the reciprocity of life and death, burial customs, rebirth, and intrafamilial reincarnation, the question of good and evil, naming rituals rooted in birth order, kinship, and events, birth marks, the existence of ghosts, the actions of powerful and traveling spirits, possession, and haunting[23] compel one to wonder if the belief in born-and-die children did not make it "intact" to North America.

Let me quickly add that between 1700 and 1810, for instance, nearly 1.2 million Bight of Biafrans,[24] as well as an equally astounding number of Yoruba men, women, and children were exported as slaves. And in North America, many of the Igbo captives were sent from the Sea Island coasts of South Carolina and Georgia to the northern plantations of Virginia and Maryland. As Michael A. Gomez points out, "The sheer size of the Igbo contingent to North America is stunning.

The Bight of Biafra, the Igbo's region of origin, accounted for nearly one-quarter of the total number of Africans imported into North America, placing it in a virtual first-place tie with West Central Africa."[25] Reinforcing A. E. Afigbo's remark that the Igbo "are probably the least studied of any African people of their size,"[26] Gomez cogently adds:

> It is beyond credulity [therefore] that the Igbo, a group with such profound impact upon African American society, has received so little recognition in the scholarly literature on North American slavery. In numerable studies on the continuity of African culture in the New World, much is made of the contributions of the Yoruba, the Akan, the Fon and the Ewe, the Bakongo, and so on. Although richly deserved, the attention afforded these groups has tended to minimize the signal contribution of the Igbo, who for reasons better explored elsewhere, have not enjoyed similar prominence and popularity.[27]

These Igbo Africans brought their language, religious memories, folk practices, political tastes and social tendencies with them, as Douglas B. Chambers also intimates in *Murder at Montpelier: Igbo Africans in Virginia* (2005). And, like Butler who suggests that slavery unwittingly transplanted also a pre-contact and extant Igbo god "Anyanwu" in North America, Wideman reckons that the belief in Ọgbañje most likely survived the Middle Passage into black American spirituality. But because "languages were stripped from us in the New World, systematically stripped," Wideman asserts in a personal interview, " . . . we lost words like 'ogbanje' as a group of people and English equivalents took their places."[28]

An instructive remark, Wideman's affirmation adds to the many voices that have contested sociologist E. Franklin Frazier's position that the exigencies of captivity in the Old World, the trans-Atlantic crossing, and New World slavery proper obliterated all vestiges of African cultural anamnesis from Africans enslaved in North America (9). Wideman's intervention is also anticipated and supported by Henry H. Mitchell, who maintains that if enslaved Africans took to Christianity, it was in part because they found its stories, parables, personages, rituals, and sacraments to be compatible with ethos, concepts and practices already in place in their syncretistic sacred religions.[29]

This study is indebted to the groundwork already produced by researchers on the subject of African religious and cultural retentions in the New World. It leans also on vast scholarship on mythology, the antebellum slave narrative, abolitionist discourse, the neo-slave narrative, black science, speculative, mythic, and historical fiction, call-and-response, signifyin(g), intertextuality, dialogue, and postmodernism relative to African American literature.[30] In addition to drawing also upon semiotics, conversation studies, critical race theories, and formal and informal interviews I had with Wideman and Due, I derive more impetus from my 2004 fieldwork in Nigeria and in pertinent findings shared in the body of anthropological, cultural, and clinical-psychiatric research on Ọgbañje and àbíkú beliefs and real-life cases. The book builds also upon the criticisms of the many Ọgbañje- and àbíkú-imprinted works in written Nigerian literature.[31]

All of this might lead one to ask: why localize the study? Why the stress on Nigeria, especially on Igbo cosmology and the Igbo and Yoruba cultural strains of the belief, if the idea of born-to-die children is evidently not peculiar to both groups but rather pervades the socio-religious imaginaries of West/African people? Put less tactfully, is this book part of what Gerhard Kubik has cynically dubbed "the Nigerianization of African-American studies, notably since Henry Louis Gates Jr.'s *The Signifying Monkey*" (22)?

Far from it. As I stated earlier, one reason for the book's geo-cultural perimeter has to do with the staggering antebellum Igbo and Yoruba presences in the New World. Besides, it is Nigerian writers who along with their international critical readerships have done perhaps the most remarkable job of exploiting and popularizing the concept of born-to-die entities. In addition and consistent with my earlier remark on the need to contextualize critiques of culturally inspired (African diaspora) texts, particularly those works that state or intimate their ethnic and/or cultural underpinnings, focusing on the Igbo and the Yoruba roots this book in place. My methodology is analogous, then, to Teresa N. Washington's recent study *Our Mothers, Our Powers, Our Texts: Manifestations of Àjẹ́ in Africana Literature* (2005). It compares also with Keith Cartwright's *Reading Africa into American Literature: Epics, Fables, and Gothic Tales* (2002), in which Cartwright, reading "America's Africanity," emphasizes the Senegambia region as his "African reference point and the American South as [his] primary crossroads of study."[32]

As it allows for warranted broadenings of subjects at hand, this book's approach also checks the temptation to essentialize "Africa." It refrains from the urge to African-diasporize Ọgbañje and àbíkú specifically and hence overindulge in, as Roland Barthes would say, the pleasure of the text—or, in this case, the pleasure of the trope. Thus, this book makes no pretensions at exhaustiveness. To reiterate Houston A. Baker Jr.'s famous caveat: every explanatory model and attempt is innately eclectic and thus can only advance an imperfect vista of the universe.[33] Therefore, for instance, Alden Reimonenq's short story "Snail" (1998) and Deidre L. Badejo's poem "Tokunbo: A Divination Poem" (1989), which feature an àbíkú character and invoke the àbíkú concept, respectively, are not treated here as discrete chapters. Nor is Beth Bosworth's time-travel novel *Tunneling* (2003), a work that depicts an unusual, white, New Jersey child/protagonist Rachel Finch whom the character Albert—a Chinua Achebe figure in the story—identifies as an Ọgbañje. I address "Snail," "Tokunbo" and *Tunneling* in the Epilogue, to further demonstrate the spirit child's conceptual capacity to inspire a theory of character and also interconnect works intergenerationally and interracially.

In addition, *Wild Seed* and *Mind of My Mind* are units of Butler's "patternist" series that also includes, in plot sequence, *Clay's Ark* (1984), *Survivor* (1978) and *Patternmaster* (1976). I concentrate on *Wild Seed* and *Mind of My Mind,* however, for two major reasons. Other than the more pragmatic goal of project management, the two novels are key texts, indeed the historical genesis of the series. As prequels, they present the ancestors of the patternists, Doro and Anyanwu. An understanding of the two works as founding pieces is imperative. They are two of Butler's three slavery narratives, along with *Kindred* (1979) which Butler says was originally intended as a segment of the sequence. But Butler kept *Kindred* as a discrete story, however, because of its demand for greater realism.[34]

Therefore, a cultural knowledge of "Ọgbañje" becomes crucial for a thoroughgoing evaluation of the entire patternist corpus. It is needed equally for a deeper study of *Kindred*'s heroine, Dana Franklin, whose character map Butler seems to have limned in part around the spirit-child archetype by harnessing Ọgbañje's stupendous capacity for telepathy and time travel. Ruth Salvaggio and Thelma J. Shinn put it more potently. Anyanwu, Salvaggio writes, is "the inspiring force for all of Butler's heroines," from Amber and Mary to the in-between and wild child Alanna. And it is *Wild Seed* that establishes the tropes reused in Butler's fictive universe (78, 80). To Shinn, Anyanwu bequeaths to the Patternists her powerful legacy of shape-shifting which animates their ability to heal.[35]

To provide foundation for the study, I create a substructure and develop interlocking discussions in chapters 1 and 2. Chapter 1 accomplishes two things. First, it unpacks insights provided on the myths of Ọgbañje and àbíkú by anthropologists and other researchers interested in the broad subjects of Igbo, Yoruba, and West/African religious universes. That synthesis is not a mere download of tedious anthropological data. Rather, it is crucial material that teachers, students, and other critical readers of the novels would also need to enhance their cultural appreciation of the texts. Second, it appends to that contextualization and conceptualization the character sketches of Ezinma and *Famished Road*'s Azaro, for the benefit of readers unfamiliar with *Things Fall Apart* and *Famished Road*. The character outlines serve also as an additional point of subsequent, critical cross-references with the African American texts.

Chapter 2 looks at Henry Louis Gates's *Signifying Monkey*. In theorizing "signifyin(g)," Gates clearly under-acknowledges the indentations of the modern

African novel on the development of its cousin, contemporary African American fiction. As the chapter amends Gates's oversight, it situates *Signifying* as a transition toward a recovery of Achebe's and the West African spirit child's place in African American literary history. It foregrounds also the contemporary neo-slave narrative, the 1960s and 1970s black consciousness and Black Arts movements against which I contextualize Butler, Due, Wideman and Morrison's thematizations of born-to-die mythology. These authors find in the spirit child concept an idiom that helps them talk about aspects of the African, African American and African diaspora experience.

Among these dimensions are, as chapter 3 discusses, Butler's exploration of the question of slavery, power, and the need for a new dispensation. She grafts these concerns onto a tense relationship between a body-snatching cult/race builder and a black female divinity's taming oppositions to his perverse New World project for immortality. Chapter 4 examines Tananarive Due's engagement with the issue of an African American born-to-die, Hilton James's in-betweenness. Due depicts Hilton's crisis of identity and belonging, his haunting by mortality and the costs of his entanglement in the dueling and also symbolic existential realms of Life and Death. Hilton's experience translates as a captivity narrative, a story of slavery and freedom.

Chapter 5 considers Wideman's manipulation of Ọgbañje as schema to treat the intertwined subjects of slavery, antebellum black evangelism, reincarnating racial trauma, as well as issues of power, black love, faith, and spiritual fortitude. Chapter 6 applies the figural and ideological tributaries of the spirit child to evaluate Morrison's exploration of the dialectics of good and evil through Sula and Beloved. I hope that, re-thought against the unifying thesis of the spirit child and with cross-references to Achebe and Okri, the African American works under study will assume "new" contexts and meanings.

In writing this book, I have had to face the same "So what?" question I sometimes ask my students during our conversations on their essay proposals: "What, really, is the point of all this?" "Why should anybody care about these nifty things you want to say?" Or, as I asked the student that day, "What's the big picture in your assertion that Tupac is an Ọgbañje? What's the broader implication of that observation?" Mindful here not to overdetermine my summation, perhaps the one conviction that this study buttresses overall is that they run much, much deeper the crosscurrents and cross-pollinations of African American and West/African formal histories, lived experiences, complex subjectivities, religious and cultural cosmologies, and their literary, intellectual, and political consciousnesses. Barely fully explored, I argue, the ties deserve more research than what exists in some studies on the subject.

Chapter 1 Ọgbañje and Àbíkú:
Contexts, Conceptualizations, and Two West African Literary Archetypes

The history of literature everywhere attests to the closeness and complexity of the relation between literature and myth [. . . as seen in] their shared traits of narrative, character, image and theme.

John B. Vickery
"Myth and Literature"

In *Myth and Meaning, Myth and Order,* Stephen C. Ausband notes that the body of lore we call mythology expresses fundamentally the primordial human quest to apprehend and organize phenomena in the world. This longing to arrange experience, this complete and unrelenting insistence on a framework of some sort, is what characterizes our humanity. When we name things, we are directly and implicitly attempting to classify those things and, in doing so, make them manageable.[1] Each human society searches for ways to give shape and meaning to its place in the world and also to explain its relationship to the supernatural. And it does this in accord with its religious cosmology and its changing experiences in space and time.[2]

That is how it has been with the Igbo and the Yoruba people of southern Nigeria. Locating themselves in what Nobel laureate Wole Soyinka calls "cosmic totality,"[3] the two societies have tried to make sense of the mysteries of life and the complexity of the human person through myth and mythmaking. In addition, because myth and literature share a number of structural affinities as Northrop Frye, Vickery above, and Jane Campbell point out,[4] we generally find in Nigerian fiction the integration, development, and allegorization of mythic motifs and ritual archetypes. In the postcolonial novel, for example, myth and ritual play other important roles beyond their exploitation as modalities of resistance and self-legitimization. Their thematic functions also include declaring "a culture's development of a civilization" and "staking claims upon and providing models for human conduct."[5]

Thus, with the qualifiers Ọgbañje and àbíkú, alongside other indigenous descriptors and urban neologisms by which they combat the mythic, born-to-die experience, Igbo and Yoruba societies try to understand their encounters with life, and in this case with events of (child) mortality, especially the type that occurs in succession in a particular family. As cultural epistemes that ensnarl numerous questions—existential, teleological, medical, obstetrical, maternal, religious, anthropological, psychosocial, ontologic, spiritual, political and philosophical—the beliefs are in their farthest semantic reaches an integral part of universal thoughts on superstition, taboos, life and death, fertility, childlessness, and abnormal childbirths. They assimilate also the concept of Sudden Infant Death Syndrome, notions of children with special supernatural powers, metempsychosis or the postmortem transmigration of the soul, the principle of reincarnation, and the precept of multiple and atypical personality, among others.

Two remarkable characteristics, however, seem to distinguish the Igbo and the Yoruba strains of the belief substantively from each other and also from many of their polygenetic counterparts in, say, Asian, Afro-Caribbean, Native American, European, Australian, and other cosmologies.[6] The first of these crucial contrasts is the willfulness and the malicious intent that the Igbo and the Yoruba generally attribute to the child's spirit-implicated anomalous behavior and its (repeated) deaths to the same mother and household. The second has to do with the nature of the ritualistic interventions that the Igbo and the Yoruba undertake in response to the experience. But even as researchers, literary historians and anthropologists caution that perceptions of and cultural practices associated with Ọgbañje and àbíkú afflictions are multifarious and have evolved over time, one thing has remained certain. The tenet of the spirit child has yet to depart Igbo and Yoruba socio-cultural reality and mythic awareness.

As with other cultures' mythic principles that are just as deeply rooted, complex, diffused, and enduring, no one can claim to know definitively when, how, or where the beliefs in Ọgbañje and àbíkú emanated in Igbo and Yoruba worlds. Arthur Glyn Leonard has suggested, for instance, that the belief in repeater death-spirits and marked children has existed among the peoples of the lower Niger possibly for millennia (212–17). A record of one Igbo mother's lament of her experience with consecutive child mortalities in an 1857–59 journal entry by native Anglican missionaries accompanying the Niger Expedition,[7] however, and also related notations on the Yoruba àbíkú (in Ellis 1894), indicate at least a pre-twentieth-century history of the beliefs. It was during the twentieth century, nonetheless, that the two myths evidently gained their most expansive, creative, and discursive publicization. They would attain greater visibility at this time through anthropological research, imaginative cultural productions, sociological studies, clinical-psychiatric inquiries, folklore, and popular media.

In addition, if as researchers such as Stuart Edelstein have speculated "a major genetic disease [Sickle Cell Anemia] triggered a new mythology," or if this inherited hemoglobin disorder substantively aided the evolution and longevity of a concept that traverses much of contemporary West Africa, then the idea of Ọgbañje, as well as of àbíkú, has a centuries' old existence, particularly among the Igbo and the Yoruba. Whether pre-existing myth or a major genetic mutation with the propensity to debilitate life at a young age, it would not be a conjecture to claim that experiences linked or likened to (Ọgbañje and àbíkú) spirits and spiritual afflictions, or whichever names and forms each belief took years back, were alive during the trans-Atlantic slave trade. They must have been extant, because hundreds of thousands of Igbo and Yoruba people, along with other West/Africans, were involuntarily shipped westward to the Americas. "Whatever the true origin of the concept," Edelstein synopsizes the foregoing hypotheses, "—pure fantasy, a historical consequence of sickle cell anemia, or some deep insight into the human condition—it is clear that the notion of repeater children, and the significance of the identifying marks they bear [in some cases], have captured a position of prime importance in African mythology" (87).

It is worth restating that in placing Ọgbañje and àbíkú in the realms of myth or the mythic, my intent is not to suggest that for the believing parents and families of such children the ideas are some grandiose fairy stories. The beliefs are not just grounded in lived experience. They are also popular in twenty-first-century Igbo and Yoruba lands, and beyond.[8] Thus, in locating them in mythology, I am simply viewing the ideas as encapsulations of the peoples' efforts to name, explain, and gain some insight and control over an encounter that has proven to be as durable as it is thematically provocative. And if myth has to do in part with the esoteric, the primal, or even the chthonic—if it articulates humankind's existential confrontations with cosmic forces, or with the activities of gods, immortal beings, and the mystifying—Ọgbañje and àbíkú entities enter mythological discourse because of their storied occultism, proteanism, supernaturality, and timelessness. I use "mythic" here also in recognition of how the continued societal fascination with the ideas in Nigeria has moved them into the realm of tabloid journalism and public talk. One can hear today in both rural and urban areas in Igboland, for instance, and even on some college campuses in Nigeria, various spiced-up, enchanting stories of this Ọgbañje child, that Ọgbañje incident or cult, or the other "Ọgbañje connection." Straddling the terminals of fabrication, euphemism, euhemerism, and authenticity, these sensationalized tales are (re)told sometimes by jesters with a dramatic flare. At other times, they are re-rendered by serious minds during casual or punditry conversations on the "shocking," violent, or generally unorthodox behavior of some contemporary Nigerian youths. These youths are casualties of the metastasizing nihilism fueled in part by the country's post-independence (1960–) and Nigeria-Biafra civil war (1967–70) nadirs.

Despite its subsumption in the foregoing remarks, this issue of variants and retellings is crucial. It deserves a bit more attention so we can clear this nagging question: With their elusive history and mutations over time and across Nigeria's ethnicities, especially, can one advance any decisive versions of the Ọgbañje and àbíkú experiences in oral tradition, written poetry, prose, and/or drama? Although he illustrates Western mythology and uses a structuralist methodology unlike the present study's more descriptive and analytical approach, Claude Lévi-Strauss offers pertinent insights that can help us tackle that question head-on.

Discussing the structural components and renditions of the Oedipus story in circulation, Lévi-Strauss notes that there is no single, authoritative version of a myth that others either replicate or falsify. The meaningfulness of mythology lies not in the random aspects of a myth's composition, but in how its different aspects come together. He adds that the problem facing mythological studies has been what he views as "the quest for the *true* version, or the *earlier* one." Instead of getting hobbled by the unending search for [and sometimes combative arguments over provenience, misrepresentation, or] authenticity, we should rather define a particular myth as being constituted by the totality of its renditions out there because a myth stays the same as much as it is considered to be so. Multiple accounts or accountings of a particular myth are not necessarily bad. Rather, they are reconstructive in that, even if they do not tell us all we need or want to know, they still reveal much so that we can at least be sure that no significant facet of the myth is overlooked in our exploration. Consequently, regardless of the many and divergent re-tellings of the Oedipus saga, each (re)construction of it remains part of the whole legend (52–58). We can therefore say the same thing about the attempted historicization and the variegations of the notions of Ọgbañje and àbíkú in Igbo and Yoruba lands, as well as in Nigerian literature and postcolonial criticism. They are *all* integral to the concepts' dynamism, as well as their socio-cultural protraction.

This chapter has two principal goals. First, it strives to synthesize in some detail the cultural anthropology of born-to-die: "Ọgbañje" and "àbíkú." Second, it extends that anthropological context by providing the character, narratological and conceptual vignettes of what I am calling the two West African literary "archetypes": the Ọgbañje child Ezinma and what I dub "the Ezinma-Ekwefi dynamic" in Achebe's *Things Fall Apart,* and Azaro, the àbíkú protagonist and narrator in Ben Okri's *The Famished Road.* The intent in succeeding a discussion of "Ọgbañje" anthropology with the Ezinma story and then "àbíkú" with Azaro's is not to imply a parallel between the fictional "Ezinma" and Igbo "Ọgbañje" or between *Famished Road*'s rendition of Azaro's in-betweenness and Yoruba "àbíkú."[9] Rather, the character geographies are to assist readers unfamiliar with the two novels. The anthropological background is needed to help explain further the appearance of the terms "ogbanje," "born-to-die," and "child spirit" in the novelists' works. Most important, I consolidate anthropological and literary interpretations of the Ọgbañje, on one hand, and the same for àbíkú, on the other, as complementary phases of my broader theoretical and interrogative agenda throughout.

Graham Allen's remarks underscore the importance of this two-pronged— cultural and literary—contextualization. Asserting that literary texts often replicate society's disputations over semantics, Allen argues that "If a novelist, for example, uses the words 'natural' or 'artificial' or 'God' or 'justice' they cannot help but incorporate into their novel society's conflict over the meaning of these words" (36). I interpret Allen's statement here to mean that when Butler and Wideman imprint their works with the provocative, ethnically affiliated belief "Ọgbañje," mobilizing it as lexeme, character, theme, and technique, and when Due does the same with the concept's Anglicization "born-to-die," and Morrison resonates the notion by creating the Sula-anticipated "child spirit" Beloved, a figure that critics have called an Ọgbañje, all four writers telescope several things at once. They signal "the routes of transmission" as well as "the tradition" in which they place themselves (de Weever 10). They also suggest that not only are significant portions of their novels' concerns, techniques, and meanings titrated on those key terms but that, as a consequence, readers and critics should upgrade their cultural literacy and critical language. And lastly, they unavoidably intertwine their novels with and thus make them analyzable through the knowledges that "Ọgbañje"/"born-to-die" have generated in research and scholarship on modern postcolonial and postmodern African letters. It is imperative therefore that we understand, first and foremost, not simply the West African fictional models re-adapted and mirrored in the African American texts. We should also begin with the meanings of Ọgbañje and àbíkú in Igbo and Yoruba worlds.

* * *

As I will point out along the way, there are subtle differences in explanations of Ọgbañje and àbíkú in Igbo and Yoruba societies, and among cultural anthropologists and literary critics. Thanks partly to centuries' old inter-ethnic and intra-ethnic migration, socio-cultural contact, and shared linguistic roots between the Igbo and the Yoruba, and among the peoples of Nigeria and indeed West Africa, there also exist a number of steady elements that one finds in discussions of the idea(s). It is these fairly consistent components that have helped shape much of the imaginative and metaphoric representations of the two concepts. As asserted, Ọgbañje and àbíkú name Igbo and Yoruba people's related, complex ways of responding to (1) the early and/or successive deaths of children in families, (2) the alien spirit cult or spirit societies believed to be perniciously responsible for such untimely thefts of highly valued human-wealth, and (3) the health-related issues as well as the (ab)normal personalities and (mis)fortunes often associated with the children and adults so designated.

Among the cast interacting in this intriguing existential drama are, generally speaking, the spirit cult and deities; the Ọgbañje or àbíkú spirit child himself or herself; the mother/parents; the diviners/priests/healers, composed of the Igbo Afa dibia and the Yoruba Ifa babaláwo; the human families of the spirit children themselves; and the larger society. To use Sam'ar Attar's theatrical parlance, these are the "characters who constitute what might be called the dramatic community" of the experience (9).

In addition, set in the spirit and human realms and traversing the two theaters, this mythic drama is played out against the wider backdrop of religions' permeation of the African cultural imagination and, more narrowly, the Igbo and Yoruba sacred cosmoses. These cosmoses stress commonly an organic universe construed as being populated by the interacting forces of the living, the dead, and the unborn. The cosmoses are inhabited also by humans and the universe's other powers and principalities: spirits, the inanimate, the "good," the "evil," and all else that abound between them. Furthermore, even with the current ubiquity of Christianity, especially Pentecostal evangelism, in the Igbo and Yoruba locales of southern Nigeria, as well as the pervasiveness of Western thought and lifestyle in much of the nation, the Ọgbañje and àbíkú dramas still assume shape. For as Donatus Ibe Nwoga acknowledges, "the contemporary Igbo," for instance, "while accepting the omnipotence and omnipresence, etc., of *Chukwu,* is still easily prone to see other causes and other solutions for problems of his life. He is quite satisfied to give God his due at mass and service on Sunday and go home and give *Amadioha* [the Igbo spirit of lightning that speaks through thunder] his due" as well (8).

The Ọgbañje and àbíkú encounters occur, then, in two syncretistic religious and cultural worlds, Igbo and the Yoruba lands, that still believe in deities, oracles, and the authority of fate. Although one's destiny is generally seen as rigid or binding teleologically, the Igbo and the Yoruba do not consider it to be absolute. For them, one's destiny could still be altered by the choices and negotiations that one makes as a pre-natal spirit and/or by the sheer force of one's post-natal willfulness or circumstance. It could also be tweaked by divinatory and ritualistic intermediation, the kind that the dibia and the babaláwo offer parents to intervene in Ọgbañje and àbíkú affliction, if seen as a peculiar and inimical kind of fate—as in being born-to-die or born-and-die (young).

More important, besieged as they were decades ago by high infant mortality,[10] the Igbo, the Yoruba, and West/Africans at large analogously place a high premium on children. They see children as the ultimate "wealth," an affirmation of marriage and motherhood, the indispensable foundation of family, and the links to immortality attained through perpetuation of both the matrilineage and patrilineage. It is when we consider the foregoing contexts that it makes more sense why the overlapping discourses of, as well as the rituals connected to, life, death, and rebirth—"rebirth" different from the discrete category of the more culturally desirable ancestral reincarnation enabled by death at a ripe old age—frame the Igbo and Yoruba attitudes to creation. They also frame both societies' dispositions to divinities, human existence, causation, and more especially to the paranormals Ọgbañje and àbíkú.

"Ọgbañje" in Igbo Metaphysics

The Igbo conception of reincarnation and human subjectivity should be clarified immediately. The English term "reincarnation" does not adequately capture the Igbo experience of the idea, argues the Reverend Dr. Anthony Ekwunife, a professor of African Traditional Religion and the Sociology of Religions at the University of Nigeria, Nsukka and also a specialist in Ọgbañje. As a result, Ekwunife adds, it might be better to envision "reincarnation" in its Igbo signification, "Ilo Uwa," that is, "coming back to the world, not necessarily being born again." In Ilo Uwa, "certain categories of the deceased in the African spiritual world of the dead are believed to be mysteriously, but in a real way, capable of incarnating their personality traits on a newborn physical body of a child, without either destroying the new unique personality of the child or substituting for it."

In addition, the Igbo commonly believe that only those who die as adults and reach the rank of ancestor can reincarnate and that the human person that reincarnates under the experience of Ilo Uwa should not be misconstrued as the born-to-die Ọgbañje.[11] Esther Nzewi supplements that elucidation. She notes, not inherently in contradiction of Ekwunife, that in Igbo thought "Every individual is believed to be an *ogbanje*" to the extent that she or he is generally "assumed to have the capacity for repeated reincarnation as self or others with increased potentials for ultimate self-improvement and self-realization with each reincarnation." Echoing Ekwunife's explanation of Ilo Uwa, Nzewi points out that in regular reincarnation rebirth takes place after an adult dies not by design but from natural or unforeseen circumstances. There exists, however, a type of Ọgbañje that the Igbo view as innately malevolent.[12] It is this group that concerns us. Edmund Ilogu describes the cult:

> This type of children form themselves into a group in the spirit world, and decide to be born into various homes, where they live for a very short while and die, all in a group, normally before reaching puberty. They form themselves into another spirit group and are reincarnated into another group of children, to be reborn sometimes by the same mothers that previously mothered them, or by their close relations. These various and often repeated comings and goings, are meant to punish these women, by tantalizing them into believing that they have got children. These Ogbanje children . . . can be detected and out-manoeuvred [*sic*] by the 'medicine man' through various devices.[13]

Of the plethora of sources[14] that confront one seeking some elaboration on this malignant or aberrant subtype of reincarnation, Christie Achebe's and Misty Bastian's inquiries into the idea are particularly fascinating, sustained, and pertinent. Therefore, I root my explanation of the belief principally in Christie Achebe's seminal project *The World of the Ogbanje* (1986)[15] and in Bastian's "Married in the Water" (1987) and "Irregular Visitors" (2002).

The malignant Ọgbañje are part-human and part-spirit beings whose existences are confounded. Achebe explains that this existential discomfiture is a result of the Ọgbañje's maintenance of a constraining, second allegiance to other supernatural forces alongside the pre-natal agreement they first made with their Chi—their "spirit counterpart" believed to be the "creative spark" of Chukwu (15–18), the transcendental and withdrawn immortal that the Igbo believe created the universe. As construed generally in Igbo cosmology, a "'normal' individual is born owing his loyalty to his 'chi'" (27). A malevolent Ọgbañje's personage is rendered more arduous, however, due to his or her entanglement in additional, insistent impositions by spectral divinities. A major part of such counterclaims is that the Ọgbañje would not complete a full, seven-time life cycle. Instead, he or she must die prematurely and not at old age, thus skewing the supposed natural order of things. Consequently, while at birth one may be that reincarnating category Nzewi above characterizes as malignant, it is quite possible for one's Ọgbañje identity and ontological tension to go largely undetected and unclassified until later in life, perhaps in adulthood (27–28).

To grasp more fully this dynamic, it is important to return, even if succinctly, to Igbo creation myth. Deserving of closer attention are Igbo deities, as well as the centrality and role of the "Chi," an idea that Emmanuel N. Obiechina deems to be a semantically "elusive," "highly complex religious and psychological" concept (62).[16] Also embedded in the Igbo myth of origins is one's role and power in determining destiny.

Chukwu created human beings in groups or sets. They are the human group called the "Otu Mmadu" and the spirit group, the "Otu Mmuo," Christie Achebe states. Within the spirit group are two important sub-leagues: one, the "Ogbanje-Elu" who inherit their qualifier Elu from the female deity of the Forest/Ala named Onabuluwa and, two, the "Ogbanje-Mmiri," associated with the River/Water deity called Nne Mmiri. These two sub-fraternities, the Ogbanje Elu and the Ogbanje Mmiri, still maintain powerful ties to the spirit domain. Thus, unlike the Otu Mmadu, they "remain part human and part spirit but equipped more with the latter attribute." Like passport or immigration officers manning the entrances into the human realm, the deities Onabuluwa and Nne Mmiri interrogate the border-crossing human sets as to each crosser's sworn oath of life Iyi Uwa—that is, his or her self-chosen and granted destiny/natural endowment—signed to at creation with Chukwu and witnessed by the companion Chi.

Collectively inescapable, possessive, wearisome, aggressive, intimidating, and highly persuasive, these female deities and their conspiratorial assistants also attempt, more consequentially, to get the journeying humans, sometimes rendered susceptible on account of having bad, inefficacious or displeased Chis, to double-cross. Onabuluwa and Nne Mmiri try to get the traveling pre-natal humans to violate or outright discard those original destiny contracts with their Chi. They attempt to lure the passers to take up new, seemingly more favorable life-gifts and concomitant allegiances suggested *and* demanded by them, Onabuluwa and Nne Mmiri (the latter deity sometimes conflated with or misidentified as Mami Wota or Mami Wata cult[17] in popular register). The idea is that, depending first on which guarded gateway (water or land) through which an individual enters the human world at birth, and if s/he acquiesces to Nne Mmiri's or Onabuluwa's pressures, the individual abandons the initial signed pact and commitment. Or, conversely, the person can have the first agreement so altered it now includes new, secondary conditions.

These contractual breaches and re-signings come with perks and retributions, however. Those immune humans, ultimately coaxed by Nne Mmiri who presides over the river entry point, become Nne Mmiri's "converts" and devotees. In addition, they might be disallowed from marrying in the earthly terrain if, consistent with the new contract, Nne Mmiri has already engaged them to water/river spirit-spouses, sometimes in exchange for earthly beauty or material successes. Nne Mmiri and her cohorts intermittently evaluate how her now earth-dwelling devotees are complying with their new pledges. Those who contravene the new obligations are tormented with symptomatic disorders, adversity, and sickness while loyalists are compensated (see Flora Nwapa's *Efuru,* 1966, and Achebe's "Uncle Ben's Choice"). A factor common to both Nne Mmiri's and Onabuluwa's cases, nonetheless, is that malevolent Ọgbañje would not live out a normal and propitious life cycle. They are instead repatriated generally at the height of their achievement or in some tragic way. Thus, in terms of the spirit child myth in Igbo thought, there are, as earlier indicated, three general clubs entering the world: (1), the Otu Mmadu: those "normal" humans that were/are able to resist Nne Mmiri's and Onabuluwa's coercions and entreaties, choosing instead to remain steadfast to their original contract with their Chi; (2), the Ogbanje Elu—"Earth spirit being[s]"; and (3), the Ogbanje Mmiri—"Water spirit being[s]."[18]

Furthermore, the pact that malevolent spirit children make with their *ndi otu,* their companions in the same Ọgbañje subgroup, is seen as obligating. In some cases, according to Christie Achebe, the pact is "sealed with bits and pieces of elements representing samples from each 'ogbanje's' body . . . such as hair, nail, wearing apparel or any material then available from the environment such as pebble." Part of this allegiance is the subgroup's agreement and choice to die prematurely and collectively.[19] A materially inclined subgroup member who, sidetracked by the lures and challenges of earthly life,[20] reneges on this ostensibly cooperative arrangement by deciding to *stay* alive past the agreed death-/return-date would be accordingly accosted by the complying counterparts with threats of sickness or accidents. The greater a member's obstinacy in conforming with the contract, the harsher and more regular the pestering from the complying preternatural members. And should the surviving but hassled member be taken early to an Afa diviner or, in more contemporary diagnoses and healing practices, to Pentecostal churches, the dibia or spiritual healer "may be able to separate the 'ogbanje's' symbolic contribution from the collective pact and so sever the link with the others."[21]

Thus, the Ọgbañje's contract with their spirit league, the *ndi otu,* is quite significant. There is also the need to nullify that contract and thus "cut" Ọgbañje from spirit-league's membership and apparent captivity. In "Married in the Water," Bastian avers that the spirit mates take the pact rather seriously because it is a covenant among peers, subject to stiff penalty. While it decides between human and spirit life, the Ọgbañje child becomes "a threat to its human kin. His/her spirit companions also act like a kind of kin, threatened with a loss of an important group member." Should the Ọgbañje, for whatever cause, attempt to breach the pact, s/he would be telepathically troubled by the spirit kin until they enforce compliance. And in "cases where a person's '*ogbaanje* nature' [*sic*] has gone previously undetected, the crisis often is precipitated by the prospect of marriage." The conflict, provoked in part by the spirit-child's double-ties to both *ndi otu* (spirit fraternity) and *ndi mmadu* (human beings), "classically occurs at the moments when the *ogbaanje* demonstrates, most concretely, his/her connection to human kin—and adds to the complexity of those relations by receiving his/her first name (just after birth), showing his/her reproductive potential (arrival of puberty), and begins to fulfill his/her lineage, and broader human, obligations by contemplating [and/or consummating] marriage."

Consequently, with so much on the line in the tenuous and adversarial drama between an intrusive outsider/force and the human family under siege by the Ọgbañje's entwistment in matrimony, parenthood, and kinship, it is no surprise "unwilling human and spirit allies engage in a kind of warfare over and through the bodies of their *ogbaanje* kin." An Ọgbañje is "a spirit that has never been ancestral." And an "uncut" Ọgbañje is liminal, "neither fish nor fowl; neither fully human nor spirit. Half of his or her loyalty is to the human lineage of his or her birth; the other half remains committed, even if unconsciously committed, to the capricious world of spiritual forces." In this split allegiance, then, the Ọgbañje can be seen as a wildcard, "an anomalous figure in his or her human patrilineage," indeed "the strangest of strangers" in a family.[22]

Working through the Afa dibia, the human family's efforts to intervene and treat the anomalous, trammeled Ọgbañje by "cutting" them from the bondaging membership of the spirit company are generally temporary remedies. Christie Achebe explains that conceived partly as an act of contrition by the contractually delinquent Ọgbañje, and depending also on the specificities of each Ọgbañje subtype and the dibia's diagnosis, the treatment modes, especially those for Ogbanje-Mmiri, could include benign bodily incisions made on the Ọgbañje client and "saraka" (token food offerings). They could also involve shock treatment, detailed rituals and, on rare instances, the enlistment of a human mediator who acts as an interpreter between diviner and the spirit cult. The treatment for the Ogbanje-Elu, the club decoyed by the forest/land deity, is considered to be more tasking. The intervention includes road-, forest-, or tree-side sacrifices made to Onabuluwa. It could also entail the now seldom employed method of Iyi Uwa excavation supplemented with medicinal antidotes. Sometimes fortified padlocks are used to symbolically bar the Ọgbañje's badgering spirit kin. Reminiscent of and seemingly derivative of the Yoruba àbíkú ritual, the diviner may prescribe jingling chains to be worn as anklets by an Ọgbañje client to frighten the group. However, all these are interim cures. They are effective to the extent that they can attenuate but not completely eradicate the spirit group's insistent interest in and tormenting telepathic pressures on their outposted and nonallegiant kindred. This is a kin that not only has infracted a pledge with the Chi but also desires to *stay*. And in *staying*, this disloyal kin contradicts, even more, the new covenant with spirit deity as well as the cult's collective pact.[23]

The etiology of this mythic belief, particularly the notion that the Ọgbanje die untimely deaths, has resulted sometimes in the reductive explanation of Ọgbanje deaths as merely high infant mortality. As Chinwe Achebe contends, however, this is not the case, because there are adult Ọgbanje. Nor could the phenomenon be scientifically translated out as a symptom of Sickle Cell Disease, she continues, even if the links between SCD and the affliction have been studied and suggested (see, for instance, Stevenson 1985, 1986, 1987, and 1997). For the Igbo, the Ọgbanje encounter remains a fascinating yet mystifying experience. It is a story all its own, one whose literary adaptation in the character Ezinma and in her relationship with her mother Ekwefi in Chinua Achebe's *Things Fall Apart* is certainly one of that novel's most memorable events.

Ezinma and the Ezinma-Ekwefi Dynamic

We first meet Ezinma as an ordinary, healthy girl in chapter five of *Things Fall Apart,* whose major setting Umuofia appears to be the present-day Umuahia.[24] This encounter occurs during the Feast of New Yam, several pages and narrative events before Ezinma is even associated directly with the identity, lexicon, and broader implications of Ọgbanje experience. We find her with her mother, Ekwefi, in a domestic scene of parent-child, mother-daughter relationship, education, socialization, and bonding.

At this point, Ezinma is almost ten years old and is described tellingly as a curious, dutiful, observant, obedient, and precocious child. She is "wiser than her years" (41) and also intrigued by (folk) stories and storytelling. Unlike her peers, Ezinma calls her mother by her name. On one occasion, Ezinma violates accepted gender binaries and cultural performance. She does not sit "like a woman" but apparently like a man, with her legs apart, a behavior her father Okonkwo rebukes immediately (44). Along with the imports of Ezinma's insinuated assumption of cultural parity with her mother, this latter infraction is significant especially in terms of the Ọgbanje's atypicality and its station as a gender-shifting spirit entity.

The narrator reveals that Ekwefi, formerly the village beauty, "had suffered a great deal in her life time" (40). Now forty-five, Ekwefi had Ezinma at age thirty-five. Plagued by the Ọgbanje spirit, however, she lost all her nine previous children in infancy. Among them are the babies she named Ozoemena: "May it not happen again," Onwumbiko: "Death, I implore you," and another she defiantly called Onwuma: "Death may please himself" (77).

If it were the case that Ọgbañje children generally die and return to their mothers for rebirth in the same family, then we should justifiably infer that Ezinma is actually each of those earlier nine children. In addition, because the children that died were both boys and girls, we adduce that Ezinma had come back, defying rituals performed to contain and normalize her and transcending temporal, spatial, and gender barriers. She had returned, androgynous, switching and shifting shape and sex in both male and female bodies, each of those returns unearthing for Ekwefi agonizing memories she would rather forget but ones she must confront. Thus if Ekwefi met Okonkwo at a historic wrestling match against Amalinze the Cat thirty years ago when Ekwefi was fifteen and if, as the narrator relays, she audaciously abandoned her former husband Anene and married Okonkwo a few years after that meeting, say, two years later at age seventeen and assuming she had her first child the next year at eighteen (the time the wandering Ọgbañje spirit entity now named Ezinma must have first infiltrated her womb and assumed human flesh), then one can argue that the present ten-year-old Ezinma is actually a woman of at least twenty-seven or twenty-eight years in "human" and Western calendar, had she *stayed* (alive) through the first incarnation. "She" is definitely an adult. She is wise beyond her years, because she has been here before.

Endowed with her mother's attractiveness, she is named fittingly Ezinma. The prefix "Ezi" means nominally and adjectivally "true," "real," "good" or "genuine" in Igbo language. And "nma" means "beauty" or "adorable." Ezi also denotes "veranda," "path" or "road." Seemingly an abbreviation of "Ezidinma," a name generally given to first-born daughters in Achebe's Ogidi-Umuoji-Idemili area,[25] Ezinma is a prayer and an affirmation and acknowledgement of that which is good. She is literally the real beauty, a true beauty or simply gorgeous, an elegance for which Okonkwo's first wife, who knows full well about her Ọgbañje identity, affectionately calls her "Nma" for short (41).

Later, as an adult woman, she would be called "Crystal of Beauty" (171). In complimenting Ezinma as "Ezigbo" (41), or the Good One, Okonkwo's first wife buttresses the authenticity of that allure. She implies, more importantly, that this Ezinma, a spirit child, is indeed a good one, *the* good Ọgbañje. Ezinma is benevolent in that she appears to have elected to *stay,* unlike her nine beguiling siblings or metamorphosed selves of the previous sojourns, one of whom (named Onwumbiko) was physically scarred at death, insulted, and unmourned.

Ezinma survives the dreaded ages of infancy. Her intermittent sicknesses, construed as part of Ọgbañje syndrome of filial impermanence, however, keep Ekwefi anxious. When, disregarding Okonkwo's pleas and Ekwefi's trepidations, Chielo the priestess of the male god Agbala/Ezinma's other-mother proceeds at night to consecrate Ezinma before the Oracle of the Hills and Caves, Ezinma becomes a blessed, special child. She is linked to divinity, a daughter of the gods, one "called," chosen, and protected by them possibly as Chielo's successor (see also Irele, "Crisis," 115–53). As Ezinma blossoms into adulthood, however, she still experiences abrupt and bewildering mood swings. Yet Ekwefi perseveres. And in no instance is Ekwefi's optimism more concretely reassured than when, years earlier, Ezinma's pact with her spirit kin is severed through a ritualized excavation of her Iyi Uwa, the location of which she volunteers to the Afa dibia Okagbue Uyanwa. Perhaps Ekwefi's Chi is not bad and apathetic after all. The above experiences explain Ekwefi's abiding love for, close friendship with, and fierce protectiveness of her only surviving child. The experiences contextualize her indignant intent to over-indulge young Ezinma against Okonkwo's predictable displeasure and threats.

Okonkwo, too, is evidently fond and defensive of Ezinma. An alert, compassionate and proactive daughter, it is she, of all his children, who is there to lend him much-needed emotional, familial, and political support during two of his most critical low points. She attends to him following his depression induced by his direct participation in Ikemefuna's ordained death. Speaking with the tonal authority of a grown-up/parent, Ezinma insists that he must finish his meal, for he has not eaten lately. And when years later another major adversity hits him—this time as the District Commissioner deceives him and other Umuofia leaders and nobility into a three-day imprisonment and the D.C.'s messengers humiliate, starve, torture, fine, and defraud the men—Ezinma is there again. She would suspend her ongoing, culturally mandated, pre-marital obligations to her future in-laws and return home promptly to ascertain Umuofia's response and also feed her physically maimed father.

Increasingly disheartened by what he concludes as his first son Nwoye's vexatious and tragic disinclination toward overbearing masculinity, as well as his supposed effeminacy, Okonkwo wishes Ezinma were a boy. He believes that she possesses "the right spirit" (66). Of his progeny, the narrator states, "she alone understood his every mood" (172). She is inspired, cognitive and clairvoyant. And though Okonkwo's life ends tragically early, and near the summit of his achievements following his confrontations with the white man, he would be gratified if not consoled to know that, if anything, Ezinma fulfilled his strong desire that she marry an Umuofia man, and not during his seven-year exile in Mbanta.

Perhaps as a way of announcing/publicizing Ezinma's portentous survival into adulthood as child, wife, and mother, Achebe brings back Ezinma in narrative discourse. She "reappears" in *Arrow of God*. In one scene, her husband Onwuzuligbo visits Ezeulu, the chief priest of Umuaro. When asked how Ezinma is doing, Onwuzuligbo responds, that is *confirms,* that she and her children are well presently, barring hunger and the unforeseen (*Arrow* 62).

* * *

In its sociocultural anthropology, its "science," and its (fiction)alization in *Things Fall Apart,* Ǫgbañje is a polysemous concept. As category, experience and metaphor, it emanates descriptors, epistemes and, significantly, archetypal themes and narrative structures that are reconstructed or resonated with various degrees of development in the Butler, Wideman and Morrison novels under study. Culturally, Ǫgbañje is a non-occidental belief. Genetically speaking, were the Ǫgbañje affliction caused by Sickle Cell Disorder, the Ǫgbañje "cell" is therefore a mutant. Or rather, the condition presupposes some form of biological mutation. And, thus, the Ǫgbañje subject to whom aberrance is generally ascribed becomes the site of physical and ideological "difference."

The Ǫgbañje can be qualified as aliens/visitors to and impermanent residents in the human/material world. They are generally intruders. More specifically, they are imperious, intrusive spirits/forces in quest for immortalizing new bodies, shapes, and identities. Their vehicle for such incarnations is the woman, a mother, with whom they are engaged in a power battle. This struggle extrapolates broadly as tension between "parasite/guest" and "host," exploiter and the exploited, enslaver/master and the enslaved, control and dissidence, voice and voicelessness, and between presence and absence. As Arthur Glyn Leonard puts it, a mother's unflinching response to the death-spirit's torment "is no act of propitiation, but one of distinct and undoubted defiance of the ancestral deities" (214).

Because of their capacity for intuitive and extra-sensory communication, the Ǫgbañje can be telepathic or space- and time-traveling telepaths. Coalesced in their alien-ness and spatial-temporal travel are the sub-themes of permeability of (cosmic) borders, separation from home/ancestry, migration, and exile. And because Ǫgbañje spirits are thieves that rob women of their babies, the belief enmeshes the questions of maternity, the plight of motherhood, abduction, loss, the repeated loss of children, or simply family members. Also at the belief's core are themes of rebirth, reincarnation, metamorphosis, transition, journey, time, history, and memory revival.

The Ǫgbañje are associated with eccentricity, beauty, bodies of water, and trees. Based on their violations of pact with Onabuluwa, Nne Mmiri and the Chi, they can be attributed with the predilection for contrariness and contractual infringement. That is, they reject conventionality and the ties that *bind.* The embodied energy of resistance and rebellion, a tenacious and uncontainable force, Ọgbañje is the problem child, one that skews what should be the "natural," "normative," and/ or stable order of things. The experience provokes these interrelated questions: How, for instance, can the same child who should be a source of joy to its mother, parents, and family, cause them and by extension the community so much uncertainty and grief? How can, or cannot the child, be such "diabolism" and "so much beneficence" all at once?

In this sense, the Ọgbañje child/encounter becomes a font for a critical and, more important, cosmologically specific deliberation of the philosophical question of good and evil. Ọgbañje is therefore a study in irony, intersubjectivity and interdependency. It offers a platform on which to interrogate the conflictive yet resolvable dialectics of positivity and negativity, construction and deconstruction. For as Christie Achebe writes, the Igbo construe Ọgbañje as the "metaphor[ic] bad child that enters its mother's womb through the back door."[26]

In addition, and consistent with Achebe's statement above, in Igboland a child could be called an Ọgbañje if she or he is erratic or ungovernable. Parental reaction to the child's death could include withholding of mourning, a punitive decision intended to deprive the child of any pleasure it was hoping to derive from the hurt its premature death inflicts. The stigmata believed to exist on the body of an incarnate Ọgbañje addresses the interplay of "difference" and (negativist) *marking*—a condition communicated also in the distinguishing, death-related names given to the entities.[27]

It is true that the return/visit of an Ọgbañje spirit to the same (house)hold excavates memory, and unearths for a mother a hurtful past on which she would like to have closure. True as well, each of its haunting rebirths complicates mothering. It sours the joys of motherhood, or simply a mother's desire to dote on a child that she cannot truly claim as hers because the child's *stay* in the family is uncertain, what with its incessant susceptibility to abduction to another place or world. Yet as in the complementarity of Death and Life, that diabolism is counterbalanced by the Ọgbañje's sometimes overlooked role as an enabler. Perhaps in no other text is that last point more persuasively modeled than in *Things Fall Apart.*

As a gendered self *and* an idea, Ezinma the problem child is still a great daughter. Even more, however, she represents ultimately for her long-suffering mother hope, renewal, liberation, triumph, and transcendence. She is a desire fulfilled, a psychic mooring, and an affirmation of Ekwefi's/a mother's motherhood, unceasing faith, and perseverance of the human spirit. At its core the Ezinma-Ekwefi subplot is a love story. Or rather, it is a story about love, the love and bond between mother and child. Ezinma's decision to *stay,* her allegoric survival, restores order into chaos.

Speaking dialectically, Ezinma, a timeless space- and time-traveler and powerful force, disrupts yet ultimately balances the natural order. She is different yet the same. Her *staying* encrypts the idea that cosmic balance, group survival and collective healing are inevitable. All three remain a certainty even when things fall apart through a spirit's encroachment on and subjection of a human person, or by the corollaries of that subjection, namely enslavement, imperialism, and colonization. Thus, the Ezinma-Ekwefi substory is more than a captivity narrative. It is also a discourse on resistance and community-involved liberation struggle. In other words, the community's participation through the energy/presence of many Umuofia villagers in the ritual excavation of Ezinma's Iyi Uwa signals the necessity of collective action in the implicit, apocalyptic defeat of a perverse order or a seemingly unconquerable dictation. That need for healing and balance is a dynamic evoked also in Ben Okri's rendering of the àbíkú encounter in *The Famished Road,* a novel that draws heavily upon the Yoruba notion of àbíkú.

The Notion of "Àbíkú" in Yoruba Cosmology

The Igbo cultural explanation of Ọgbañje in terms of repetitive life journeys is a major point of contrast between Ọgbañje and the Yoruba view of àbíkú. However, unlike the journey-focus of Ọgbañje and its stress of Iyi Uwa, both of which are distinctly Igbo, àbíkú emphasizes mortality. It represents mortality as an existential given by virtue of the concept àbíkú being attached to "íkú," the Yoruba force or agent of death. Nevertheless, the Yoruba associate the àbíkú with conditions and descriptors reminiscent of the peculiarly Igbo notions of *ndi otu,* Nne Mmiri, and Onabuluwa.

The àbíkú are the "born to die," the Reverend Samuel Johnson explains. They are a category of children who are "supposed to belong to a fraternity of demons living in the woods, especially about and within large iroko trees and each one of them coming into the world would have arranged beforehand the precise time he will return to his company."[28] Also called "eleri" or "spirit children," H. U. Beier adds, they belong to an "egbe" or secret *society* that deputizes some of its votary and rapacious members for a [brief] earthly, human birth and life. Beier adduces that the àbíkú

> spirit is said to enter the womb of a pregnant woman, where he "drives" out the real child. The phrase "drives out," however, does not actually mean what it seems to

indicate at first ... people did not conceive of the original child to die, nor did they actually imagine it to go from the womb to some other place. The spirit child is, in fact, considered the legal child of its father, if only it can be persuaded to remain in this world. Once it has been prevented by charms from returning to the spirit world, the Yoruba do not feel that it disturbs the lineage system in any way.

It may perhaps be said that the child is conceived of mostly as a human child *possessed* by the spirit, and sometimes as a human child replaced by the spirit. This "double-think" results clearly from the ambivalent feelings towards the child, and it is typical that the Yoruba does not feel any necessity to solve the ambivalence by deciding to adopt the one or the other attitude.[29]

Because an àbíkú stays in communication with its egbe, Beier asserts, it remains a source of anxiety for its parents, particularly its human mother, given the àbíkú's temporal impermanence and predisposition to die young. In its often malicious motivations, Beier states, the àbíkú also becomes the cause of undue financial distress for its parents, who are generally willing to sacrifice, if not overindulge, their spirit child's ontological proclivities and material entreaties in hopes that the child would *stay*. The àbíkú is bound to submit to its spirit confederates' requisitions for sacrifice, a burden it transfers to its desperate, acquiescing parents. Most àbíkú have "frequent visions of their companions. Some will associate their visions with water or trees: and nearly all will have them when alone. . . . the spirits will frequently tempt the child to throw itself into the water or do other dangerous things that may result in its death. . . . When the time comes, usually before the ages of four and ten years, the spirits will request the child to return to them. Even though the child is very attached to its mother, it cannot resist the call of the spirits and will 'go.'"[30]

The àbíkú will return, by dying, to its usual home: spiritland. In other words, the earthly terrain is not really the àbíkú's home. In cases where the àbíkú contravenes the pact by deciding to *stay* alive in the human world instead, writes E. Bolaji Idowu, the oracle generally recommends the surrender of an alternate to recompense the terms of the broken pact. The replacement is also a condition required to hinder the àbíkú from being abducted by its companions. The need for this forfeiture of a substitute increases at the point the àbíkú is perilously sick or upon prompting by the oracle itself (123). Every àbíkú's scheme is therefore to "return affluent to its abode after having ["stolen" from and turned] its parents into a wretched couple" financially and emotionally. It is no surprise, then, that the Yoruba so dread the àbíkú experience that they have a special wish for a new wife: "*O ko ni pade Abiku* (May you never come across an *Abiku* child)."[31] In hopes of escaping the àbíkú mischief, expectant mothers are advised to stay away from, at specific times of the day, such areas as trees and bodies of water believed to be àbíkú-haunted sites. In addition, some pregnant women go as far as wearing medicinally fortified hair ornaments and waist girdles to deter the àbíkú spirit from infiltrating their wombs.

The foregoing published collage on àbíkú squares with views on the myth that an Oyo-Yoruba Ifa babaláwo, Babalola Ifatoogun, relays to Douglas McCabe. Noting that the spirit children have other names in Yoruba though the term àbíkú has gained the most currency, McCabe quotes Ifatoogun as describing the àbíkú similarly as "'thieves from heaven,'" as a "'club' (*egbé*) of 'heaven people' (*ará òrun*)" whose chief aim is to drain wealth from "*ilé aráyé,* the 'houses' (*ilé*) of the 'world people' (*ará-ayé*)." These celestial robbers do this by camouflaging their felonious mission and by amassing parental pity and love. Given the nature of this situation which translates into a serious rivalry between homeowner and intruder, Ifatoogun reasons that the earthlings' seemingly only viable counterintelligence against this lawless, peripatetic spirit club—in short the parents' or household's offensive against unremitting theft—is to "spiritually" restrain the rogue, destabilizing àbíkú. But to accomplish this, the *ilé* must first and foremost identify and decode, through the babaláwo's divinatory skills, àbíkú's confidential oath to its spirit compatriots as to the exact time, occasion, and manner of its stipulated return back to heaven.

Armed with this critical information, the *ilé* can now hopefully move to actuate the desired spiritual subjugation or arrest of the àbíkú by doing the following: The *ile* can bind àbíkú by impeding the situations that enable the àbíkú's return/death. It can also restrain it by broadcasting that the àbíkú's concealed schema has been unraveled. Or it might choose to alter (that is, mutilate or mark on) the àbíkú to render it unknowable and unacceptable to its club mates upon their arrival to kidnap him from the human terrain—where the àbíkú is seen as one incarcerated—and from there take it back to paradise, their land of immortality.[32]

The babaláwo's role in àbíkú mythology is evidently major. But the problem remains that the àbíkú disrespects the babaláwo, whose skills it implicitly mocks. For in re-incarnating ultimately, in spite of the babaláwo's efforts to hinder its return, the àbíkú tricks the diviner himself. It negates the anticipated efficacy of the diviner's expertise and ritualistic intercessions and thus renders his intervention provisional and him useless to the forlorn parents.[33] The àbíkú is able to avoid prescribed firewalls and apparently resists, surmounts, and ridicules them by refusing to *stay*. Alongside the *ile*'s countermoves discussed above, the other hurdles range from naming rituals and postnatal parental vigilance to postmortem ceremonies of cadaver disfigurement. Like their Igbo variants, the Yoruba àbíkú names, which demonstrate the àbíkú's mischievous goals have been expected, are generally supplicatory, conciliatory, flattering, desperate, accusatory, rejective, anxious, indignant, commanding, persuading, sarcastic, incantatory, affirmative, and hopeful. Collectively, they relay the state as well as the extent of parental/familial ordeal and sentiment.[34]

In addition to names, charms are also used as parts of parental vigilance to induce and indirectly control the àbíkú so that it *stays*. But the àbíkú's death after these interventions could provoke an even harsher somatic response. In such cases parents may "become so frustrated and demoralized that they may resort," as hinted above,

> to punishing or torturing the corpse in such a way as to leave definitive, visible signs of physical punishments or torture on the body. Actions of this sort are not merely acts of despair, however. The Yoruba believe that the Abiku will be excommunicated from the assembly of its spirit-comrades should it appear to them with any of those marks of ordeal over its body, and that therefore when it is reborn, it must necessarily stay alive, having been ostracized by its fiendish colleagues of "the region beyond."[35]

The bodily incisions are intended to do more than punish, stigmatize, and shame the àbíkú. They serve also to enable parents to identify the reincarnated spirit, if and when reborn as another child. And if reborn, the tortuous and torturing drama begins all over. It is the idea of the àbíkú's willfulness, capriciousness, and intractability that Wole Soyinka's works along with those of Amos Tutuola inform Okri's figuration of Azaro below, as portrayed in his splendid poem "Abiku."[36]

The Famished Road *and Azaro's Àbíkú Impasse*

Described respectively by the *Boston Globe* and *The Wall Street Journal* as "A masterpiece if one ever existed" and "Something approaching a masterpiece of magic realism" (dust jacket), Ben Okri's *The Famished Road* features Azaro's àbíkú saga. Named Lazaro after the Christ-resurrected biblical Lazarus, Azaro (the self-raised black Lazarus) is the story's narrator. His life as a born-to-die, which Okri extends in *Songs of Enchantment* (1993) and *Infinite Riches* (1998), holds together the novel's dizzying plot.

The stunning spectacle that is the text's five-hundred-page narration is set in motion by Azaro's state of in-betweenness. Azaro is caught between spirits, ghosts, and human beings; between life and death; between past, present, and future; and between dreams. He is also caught between the fantastical and real. Like Ezinma, he is characterized as dreamy, a space- and time-traveler, a vagrant, exile, and a capricious child. At one time Azaro vengefully makes his parents suffer three days for punishing him by almost willing his death. "You are a stubborn child," his Dad admonishes him, and "I am a stubborn father. If you want to return to the world of spirits, return! But if you want to stay, then be a good son!" (325).

Like the unnamed narrator in James Weldon Johnson's *The Autobiography of an Ex-Colored Man* (1912) and the writhing speaker torn between his American nativity and his African blood in Countee Cullen's Harlem Renaissance poem "Heritage," Azaro is doubly conscious. He is depicted as "a child who didn't want to be born, but who will fight with death" (8). He is "a child of miracles" (9), a mind-reader, a figure gifted with supernatural powers of insight and foresight. And judging by his awareness and mature interpretation of both historical and contemporary world events much older than his human age, it is clear that he, like Ezinma, is a child-adult, an old spirit that has been here several times before.

Azaro starts the narrative and simultaneously his earthly journey by going back in time, to the myths of beginning. Situating himself self-consciously in àbíkú experience, he takes us through his plight as a spirit in human body. He is born into a family he helped impoverish—to an overworked mother-trader and an irritable, unprosperous father heavily in debt after spending so much in ritual efforts to keep him alive.

Also at the center of the book's tension is Azaro's seditious secession from the spirit world. Shaping its narrative axis is his desertion of his spirit playmates, with whom he made a pre-natal pact, *and* his decision to *stay* in the human/material domain the difficulties of which he readily accepts to endure. Because of this resolve to tarry with his human family and parents called simply Dad and Mum, Azaro incenses his mates in the spirit colony. This colony, we are told, is ruled by a powerful king, "a wonderful personage who sometimes appeared in the form of a great cat" (3). Feeling bereaved of a relative, a fellow colonial implicitly held captive in the material sphere, Azaro's otherworldly kin promise to make his life "unbearable" should he refuse to come home, unlike his alter ego and the other àbíkú child in the text, the young boy Ade, who elects to *return*. As they use various tactics and abductors, animate and inanimate, Azaro's spectral mates try to snatch him. They hunt and haunt him with unsolicited visitations, apparitions, apocalyptic premonitions, invasive subconscious chatter, persistent reminders of his allegiance, spatial transplantations, time and memory warps, physical violence, and near-death experiences.

The Famished Road takes us through a universe of the surreal and overlapping realities that àbíkú (Azaro) himself embodies. This is a world in which the unifying metaphor of road, or rather a mythic, famished road that has been under construction the past two thousand years, construes earthly life as a journey of cyclical, unending, an eternal becoming. It is a life fraught inevitably with physical accidents and human suffering. The misfortunes notwithstanding, Azaro longs to *stay* indefinitely with his human family but he maintains one leg in the spirit world, and thus suffers a crisis of identity and belonging. He loves (earthly) life but is shadowed closely by Death's agents—Death's bounty-hunters—even in public spaces, and as he interacts with the story's other intriguing characters that include the enterprising bar-owner Madame Koto, her human and spirit customers, and Jeremiah the photographer. In short, Azaro's encounters with the sick and hungry beggars, the maimed and volatile members of his penurious neighborhood, all call attention to Okri's positioning of *The Famished Road* as much more than an àbíkú tale. Like Achebe, Okri is preoccupied also with the human predicament. The narrative incidents disclose the text's concern with the intersections of the mystical, spiritual, and political with gender, power, violence, terror, corruption, suffering, and mass revolt.

Active in the saga are the Party of the Poor and the Party of the Rich. Both are depicted as deceptive, corrupt, ruthless, and rat-like. The story becomes more fascinating as Dad joins a different party from Madame Koto, whom Teresa N. Washington relates to Naylor's *Mama Day* and also ascribes with *Àjẹ* force (245–72). In addition, hoping that brute strength might extricate him from his penury, Dad trains as a boxer. He takes the name Black Tyger, and fights opponents named Yellow Jaguar, Green Leopard, and a non-human opponent dressed in white. This last fight almost kills him. As the story closes, reeling off a succession of epiphanic prophecies, one by Ade whom Azaro unmasks as having reincarnated in different nations, one of those rebirths uncovering Ade as formerly a white slave trader (481), Azaro meditates on his life as a spirit child. Azaro's father awakens suddenly from three days of recuperation. He too survives, thus symbolically surviving Death and lives on, as does Azaro. And in what the novel builds as a moment of familial and marital reunion, Dad shares his visions of human suffering, racial oppression, power, global justice, and a new world order.

Okri withholds the name of the country in which the novel is set. And thus the story's nameless Mum and Dad could be seen as every woman/mother and man/father struggling to save, claim, and raise a special child. Okri similarly allegorizes his themes of Life and Death and the tension between both phenomena. His approach to both subjects is rooted not in a Western or a universalist understanding, however, but rather in Yoruba cosmology, folklore, and folk practices. Furthermore, though Okri's nameless country might destabilize critical and geographical certainties,[37] we can infer at least that the nation is Nigeria. It quite likely is Nigeria in its emblematic history of independence, postcolonial politics, transitions, ethnic conflicts, socio-economic travails, and more. These are crisis points that for years stymied if not stunted the identity, growth, and "maturation" of Nigeria, a country that Soyinka represents as a half-child, an àbíkú, in his scathing play *A Dance of the*

Forests (1960). These crises have turned the country's youths into physical, spiritual, and emotional migrants dispersed all across the globe, drifters whose subject and identity formation is not only heavily circumscribed but also hybridized.

The àbíkú's metaphoricity resonates the Ọgbañje's epistemes exfoliated earlier. As a result, it would be redundant to rehash the same descriptors. Nevertheless, Okri's rendering of alternative reality and a born-to-die's dilemma of existence *and* Achebe's construction of Ezinma's Ọgbañje story are refined, extended, and echoed in contemporary African American narrativizations of slavery, slavery's aftermaths, implicated themes, and (postmodern) black subjectivity. Those conceptual, thematic, and stylistic transformations of the spirit child myth in the New World texts of Butler, Due, Wideman, and Morrison are neither accidental nor unrelated. Rather, they are grounded in the very workings of intertextuality. But most important, they are substrata of African American literary, cultural, intellectual, and political—one might say "postcolonial"—responses to late twentieth-century American history and African diaspora experience.

Chapter 2   Chinua Achebe, the Neo-Slave Narrative, the Nationalist Aesthetic, and African American (Re)Visions of the Spirit Child

[L]et us remember that, whenever we encounter repetition in cultural forms, we are indeed not viewing 'the same thing' but its transformation. . . .

> **James A. Snead**
> "Repetition as a figure
> of black culture"

Over the last three decades, literary historians, theorists, and critics have increasingly directed attention to the intertextual character of African American literary production, a complex interplay discernible even in the classic slave narratives penned and dictated by Africans and their descendants enslaved in the New World. Using various tools, from the vernacular call-and-response and (post)structuralism to dialogism and black feminist/womanist methodologies, they have alerted us to the web of internal linkages among novels of the African American literary tradition and between those novels and the fiction of other racial, ethnic, national, and religious groups. Of these studies, however, Henry Louis Gates's *The Signifying Monkey* (1988) is worth highlighting. I mention *Signifying* for its germane advocacy of comparativist exposition of African American texts. Beyond that, though, it complements the present endeavor in terms of both projects' shared interest in West African and more specifically Igbo and Yoruba historical, literary, religious, and aesthetic inheritances of black America. Such heritages are evinced in, for example, *Signifying*'s invocations of the Igbo Olaudah Equiano and the Yoruba trickster figure Esu. Quiet as it's kept, Esu as a polysemous, mythic trope shares with àbíkú—and by implication Ọgbañje—complements that Gates does not recognize in his contextualization of that god and guardian of the crossroads.[1]

At any rate, I want to suggest in this chapter one or two ways in which *Signifying*'s perspicacious conclusions about the African American literary tradition should be extended. The intended amplification pertains to the Ọgbañje/born-to-die concept, Chinua Achebe, and the criss-crossings of African American and West/African cultures and literary imaginations. Gates understates the interactions of African American and modern African fiction. Nonetheless, I would like to position his important argument as a transition toward a meditation on the 1960s emergence of the contemporary neo-slave narrative, the genre to which, I argue, all six focal African American works belong. It is in light of that form and, just as important, the cultural imperatives, aesthetic stances, and gendered politics of the 1960s and 1970s black consciousness and Black Arts movements that I shall attempt to ground Butler, Due, Wideman, and Morrison's texts in scrutiny. It is against those backdrops that I propose that we re-evaluate the four authors' semantic mimesis, complex character and thematic reconstructions, and other ideological reverberations of Achebe's and Okri's "archetypal" fictionalizations of Ọgbañje and àbíkú mythologies.

As we saw in the last chapter, the theme of born-to-die, in both its sociocultural anthropology and its literary dramatizations in the Ezinma and Azaro experiences, can be seen as a metatrope. It qualifies as a multi-performing, genre-transcending mythic idea around which a writer can develop a story's subplot or shape its characters and entire narration. As evinced by the focal works, the spirit child idiom lends itself liberally to novels in various, loosely applied generic markers: science/speculative fiction, magical realism, historical novel, and postmodern text.[2] In these instances, the reformatted paradigm of the spirit child performs superbly in the novelists's signifying practices, indeed in their realization of title, character, theme, narration, philosophy, and more.

Signifying on Signifying: What Has Achebe Got to Do with It?

In addition to contending, as does Houston A. Baker Jr., that all explicative hypotheses are text-generated, text-specific, and generally subsume a level of bias,[3] Gates explains that the earliest practitioners of black American letters (curiously, slaves and former slaves) wrote mainly to inscribe their humanity. And through writing, they reasserted their intellect and creativity, which Western historiography castigated as either non-existent or inconsequential at best. Of particular instructiveness, however, are Gates's remarks on how, largely because of their polygenesis, works of the African American literary tradition tend to mirror the socio-historical circumstances of their evolution. Consciously or unconsciously, they interact with their times. They also engage with other works in a dialogue that affirms, reverses, and/or extends antecedent or contemporary authors, texts, themes, and literary conventions. It is this latter insight that is paramount here in terms of establishing a point of departure and drawing attention to the African novel's, specifically *Things Fall Apart's*, under-studied fingerprints in late twentieth-century African American politico-literary culture.

Signifying posits correctly that black texts are inherently polyreferential. Double-voiced, they are an expressive hybrid because their literary predecessors are not only black texts but white ones as well. Consequently, African American writers sometimes replicate received occidental canonical texts and tropes. They do this, however, with a veritable sense of racial difference rooted in the black vernacular tradition of "signifying," which Claudia Mitchell-Kernan defines concisely as "a way of encoding messages or meanings which involves, in most cases, an element of indirection."[4] The writers also "read [and revise] each other," Gates stipulates, "and seem intent on refiguring what we might think of as key canonical topoi and tropes received from the black tradition itself" (xxii). Among such recurrent, cardinal motifs of the tradition are "[t]he descent underground, the vertical 'ascent' from the South to North, myriad figures of the double and especially double consciousness" (xxv), and others. It is mainly through this schematic of replication, change, and continuity, and not on the basis of skin pigmentation, that a "literary tradition" is constituted.[5] Thus, because of the canonical African American text's propensity to network with other black texts, and because of its pluralistic nativity, it is necessary that students of African American literature keep its dual descent in mind and approach the tradition's fiction, in this case, from a comparativist standpoint. For Mary Helen Washington, we can visualize the African American literary tradition as "a grid in one of those airline magazines that shows the vast and intricate interweaving patterns of coast-to-coast flight schedules."[6]

It is not a case of misreading to say that Washington's clarifying graphic of "coast-to-coast" literary topography implies that the authorial, thematic, and formal collaboration in question does not quite extend to either continental or other African diaspora locales and letters. Nor is it reductive to adduce that the charted literary bond starts with, stops at, and thus is framed within the limited perimeters of black American racial encounter and literary production in *North America*. The anthology *Black-Eyed Susans,* in which Washington's cited, introductory statements appear focuses on African American women authors. Given that, it would be hard to argue in this case that the circuitry of those intersecting flight routes that plot the coordinates of African American literary history and tradition is not specifically national or sub-regional. In other words, it seems apparent that the coasts in question are those of the United States. And in spite of its undertone of a global literary Africanity, a Paul Gilroyian black Atlanticism, if you will, *Signifying*'s concern is with a hemispheric literary canon when Gates talks about not only black, black texts, blackness, and texts of blackness but likewise those exchanges that enable the advent of a group's praxis of letters.

To be clear, the above observations are not intended to suggest that the cultural integrity, canonic implications, and seminal vision of *Signifying Monkey* are in any way compromised by its specific focus on illustrative African American writers and texts. Nor, as in the case of Washington's image of coast-to-coast grid, is anything remotely wrong with a scholarly stress on African American women's distinguishing, creative sisterhood, a literary and political partnership that Alice Walker, Barbara Christian, Michael Awkward, and many other scholars have diligently diagrammed.[7] The point is that, if left unaddressed, uncorrected, and "demask[ed]," to mime Lawrence Hogue's term explicative of Michel Foucault's notion of discursive formation,[8] *Signifying* would go on leaving us with a certain insoluble impression. It would entrench the postulate that along with the transformative impact of Anglo American and continental European literatures, the "black texts" that have left the heaviest direct or indirect legacy on the development of the contemporary black American novel are those written specifically by fellow North American blacks.

This insinuation—that there exists little or no significant, mutual, and sustained reciprocity between the creations of the contemporary African American novel, and postcolonial African fiction—should be amended. It should be rethought and revised specifically because it diminishes, if not disregards, the thematic, aesthetic, and cosmological impresses of modern African novelists, texts, and narrativized tropes. Such stamps are evidenced in the undeniable signatures of Chinua Achebe, *Things Fall Apart,* and the Ọgbanje/born-to-die concept on late twentieth-century African American novels.

A pathbreaking and perennial classic translated to over fifty-five world languages, one whose golden anniversary in 2008 would not go unnoticed, *Things Fall Apart* is Africa's most widely read novel to date. It is also the one African text that many contemporary African diaspora authors and critics acknowledge reading either in school, alongside other black and white writers, or during their own periods of literary apprenticeship. More important, it is arguably the novel that is, through its first and subsequent American editions and overall popularity in the

West, quite likely most responsible for acquainting North American readers of the 1960s and beyond with the "Ọgbañje" concept. Preceded only by Amos Tutuola's excerpted fabulation of the "born and die" in his mesmerizing piece *My Life in the Bush of Ghosts* (1954), *Things Fall Apart* presents through the Ezinma/Ezinma-Ekwefi encounter one of the premier, extended, structural, political, and philosophical depictions of Ọgbañje character and experience in continental African fiction. Even though other oral and plastic forms, as well as literary endeavors by native Africans in indigenous, Arabic, and colonial languages anteceded it, *Things Fall Apart* is the work whose publication is identified as the inaugurating event of modern African fiction. And not only can its thematic and formal prints be spotted on the projects of other equally venerable postcolonial (African) writers[9] and on the evolution and trends in the postmodern African novel (Quayson 2004), but also it has more positively re-invented black Africa. It has represented the continent's history, cultures, and thought for the (post)modern world. As the preeminent flag-bearer of African fiction's heft on the global literary carnival, *Things Fall Apart* has garnered more visibility and prestige to the African novel whose viability and vibrancy were initially assailed by racist European and Anglo-American reviewers and even by Western-minded African critics. As Ernest N. Emenyonu puts it, *Things Fall Apart,* whose author he adulates as "Omenka: The Master Artist," is the novel that "was to change the course of World Literature in English."[10]

The above facts, which Simon Gikandi calls "Achebe's seminal status in the history of African literature," and his keen grasp of "the archaeological role of the novel"[11] were confirmed again in events that occurred in the past twenty years. For a sample: just recently, in June 2007, Achebe solidified that pioneer status by winning the second-ever Man Booker International Prize.[12] And, some years after the editors of *Matatu* devoted a special volume (no. 8) of the journal to a criticism of Achebe's last novel *Anthills of the Savannah* (1987), Howard University's English department dedicated its 1998 Annual Heart's Day ceremonies to "The Achievement of Chinua Achebe." The multi-topic conference papers presented as part of the occasion would culminate in a special edition (volume 25.2 [2002]) of *Callaloo: A Journal of African Diaspora Arts and Letters* dedicated to Achebe.[13] A similar tribute came in 2000 during a two-day conference organized by Bard College, New York, where Achebe holds an endowed professorship, to commemorate his seventieth birthday. Among the dignitaries that attended from various parts of the world were luminaries of African American literature, including Toni Morrison, John Edgar Wideman, and Sonya Sanchez.

Achebe's African American and African diaspora peers, admirers, and well-wishers comment on his extensive intellectual contributions to African peoples, world letters, and humanity at large. They remark on, among other things, his impact on them as fellow (black) writers of fiction who have to tell their own stories using a European mode—"the novel"—as well as "English" language. Like Achebe, black diaspora writers, though possessing an enviable operational mastery of "standard" English, French, Spanish, Portuguese, Dutch, and other languages, have also had to inflect these European and Romance dialects with their own accents and intentions and thus have permanently bent them to shoulder the weight of their humanity. Achebe celebrators also credit his work with heightening their knowledge of the cosmology, strengths, internal tensions, and philosophic depth of the (pre-conquest) Igbo/African people of Umuofia as they confront, survive, and try to transcend, as does black America, the predative encroachment of a domination-minded white world. Akin Adesokan notes in his coverage of the birthday occasion that Sanchez even "links Okonkwo's act of resistance [in *Things Fall Apart*] to the spirit of rebellion, the sense of historical duty which inform[ed] the creative choices of the Black Arts Movement of the 1960s."[14] For many a 1960s African American student who defied southern apartheid and white power blessed by the Supreme Court in *Plessy v. Ferguson* (1896), just as imperialist Europe was scrambling for Africa and as the Igbo/Umuofians were dealing with British missionary-espionage, *Things Fall Apart* was among the inspirational texts to read. As Catherine Lyn Innes recalls, for her students at Tuskegee Institute, Alabama, at the peak of the Black Power movement, Okonkwo the novel's towering figure of manhood, resistance and self-determination symbolized "'a real Black Power.'"[15]

Matching Okonkwo's opposition of white power and *Things Fall Apart*'s political legacy are Achebe's incisive opinions on African/black empowerment and aesthetics, enumerated in such seminal essay collections as *Morning Yet on Creation Day* (1976), *Hopes and Impediments* (1988) and *Home and Exile* (2000). In these volumes, the first *Morning* released at the twilight of the Black Arts movement, Achebe displays that depth of intellectual acumen for which Emenyonu duly hails him as "the forerunner-theoretician of African literary criticism" and a "Philosopher-critic."[16] Achebe ponders issues that African American political activists, artists, critical theorists, and literary historians, or just scholars, teachers and students of African American history and literature of any era, would find rather familiar, timely, refreshing, or at least provocative. But they would resonate the most with the innovators and trustees of the 1960s and 1970s Black Aesthetic, a historically elastic movement that interestingly coincided with Africa's equally Afrocentric and nationalist *bolekaja* critical school.[17]

Of interest to Achebe in the essays are, in permutation: historicity, the question of African peoples' humanity, "chi" and the individual in Igbo thought, the inextricability of self and community, and the power of names and self-naming. Others are the identity, membership and audience of African literature and its creators, the audacity and errors of colonialist criticism of African/black letters, and the place of (colonial/English) language, universalism, folklore, myths, myth-making, ideology, protest, and war in the African novel. Achebe talks also about the process-oriented Igbo art and aesthetic reified powerfully, he invokes, in the collectively and lavishly constructed, sublime, mediative, functional, and yet ephemeral *Mbari* houses of Owerri *and* in the spectacle and mobility of the Ijele masquerade in which Achebe finds subsumed "other forms—[dance,] sculpture, music, painting, drama, costumery, even architecture" ("Igbo World" 65). He reflects on the axial significance of the River Niger, Onitsha, and Onitsha market in Igbo Christianity, modernity, cosmopolitanism, mythopoesis, literary history, capitalism, and education. Achebe addresses the politics of publishing (in Africa), the interpenetration of art and politics, and the novelist's role as teacher, cultural custodian, community activist, generational bridge, and nationalist. He tackles as well the oddities of postmodernism, the presumed "innocence of stories," and the importance of "re-storying"[18] in a colonized people's transcendence of their trauma, their healing of their damaged group psyche, and their reclamation of their land, history, story, and human dignity.

This subject of the veracity and redemptive potential of self-narration, which Achebe raises in *Things Fall Apart* and revisits in *Anthills of the Savannah,* is echoed in Wideman's *The Cattle Killing.* It is approximated also in the title of Wideman's short story collection *All Stories are True* (1992). The story is often told about how some canonical African American male writers—notably James Baldwin, Ralph Ellison, and Ernest J. Gaines—have at various times not only self-identified mainly with white writers Mark Twain, William Faulkner, Ernest Hemingway, T. S. Eliot and Russian authors but also claimed that they inherited little of aesthetic significance from their black male precursor, particularly Richard Wright. Unlike his predecessors and contemporaries, however, Wideman has no anxieties about acknowledging his debt to Achebe's traditional yet sophisticated vision of the novel. Nor has Morrison, who appreciates portals that Achebe "figuratively opened for her."[19]

In an interview with Christina Davis, Morrison, responding to a question on her literary closeness to or kinship with any African writers, affirms that alongside her epiphanic discovery of such African authors as Guinean novelist Camara Laye, Wole Soyinka's plays, and Ghanaian writer Ayi Kwei Armah, "Chinua Achebe was a *real* education for me, a real education."[20] Further, in her introduction to a new edition of Laye's *The Radiance of the King,* Morrison again talks about how her sighting of Achebe in the 1960s was "more than a revelation—it was intellectually and aesthetically transforming" (18). At the Achebe birthday conference, Morrison described that debt to Achebe as "very large, [it] had no repayment schedule, and was interest-free" (Sengupta, "Chinua Achebe").

Morrison expounds on the substance of that philosophic and creative transformation. It has to do with Achebe's ingenious alteration and enlargement of the "traditional" novel form, his *Africanization* of the mode by what Wideman sees as Achebe's "switching of perspective, [his] putting an African sensibility at the center of the novel ... [and his use] of cultural items, the language and the spiritual perspective of the Ibo culture."[21] Also, one cannot help but discern how some of the most striking attributes of Morrison's fiction—her dialogue construction, her precision with, and her oralization and auralization of the racism-inflected English language—favor what Achebe scholars praise as his linguistic brevity. They remind one of Achebe's sharp ear for the undulation, the cadence, of the spoken word, his deceptive, unembellished prose, and his insurrectionary Igbonization of the Queen's tongue with proverbs and the Igbo art/act of conversation. This Achebe signature, Morrison acknowledges, has helped her write back contrarily to and dismiss as inconsequential a scrutinizing white gaze. And, although it might just be coincidental, there are also noteworthy parallels in racial-political intents between Achebe's accusatory re-reading of Conrad in "An Image of Africa: Racism in Conrad's *Heart of Darkness*" (1975) and Morrison's daring and incriminatory revelation, in *Playing in the Dark: Whiteness and the Literary Imagination* (1992), of the racist treatment of "Africanist" presence in works by some of the most valorized white writers in the United States. Indicted to various degrees in *Playing* are Henry James, Hemingway, Willa Cather, Flannery O'Connor, Harriet Beecher Stowe, Edgar Allan Poe, William Faulkner, Mark Twain, Herman Melville, Nathaniel Hawthorne, and William Styron. Similarities abound as well between Morrison's statements in the essays "City Limits" and "Rootedness" that she writes "village" literature and Achebe's declarations of his artistic and political creed in *Morning* and *Hopes*. But did Morrison also glean from Achebe, as he exemplifies in *Things Fall Apart*, how to fluidly naturalize horror and the supernatural (as in the Ezinma story) or make community the protagonist, the dominant presence and voice in a novel, as Morrison does in *Sula?*

In view of the above, and given that what one might call the "Achebe impact" on or his apparently significant contributions to (black) American intellectual life and history are not unknown in the U.S. years before the 1988 publication of *Signifying* (for instance, the Achebe critique of Conrad was delivered at the University of Massachusetts in 1975), it is rather baffling that the only contemporary African creative writers of note that Gates indexes in theorizing signifyin(g), vis-à-vis African American literary tradition, are Anthony Appiah and Wole Soyinka.[22] Even more curious is that the bulk of his reference in *Signifying* to Soyinka focuses on an observation that a character's statement in Soyinka's 1963 play *The Lion and the Jewel* parodies Shakespearean blank verse (107). It appears that this is Gates's notation that African writers, as do their African diaspora cousins, also signify on Western literary structures. That is true.

Yet it is really not anything new to students and critics of African literature. Most African novelists and novels focus on the experiences of Africans *on* the continent. They also appropriate from, parody, satirize, and directly challenge some classics of Western literature, as exemplified in Achebe's titular, epigraphic, intertextual, and modernist conjurations of W. B. Yeats and T. S. Eliot. The literary assault is illustrated also in Achebe's counterpoising of *Things Fall Apart, No Longer at Ease* and *Arrow of God* as revisionist, contrapuntal, and certainly signifyin(g) responses to Joseph Conrad's *Heart of Darkness* (1902) and Joyce Cary's *The African Witch* (1936) and his *Mister Johnson* (1939). As does Rudyard Kipling with colonial India in *Kim* (1901), Conrad and Cary treat Africans as calibanic palimpsests for the inscriptions of Europe's imperial/colonial project on Africa.

Also, as the historiography of modern African literature discloses and illustrates in the comparable themes and styles of the hundreds of novels that comprise Heinemann's African Writers Series (AWS) for which Achebe was founding editor, members of the older guard that achieved literary prominence from the mid- to late-1950s through the early 1980s and into the 1990s, also read, revised, and amplified each other. They discoursed on national, regional, continental, formal, and even gendered levels. And, construing themselves as part of a nascent African literary renaissance, one that is postmodern, borderless, more diasporic and certainly quite daring in its appropriative gestures and rhetorical echoes, some of the most recent African-born writers also pay tribute to their African American precursors and contemporaries.[23] Even Achebe himself has acknowledged the humanistic and intellectual impression that James Baldwin's works, particularly *Go Tell It on the Mountain* and *The Fire Next Time!,* had on him as early as 1963, the first time he visited the United States and met with John Oliver Killens, Langston Hughes, Ralph Ellison, Paule Marshall, LeRoi Jones (Amiri Baraka), and Arthur Miller.[24] Achebe discovered a kindred spirit in Baldwin's intent to tweak the English language and force it to carry the black experience. But more important, he describes his initial encounter with Baldwin's writing as "a miraculous experience. Nothing that I heard or read or seen quite prepared me for the Baldwin phenomenon," Achebe says.[25] In his meditation "The Day I Finally Met Baldwin" (2002)

Achebe recollects that memorable encounter with Baldwin, who saw in resourceful Okonkwo his own father.

These crosscurrents, these bi-directional, trans-Atlantic meetings of twentieth-century African American and African literary imaginations, demonstrate that things, not surprisingly, sometimes have a way of journeying back full circle, like Ọgbañje. It seems to me, therefore, that we should re-plot and stretch farther eastward to various coasts and points in West/Africa and then back to the Americas, to the Caribbean island nations, and to Europe, those flight lines in Washington's picture of the African American texts' coast-to-coast geography of intertextual repetitions, revisions, expansions, and echoes. Those rootings and routings, to call on Gilroy, look more authentic and complete if drafted diasporically.

Thus, with the mythic drama of the spirit child serving as yet another powerful metaphor that can help us delineate further the heuristic kinship of African American and West African world views, texts, contexts, and aesthetics, it becomes imperative that we expand our critical comparisons of those cultural, literary, and philosophic equivalencies from their current emphasis on the more popular areas of interplay. For intermittently we hear scholars interested in such synergies declaim that, yes, both African American and postcolonial African arts and letters are in part socially utilitarian and especially Marxist in their collective didacticism and their thematic as well as formal interest in grassroots/proletariat struggle against imperial domination and (capitalist) exploitation. Critics reflect that twentieth-century Afro-Caribbean and African literary histories share the Harlem Renaissance's influence on the thirties and forties Negritude movement and the Negritude's goal of rehabilitating diasporic black humanity, soul, identity, culture, art, and civilization on par with if not higher than those of Europe.[26]

Africanist scholarship espouses that African America and Africa are bound by their common ties to discourse of Ethiopianism and that postcolonial theory could also be usefully applied to African American texts.[27] We read as well that African American and African writers analogously tackle themes of oral tradition, satire, gender, family, motherhood, and the mother-daughter experience. There are persuasive studies on both groups' corresponding ruminations on linguistics, voice and voicing, community, the ancestor figure, and the (god)dess archetype. Other readings note African and African American thematic investments in Christianity and African religions, conjuration, the trickster/picaresque tropes (especially the ubiquitous Esu Elegbara), and other folkloric concepts. Interestingly, these unifying ideas are seldom discussed in terms of African American texts that consciously or otherwise refashion, extend or simply echo specific modern African novels, or vice-versa.

It is illuminating what unravels when those crossroads are traveled relative to signifyin(g). Specifically, in bridging each of the focal African American texts and a West African precursor (for instance, though not in this order: *Wild Seed, Mind of My Mind, The Cattle Killing, Sula, Beloved* each with *Things Fall Apart;* and *The Between* with *Famished Road*) and then interrogating them using the tropological repetition-revision-and-extension sublogos of signifyin(g), some "new" insights emerge. It becomes clearer that what Butler, Due, and Wideman especially have done, subsumed in their dominant concern with the African, African American and American experience, is re-frame the literarized, mythic spirit child. They have expropriated and (re)modeled Ọgbañje /the born-to-die toward elaborate treatments of the one mammoth, racially consequential, and "living dead" encounter explored also in Morrison's texts but addressed minimally in *Things Fall Apart* and African fiction in general, namely, the Middle Passage and New World slavery.[28]

Beside works by such African authors as Pita Nwana, Ayi Kwei Armah, Bessie Head, Yambo Ouologuem, Ama Ata Aidoo, Kofi Awoonor, T. Obinkaram Echewa, and Isidore Okpewho,[29] *The Slave Girl,* the 1977 novel by the expatriate Nigerian writer Buchi Emecheta, is a notable exception to anglophone African novels' reticence on (trans-Atlantic) slavery. Significantly, in *Slave Girl* Emecheta associates the Ọgbañje experience with domestic slavery in early twentieth-century Igboland through the eponymous Ọgbañje/slave character Ojebeta.[30] However, it is neither *Slave Girl*'s gendered exploration of "Ọgbañje" that Butler and Wideman transcode. Nor is it the other Ọgbañje- and àbíkú-centered works in Nigerian literary corpus that they positedly mine.[31] For one thing, Butler's *Mind of My Mind,* which features the Patternist ancestor Doro whom we discover later in *Wild Seed* (1980) to be an Ọgbañje, was published in 1977, the same year as *Slave Girl.* Thus, it would be illogical to contend that Butler was familiar with Emecheta's story prior to its publication.

As hinted in the introduction, the signs to Butler's cultural contexts, literary antecedent, and our fullest appreciation of *Wild Seed* and *Mind of My Mind* lie elsewhere. The clues reside in much more than Butler's development of Doro's and Anyanwu's characters, as well as their chance encounter, around Igboland, Igbo history, myths, and culture. The hints go beyond her interest in Igbo women's experience with motherhood, power and sociopolitical revolt, and Igbo people's rejection of imposed rule and their penchant for egalitarianism. The arrows point directly also to the cultural and aesthetic marks of *Things Fall Apart,* which Butler recognized in an unpublished, 1991 private interview with Margaret O'Connor. In that exchange, Butler states, "*Wild Seed* was almost entirely library research. . . . an earlier reading of the novels of Chinua Achebe ignited my interest in Igbo people."[32] Unfortunately, the Achebe impact is overlooked by most reviewers of *Wild Seed*. Most recently in *Our Mothers, Our Powers, Our Texts,* for example, Teresa N. Washington relates Butler and *Wild Seed* not to Achebe and *Things Fall Apart* but instead to Soyinka and his drama *Madmen and Specialists* (1988).

Nevertheless, *Things Fall Apart*'s narrator profiles an Ọgbañje as "one of those wicked children who, when they died, entered their mother's womb to be born again." The narrator adds that the spirit child Ọgbañje is a "wicked tormentor" mired in an "evil cycle of birth and death."[33] Butler signifies on Achebe. She repeats and extends *Things Fall Apart* in, among other ways, her "framing" of Doro's character thusly: "He was like an ogbanje, an evil child spirit born to one woman again and again, only to die and give the mother pain. A woman tormented by an ogbanje could give birth many times and still have no living children. But Doro was an adult. He did not enter and re-enter his mother's womb. He did not want the bodies of children. He preferred to steal the bodies of men" (*Wild* 12).

The lexical, syntactic, and conceptual parallels in the above depictions are clear. From that sketch of Doro's genes emanates Butler's elaboration of him as a time-traveling and power-driven alien, invader, enslaver, and eugenicist colony builder that is at once spirit and matter. From it flows her portrayal of him intersubjectively as a trickster, body snatcher, a serial-killer, an immortality-seeking entity, and a contract breaker that inhabits, destroys, discards, and over again re-invades generations of human bodies with ease and repeated impunity, consistent with the Ọgbañje's ontology and figurative extensions. Also, as a wife and mother toughened after bearing forty-seven surviving children to ten husbands, Butler's powerful and insubordinate heroine/healer Anyanwu—implicitly a sun deity, earth mother, and racial ancestress who in colonial America undergoes a name change—evokes yet reverses the motherhood plight of Achebe's Ekwefi: a brave and rebellious woman who after several maternities and bereavements tells Death to please Himself. And the Anyanwu-Doro opposition—that is, woman versus a controlling and exploitative force—also signifies on the Ezinma-Ekwefi dynamic in that Butler genders Doro, her "Ezinma"/Ọgbañje *and* enslaver figure, as male. John R. Pfeiffer is one of the very few critics, including Sandra Y. Govan, Sandra M. Grayson, and recently Bernard Bell, who have remarked on Achebe's influence on Butler. Pfeiffer keenly observes that in *Wild Seed* Butler's deliberate "accreting" of "detail in relatively short sentences" resounds *Things Fall Apart*'s narrative style (152). As we shall see, Butler echoes Achebe in many more ways.

Just as Butler takes her cue from Achebe's structuring of Ọgbañje and his treatment of indigenous Igbo life and Umuofia's experience with colonization,

Tananarive Due's *The Between* (1995) likewise reminds one of Ben Okri's rendering of the conundrums of àbíkú/born-to-die subjectivity in *The Famished Road.* What is noteworthy about Due's case, however, is that unlike Butler and Wideman's imprinted novels and Morrison's imbricated ones, *The Between* does not engage directly with the subject of "slavery" or enslavement through characterization or narratology. But one *senses* it. Due topicalizes slavery and its child Jim Crow by express and allusive reference on the novel's first two pages. Here the narrator talks about a street named after the antebellum abolitionist, black autobiographer, and orator Frederick Douglass. The narrator also describes the protagonist Hilton James's migrant grandmother Nana (Eunice Kelly) in ways that conjure up Sojourner Truth's famed meditation on her masculinized womanhood. Also mentioned is school segregation, slavery's other child.

The story follows Hilton's ordeals as a part-human, discernibly part-spirit born-to-die that straddles uneasily both the corporeal and disincarnate spheres. Captive to the material realm, as is Azaro in *Famished Road,* Hilton is subjected to extreme pressures by Death, which hounds him to rejoin the otherworldly fraternity. This unseen fraternity's telepathic insistences that Hilton return "home" assume the form of dreams, directives, terror, and control. Thus, *The Between* reads as Due's initial sculptings of the theme of "subjugation" or, by extension, enslavement. A writer who majored in Nigerian literature for her Master's at Leeds, learned about the West African "born-to-die" idea while in graduate school, and has intensely studied "Yoruba belief systems, vodou and Santeria,"[34] Due reclaims and reintroduces that subject of slavery/enslavement proper in her next novel *My Soul to Keep. My Soul* anticipates Due's third novel, the award-winning epic *The Living Blood.* All three works can be seen as forming a conceptual trilogy, with *The Between* situated as their thematic and stylistic understructure.[35]

In his case, Wideman stated to me in an interview that he did not research Ọgbañje formally before restructuring it in *The Cattle Killing* (1996). In the novel, Wideman transmutes Ọgbañje as pretext to retell and contemporarize slavery and the epic sagas of some of those wandering souls—the antebellum, itinerant black revivalists and evangelists—whose conversion narratives/spiritual autobiographies/slave texts receive new emplotment, force, and political significance in Wideman's remarkable craftsmanship. "What I know about ogbanje," Wideman allows, "is actually derived from my reading of Achebe, and thinking about *Things Fall Apart.* When I came across the idea, specifically for the first time in Achebe, what happened is that a very important idea [that he had been pondering for long] suddenly had a specific name, a specific provenance, for me. And it was like meeting an old friend."[36] Wideman recomposes and also improvises on the Ọgbañje drama as follows:

Certain passionate African spirits—kin to the ogbanji [*sic*] who hide in a bewitched woman's womb, dooming her infants one after the other to an early death unless the curse is lifted—are so strong and willful they refuse to die. They are not gods but achieve a kind of immortality through serial inhabitation of mortal bodies, passing from one to another, using them up, discarding them, finding a new host. Occasionally, as one of these powerful spirits roams the earth, bodiless, seeking a new home, an unlucky soul will encounter the spirit, fall in love with it, follow the spirit forever, finding it, losing it in the dance of the spirit's trail through other people's lives.[37]

Wideman's *The Cattle Killing* bears out the above claim of familiarity. Unfortunately, in spite of his interview statements regarding Ọgbañje, its ethnic origins and artistic and philosophic thrusts in the novel, critics have yet to investigate that cultural background. Nor have they disseminated Wideman's re-envisaging of the Ezinma character and experience/the Ezinma-Ekwefi relationship or, even more, diffused the above framing passage into an analysis of the story, its characterization, thematics, narrative structure, and more. Looking at the way both Butler and Wideman treat Ọgbañje, however, there can be no doubt that for them the idea is not a stranger. It is, rather, a complicated religious principle whose bedrock postulate of alternative reality and an integrated universe is not alien or bizarre. As pointed out in the Introduction and buttressed in studies such as Robert Farris Thompson's *Flash of the Spirit* (1983) and Elliot J. Gorn's "Black Spirits: The Ghostlore of Afro-American Slaves" (1984), spirits-related beliefs such as Ọgbañje permeated and still permeate African American syncretistic folk thought. "Spirits" also interconnect African diaspora's cultural continuum, as Morrison's works illustrate.

Further, as earlier stated, Morrison does not use Ọgbañje, àbíkú, or born-to-die in either *Sula* (1973) or the explicitly slavery story *Beloved* (1987). Although published earlier than some of the focal texts, both novels are discussed last in this study for purposes of category differentiation, intellectual vision, and structural cohesion. Critics such as Karla F. C. Holloway (*Moorings* 183), Brooks De Vita ("Not Passing" 10), Dathorne (2001), and Ogunyemi (2002) have divined Beloved as a spirit child and Ọgbañje figure. I argue that not only is *Sula* a captivity narrative and that the character Sula is a precursor of Beloved, but that both characters are Ọgbañje spirit children. A deep appreciation of the philosophic range of the Ọgbañje idea, particularly Ezinma, makes Sula's unearthliness less startling, less culturally unrivaled, or indeed unprecedented literarily. I say less shocking and not an uncharted territory because of what Morrison said about Sula's character and about *Beloved*. In their interview "Intimate Things in Place" (1976), Morrison told

Robert Stepto that part of the difficulty she had in "describ[ing Sula as] a woman who could be used as a classic type of evil force" (12) was that she, Morrison, "didn't know anyone like her." But she "knew women who looked like that, who looked like they *could* be like that" (15). Also, Morrison shared with Gail Caldwell in another interview that she "didn't have any literary precedent," apparently in African American letters, "for what [she] was trying to do with the magic" realism, that is, the folkloric and supernatural dimensions of *Beloved* (242–43).

Morrison's remarks to Stepto, coupled with many readers' potential unfamiliarity with the Ọgbañje concept, specifically, might have had the unintended effect of steering subsequent criticism on Sula/*Sula* toward other contexts and texts than Ọgbañje and *Things Fall Apart*. For instance, consistent with the ongoing historiographic chartings of a viable tradition of black women's literary, feminist, and womanist expressivity, some reviews have observed interfaces between *Their Eyes Were Watching God*'s Janie Crawford and *Sula*'s eponym. Morrison certainly appreciates those efforts to link, in particular, twentieth-century generations of African American women writers whose matrilineage is often traced to Hurston, thanks mainly to Alice Walker's recuperation of Hurston as literary ancestress. But as Morrison stressed to Gloria Naylor, however, she actually had not read *Their Eyes* before writing *Sula*.[38] Invariably, the character Beloved has been tracked to several source-springs. And the cultural, semantic, and political results of such lines of inquiry have been mixed, to say the least.

These tracings not withstanding, both Sula and Beloved have additionally, in Ezinma, more than a West African religious "explanation" and *another* literary forebear. The two eponyms reconnect with an ontological kin as well. Ezinma's rebirths and return to Ekwefi make Beloved's spiritual/physical reincarnation to Sethe less mystifying, infeasible, and atypical. Ezinma's diabolism and beneficence relative to her mother Ekwefi and her father Okonkwo nullify binary opposition and provide a philosophic site for further evaluation of Sethe's infanticide. That is, given the inhumane crucible of slavery that nurtures Sethe's enactment of agency but again the idea of a mother killing her own child, denying the child life and chance, and polluting *Ala* (the sacred earth) with her child's blood, we cannot adjudicate Sethe's infanticide as completely unconscionable. Nor is it, on the other hand, totally morally defensible. Most important, however, seeded in the subplot of the Ezinma story is (1) the need for healing for Ekwefi, the Okonkwo family and Umuofia people at large, and (2) the demand for cosmic order. Absorbed in it is the obligation to restore balance through the ritual exorcism of a seemingly intractable evil/presence/memory (insert: Ọgbañje's or, by ideological extension, Europe's invasion, enslavement and colonization of black body and mind).

Thematized earlier in *Things Fall Apart,* such requisite ritual intervention and familial, communal and by extension racial healing are central in *Beloved.*

We can begin to see then why an informed comprehension of *Things Fall Apart, Famished Road,* and the anthropology of Ọgbañje/born-to-die enhances greatly and indeed is crucial for our broadest cultural, critical, and comparativist apprehension of the African American novels in this study. Such an understanding relativizes those New World and African novels and further ethnically roots their salient Africanisms. It also helps clarify subtleties of the Butler, Due, Wideman, and Morrison metanarratives of the living-dead that some readers may find arcane, obfuscating, or just implausible.

Dearly Departed: The Born-to-Die Keep "the Dead" Alive

As we gain more preliminary clarity on the foregoing, however, I would next like to consider, as a question, the following point hinted at in the beginning of the chapter. How is it that the theme of enslavement, allegorized in the drama of the born-to-die, appears in virtually all of the studied works which, as it turns out, were released at a certain moment in American political and African American racial and literary history? Put another way: why is it that the Ọgbañje- and àbíkú-implicated topic of enslavement—or slavery's residual vestiges in other attempted or realized enactments of power—recurs in one way or another in each of the imprinted and imbricated novels?

One quick answer would be to allude to the point that underneath the death-and-life drama enacted between an Ọgbañje-àbíkú child and his/her parents is, as earlier intimated, an ongoing struggle for power, control, and self/autonomy. It is a putative epic power battle waged between the cruel, power-abusing Ọgbañje-àbíkú, as Soyinka deems the spirit child, and the child's parents who, held hostage by worry over the child's survival, and together with the diviner, constitute a counter-offensive coalition. Broadened into other spheres, what we have at play is the real yet analogic rivalry between oppressor/oppression and the oppressed, delimitation and revolt, and "evil" and "good." The eminent sociologist Orlando Patterson might characterize that adversarial relationship as the primordial tension between and interdependency of slavery and freedom.[39] We can extrapolate then from Patterson's thesis, which Morrison endorses in *Playing in the Dark,*[40] that the Ọgbañje-àbíkú existential spectacle mimics, on one hand, the wider African American racial conflict with and within a dominating white world. It infers, on the other, the more personal and dogged quests by individual black men and women to achieve unfettered human agency by subverting not simply white domination of black life but also intraracial violations of the black (gen-dered) self.

A weightier response, however, is that the Ọgbañje/born-to-die implicated theme of enslavement traverses, unifies, and helps dialogize the works for a number of other social, intellectual and artistic developments in American and African American history. It is clear that in *and* through their fiction, Butler, Due, Wideman, and Morrison intend to continue their antebellum forebears' literary testimonies. All four authors are concerned, as is Achebe, "to tell a free story."[41] But they want to bear witness without a white abolitionist's, amanuensis's, or colonialist's prefa-tory authentication. They simply want to express themselves without those socio-editorial proscriptions that stressed rhetorical persuasiveness and sentimentalism but pressured many an antebellum slave-scribe against subjectivity and rage, against "dwelling too long or too carefully on the more sordid details of their experience"[42] and the inclusion of Africanisms in their narratives.[43]

Butler, Due, Wideman, and Morrison aspire then to (re)link the New World with Africa. Bringing a healthy and unencumbered attitude to African cultural survivals in the New World, as did Zora Neale Hurston, these writers are not afraid to be called "superstitious." And thus they embrace the reality of alternative reality. Like Achebe, they exploit the past and those besmirched "Africanisms" to explain the present and philosophize on the complexity and irreducibility of the human person. As writers of "retrospective fiction,"[44] as artists interested in enunciating the meanings and depths of holistic black liberation,[45] Butler, Due, Wideman, and Morrison want in various ways to revisit and re-envision history. Insisting that the trans-Atlantic slave trade *was* and *remains* "a *mass experience*," a catastro-phe (Lukács 23)[46] that reshaped and permanently entangles Europe, the Americas, and Africa, they want to re-articulate history. They intend to recover into pres-ent memory, experience, and discourse some of the brutal past's buried, unburied, and/or distorted stories relative to African-descended people. Black people's New World blues is not merely centuries old. It also sometimes defies representability through the romantic, realist, or even naturalist modes of American literature. The writers under study here seek a vernacular code that is startling, pliable, and vehicular enough to help them navigate slavery and the reparative journeys back.

Foremost among the more "precise" reasons, however, is that the six focal Afri-can American novels are late-twentieth century outgrowths and ostensibly formal, thematic, and political continuations and resonances of the "Neo-Slave Narra-tive." Ishmael Reed neologized the term in 1969 in connection with the 1960s new, revolutionary black confessional writing,[47] whose structural and thematic ground plan was laid centuries ago by antebellum black autobiographers.[48] Literary historian Bernard W. Bell then applied the phrase to those "residually oral, modern narratives of escape from bondage to freedom."[49] The narratives were incubated before the 1960s civil rights and black consciousness movements. But they have grown in number, concerns, and styles following Margaret Walker's publication of *Jubilee* in 1966. Collectively exhibiting the features mentioned above, neo-slave narratives engage with the experiences and repercussions of New World slavery as their main preoccupation, integral theme, or organizing metaphor. As Ashraf H. A. Rushdy explains, these "modern or contemporary" stories of slavery generally have "fictional slave characters as narrators, subjects, or ancestral presences." The texts are cohered by their historicist portrayal of slavery as a "phenomenon that has lasting cultural meaning and enduring consequences." They also "assume the existence of a vital slave culture that prevented slaves from becoming docile or absolutely servile automatons found in the stereotypes of the plantation romance tradition." Neo-slave narratives insinuate themselves among various literary categories and discursivities, including antebellum slave narratives, postbellum slave narratives, and abolitionist novels. *Jubilee* signals the shift from "modern" neo-slave narratives, which according to Rushdy date back to such works as William Wells Brown's *Clotel* (1853) and Martin Delany's *Blake* (1861), to the contemporary types.[50]

In his seminal work on the topic, *Neo-slave Narratives: Studies in the Social Logic of a Literary Form* (1999), Rushdy reinforces this. He also adds to it important insights that aid a generational placement of the novels under interrogation. Rushdy notes that the writers of the 1970s, 1980s (and now 1990s) neo-slave narratives address the late-1960s socio-cultural and political climate. As novels published after the 1960s, these later narratives align themselves as belated participants in a preceding cultural conversation (17). However, this race- and slavery-implicated conversation did not begin in the twentieth century at which time the vagaries of black-white social relations inundated the works of some of America's, particularly Southern, fiction writers. Rather, slavery and the slavery debate inflected Enlightenment exegesis and the Romantic imagination. The disputation reaches back to the eighteenth- and nineteenth-century racial, philosophic, and political questions over the intrinsic worth of blackness and black racial humanity. At issue were, among other things, whether the propertized black person should be constitutionally and electorally counted as a whole or fractioned human being and whether, as proffered in the 1857 Dred Scot case, the American black individual was in fact a U.S. citizen or an alien. The colloquy registers also in Reconstruction literature and in the 1930s, particularly in the socio-intellectual responses to the thousands of interviews conducted by writers of the Federal Writers' Project (part of the Federal Works Progress Administration, WPA) with the last surviving African Americans born into slavery.

Recounting the history and mission of the WPA interviews is outside the scope of this study. However, historians of the subject have already brought sensitive perspectives on it. In addition, scholars have cautioned against simplistic interpretations of the interviews, given problems of interview quality, former-slave candor, and editorial intrusions.[51] Yet the former slaves' testimonies foretell some of the crucial issues that preoccupy the African American writers in this study, issues the deliberation of which the writers encrypt in their translations of the spirit child. They include: "Africa," the Igbo presence in North America, and the now legendary Igbo slave revolts through mass, self-affirming, and repatriative suicides or "flights." Others are the postbellum survivals of African religious beliefs and cultural practices, the questions of orality and text, history and historiography, fiction and fact, authorship and authority, memory, community, spirituality, gender, maternity, race relations, racial identity, and more. The WPA interviews provide important answers, from the ex-slaves' previously denied voice and viewpoint, to what slaves thought, knew, and felt about their bondage and freedom. Those testimonies offer "[p]ossibilities for learning about the experience of being black in the United States," Marion Wilson Starling writes (xix). Regardless of their inconsistencies, the former slaves' self-narrations anticipate the 1960s and 1970s black consciousness movement's insistence on rebellious self-naming.

For New World black people who had been compelled to (un)name, rename, and write themselves back into humanity, the existential density and relevance of that self-(re)creation cannot be underestimated. As John Edgar Wideman states in his reading of Charles Chesnutt's works against the milieu of the WPA narratives, "[t]he absolute power of the master licensed him to name his chattel" (67). And in doing so the master exerted control over his human chattel's perception of reality, truth, beauty, and history. The WPA interviews helped keep the experience of slavery alive in national consciousness during and after the Great Depression years. In fact, the publication of and academic/intellectual responses to the interviews would usher into the historiography of slavery in the 1950s what C. Vann Woodward calls "a neoabolitionist mood." Partly on account of the interviews, equal evidentiary weight was granted to both the white master's version of truth on the peculiar institution and the (former) slave's freer remembrances, disputations and reinterpretations of history (49). "[C]ontradict[ing] the masters' version of slavery by presenting the black slave's views" was risky especially for nineteenth century slave narrators who had to be diplomatic so as not to antagonize their white audiences, Frances Smith Foster notes.[52] The rediscovery of the slave narratives in the 1960s, Charles Johnson contends, ostensibly disrupted mainstream America's tendency since Reconstruction to reduce if not forget the slavery experience. The resurrection of those stories also unsettled black people's "soft-pedal[ing]" of the subject, as evinced in Dr. Martin Luther King Jr.'s proclamation that "The Negro understands and forgives and is ready to forget the past."[53]

Rushdy explains then that, just as they obdurately remember the past and respond to and challenge the white writer William Styron's *The Confessions of Nat Turner* (1966), a fictional autobiography denounced by African American intelligentsia,[54]

> The Neo-slave narratives of the seventies and eighties enter th[e] specific intellectual debate over race, especially as the debate plays itself out in discerning the relationship between the history of slavery and the social significance of contemporary racial identity. [They] take up the issues raised by the anthropological idea of race as a performed and regulative social category, question the politics proscribing cultural crossing, and develop statements on the liberating effects that come with acknowledging the pliability of racial identity. [They also] articulate the problems that arise when intellectuals focus on the performance of social identity without considering the role of power and the effects of powerlessness in these performances.[55]

In addition to underlining the role of power and its positionings in American race relations, the contemporary neo-slave narrative, Rushdy continues, raises also the critical question of the interplay of "slavery and postmodern black identity."[56] A 1960s and post-1970s phenomenon, if we go by Madhu Dubey's timeline,[57] this "postmodern" black identity is neither provincial, static, nor circumscribable. Rather, it is an untotalizeable difference, a being quite "polycentric."[58] With its fragmentation and propensity for unbridled mobility, its "identity . . . specifically constituted in the experience of exile and struggle,"[59] the postmodern black subject is and has always been a traveling and oppositional complexity. Crossing, re-crossing, and violating formerly rigid geographical, racial, and class separations and also gendered borders, that subject negotiates concurrently even if conflictively multiple experiential spaces, consciousnesses, and identity affiliations. Like spirit children generally, or like Azaro more specifically, he or she is the ultimate in-between. For African America, however, this (postmodern) condition of decentering, motion, and repositioning that predisposes black life and black self-cognition to flux has its beginnings in that initial Europe-Africa encounter and, subsequently, in the ancestral deracination and dispersal of native Africans by slavery. It has its onset in that peculiar institution's perverse, Ọgbañje-like intent to transform the black woman's body as an instrument of self-perpetuation.[60]

That use, misuse, and effacement of the black woman and her body account in part for the dominant weight of gender issues in the contemporary neo-slave narrative and in the texts under study. Because of them, we find black women writers of contemporary neo-slave novels seizing on the genre. Like their black male counterparts, today's black women authors of the form endear themselves to the theme of the Middle Passage with renewed vigor and a consecratory earnestness. In re-casting history, they indict America and stress the degradations their enslaved foremothers suffered. The women artists restore face and voice to their forebears and also dignify their vital and underappreciated contributions to the survival of the slave and free communities at large.[61] In their works, the African American women writer-descendants of the African ancestresses intend to do more than reconstruct besieged black motherhood and womanhood. They want to emphasize that their beloved forebears were most definitely more than chattel.[62]

However, while *Beloved* is valued as the quintessential neo-slave text, the rest of the works examined in this study—*Wild Seed, Mind of My Mind, The Cattle Killing, The Between,* and *Sula*—hardly make recurrent lead-essay appearances in extant criticism on the genre or on the postmodern slave narrative (see Spaulding 2005). As I have been arguing, these five texts also address directly or at least hint at the theme of enslavement. Their publications within the elastic timeframe of the contemporary neo-slave narratives (1960s–), their group depiction of literally enslaved or simply contained characters, as well as materially captive and destabilizing subjectivities, and thus their implicit participation in the discussion of slavery, race, memory, and the aftereffects of slavery on (post)modern black community, life, and identity, place them squarely as contributors to the historicity, conventions, and stylistics of that literary type.

Further, the subject of slavery traverses the above character-roster and topics thematized by the focal narratives and allegorized in the anthropologic, archetypic, and literary born-to-die. Relatedly, contemporary fictionalization of the Middle Passage and antebellum slavery experience imposes some technical demands on the creative writer, who has to look back in time. It is also against this backdrop of the challenges of narrativization that we should apprehend, even more, Ọgbañje/born-to-die's conceptual appeal to the writers and the multiple ways its adaptation shapes their works.

Although inflicting scars that remain visible in the present, the experience of the Middle Passage and antebellum slavery occurred in an earlier time. The experience embeds, among other things, the issue of alien invasion, a foreign entity's or an enslaver's power encroachment on another's self, body, family, and homeland. It assimilates questions of displacement, exile, repeating trauma, life, death, survival, and more. As illustrated in narratives such as Walker's *Jubilee* (1966), Gaines's *The Autobiography of Miss Jane Pittman* (1971), Charles Johnson's *Middle*

Passage (1990) and *Oxherding Tale* (1982), David Bradley's *The Chaneysville Incident* (1981), *Beloved, Kindred* (1981), Ishmael Reed's *Flight to Canada* (1976), J. California Cooper's *Family* (1991), and Phyllis Alesia Perry's *Stigmata* (1998), among others, imaginative exploration of those multifarious, slavery-grown topics *from the present time* require "journeys" back to and from the past. The contemporary neo-slave novel sometimes needs, then, as framework, what I call a "characteridea," a character-cum-idea that has time-travel potential. Or rather, the novel benefits from the telekinetic, affective, and ideological possibilities of a supernatural intermediate. It could use the services of a "living dead" entity, a spatial-temporal traveler that as vocabulary synthesizes slavery-generated topics and, like an Ọgbañje/born-to-die spirit specifically, can also spiritually and physically inhabit multiple bodies and is shackled not by space, time, history, gender, sex, or even mortal (white) power. It is this—the African American writers'—recall and enlistment of the otherworldly for duty in narrative construction that Kathleen Brogan has addressed. Brogan observes that twentieth-century American ethnic writers of haunted tales have had to conjure ghosts [and spirits] as median "to perform cultural work" (17). The writers have had to deploy the preternatural and mythical to excavate "individual psyche . . . [and] group consciousness" and to salvage as well as rewrite "group histories that have in some way been threatened, erased, or fragmented." That the authors have to resort to the mystical to recoup past history shows the difficulty of that recovery effort and how any such retrieval becomes essentially figurative (5–6).

Also significant and inseparable from the foregoing, chattel slavery or in fact any kind of captivity inevitably incites resistance. In other words, acts of bondage, in whatever form they come, stir the human impulse for liberation. And we can associate liberation with resistance, freedom, literacy, voice, choice, self-determination, wholeness, or the vertical south-to-north ascension in African American thought and life. Whatever the terminology, that quest for complete and unconditional human agency has been, as W. E. B. Du Bois stated, black America's spiritual striving since the first and Dutch-traded Africans were brought to Jamestown, Virginia, in 1619. In one way or another, that struggle for emancipatory (self)authorship has been a leitmotif in the African American novel from its earliest beginnings.

The born-to-die's other conceptual appeal lies therefore in its satisfying of the writer's need for a trope that interiorizes epistemes of infraction. The spirit child drama provides an ideal stage in which a writer can build a case against hegemonic power, as well as the reaches of gendered and/or artistic containment. Were the Ezinma-Ekwefi tension an exemplar, then the Ọgbañje event becomes a site for creative, critical, and philosophical exploration of the interrelated matters of exploitation, regulation, and resistance as they relate to, for instance, (black) women as wives, mothers, and daughters; as they relate domestically, intraracially, nationally, and artistically. In short, the Ezinma-Ekwefi encounter offers a platform for novelistic response, by both black women and men alike, to caller-issues of aesthetics. And here, the 1960s other major literary moment—the Black Arts movement and its nationalist aesthetic—comes into play. That age sheds more light on the other ways the ideas refracted in Ọgbañje/born-to-die are woven, sometimes fairly indecipherably, into the focal works' collective concerns and styles.

Blackness, Maleness, Revolutionary Art, and the Spirit Child

Concurrent with the 1960s emergence of the contemporary neo-slave narrative is the black consciousness movement, specifically the Black Power and its cultural arm the Black Arts movement. Like its precedent the "New Negro" or Harlem Renaissance, the Black Arts movement witnessed a widespread effusion of African American radical creativity in poetry, polemics, debates, theater, art, music, fiction, and literary criticism. In *Performing Blackness: Enactments of African-American Modernism* (2000), Kimberly W. Benston helps us date the age. Benston places its heyday between 1964 and 1974. The former historical marker designates the time Malcolm X, a major icon of Black Power insurgency, parted ways with the Nation of Islam. The latter represents the moment Imamu Amiri Baraka (LeRoi Jones), one of the movement's chief architects and spokespersons, abandoned "absolute black nationalism" in favor of an internationalistic Marxism. More significant, this epoch was one in which "the category of 'blackness' served as the dominant sign of [an] African American cultural activity" (3) that produced over one hundred variously published anthologies of African American literature between 1965 and 1975.[63]

It might be better, however, to consider this timeframe to be stretchable. For, as Benston rightly discusses in *Performing,* the 1960s and 1970s social movements and black racial uplift campaign are, significantly, a living-dead, "a still-living moment," as Benston characterizes it. They are both a moment when a concerted attempt to "transform representation into presentation became the hallmark of a fresh chapter in the history of African American cultural expression" (2). If that consciousness persists today, and it does, then it is arguable that African American literary production of the post–Black Arts movement era, and thus the works under study, are direct offspring and extensions of that cultural watershed. Or it could be said, at least, that the six African American texts in focus are implicated in the era's ferments.

That is not to say, though, that the late-1960s and early-1970s literary renewal has not undergone any thematic and/or formal shifts. Rather, African American belles lettres from the 1970s and 1980s have sought to illuminate socio-cultural, economic, political, psychological, and aesthetic currents that affect late-twentieth through early twenty-first century African America.[64] And perhaps in no areas of the African American literary tradition are the shape-shiftings in question more glaring than in the growth of the women's movement, Afrocentricism, and diaspora studies. Also worthy of note are the much publicized *canon* debates waged between Henry Louis Gates Jr., Joyce A. Joyce, and Houston A. Baker Jr. over the place of (post)structuralist theories in African American literature. Add to those the positive academic and commercial reception of black women/feminist writers since the 1980s. Another significant departure is the cultural hybridity, the class and political tastes of the works by artists of the "New Black Aesthetic" (NBA), as Trey Ellis calls them. Among this "Post-Soul" group are those authors of African American popular fiction and romance novels who are generally regarded as members of the so-called Terry McMillan era. This NBA generation declares itself markedly different from the New Negro and Black Arts renaissances. It is also busy with inventing what McMillan sees as an oeuvre unlike the 1960s angry, protest, and preachy art hamstrung by race, racism, and sociology. Their goal, McMillan declares, is a pulpy, warm-hearted, more entertaining, and universalistic fiction.[65] As James Edward Smethurst points out (73–75), however, the creative liberties desired and enjoyed by this new breed are indebted to the bruising culture wars fought partly by the 1960s and 1970s black cultural activists. For it was those same activists and intellectuals who cleared the way by refusing mainstream intent to have the already segregated black letters continue to stand trial at "the Wheatley court." This antebellum, men-only "court," as Nellie Y. McKay argues, "remains in session" even at the dawn of the twenty-first century.[66]

The Okonkwo-esque masculinism and ethnocentrism of the Black Power and Black Arts movements courted gender trouble, or what critic Chikwenye Okonjo Ogunyemi could rephrase titularly as African America "wo/man palava" (1996). The movements' aura of virility inevitably exposed the anecdotal dirty linen of intraracial gender infighting. (And this bears directly on McMillan's and Ellis's quests to free their NBA peers, including Due, from the 1960s philosophy of black arts and racial identity.) More exactly, the two concurrent and mutually reinforcing movements drew attention to the issues of black male chauvinism and black women's experiences in African American liberation struggle. Related to that, the era's radical nationalists and cultural workers sometimes promoted well-meaning but prescriptive ideas of group particularism. Couched in their notion of distinctive black collective experience and art are presumptions of racial normative.

The normative postulated a uniform black community and racial self. But then *that* racial self was construed at the time as the (black) male. Macho, leader, fighter, and defender of black people,[67] *the black man* was heterosexual, bohemian, nationalistic, Pan-African, and enraged. He was empowered by his rage and was not an invisible man. The black man respected the historical role, power, and successes of the black church and especially the black preacher, dead and alive, stationed and itinerant, in African American racial survival. The black man was tired, however, of Gandhian civil disobedience, of holding hands, marching, singing, dreaming, going to jail (and later to Vietnam)—and still not overcoming. Thus, disenchanted with the timbre, speed, compromises, and supposed passivity of non-violent civil rights activism amid persistent white supremacy, the black man decided to change tactics. He would instead abide by Malcolm X's hortatory injunction to "stop singing and start swinging" onto freedom, for it was *swinging* and not singing, Malcolm exhorted, that got Muhammad Ali his World Heavyweight boxing crown.[68] The black man was resolved, therefore, to rehabilitate his (racial) manhood and African/ancestral names. He would wage a revolutionary and retaliatory war with white America, with its years of antiblack terrorism, neo-slavery, domestic colonialism, and pervasive Eurocentrism (Van Deburg 257–65). "[F]or the first time in this nation's history," Stephen Henderson reflects, "the Black man was putting his oppressors in the *political dozens.*"[69] And the 1960s and 1970s literature was poised to help in that goal by "consolidating the African American personality," reaffirms Larry Neal, another of the Black Aesthetics' key visionaries and theoreticians.[70]

As many others, more recently Rolland Murray (2007), have similarly commented in retrospect, however, the sociopolitical and literary attempt to homogenize African American racial subjectivity was misguided. It is true that the Black Panther Party—the period's sartorially most ultra black and militaristic black organization—did condemn sexism and was also the first major black group to ally with both the women's and the gay rights struggles.[71] And no one discounts black America's unifying history of slavery, careerist Jim Crow, and unrelenting racial injustice. Yet the campaign for authentic blackness—to echo Martin Favor—the jostling for who was the "blackest"[72] and could like James Brown say it most loudly and proudly was rather interesting. For as beautiful as "black" suddenly became in the 1960s and 1970s, a mere two or three decades earlier it was an insult to call someone or one's then "Negro"/"Afro American" self "black," much less "African." The authenticity crusade was also divisive, intolerant, and "shackl[ing]" of intraracial difference (Lorde 136), given the heterogeneity and the long history of public and sometimes heated ideological disagreements among black people.[73]

And, because the period's cultural production was framed as the "aesthetic and literary sister of the Black Power concept,"[74] the partisan exponents of Black Arts espoused a radical black nationalist agenda. They sought not just intellectual independence from white control but also the decolonization of black letters, as did their African contemporaries the Chinweizu-led *bolekaja* critical fraternity. The exponents endorsed Du Boisean literary propagandism, disfavored his idea of black duality and, like Achebe, abjured (Alain Lockean) universalism and art-for-art's-sake.[75] Moreover, staging that strident censure of ancestors that inspired Octavia Butler's neo-slave narrative *Kindred,* they also chastised African American cultural movements of earlier times. But drawing their particular ire was the "New Negro" or Harlem Renaissance. Ignoring that it "was the production of a people just up from slavery (with millions still slaves) who had to produce their art in an extreme racist context that disjointed and depreciated their effort" (W. D. Wright 145), they upbraided the New Negro academy. This modernist coterie was reproved for its bourgeois affectations, code of racial respectability, and its conscious and unconscious stimulations of white intrigue with notions of black primitivity and exoticism. It was reproached also for pandering to agencies of white power (white aegis, publishers, readership, and critical judgments) and for lacking sufficient anger and telling "half truths."[76] In short, to Nathan Huggins, who downgraded the movement, the renaissance was a failure; its implosion the unfortunate result of the movement's intelligentsia's fatal error of ethnic provincialism, their failure to insist on their birthright as American citizens (see also Baker *Modernism,* 9–14).

The aestheticians also admonished the post–Harlem Renaissance era. They generally elevated Richard Wright's literary protest over James Baldwin's earlier moral suasion and Ralph Ellison's noncommittal individualism and his subordination of ideology to seditious style (Grayle 1975: ix–xx). But they also eschewed "protest" art if all it did or seeks to do is scream for white attention. They alleged, furthermore, that African American writers of the 1940s and 1950s were, significantly, ambivalent toward Africa and folklore.[77] Those forties and fifties writers were said to suffer from a sense of "anguish and aimlessness" that "drove most of them to early graves, to dissipation and dissolution."[78] What the aestheticians insisted on, invoking the authority of utilitarian African art (which *Things Fall Apart* and Achebe's other works partly exemplify), was that "all Black art, irregardless of any technical requirements, must have three basic characteristics which make it political, weaponized and ultimately revolutionary. In brief," Ron Karenga outlines, "it must be functional, collective and committing or committed" (33). Often privileging content over form and "[d]iscarding the mimetic and textual aspects of literature,"[79] they maintained that black art must be devoted to the African American community. It should address blacks and their confrontations of "the many-headed beast of U.S. racism" as Kevin K. Gaines describes it (xvi). The

art, relevant, responsible and judged by aesthetic benchmarks set by blacks themselves, should expose whites and help black America awaken to its long-trampled
unassailable rights to full humanity and citizenship in a nation where "[e]verything
that came out of Europe, every blue-eyed thing, is already an American"[80] except
the *alien*ated blacks.

Needless to say, black women, like black men, shared that political and cultural
ideal. Not only were black women some of the Black Arts movement's "key poets,
theorists and revolutionists,"[81] they also willingly risked their lives for the dream.
To outfox the government's feint of divide-and-conquer[82] and project an image
of intraracial solidarity, among other things, however, the women were enjoined
directly and indirectly to stress racial emancipation over gender, sex, class concerns
and even religious discords. "Whether we are Christians or Muslims or nationalists
or agnostics or atheists," Malcolm X once admonished his listeners, "we must first
learn to forget our differences. If we have differences, let us differ in the closet; when
we come out in front, let us not have anything to argue about until we get finished
arguing with the man" ("Ballot" 25). Yet as the women were opposing white power
and concomitantly helping uplift the race, the male leaderships of not only the civil
rights movement and the Nation of Islam but also the Black Power and even the
Black Arts organizations occasionally subjected many of them to conducts that
were exploitative, silencing, disempowering, and sexist.[83] Consequently, the black
woman found her place in the movements and her relationship to the larger black
community to be paradoxical if not precarious. For it was *that* same gender-stifling
"community" whose survival the women were pressed to champion in the midst of
such intraracial masculinism, misogyny, and homophobia.[84]

The black woman—whose "assigned" role in the struggle was maternal and who
was told by her brother, as Audre Lorde retrospects, that her "only useful position in
the Black Power movement was prone" (137)—was assaulted even more. She was
miscalled a matriarch and the castrator of the black male. That was the portraiture
painted by the New York senator Daniel Patrick Moynihan's controversial 1960s
sociological report on the state of urban U.S. black family. Resorting to what Angela
Davis would later deplore as "the myth of [black] matriarchate" "repeatedly invoked
as one of the fatal by-products of slavery" (4), Moynihan adjudged the black man
as overshadowed by his strong black woman. He also assessed the black family as
unstable, deviant from the patriarchal pattern of mainstream (white) America, and
mired in a "tangle of pathology" (29). And the black underclass, the poor and more
pertinently the unmarried black mother were together chiefly to blame.

The black woman saw herself singing what one would say amounted to a bi-
directional, Sonny Boy Williamson's "Win the War Blues." Speaking in tongues,

she sang the blues at home, testamentally decrying her black brother's intraracial politics, interracial desires, and his frustration and repressed rage sometimes misdirected domestically.[85] Outside, she sang it equally combatively with the interactive liberal and conservative programs of mainstream white America. She also had to contend with the overt and obscured racism of white feminists.[86] Calling for women's sisterhood and a legally enforced end to inequality but really emphasizing gender and class discrimination, Second Wave and radical white feminists, who like other emergent aggrieved voices ironically drew strength from the civil rights and Black Power demands, downplayed "race." They sometimes outright dismissed the racial, ethnic, sexual, and religious persecution and complaints of colored women, in this case the African American woman who initially was circumspect of joining the Women's Liberation movement for fear of intraracial vilification and black-male disaffection. To black womanist writer Alice Walker who recaptures the era in *Meridian* (1976), it may well be no surprise that, as Paula Giddings writes, the 1960s would end up labeled "The Masculine Decade" (Giddings 314), an Okonkwo-esque epoch, despite the layered histories, structures, memberships, alliances, goals, strategies, achievements, and particularly the gendered moorings of the period's various social movements.[87] What is irrefutable, however, is that the black female—beloved yet demonized like Ọgbañje-àbíkú, visible yet alienated, insider yet outsider—was vital to the period's political, cultural, and literary causes.

To black feminist science fiction writer Octavia Butler, who like Walker was a college student in the 1960s and also participated in the era's black consciousness drive, it was not simply the boundless freedom of science fiction that attracted her to the genre.[88] It was also the racial and gendered enlightenment spurred by the period that enabled her decisive thematic intervention in the speculative mode. As Frances Smith Foster attests, Butler's artistic intent was revolutionary. She "consciously chose to introduce the *ism*s of race and sex into the genre and obviously did not set out to write 'fine, old fashioned [sci-fi].'"[89] Butler's refusal to be further alienated and "(e)raced" from both history and text[90] compelled her to meddle, even more, in the white-female-dominated landscape of feminist science fiction, particularly. While the women's movements empowered "*white* feminist voices" to gain ground in sci-fi beyond "the erasure of past tokenism," Elyce Rae Helford remarks, the case was different for the "womanist fibulat[or]" Butler. Her early works suffered the racism and sexism of white science fiction publishers,[91] some of whom opposed the inclusion of black characters on the conviction that black figures alter and distract sci-fi stories from their intended complexion.[92]

In addition, "recent [sci-fi] publications that deal with Africa as inspiration" negativize the continent as "an alien and mystifying place." This, needless to say, is a racist picture propelled by the enslaver's, colonizer's, and Western traveler's tales of Africa as "'the dark continent'": an Other, different, frightening, and disempowered.[93] But even as Butler counters these stereotypes, irreversibly reshapes the genre, thematizes slavery and colonization, and empowers the margin, she—as do Achebe, Okri, Due, Morrison, and Wideman—"rejects a one-dimensional understanding of [life's] complicated processes." And thus her stories, in this case *Wild Seed* and *Mind of My Mind,* neither "romanticize[] the position of difference"[94] nor attempt to cement black racial humanity.

To Wideman—who also came of age during the 1960s, began his teaching and literary careers then, and is unapologetic for writing thematically and formally devious novels such as *The Cattle Killing*—the idea of an easily readable, classifiable, hermetic, and by extension confinable black humanity is vexing. The unsavory notion of a race-shackled and thus captive black text displeases him. To Wideman, such a premise is antithetical to the spirit of liberatory blackness and artistic innovation. What "a writer wants is freedom of expression," Wideman writes in his preface to the Terry McMillan–edited collection *Breaking Ice: An Anthology of Contemporary African-American Fiction* (2000). The writer needs that freedom, Wideman emphasizes, to create stories that "transcend stereotype." S/he needs it to produce works that debunk the Emperor's "fantasies of superiority." Such works ought also to contain cultural signifiers that situate one firmly within a particular tradition, even as one's works also review and critique that tradition (vi–ix).

As we review the Black Arts movement in the broader scheme of things, placing it specifically within the call-and-response layout of African American literary production, we might surmise a few things. It was the overriding project of the *Native Son*–inspired Second Renaissance, as C. W. E. Bigsby says of the era (9), to forge a fresh, unique, raced, and counter-hegemonic aesthetic intended to shape and sustain the 1960s, 1970s, and post-1970s generations of African American arts and critical praxis. To distinguish itself, the movement excoriated its antecedents, particularly the Harlem Renaissance, whose racial politics it found wanting and whose literary output it valuated as partly "mediocrity," as Amiri Baraka estimated.[95] Although it touted its urbanity, novelty, assertiveness, and sophistication, among other attributes, the self-declared "New Negro" of the turn-of-the-twentieth century was in many ways tied inseparably to the "old Negro" of the earlier times by the umbilical cord of racial history, memory, uplift, artistry, and more.[96] Similarly then, and in what rarefies the relativity of good and evil, the 1960s and 1970s literary revival, despite its deprecation of precursors and its claims to newness, inevitably took its spark from the past, especially from the positivist fortitude of the same unduly stigmatized Harlem Renaissance.[97] And thus the nationalist aesthetic is better appraised intergenerationally. It cannot be fully understood outside of those fluid, epochal conversations, contestations and continuities that, while situating the (black experiential/literary) past as a returning, remembered, shape-shifting, and still-influential dead, also help periodize, in this case, twentieth-century African American literary history.

Most significant, however, the Black Arts movement, indeed the 1960s and 1970s, can be said to have bequeathed the African American novels under study a dual inheritance that the spirit child idea helps the novels and authors play out. That is, on the one hand, both the movement's (literary) stress of black empowerment and its propagation of a decolonized Black Aesthetic subsisted on Africanisms, oral/folk tradition, indigenous myths, legends, symbols, metaphors, and iconology would stand as one of the era's most enduring visions for and legacies to the focal New World novels. Invigorating the creation of contemporary neo-slave texts and, in turn, energized by the age's Pan-Africanism, the demanded establishment of Black Studies programs, emergent black presses, Frantz Fanon's acrid illuminations of the colonial condition relative to blackness, the crumbling of Europe's overseas empires, and the independence of several African diaspora nation-states including Nigeria, the movement would be credited also with helping galvanize more concerted, though at times ambiguous and adventurous, pilgrimages by black Americans to their African ancestry and religious roots. These are shared roots that works such as *Things Fall Apart* and *Arrow of God*—both anticolonial and historically antiphonal masterpieces that together dramatize tradition, loss, skepticism, and Achebe's proverbial defense of alert "return" to a consequential past—brought to black America's attention. They transmitted those roots to the New World *a la* Igbo worldview, Africa's experience, and the myth of Ọgbañje. On the other hand, "while assaulting racist strictures," the movement's creators, theoreticians, and "critics often employed new strictures of exclusion and created a new hegemony."[98] Their insistencies on centripetality, on racial uniformity and manhood, risked ossifying black (gendered) humanity, art, and themes.

It is the foregoing remnants of antebellum slavery and the subtleties of "enslavement"—subjugation, colonization, control, regulation, and the like—that are thematized and complicated in the post-1960s and 1970s novels of Butler, Due, Wideman and Morrison. In the texts the re-envisaged Africanism/the spirit child, plays a role in the novels' polydirectional "journeys" back to slavery times. The trope also animates the novelists' literary acts of (gendered) resistance to control and a convergent aesthetic (Jennifer Jordan 39–55).

What unfolds therefore is that the imprinted and imbricated neo-slave texts in this study are doubly double-voiced, centrifugal, and multi-referential. On one hand, they are, as we have pointed out, cosmologically informed works whose formal foreparents are both white Western and African diaspora texts. On the other, they memorialize historical slavery and reflect on its aftermaths on black community, life, and identity. The texts respond affirmatively to the Black Arts movement's enduring call to African American writers to "rediscover Africa as source of race pride," consider "the political relevance of modern Africa to the rest of the Black World,"[99] and to search for and use transgressively relevant principles of "Third World" cultures. The focal works do that evidently, particularly in their adaptations of one such (African) principle, Ọgbanje/born-to-die. But the texts also destabilize the absolutisms of the period's "still-living" aesthetics and the era's restrictions on the black (female) self. The novels also express an awareness of recent developments in United States' and black diaspora history. In other words, the works stay current even as they look back on, journey to, and address the slavery past, and also signify on African fiction's general silence on trans-Atlantic slavery—that cyclically returning and haunting racial trauma.

Take, for first example, the two imprinted neo-slave texts *The Between* and *The Cattle Killing*. Both came out in the mid-1990s, a decade of counterhegemonic multiculturalism. The 1990s was a time when increased black racial and gendered shattering of the color, class, and professional bars, and those bars' imports for racial membership, racial crossing and identity, agitated white supremacist resentment. It was an era when various 1960s civil rights gains were threatened or even stripped. In addition, conservative think tanks, extending what James Berger elucidates as the 1980s "neoconservative and Reaganist denials of race as a continuing, traumatic, and structural problem in contemporary America" (408), hailed the period as marking the end of racism.

The decade was also marked by globalizing economies and greater migration of black diaspora and colored peoples and labors across (inter)national borders. The period witnessed reports of widening spread of HIV and AIDS among blacks and of black children increasingly exposed to urban violence. It also registered a number of well publicized, injustice-provoked violent events and demonstrations in American cities and streets. Perhaps the most memorable of them occurred after an all-white jury acquitted white police officers in the videotaped beating of black motorist Rodney King. And lastly, the time saw some intensification in African American interest in post-Apartheid South Africa. Reinforced by such organizations as Randal Robinson's TransAfrica, this post 1960s re-connection with the homeland was heightened by Nelson Mandela's emancipation/resurrection from a twenty-seven-year incarceration (read: captivity and death) in Robben Island. These issues, though not in their specificities, made their way into Due's and Wideman's novels.

Through its setting in multiethnic Miami as well as its leitmotif of migration, Due's debut *The Between,* also deals with issues of race, class, gender, and AIDS. It appeared amidst the 1990s congressional wrangle over proposed drastic amendment to the nation's immigration legislation—a volatile and polarizing reform a strain of which President George W. Bush attempted unsuccessfully and to his political detriment. Migration is a topic for which the myth of born-to-die child/ the Azaro story holds promise, through àbíkú's ideological entanglement in questions of borders and border crossings, displacement, exile, belonging, double vision, and identity-formation. The theme of immigration evokes the pressures between (citizen)ship and (alien)ation, center and margin, insider and outsider, home and away, and between separation and family reunion. *The Between* engages with these matters.

In the same vein, through his masterful exploration of Ọgbañje as character and framework in *The Cattle Killing,* Wideman reveals a broad consciousness of African diaspora history. With "Ọgbañje" as archetype and glue, Wideman is able to establish and link the following as related offspring of the initial Europe-Africa encounter: antebellum slavery; implicitly the Igbo experience with colonization and infant mortality/losses of children charted in *Things Fall Apart;* the 1856–57 Xhosa cattle-killing incident in South Africa; and black Philadelphians' experience during a late eighteenth-century fever outbreak. Wideman views this fever plague, which white citizens of Philadelphia blamed on black West Indian refugees escaping unrest in their homeland at the time, as the antebellum equivalent of the present AIDS epidemic. Like its predecessor the fever plague, AIDS, we might recall, was initially blamed on Africans and the black race.

Consider, as a related example, *Sula.* An imbricated novel, *Sula* is illuminable by Ọgbañje's evocation of views on complex if not mystifying subjectivity with respect to race, the black woman, and to socio-literary portraitures of her. In *Black Women Novelists and the Nationalist Aesthetic,* Madhu Dubey argues correctly that Morrison uses Sula's character refutatively. Through Sula, Dubey contends, Morrison set out not merely to respond to but to displace the 1960s societal and black nationalist aesthetic's constructions and stigmatization of the black female. To Dubey, the black female self was and is depicted as a figure who straddles the poles of the overseen and the unseen. She is coherent yet fragmented, the totally known but an enigma (4–5). In short, the black female is a figure that confounds accepted meanings and referents of "good" and "evil," as resonated in the Ọgbañje/ child Ezinma; in Sula's positivity and de-constructiveness; in the irony of Beloved as spirit and child, demonic presence yet an enabler; and in the more ethical questions raised by Sethe's infanticide. Dubey asserts that Morrison's adoption of a "nonrealist" mode in *Sula* (an approach she continues in *Beloved)* serves to challenge fixities. Like Butler's, Due's, and Wideman's works, Morrison uses post-modernist literary techniques to suggest that "the notion of a whole and unified self [is] an unrepresentable, imaginary ideal." Thus her "figuration of black feminine identity" in *Sula*/Sula "may best be understood as a contradictory interplay between presence and absence, wholeness and fracture" (5). This conflictive view of the black woman predates the 1960s and 1970s tempestuous political scenes. It has its beginnings in racial slavery—that overarching hurt that in one way or another preoccupies the African American authors and novels in this study.

* * *

By virtue of the foregoing discussion on the 1960s and 1970s sociopolitical climate, the period's nationalist aesthetic, and its ties to the contemporary neo-slave narrative, I am aiming to ground a key part of my argument. As we might recall, it is Gates's proposition that African American writers generally bring to their repetition, revision, and resonance of both indigenous and received texts and tropes a sense of signifyin(g) black difference. If so, I am contending that in terms of the African American writers' direct adaptations of the literary and, by default, the anthropological and cosmological spirit child, and also the philosophic echoes of the idea in the works under study, *that* signifyin(g) black difference materializes most powerfully in specific ways. It evinces in the authors' subjections of that West African mythic belief—exemplified in Achebe's and Okri's works—to the topic of New World slavery, slavery's contemporary tributaries, (intraracial) gender politics, and black-white power struggle. It manifests in African American novelists' adoptions of the belief to explore the complex aftermaths of *acts of captivity* on not just antebellum and postmodern black humanity but on texts that, while responding to the 1960s and 1970s cultural calls, also revolt through character, theme, and formal devices against the period's restrictive conceptions of blackness and the functionality of black art.

In other words, one could say that Butler, Wideman, Due, and Morrison approach the spirit child principle with an intent at "denigration." That is Michael Awkward's invertive term for African American novelists' inclination to *blacken* received epistemologies by injecting into them alternative black ways of knowing.[100] The four novelists' graftings of the spirit child trope onto the theme of "enslavement," (black) power, black empowerment, racial liberation, and survivalism stand as one of their most remarkable, signifyin(g) re-workings or *African Americanization* of the derived, ethnically and culturally specific, notions of Igbo Ọgbañje and Yoruba àbíkú.

If there exists one mythic germ whose encapsulation and refraction of multiple archetypal figures and discourses make it a revealing study on the various character profiles, thematic concerns, and the narrative strategies featured in the works under study, it most certainly is the spirit child. For, as the analyses that follow demonstrate, the idiom services the creation of a character that is simultaneously (an alien) spirit and matter, a telepathic time traveler, an androgynous invader given to the atrocity of controlling and transforming the (black) woman's burglarized body/womb into a vehicle for mischief and intended immortality (Butler). It lends itself to the figuration of, relatedly, fated spirit-human personas that struggle with and are tormented by Death and by their double descents and identities, especially their dueling and allegoric affiliations to, on one side, the *ancestral* spirit world and, on another side, the material sphere codified in the human family, in wife, children, relatives, friends, job, earthly possessions, and others (Due). It facilitates authorial imagining of reincarnating characters, especially a nineteenth-century itinerant evangelist and an intrusive narrator that undergoes multiple rebirths and also traverses historical and racialized moments (Wideman). Similarly, as "spirit child," Ọgbañje resonates in a novelist's construction of related, spirit children with supernatural powers: entities whose relationships with their earthly parents and the larger society become a venue to meditate on both the possibilities of closure and healing from slavery *and* the semantics of good and evil (Morrison).

Inextricable from its possibilities for characterization and its collapsing of cosmological, political and philosophic themes, Ọgbañje/born-to-die mythic drama also interiorizes certain settings, plots, and subplots. For instance, the existential drama in which an Ọgbañje or àbíkú entity performs takes place in the alien universe of spirits and the concrete world of human beings. As contextualized in the earlier chapter, the concept absorbs patterns, conflicts, and situational ironies. It lends itself fully to the goals of a writer interested not in occidental, progressive linear time but in discontinuous, simultaneous, and recursive temporalities. The spirit child's rootedness in complex if not an amorphous and de-centered existence supplies some of the raw materials for an author of science, speculative, and "magical realist" fiction. The intricacies of the spirit child's life arm a novelist intent on creating a difficult postcolonial and postmodern black text and on treating black racial subjectivity as irreducible. Simply put: if not Ọgbañje/born-to-die, what better "symbolically anthropological" is there for the author of a contemporary neo-slave narrative who desires a protagonist that, while in the mortal present, can travel freely, physically and spiritually, back and forth in time and space, and is part of the dead/Death, the living/Life and the unborn/Hope?

Chapter 3 Of Power, Protest, and Revolution

Wild Seed *and* Mind of My Mind

If there were only one reason why blacks should read science fiction, it would be the writings of Octavia Butler.

But, of course, there are more.

Charles R. Saunders
"Why Blacks Should Read
(and Write) Science Fiction"

Whether measured by creative output, philosophic depth, commercial popularity, academic reception, or critical accolades, Octavia Butler would rank highly in post-1960s African American literary and intellectual history. A winner of some of science fiction's most prestigious awards, Butler stands as a major force in the speculative genre. But she is exceptional for other reasons. She is a black woman in the field, a writer who professed herself a feminist and also explores such provocative and persistently contemporaneous issues as race, difference, racism, slavery, colonization, miscegenation, incest, genetics, identity, sexism, and power. *Wild Seed* and *Mind of My Mind* are two of Butler's stories in which the question of power and power's dynamics, scope, intricacies, misappropriations, and subversions are central. These issues and others are a 1960s and 1970s preoccupation.

As do the other imprinted and imbricated novels in this study, then, *Wild Seed* and *Mind of My Mind* together dramatize a civil rights, Black Power, and Black Arts movement sensibility. Like *Kindred,* both novels respond to the 1960s and 1970s, specifically in terms of Butler's journey back to black America's Igbo/ African ancestry. They address the eras also in their black feminist and womanist consciousness, as well as in their unified concern with black religious and cultural heritage, spirituality, community, (double) consciousness, kinship, and, in this case, the interplays of slavery, gendered injustice, protest, and self-determination.

As hinted earlier, Butler said that she wrote *Kindred* as "a kind of reaction to some of the things going on during the sixties when people were feeling ashamed of, or more strongly, angry with their parents for not having improved things faster." And thus she "wanted to take a person from today and send that person back to slavery"[1]—which makes Gregory E. Rutledge's intervention quite pertinent.

Rutledge is concerned that some "*traditional* scholars" of African American literature might hesitate before equating futurist and black science fiction's interests and its "patently hedonistic" indulgences, as he refers to it, to the Black Power/Black Arts movement's racial cause. He cautions that it would be a mistake, however, to discuss the sister movements without acknowledging what he dubs the "Pro-black" angles of the collective futurist, science, and speculative fictions of Samuel R. Delany, Octavia Butler, Charles R. Saunders, Steven Barnes, and Nalo Hopkinson. Perhaps most important, Rutledge proposes that "if literary critics evaluate the creative efforts of Black futurist fiction authors without a cultural predicate grounded in the Black experience, they might produce an intrinsically deficient exegesis" (128–29). Such an interpretation might be lacking even more if it ignores the possibility that African American futurist and science fiction might be pollinated by or is in dialogue with some postcolonial African novels. *Wild Seed* and *Mind of My Mind* together give expression, then, to science fiction's chiasmatypy. Both stories disclose not just the genre's formal investments in intertextuality but also the cascadings of biology, history, religion, myth, folklore, science, and literature. Butler's novels may address "universal" topics, as Charles R. Saunders asserts (400). But in terms of her portrayal of the black experience in dystopic America and her figuration of Ọgbañje Doro and the sun woman Anyanwu, among other things, her cultural, literary and historical scaffolds are autochthonous. They are rooted in part in the lived history and cultural imagination of the Igbo of southeast Nigeria.

This chapter undertakes an intertextual and histo-cultural explication of *Wild Seed* and *Mind of My Mind*. I would contemplate, initially and foundationally, some of the ways in which these two contiguous novels, especially *Wild Seed,* are inspirited by Butler's critically understudied, signifyin(g) dialogues with Achebe. Of particular interest is what I have posited as Butler's transcodings of Achebe's archetypic rendition of the Ọgbañje myth. Also noteworthy is Butler's exploration of the theme of "difference," which Achebe equally narrativizes powerfully in the Ezinma and Nwoye substories of (genetic) mutation and social alterity. Butler sets *Wild Seed* around the 1690s, almost exactly two hundred years before the 1890s backdrop of *Things Fall Apart*. She ends it just before the onset of the American Civil War in 1861, three decades before 1890. In doing so, she extends Achebe indirectly by narrating a "missing" though crucial "link" in the chain of Igbo historiography—the Middle Passage years—to which Achebe only alludes in *Things Fall Apart.*[2]

I consider, next, how *Wild Seed* and *Mind of My Mind,* particularly *Wild Seed,* are shaped by and thus are able to engage with the titular topics of (oppressive) power, radicalism, and change through Butler's graftings of additional facets of Igbo history, culture, myths, folklore, and gender relations. I would contend, in closing, that Butler seems to have been drawn to the Ọgbañje belief and experience for more than anthropological, historical, and artistic goals. There is something in the spirit child idea that appears to hit close to home for her. It should also be stated outright that if the analysis that follows the foundational discussions below seems to focus disproportionately on *Wild Seed,* it is intentional. *Wild Seed* receives more critical coverage because it is the longer and clearly more historically, culturally, and technically seamed of the two works. Moreover, the Anyanwu-Doro rivalry plays out more thoroughly and intensely in it than it does in *Mind of My Mind,* whose plot follows Mary's formation of the Pattern as well as the apocalyptic events subsequent to it.

Before They Depart:
Profiling Doro as Ọgbañje and Anyanwu as Alpha Quadrinity

Mythology's importance to science fiction cannot be overstated. It is for that reason that C. W. Sullivan's remarks on folklore's benefits for fantastic and science fiction are a good place to start. Sullivan argues in "Folklore and Fantastic Fiction" that although the terms folklore, fantasy, and science fiction appear to be incompatible, in practice they are not. The "writer of fantastic literature, the creator of impossible worlds, has need of and uses folklore to make those imagined worlds accessible to the reader." This is "much the same way, if obverse, as the modern critic might use a knowledge of folk materials to gain access to . . . meaning(s)" subterfuged in texts. Sullivan explains that "[s]ome part of the creative process through which the mimetic and the fantastic elements are combined—or reconciled—into a logically-coherent Secondary World must also include a strategy or strategies by which the reader will be able to connect with . . . understand, and . . . decode any meaning inherent in the story set in that Secondary World and also decode that Secondary World itself." Thus, "[t]here must be enough of the familiar, the mimetic, within the story so that the reader can understand the nature of the unfamiliar, the fantastic." Authors of fantasy and science fiction need "more than just motifs and other individual elements from tradition" to cohere the universes they envision. They require also such "myths, legends, folktales, or ballads [that are in] themselves sufficiently fantastic that nothing needs to be added and a retelling, usually expanded, is the result." The "traditional tale provides [then] something like the skeletal structure of the plot, and the author fleshes that structure out to present a theme that may or may not have been implicit in the original" (279–84).

Butler's characterization of Doro and Anyanwu as shape-shifters and her drawings of the Anyanwu-Doro spectacle illustrate Sullivan's remarks. Butler restructures narrativized and thus familiar Igbo myths and subjects them to fresh uses for the purpose of reader accessibility, as Sullivan mentions. Thus, before tracking Doro's slave ship *Silver Star* as it departs from the West African coast and transports its human cargo to Wheatley, New York, it is important to first ground and visualize Doro in the contexts of Ọgbañje drama, a recognizable/antecedent text *Things Fall Apart,* and my discernment of a hint of sickle cell disorder in Doro's character profile. We might also place the contexts for the character Anyanwu against a matrix of cultural models to clarify on whose mythic authority she defies Doro. In other words, as I shall explain, Anyanwu challenges Doro effectively because she is much more than a wild seed and shape-shifter.

* * *

The Ọgbañje myth deepens Butler's lineaments of Doro. It also enables her to realize *Wild Seed* and *Mind of My Mind*'s other formal components. Butler incarnates in Doro a number of the Ọgbañje's ontologic and conceptual attributes enumerated in chapter 1. In addition to finding in Achebe's "skeletal"/archetypic Ọgbañje tale the seeds for her constellar figuration of Doro, Butler also reverses *Things Fall Apart* by gendering her novels' Ọgbañje diviner as female. The Afa dibia Okagbue Uyanwa's male role of prophesying Ekwefi's child Onwumbiko's Ọgbañje identity is performed in *Wild Seed* by a woman. In other words, it is Anyanwu who, functioning also as dibia, shortly after first encountering Doro foretells him twice: "You are a spirit." Anyanwu's elaboration on that divination is expressed in the narrator's derivative description of Doro as an Ọgbañje. Butler extends Achebe equally by upgrading and thus making more brazen and malignant the cannibalistic appetite of her story's spirit child. The Ọgbañje spirit that menaces the Okonkwo-Ekwefi family goes after infants. But Doro, in his bravado, relishes much older victims in a flagrant display of machismo that Anyanwu refuses to condone. And she lets him know that during their conversations.

Wild Seed and *Mind of My Mind* also evince an Achebean impact through character dialogue. The imprint shows in the form of Butler's seeming re-

rendition of the tense, cosmic palaver between Ọgbañje (as mortality and mortality's agent) and woman-mother. What one "hears" in Anyanwu's and later in her granddaughter Mary's various exchanges with Doro—in both women's entreaties, admonitions, condemnations of, and verbalized shock at, Doro's repeated killings and their supplications that he not kill anyone else, especially children—seems to be a recasting of Ekwefi's motherhood ordeal. We adduce from Ekwefi's deceased children's names that Ekwefi's attempts at a negotiatory conversation with anthropomorphized Death have become calls denied a (favorable) response. Like Ekwefi's attitudes to Death, Anyanwu's and later Mary's reactions to Doro would shift tactically, fluctuating from plaintive and frustrated to aggressive and sarcastic forbearance. Anyanwu's defiance of ravenous Death by warning Doro, the earliest time it/he intrudes into her human/woman space, "You will not trouble my children" (*Wild* 26), sounds like a paraphrase of the Ọgbañje name "Onwurah-Death leave the child."[3]

Butler's most provocative dialogue with Achebe is in her poignant play on the Ọgbañje's gender. She transcribes the Ọgbañje's locus as a sign of "difference" to make broader cosmological, gendered, racial, and political statements relative to power and the need for Anyanwu's and Mary's revolutionary resistances. In *Things Fall Apart,* an Ọgbañje, described as a wicked spirit/child that plagues its mother (or plainly the source of a woman's sorrow), is figured female, in Ezinma. Butler counterpoints that such a dubious honor should go to a male, Doro. Butler inverses the Ọgbañje relationship with the mother by intimating that, while Ezinma in all her occult powers does not kill but rather *stays* in nurturing empathy with Ekwefi, Doro's ascension to solipsistic power and immortality is predicated contrastively on post-transition matricide. Interestingly, it is in the narrator's recall of both the matricide and Doro's past that one finds significant evidence that Doro seems to be in part Butler's signifyin(g) (re)incarnation, synthesis, and science-fictionalization of Okonkwo's two heteroclite children: his "strange" daughter Ezinma and his "problem" son Nwoye. The "irregularities" of these Okonkwo offspring echo in Butler's exploration of the tension between power-inflected Othering and revolt.

As an Ọgbañje, Ezinma is one of *Things Fall Apart*'s dominant sites of alterity. We noted in chapter 1 that Okonkwo wishes that Ezinma were a boy to compensate for his "loss" of Nwoye to purported effeminacy. And worse, Okonkwo would lose and implicitly sacrifice Nwoye again, this time to the white man who exploits Umuofia's caste system to build a resilient Christian church, peopled first by the village's stigmatized wild cards. Among them are slaves, twins, mothers of twins, supposedly unmanly males, lazy children, the "*efulefu,* worthless, empty men" without title (*Things* 142), and especially the *osu*—Umuofia's cult slaves and community outcasts (154–59).[4] It is these socially susceptible Others, these early converts to Christianity whom Chielo berates as "the excrement of the clan" (142), that readily embrace or rather are enticed into seizing the empowerment offered by the white man's faith and colonial institutions.

That issue of intraethnic/intraracial ostracism recurs in and is foundational to *Wild Seed*. It is apparent when Doro's confusion about Anyanwu's statement that she bore no culturally abnormal children prompts the narrator to explain that such children, for instance, "twins . . . children born feet first, children with almost any deformity, children born with teeth . . . were thrown away" (*Wild* 26). In addition, the Umuofia wild cards find kindred in the ironically priceless "wild seeds" that serpentish Doro would slyly recruit, as he does Anyanwu and Others like her from elsewhere, to found his colonial America society. These "special" people are the talents that Doro, contemptuous of gods, scouts during his "missionary," albeit predatory, foray into Igboland. As the sacrilegious Doro tells Anyanwu, herself a once-enslaved, socio-gendered Other attacked because of her long-concealed, mystical and inherited powers of shape-changing which she calls her "greatest difference," "Their differences have made them outcasts. [And so t]hey are glad to follow me" (*Wild* 10, 18). Butler here addresses the insidiousness of domestic polarization. She draws attention to the role that homeland injustice played in black peoples' loss of valuable human and intellectual capital to the agents and ravages of colonization in Africa and, before that, to New World slavery.

That Butler's intent is to validate the margin is clear. Reminiscent of Gayl Jones's remark about how the mainstream-proscribed Black Arts movement paradoxically erected its own preclusive strictures, Butler demonstrates mythically also how the periphery could quickly turn into an oppressive "center." She shows, in short, how "difference" or differential power could easily be perverted, especially if its cause is driven by the desire to over-compensate for a lack, the past, or a grievance. Okonkwo's extreme and unconceding masculinism and his habitual impatience with Others, for example, are stirred partly by his overpowering quest for rehabilitative nobility, one that would restitute his own haunting past, his "history" and existential "difference" as the son of an untitled loafer. Along those lines, through her seeming transposition of Ezinma's and Nwoye's experiences of aberrancy in Doro's intersubjectivity, Butler is able to explain Doro's fetishes. In other words, Butler situates Doro's oddity with body consumption and thus his power complex in the context of an agonizing abnormality, that is, a genetic mutation. Doro's allusive *sickling* requires convalescence for its correction and a continuous transfusion of new blood and anti-sickling-bodies, hence his desperate need to kill and kill again for a healthy and eternal life.

My point is that Doro appears to be also a mythicized sufferer of the physically debilitating genetic condition, Sickle Cell Disease. As stated in the introduction and subsequently, some researchers have suspected this devastating disorder in the evolution of the belief in Ọgbañje in Igboland, West Africa, and beyond. The complications of the illness are also suspected in the unusual behaviors and successive deaths commonly associated with children so categorized. Some clarification is in order here regarding the above claim and my hypothesis about Butler's seeming fluid fusion of Ezinma's and Nwoye's breached ontologies. Let us look momentarily at what the novel divulges and also insinuates about Doro's childhood. The narrator discloses that Doro was, among other things, a "sickly" and "stunted" child, the last and only living of his mother's several children. He was odd, frighteningly bedeviled, and convulsive. And although his "were a tall, stately people," it was evident early on that he would not reach a comparable physical height and bearing (*Wild* 177).

The above revelations bring to mind the Ezinma/Ezinma-Ekwefi story. The following "familiar" structures are notable in them: Like Doro, Ezinma is an embodied spirit and part of the (super)natural. Similar to Doro and to his unnamed mother's eleven bereavements, Ezinma is Ekwefi's last and only surviving child after many failed maternities. Ezinma, like Doro, has siblings that died after showing promises of life, of *staying*. She and Doro are sickly. And although "strange," as is Doro, she too is precious and shielded by her parents. Now, interwoven cleanly into Doro's childhood saga is the tale of a young man who abnormally does not measure up to parental standards and social expectations—suggestively a Nwoye story. Or rather, it mimics the Okonkwo-Nwoye father-son genealogical impasse. Inscribed in that tension is the irony of fate and the question of a mutated or "sickled" bloodline, both of which Butler appears to repeat and reverse to empower Otherness. Here are the additional pertinent assertions: people "whispered" about Doro, rumoring that "he was not the son of his mother's husband." Yet his poor father, "if the man was his father—claimed him" proudly, despite Doro's deviation from the common gallantry of his ascribed Nubian descent (*Wild* 177).

The narrator associates Doro with Egyptian ancestry. This identification certainly bolsters the story's epic scope. It also augments its geo-historical and thematic expansiveness through Butler's allusion to biblical Egyptians' history of slaveholding and her implication of Arab merchants in the trans-Atlantic slave trade. Doro's Eastern descent does not, however, negate an amplification of his biological, physical, and social imperfections in the context of Nwoye's (childhood) plight as a "misfit" when weighted next to his father Okonkwo—Umuofia's statesman and paragon of stateliness. On the contrary, there is much heuristic value in such a juxtaposition, beside Butler's subtle yet provocative suggestion that the Egyptians and the Igbo—themselves geographical Easterners, ethnically situated in the path of the rising sun, as the Igbo's civil war Biafra flag announces—might have crossed paths in antiquity (*Wild* 8).[5]

In "'Beloved Pawns': The Childhood Experience in the Novels of Chinua Achebe and Mongo Beti," N. F. Inyama examines the Okonkwo-Nwoye conflict. Inyama provides an important cultural and psychological prism by which to assess more deeply that tension and its resonances in the matrix of Butler's gender theses. "Okonkwo's cruelties to Nwoye," Inyama notes, "are coloured [*sic*] by his own peculiar perception of the importance of the first son in Igbo family culture: the first son is seen as the most potent proof of a man's manhood and an assurance of family continuity. But in time with his partial perception of the significance of things in his culture, Okonkwo sees the upbringing of his son as an enterprise in the projection of his own self-image" (37).

The above helps explain why, to Okonkwo, Nwoye who does not copy and perpetuate the father-as-normative is metaphorically a mutant. In fact, Okonkwo scorns Nwoye evocatively as a "degenerate" (*Things* 153). Ironically a mirror of Okonkwo's own less achieving father Unoka, Nwoye deviates from the norm and hence would not be "stately." He would not because, having a Chi different from his father's, being in touch with his female side, and as the proof of nature's and biology's supreme paradoxes, Nwoye strays from source and expected nobility. It stupefies Okonkwo that he, "a flaming fire," Umuofia's greatest living warrior and diplomat whom his people apotheosize as "the Roaring Flame," "could . . . have begotten a woman for a son." How, he grieves, does "Living fire beget[] cold, impotent ash"? Recalling the narrator's statement that people gossiped about Doro and the possibility that he is the product of adultery, Okonkwo introspects that "Perhaps he [Nwoye] was not his son. No! he could not be. His wife had played him false. He would teach her!" (*Things* 153).

Furthermore, people such as Obierika Okonkwo's greatest friend and Okonkwo's cousin Amikwu talk about Nwoye. They whisper about him, particularly when he dares to commit the taboo of converting to Christianity. Following the white man and the Bible, Nwoye counter-rebelliously disowns his biological father in favor of God as progenitor. He also gets baptized as Isaac, a "sacrificed" personage that Butler implicitly reclaims and empowers as Doro's beloved son Isaac. In figuring Doro's father as a poor yet appreciative man who, unlike Okonkwo, does not forfeit but rather is glad to have a son regardless of the son's "difference"—his scraggliness, diminution, and peculiarity—Butler subordinates wealth, social power and racial descent to the primacy of life and children embodied philosophically in the Igbo names Ifeyinwa and Maduka.

More important, by using a reversive depiction of Doro's father to denounce Okonkwo's male chauvinism and his preoccupation with patrilineage, Butler signifies on the 1960s Black Power/nationalist movement's positing of Okonkwo-esque patriarchal maleness and potent masculinity as racial idea, ideal, identity, and longing. More so, when Anyanwu tells Doro, as they walk to the coast, about her daughter "who had married a handsome, strong, lazy young man" only to abandon him for a striving and less imperious husband (*Wild* 26), Butler insinuates black/female empowerment. She also alludes to young Ekwefi, who deserts her husband Anene to marry Okonkwo instead. Butler signifies then on *Things Fall Apart*'s and the 1960s discourses on repressive masculinity and valor by having the self-determining runaway bride remarry Okonkwo's alter ego, minus the laziness. And, like Anyanwu's people's "loss" of her to Doro's New World mission, Nwoye's defection with the missionaries could be seen as Okonkwo's real though power-orchestrated "loss" of a child because of some hint of sickle-ness.

I hinted earlier that Butler might be implicating sickle cell anemia in Doro's Ọgbañje character profile and life. The narrator's description of Doro as a "sickly" child evokes the descriptor "sickle" and hence points to "sickle cell." More than that, though, Doro exhibits some of the many and complex symptoms of that powerful and dreaded disease. Two of the syndromes are infection and compromised immunity. That Doro is vulnerable to intravasation seems apparent. One infers this at the moment "a small cut" in his hand becomes infected so fast with microbes that Anyanwu has to treat him by dentally injecting him with her own healing antibody (*Wild* 28–29). Other signs of Sickle Cell Disease are "[d]elayed growth and puberty in children and often a slight build in adults,"[6] chronic pain, periodic acute attacks called "crisis" and decreased life expectancy. Because there is no absolute cure for the ailment yet, sickle cell anemia patients depend sometimes on the best available intervention such as bone marrow transplants and, suggestively, blood transfusions. These remedies help them live longer and healthier lives.[7]

The painful and potentially life-threatening "transition" that hits Doro first at age thirteen—a growth moment he expects his breeds to experience in different ways—could be seen as sickle cell "crisis." Ezinma suffers such a major "fit," one that had her "shivering on a mat," on the night a traumatized Ekwefi rouses Okonkwo from sleep with the lament that "Ezinma is dying" of what Okonkwo immediately determines consolingly to be "*iba*" (fever) which is caused, interestingly, by malaria parasites. Researchers have traced evolutionary links between sickle-cell trait and *falciparum* malaria.[8] Given that, it becomes quite certainly provocative then that Ezinma's "crisis" episode occurs just moments after a mosquito bites Okonkwo, prompting the explanatory myth of the skeletal mosquito's infestive and infective attraction to the human ear (*Things* 75–86). It is equally telling that it is after

Doro's earliest major attack that he takes his nearest first victims, paradoxically his mother and soon after his father, in what registers as emergency blood/body transfusions. With his longevity riding on continuous and sometimes urgent blood and "body" replacements, Doro realizes he must kill; hence his parasitic and vampirish appetite. Each time transgenic Doro takes possession of another's body or, rather, anti(body) is a moment of felicity, indeed an event of blood transfusion that revives and "always [puts him] in a good mood" thereafter (*Wild* 37). More significant, however, each chronic seizure betrays and magnifies his dependency. As coauthors Anionwu and Atkin observe, sickle cell disorder does not just complicate its sufferers' self-identity. It also escalates their inevitable reliance on others such as family members who become care providers (68). Doro finds then in his interminable consumption and his endless deaths and rebirths, a window for immortality and with it an enormous psionic power that he mishandles.

This possible Sickle Cell Disease and malaria parasite connection aligns Doro, then, and by default Ọgbañje, as the axis where biology, environment, culture, myth, folklore, science, fiction, history, and spirituality intercross. Their intersection generates for Butler the theme of genetics, mutation, and abnormality/difference, identity, power, survival, and opposition. Butler masterfully frames all these concerns within the context of gender and African people's involuntary trans-Atlantic migration to and enslavement in the New World. Butler recycles her interest in the genetics leitmotif, which she calls "one of my favorite questions, parent to several of my works" (*Bloodchild* 69), in the rest of the Patternist narratives. She explores the theme again in "The Evening and the Morning and the Night" (1987), *Dawn* (1987), *Adulthood Rites* (1988), and *Imago* (1989). Still common in West Africa, Igboland, among peoples of African ancestry and those of Mediterranean and Middle Eastern descent and some whites, sickle cell anemia was brought to North and black America through the slave trade.[9] As hinted in the Introduction, the disorder was in part responsible for the sometimes unexplained deaths of many slave infants and teenagers.[10] If timed by Doro's timelessness, and should the miscreant Doro exteriorize the sickness, Ọgbañje malignancy, slavery, a "capitalist,"[11] colonization, and male ideology of power and Death, then it seems the disease has for centuries ravaged black racial humanity. It continues to rob African diaspora and in this case black American mothers of their children, nieces and nephews, and siblings of immediate family. To Butler, that cycle, that power play, must be protested if not broken. And women, through whose bodies the phenomenon seeks perpetuity, must ultimately have a hand in its cessation.

Enter Anyanwu, the Alpha Quadrinity

One cannot begin to fully and critically appreciate the immensity of Anyanwu's physical, mental and cosmic powers, as well as her pioneering, gendered, and pre-feminist revolts against Doro's shape-shifting hegemony without understanding first her cultural models, meanings and firewalls. Anyanwu is mythically speaking what I call an Alpha Quadrinity. She is Atagbusi, Anyanwu, Ala and Agbala incorporated. Her Atagbusi powers of metamorphoses are augmented by the associative forces of Igbo sun deity "Anyanwu," Agbala's priestess Chielo, and the Igbo Earth goddess Ala/Ana/Ani. Anyanwu is a multi-spirited interventionist that evinces both Igbo hospitality and the historicized Igbo distaste for autocratic power. In other words, Ndi Igbo, the Igbo from whom Anyanwu descends, are known to value republicanism over extremism.[12]

In an interview with Larry McCaffery, Butler admits that of all her novels, *Wild Seed* was the hardest to research. To write about the Igbo she had to engage with Igbo people's intra-ethnic and linguistic heterogeneity. "I found a huge ethnography about the Onitsha Ibo [*sic*] that was very useful," Butler states, "and before somebody torched the L.A. Public Library, I also found a book called *The Ibo Word List,* with words in five different dialects. It was a wonderful old book, shabby and falling apart, and it helped me get the language I needed" (66). Concerning the character "Anyanwu," Butler adds:

> For a while I didn't know how I was going to relate Anyanwu to the Ibo. The solution came from a footnote about a woman named Atagbusi in a book called *The King in Every Man,* by Richard N. Henderson. Atagbusi was a shape-shifter who had spent her whole life helping her people, and when she died, a market gate was dedicated to her and later became a symbol of protection. I thought to myself, This woman's description is perfect—who said she had to die? and I had Anyanwu give "Atagbusi" as one of her names. I gave Doro his name without knowing anything about his background, but later on I looked up "doro" in a very old, very tattered Nubian-English dictionary and discovered that it means "the direction from which the sun comes"—which worked perfectly with what I was trying to do. And Anyanwu ties into that since "Anyanwu" means "sun."[13]

Butler is right about Robert G. Armstrong's *A Comparative Wordlist of Five Igbo Dialects.* It is in this ethnolinguistic study that she found the English word "Sun" translated as "anyanwu" in the Awo Idemiri/Olu dialect group. Published in 1967, and produced with an older typewriter, the work is set in stencil and unpaginated. Butler is also correct about Henderson's scholarship on Atagbusi's legendary transmogrification.[14] Henderson (1972) says a bit more on Atagbusi, however. In addition to sourcing Butler's Igbo kinship terms such as "*Nwadiani*—daughter's child" and "*Nneochie . . .* Mother's mother," Anyanwu's "Ado and Idu" lineage, the word "Orumili" for River Niger, he examines other specificities of Onitsha geographical location, its migration history relative to Benin, and Onitsha people's cultural attitudes to motherhood and children.[15] Some critics such as Dorothy Allison have expressed frustration with Butler's female characters' affirmations of motherhood, children, and family.[16] Reading works like Henderson's, which examine Igbo responses to those issues, would help clarify for readers that Butler sometimes writes from a specific cultural domain, as she does with the Igbo Anyanwu.

Nevertheless, Henderson asserts that people believe that Atagbusi routinely appears "in the great market on market days and entices people into it with her magic fan." It is also said that she hails from a small clan "*Ôkposi-éke*" known for its "native doctors and responsible for magical protection of the northwestern bush outskirts of the town" (311). Anticipating Henderson by fourteen years, Achebe had rendered the Atagbusi lore as the story of the bustling market of Umuike [a fictional Onitsha market] whose size, density, prosperity, and dominance are traced to "a great medicine" which at dawn on every market day "stands on the market ground in the shape of an old woman with a [magic] fan." With this fan "she beckons to the market all the neighboring clans" (*Things* 113). Achebe reuses this myth a year later in his 1959 short story "The Sacrificial Egg"[17] and, again, in the 1964 epic *Arrow of God* (18-19).

To contextualize Anyanwu's dilemma in Igboland and therefore a major part of her motivation to oppose Doro and slavery, Butler draws on Henderson's remarks about certain contradictions inherent in Onitsha's parabolic gender politics. Traditional Onitsha society venerates powerful, mystical women such as Atagbusi as "prophets and as agents driving evil from the community." Yet it condemns them as *amusu* or "'witches.'"[18] Butler transplants that discrepancy into her figuration of Anyanwu as a formidable, protective force yet a woman whom her people malign as an evildoer. Appropriating Henderson's lexicon above, the narrator asserts that Anyanwu is reputed to have "highly accurate dreams." She also makes "medicine to cure disease and to protect the people from evil" (*Wild* 10). She is still accused of witchcraft and compelled to repress the very clandestine powers that enable her security of her kin. This tension in Igboland manifests in how the traditional Igbo see "a man [as] the head of the family and his wives do his bidding." Yet the Igbo name their female children "Nneka—'Mother is Supreme'" (*Things* 133).

In addition, there are nominal, metaphysical and metaphoric connections of the word Anyanwu with Igbo sun deity and fertility cult also called Anyanwu. Those links make the character Anyanwu's declaration of herself as her people's oracle acceptable. Adding yet another layer to Anyanwu's character strengths, the associations also resolve in mythological terms why Anyanwu is both a confident and courageous adversary to Doro and a life force. At first glance and also on an intertextual level, Anyanwu radiates the esoteric authority of the powerful Agbala prophetess Chielo. A priestess unclad in "priestly regalia" in *Things Fall Apart*,[19] Chielo is an ordinary market trader during the day. But then at night, especially when her god possesses her, she transforms into something other than woman and human being, and thus becomes herself a shape-shifter of considerable powers. Not even Okonkwo in all his success, size, belligerence, and bravery can deter or disrespect this extraordinary mediator of the sacred, the secular, and the profane realms. Looking more closely, however, Anyanwu is more than a Chielo, whose strong deity Agbala is also venerated, interestingly, as "Anyanwu."[20]

Butler's Anyanwu externalizes the attributes of the male-figured Igbo sun god "Anyanwu." In traditional Igbo religion Anyanwu is sometimes discussed next to Chukwu, whose abode is the sky. As divinity, Anyanwu is among the pantheon of other Igbo gods and spirit entities. They include "Igwe," the sky god; "Amadioha," the god of thunder and lightning and, quite significantly, the most powerful, ubiquitous, and feared of Igbo immortals—"Ala"—the Earth goddess and mother under whose jurisdiction and care lies "[t]he field of morality."[21] It is perceptive therefore that Thelma J. Shinn should describe the character Anyanwu as "the female principle of life itself . . . [the] Great Mother."[22] As deity and icon, the sun god[dess] is timeless, esteemed, enlightening, en-lightning, watchful, all-seeing, and far-reaching. She is the fountain of creativity, fertility and reproduction. Warm and nurturing, she is compassionate, protective, and healing, but also fiery and unforgiving. Astral, Anyanwu is a companion on one's life journey, from that journey's rising (at birth) to its setting (in death). Anyanwu is thus part of Igbo "calendrical and cosmic cyclic components."[23]

The Igbo "woman" that boards Doro's slave ship *Silver Star* is far from ordinary, as she herself acknowledges. She is an oracle and a mystic who, consistent with her people's social grace, is quite cordial to a stranger (Doro). For not only does she, as mother, feed the ravenous wayfarer Doro an Igbo delicacy—pounded yam and soup—but she also welcomes him to her home with kola nut, "the greatest symbol of Igbo hospitality."[24] As it would turn out, however, Doro's predatory mission and his race-building project are neither honorable nor humane. Most of all, Anyanwu hails from an African people who were not obsequious, ensuring that New World slave traders in South Carolina and Georgia, for instance, were hesitant to procure them.[25] Hailing from an Onitsha Igboland that historically was not patriarchal but rather matriarchal,[26] Anyanwu disaffirms that her Chi destined her to be someone's chattel, whether in Onitsha or in colonial America. And in her rebelliousness on board the *Silver Star* and later in New York (with Doro/Lot's children) and in Louisiana (her liberating Canaan), she maintains her people's antebellum and particularly Igbo women's legacy of insubordination to "foreign" rule. She would help graft onto antebellum and postbellum African America her Igbo history, cosmology, customs, art, and aesthetics. Anyanwu's "decorative and utilitarian" pottery and basketry are not the only indicators of this formal syncretism (*Wild* 141). As Ala, Anyanwu's authority and legitimacy reach even the Owerri Igbo whose splendid visual displays, the Mbari houses, are built on "land" and upon Ala's command.[27] As a result, Anyanwu the Earth goddess figures equally as a patron(ess) of Igbo art and artists (Achebe "Writer," 48). She embodies those elements of ritual, communality, functionality, and regenerativity which Achebe in chapter 2 associates with Igbo aesthetics, elements that Doro/slavery brought incognito to the New World.

Leaving Home for "Home" Distant and Dystopic

Butler African-Americanizes and thus extends the foregoing "familiar" cultural, mythic, and political paradigms. She also reconfigures "skeletal" structures from *Things Fall Apart* by developing both the structures and the paradigms into two contiguous neo-slave narratives, plotted trans-continentally and interested in the topical subjects of power, resistance, and apocalypse. One engrossing feature of *Wild Seed* as a neo-slave text is how Butler meshes factual history and imagination, and also spends time recapturing the captives' long departure through the hinterland. She also recreates activities in a slave factory on the West African coast and follows the trans-Atlantic crossing proper. Butler mentions the notorious slave ports of Bonny and New Calabar (from where many Igbo kidnapees, called Eboes by their white captors, left home). She incriminates infamous European expansionist enterprises such as the Royal African Company.[28] Butler illustrates the sounds, horrors, and foulness of slave merchandizing, noting how the branding of new slaves leaves in the air the "smell of cooking flesh" (*Wild* 37). This scorching and trade-marking of black flesh is supervised by Bernard Daly—a racist English factor, an employee of the Royal African Company, and also fortuitously Doro's man. Unshaven, unclean, and emaciated, Daly avails himself of the African woman's body, emboldened by the enslaver's sense of power and entitlement. He enjoys three African women as wives and has fathered children with them. It is ironic, therefore, that Daly dehumanizes the same Africans as cannibals when his lungs consume the spices of blistered human tissue.

Daly's sentiment—his resort to "the white-held stereotype of the bestial other" implored by Europeans since Christopher Columbus to justify their enslavement, colonization, vampiric capitalist exploitation, murder, and human/bodily depletion of nonwhite peoples[29]—is mutual, apparently. As Butler's counterhegemonic insertion of "the cannibal trope"[30] shows, and as verified in Anyanwu's consternation, enslaved (Igbo) Africans equally saw the white man as visually shocking and cannibalistic. Like the distrustful local residents of the Onitsha Waterside, who on July 26, 1857, bolted on seeing "the Europeans with long beards and full whiskers,"[31] Anyanwu cringes the first time she sees a white man. Her fright not only reminds one of, but also precedes, the terror that *Things Fall Apart*'s Abame people would years later feel on first encountering a real Caucasian, an enslaver-turned-missionary, not a leper or an albino as Umuofians had feared. It brings to mind just as vividly the chill that befalls Olaudah Equiano, that other Igbo slave, autobiographer, seaman, orator and abolitionist who in his *Interesting Narrative* (1789) initially sees his white captors as hideous cannibals and abducting "bad spirits."[32]

Furthermore, Anyanwu's long trek with Doro from Igboland and the inland territories to the shore echoes if not retraces Equiano's torturous foot travel from his village of Essaka, through the African interior, and on to the Atlantic coastline. But just as Linda Brent's (Harriet Jacobs's) gendered *Incidents in the Life of a Slave Girl* (1861) implicitly responds to and revises Frederick Douglass's 1845 male, canonically dominant and "master"-slave story, Butler through Anyanwu's captivity converses with but also historically subordinates Equiano's experience to his kinswoman Anyanwu's ordeal. In other words, she predates Anyanwu's 1690 story and her arrival to the New World almost a hundred years before Equiano's 1789 narrative. And because, as Ala, Anyanwu is figured as Earth Mother, as an Igbo mother and black racial ancestress, and also because she and Equiano hail from the same geographical zone—the Onitsha-Benin axis—the narrative Equiano becomes one of Anyanwu's many and sometimes "unidentified" descendants.

The sight of *Silver Star,* Doro's anchored, sturdy slave ship named after an 1856 clipper vessel, shocks not just Anyanwu. It scares her youngest daughter's child, Okoye, who had been kidnapped. She is already branded, but is bought/freed by Doro to appease Anyanwu and also reconnect her with her Igbo diaspora, her several and scattered descendants, including Udenkwo. Butler harnesses the story's maritime intermission, the occasion of the trans-Atlantic voyage proper, and Anyanwu's ineluctable adaptation to pre–Civil War North America to tabulate the real human cost of enslavement. As Anyanwu's moodiness shows, perhaps the first and most devastating tragedy of forced, trans-Atlantic migration and New World human propertization is the very permanency of the exile and the severity of cultural loss. To Anyanwu, the core problem is not about the quirks and prejudices of early European settlers. The issue is not that she, gifted naturally with a powerful perceptivity, "misreads" Doro's procreative intentions with her body and mind. His stated goal is to harness her difference, her rare bloodline, and healing abilities. Nor is it that she misjudges and mistrusts the proven capacity of her paranormal endowment to insulate her against harm, both sensorially "perceived" and physically real. After all, she has emphasized to Doro that she cannot be his slave, although she agrees to marry him and mother his children so as to actualize her desire "to have a man who was as different from other men" as she is "from other women" (*Wild* 52).

In addition, when threatened, she herself can murder an enemy just as fast and as coldly as Doro. She demonstrates this when she morphs into a leopard and defensively kills Doro's own son Lale Sachs. Lale had infiltrated her mind, projecting into her thoughts amorous pictures of her having sex with both him, Lale, and Isaac, Doro's favorite son. Doro pressures Anyanwu into an incestuous marriage with Isaac with the aim of saddling her into obedience with maternity and motherhood. Like the androgynous Ọgbañje, Anyanwu can fluidly but transgressively assume male and female bodies, as well as black and white identities. For instance, in Louisiana she incarnates as a white plantation owner Edward Warrick. She can also turn into animals: the royal python, an eagle, a leopard, a dolphin, and a dog; and in animal form she can elude Doro. As a female dolphin she experiences freedom and tranquility by being one with an intelligent creature of the deep. Unlike her male counterparts, the novel's female dolphin is neither obsessively competitive nor territorial.

Anyanwu ably navigates all that. But what distresses her to the point of contemplating oceanic suicide en route to the New World is the sobering realization hinted at earlier. Once uprooted, she knows, she and her fellow captives would become permanent exiles. They would have to make new "homes" in a land far away, strange, and chaotic. Perhaps she had made a perilous and irreversible covenant with the Devil. Approximating the pains of "social death" (Patterson *Slavery*, 38) and the nostalgia for roots are the other hard realities of involuntary departure. Among them are suffering racial slights and epithets, losing or evanescence of ancestral names that are culturally and experientially inspired, event-specific, and sometimes panegyric; acquiring literacy in new and foreign languages; and meeting new sartorial, social, and dietary requirements.

For instance, upon disembarking in Doro's multiethnic New England settlement named evocatively Wheatley, Anyanwu is compelled to don a petticoat. Although an Igbo/African woman, she is to behave like an Anglo-Saxon lady. In addition, she is served animal milk, much to her disgust and sense of cultural abomination. Anyanwu would discover that in America the politics of beauty, race, blackness, Indian-ness, and whiteness equates to discourses of caste, slavery, and freedom. She would become aware also of the black discontent and incendiary uprisings in New York that altogether, as John Hope Franklin authenticates, culminated in the witch hunt, arrest, prosecution, execution, lynching, and burning of dozens of blacks, as well as four whites who were hanged (59–60). She would have to find her voice and also adopt a new conception of time. Whereas her Igbo people have a four-day market week, namely, Nkwo, Eke, Oye, and Afo, in America the weekly calendar stretches seven days. Other things to learn included new marriage customs. Her unceremonious marriage to Isaac, Doro's son, lacks the familial and appropriate liturgies obtained in Igboland. Doro adulterates kinship and "kinship networks," which Butler manipulates structurally "to build dramatic complexity" in the novel.[33] Thus, Anyanwu finds herself bedding father and son, bearing for them eight and five children respectively. Young, lonely, in need of companionship and understandably petrified of Doro, Anyanwu's descendants Okoye and Udenkwo get married, a coerced nuptial that is both incestuous and a sociocultural travesty. And last though not least, Anyanwu also has to reconcile the Biblical postulates of New World Christianity with the complex precepts of traditional Igbo religion and beliefs to which she is heir and avatar. Through the above perverse unions Butler inveighs slavery's insensitive defilement of the cornerstones of indigenous Igbo marriage tradition whose purpose, integrity, playfulness, ritualistic dimensions, and ceremonial grandeur Achebe painstakingly solemnizes in both *Things Fall Apart* and *Arrow of God.*

One is not surprised then that, arriving in colonial yet colonizing and racist North America with a strong sense of her personal identity and cultural heritage, Anyanwu appreciates the need to maintain control over her language, children, and especially their names. The aspects of her life that include motherhood and indigenous culture and history remain defiantly outside of Doro's jurisdiction and expanding empire. While Doro jovially calls her Sun Woman and in his compounding power drive continues to acquire new settlements and territories in Canada, Brazil, Mexico, and Kentucky, Anyanwu converses with her children as though she was still in Igboland. She would not acculturate or assimilate uncritically. She refuses to take a European name or address her children by the European names she gives them superciliously at Doro's clamoring. Quite significant, and indeed remarkable, her children are fluent in Igbo language. And although her New World name Emma means ancestress, which complements the Ala component of the Quadrinity, she still identifies herself as Anyanwu, Atagbusi, and her given name Mbgafo [*sic;* Mgbafo].

Butler gestures toward *Things Fall Apart, Arrow of God,* and the story " The Madman," in her choice of her characters' Igbo names, especially Anyanwu's marital and birth names, as well as the Igbo names of some of her descendants. Thus it is not the case, as Bernard W. Bell states, that although Richard Henderson's and Achebe's impact "in the construction of *Wild Seed*" is "major," "this [Achebe] influence is not apparent in the language of the novel" which Bell describes somewhat limitingly as "a blend of historical romance and parapsychological realism."[34] For example, Anyanwu's grandson Okoye [Male Child Born on Oye Day] has nominal precursors in Okoye, Okonkwo's father and Unoka's neighbor and creditor and in another Okoye, Akukalia's brother in *Arrow of God.* Anyanwu's descendant Udenkwo [female child born on Nkwo day, transcribable as The Great Event of Nkwo Day] has cognates in Udenkwo, the new mother unable to assist with preparations for Obierika's daughter Akueke's marriage in *Things Fall Apart* and Udenkwo, Nwibe's junior wife in "The Madman." It has an additional literary root in Udenkwo, Akuebue's insubordinate daughter in *Arrow of God.* Butler also apparently borrowed Anasi—Anyanwu's endearment name as a first wife of her young husband—from Anasi, the regal first wife of Okonkwo's prosperous benefactor, Nwakibie. Anyanwu's name Mgbafo [Female Child Born on Afo Day] celebrates a fellow victimized woman Mgbafo, Uzowulu's runaway wife whose physical abuse case is adjudicated by the ancestral *egwugwu* in *Things Fall Apart.*

Additionally, Anyanwu's son Peter is Chukwuka [Chukwu is Supreme], a theophonic name invoked by Umuofia's Akunna while discussing polytheistic Igbo religion with the District Commissioner Mr. Brown. In Igbo world, the name Chukwuka is also an abbreviation of "Chukwu-ka-dibia": Chukwu is Mightier than the Dibia or, rather, is greater and stronger than both the diviner/fetish doctor and his healing power, or whatever diabolism a malevolent doctor concocts or conjures. Anyanwu names another child, Stephen, Ifeyinwa [There's Nothing Like a Child or Nothing Compares with a Child]—ironically, a predominantly female name in Igbo culture. Margaret's Igbo name is Nneka [Mother is Supreme], taken after another long-suffering and culturally castigated woman and mother, Nneka, in *Things Fall Apart.* Nneka is Amadi's pregnant wife and a new Umuofia Christian convert whose previous four sets of twins were thrown away. And Helen's is Obiageli [short for Obiageliaku or Obiageriaku: a female Child Born into Wealth]. Anyanwu names Obiageli (whose namesakes are Nwoye's sister, and Ezeulu's daughter in *Arrow of God*) after her barren white friend, Helen. Then there is Ruth, given the male name Nweke [Male Child Born on Eke Day], after Ezeulu's son and Obierika's companion on his first visit to Okonkwo in Mbanta.

Like proverbs and aphorisms in general, Igbo personal names, praisenames, endearment phrases, and titles are more than appellations. As evinced in Ọgbañje onomastics, Igbo names are integral to Igbo metaphysical and epistemological systems. The names are in principle and practice shrunken statements and narratives. Or as Ebo Ubahakwe describes them, they are "short forms of longer expressions" (2). In them are compacted, voiced, and "written" some of the voluminous chapters of Igbo philosophies of existence.

As a result, in addition to signifying Butler's tacit affirmations of Achebe and her sometimes revocative dialogue with his novels, Anyanwu's stance that her offspring take Igbo names represents much more. It reveals also her exercise of parental discretion and her continued observance of an endogenous customary rite of passage. Her decision is equally insurrectionary, a tactical cosmological and ideological assault on Doro. It affronts the colonizing New World, especially the white slave traders' and slaveholders' self-arrogated right to (re)name, misname, define, and thereby disempower the enslaved. Understanding the transformative power of words, Europeans knew that "[s]imply by applying a certain vocabulary one can easily turn Gods into idols, faces into grimaces, votive images into fetishes, discussions into palavers and distort real objects and matters of fact through bigotry and prejudice" (Janheinz Jahn, *Muntu*, 20). But as John Blassingame argues in *The Slave Community*, maintaining links with ancestry was among the ways Africans fought their bondage (25). One of such seams is language, and Africans who insisted on their linguistic ties to their homelands were seen as "stubborn and proud" (22).

Through naming, conversations in Igbo language and other domestic rituals with her children, the conceited outlaw Anyanwu sows Igbo philosophy in the New World. More important, however, she continues to challenge slavery and its identity matters. For in the name "Chukwuka," for example, Anyanwu keeps alive and interjects into Christian America and colonial American Christianity the Igbo conception of the transcendental divine, as well as the powerful, tutelary deity of Arochukwu.[35] She also seems to sneer that neither the monotheistic Doro, slavery, whites, nor the New World is all powerful. Anyanwu additionally preserves and interposes, by way of Chi-Ukwu, Igbo creation myth as a complement if not counterpoint to the Genesis version of earth's and human evolution. Also affirmed incantatorily in the name Chukwuka ("God is mightier than . . .") is an ethos of faith and perseverance. Ifeyinwa prioritizes humanity as does Maduka, a name that espouses the unrivaled Igbo "respect of the individual personality" on account of the "chi," although the idea of individualism has historically been conceded to the West, particularly to America's Ralph Waldo Emerson (Achebe "Writer," 49–57). Ifeyinwa deemphasizes territorial wealth or other worldly acquisitions. The name is antithetical to and thus an implicit denunciation of New World mercantile capitalism, its commodification of that which should be unpriced and priceless, namely, children/human beings. "Nneka," a name that also celebrates matrilineage and has "no male parallel or equivalent,"[36] expresses the preeminence of motherhood. It enunciates, as it were, that a mother should be validated and venerated instead of enslaved and exploited. "Nweke," "Okoye" and "Udenkwo" all derive from Igbo commercial arenas, the Eke, Oye and Nkwo markets and their dedicatee spirits. The names also refract Igbo people's pre-colonial and pre-industrial *thoughts* on event-marking, record-keeping, and "periodicity," as well as a consciousness of time, which the Igbo structure ecologically and chronologically.[37] This mathematical, macro-ordering of temporality, along with Igbo awareness of a market economy, long-distance trade, and the use of money, among other things, preceded Europe's presence in West Africa.[38] It is more so noteworthy that in the Nri myths of Igbo ethnic origins, those time-marking, four market days Eke, Oye, Afo and Nkwo have as their symbol "(*ubosi-nano,* four days)": the Igbo celestial force or deity that "guard[s] the secrecy of time."[39]

In all, through her own and her descendents' names Anyanwu refuses to compromise on her right to self-determination. Using Anyanwu's cultural agency as a launch pad, Butler reinforces Joseph E. Holloway's findings that "Africans arriving in Colonial America . . . did not forget their traditional naming practices at first." Rather, they retained the habit of "naming children after the days of the week, months, and seasons"—a custom that African Americans continued and later modified.[40] Through Anyanwu's act, Butler also advances the 1960s emphasis on self-naming, ancestry, and racial pride. Such self-definition, which slaves recognized (Gutnam 185–256), is needed for African-descended people who for centuries were denied their rightful, beautiful, and functional group and personal names.

A beauty herself, Anyanwu bears Doro many beautiful children. In addition, displaying Ala, Atagbusi, and Agbala's combined powers of compassion, healing, and protection, she affirms life in motherhood. She also excels at helping Doro's seeds—his latents—endure their physically torturous transitions. This way, she shows further her immense resourcefulness, her potential to produce and contribute to family and society. But nothing short of her complete surrender and servility would satisfy Doro. It irks him that she would not nor does she intend to be tamed, despite the time and the energy he and Isaac expend trying to elicit her submission. Blinded by totalitarian power, Doro cannot see that in Anyanwu he has, as Isaac reminds him bluntly, a woman who "can be everything you need if you let her—mate, companion, business partner, her abilities complement yours so well. Yet all you do is humiliate her" (*Wild* 143). He demeans her, a deity, in many ways, including mating her with a filthy, sick, grotesque, and racist Virginian named allusively Thomas. That is how Nweke, Anyanwu's powerfully telepathic child was born, although like Ọgbañje, Nweke dies in infancy. Doro is so consumed with winning what the narrator describes aptly as his "old [Ọgbañje] tug-of-war" (*Wild* 265) with woman/Anyanwu he tracks her down and tries to intimidate her everywhere she escapes. For instance, he interferes in her ongoing healing of Thomas, whom he subsequently kills just to spite Anyanwu. Having antagonized "that thing he was, the spirit, the feral hungry demon, the twisted ogbanje" (*Wild* 173), Anyanwu knows she is imperiled, for Doro decides she should die once he exhausts her utility to him.

But in a defensive-offensive move, Anyanwu resolves to make herself an even more formidable antagonist to Doro. Her determination to maintain agency, to assert maximally her Quadrinitarian authority, would be actuated on a plantation in Avoyellas Parish, Louisiana. She had, in the body of a dolphin, vanished to this location where she eludes Doro for a century. To her neighbors, she is the reclusive, mysterious white planter and widower Edward Warrick, owner of several slaves and a Big House, a suggestively "solid, permanent-looking" structure with adjoining slave quarters (*Wild* 201, 203). Butler hints, however, at Anyanwu's imminent, decisive opposition in the closing section of *Wild Seed,* Book III, which Butler allusively subtitles "Canaan 1840." Butler also uses Anyanwu's gendered, symbiotic, and protective leadership of this women-administered plantation as a space to dignify anomaly, to further expose the horrors of slavery, and to inveigh violent and disabling male governance and attitudes toward power. For example, Anyanwu takes another's life only in defense of herself or of a loved one. She evinces this in her murder of Joseph Taylor, whom Doro sent to disrupt her Edenic society where she "practic[es] humane eugenics."[41]

In contrast, Doro kills selfishly. He transfuses unsickled and unsickly new bodies and blood to maintain control and prolong his otherwise at-risk longevity. Doro intends to destroy anyone capable of accessing and containing him telepathically. That is what Anyanwu dares by blocking his insight on her mystery. Anyanwu had spent years cultivating and earning her people's trust. But Doro's Ọgbañje-intrusion into her new sanctuary erodes that confidence. It deteriorates so fast that even her children become skeptical of her, just as the Umuofians, especially those inveigled by the disruptive and furtive white missionary, now question their oracles.

Anyanwu's Igbo people have a certain world view that would help clarify her thinning patience with Doro and the drastic action she subsequently takes. That cosmological injunction is coded in any one of these semantically related dictums: *Ịjụrụ mmadụ ọfọ; Ịjụrụ mmadụ ogu;* or *Ịjụrụ mmadụ ọfọ na ogu.* Victor Uchendu explains that *ọfọ,* an aspect of Igbo ethos of transparent living, is "the symbol of ritual authority" invoked to profess or legitimize one's innocence (17). *Ọfọ* is "the god of justice and truth on the Niger," Arthur Glyn Leonard adds (301), noting that "those who, having a grievance, consider that right is on their side, or, in fact, that they are altogether right," appeal to *ọfọ* (420). *Ogu* is "a deity of protection" which is also petitioned in matters of "disputation and litigation with others" (412). The above dictums translate loosely, in this context, as follows: summoning *ọfọ* or both *ọfọ* and *ogu;* warding off an opponent; feigning passivity for peace; wishing to be left alone; or simply giving someone, particularly one's enemy, a long rope—before one takes justifiable, retaliatory, even excessive action. This cultural mandate—this Igbo practice of exculpable self-defense covered also under the goddess Ala's ordinances of ethics, civility, and fairness—is what Anyanwu importunes by leaving Doro for a century. It is *ọfọ* and *ogu's* advocacies of right and judicious self-protection that she activates by circumventing Doro's threats on her life and her children's lives to seek refuge in Louisiana. She avoids him not because she is cowardly. But when Doro, ignorantly and predictably, misreads those cultural signs, Anyanwu decides to retake full ownership of her body and life. For as the Earth mother Ala, she can create but also destroy.

To deny Doro the joy of victory, Anyanwu elects to commit suicide—in Doro's face. Cleared by *ọfọ* and *ogu,* Anyanwu's recourse to transcendental self-creation is not simply gendered. Nor is it a case of what Huey P. Newton describes as "reactionary suicide" or a mere "death wish" (2–6). Her act must also be viewed within a wider literary, historical, and political lens. Put simply, her resolve is corroborated in and magnifiable by other Igbo captives' spectacular performances of black power in the New World. Having directly and personally challenged the white District Commissioner George Allen (see *Arrow of God* 32) by slaying his native informant, Okonkwo anticipates inevitable imperial capital punishment. But he refuses the white man the pleasure of a power-kill and embraces instead an act of militancy and martyrdom. Anyanwu's initiated counteroffensive may baffle rationalism and alarm radical feminism. But her choice is also not inconsistent in spirit and intent with Okonkwo's mode of resistance which, though a cultural taboo in Igboland, nevertheless occurred. Nor is it incompatible with the examples of those "mindless" Igbo slaves who so disdained bondage and sought to sabotage plantation economy and slavocracy in general by committing mass suicides or, as I prefer to call them, revolutionary life-takings.

Upon setting foot in North America and rejecting a life in chains, which they foresaw, a group of Igbo captives "freed" themselves by drowning in South Carolina's Dunbar Creek. To many South Carolina and Georgia planters, Igbo mass revolt, which occurred also on plantations in Haiti and beyond, suggested an ethnic penchant for depression and self-annihilation. (The British called it "Ebo melancholy" [*Cattle Killing* 103].) But as Michael A. Gomez rebuts, New World Igbo suicides were often "dramatic," "very emphatic," "decisive," "irreversible," and "sensational" (120, 124). Inspired also by religious imperatives and the promise of a return to homeland, Igbo suicide represented "the ultimate form of resistance, as it contained within it the seed for regeneration and renewal" with ancestors in Africa (120). The Dunbar Creek episode and, as Gomez explains, the other Igbo suicides have gained currency as the myth of Ebo/Ibo Landing and the legend of flying Africans.[42] It is no surprise, then, that in his poem "The Ballad of Nat Turner," Robert Hayden figures antebellum Igbo rebels/warriors as Nat Turner's co-conspirators.[43]

Nevertheless, what makes the rebel and warrior priestess Anyanwu suspend her life-taking in progress is Doro's disempowerment. Reversing him into a slave, she "breaks" him with her resolve and forces him to concede narcissistic power upon demand, as Frederick Douglass would declare years later.[44] For the moribund Doro realizes at that moment how desperately and profoundly he depends on her for life. During their first encounter in 1690, he dominated the tone and terms of their covenant, but not this time. Although tired, she secures from him, in the Epilogue, her manumission from breeding and his proprietorship, as well as his pledge not to kill her descendants. Anyanwu knows, however, that she cannot eradicate completely Doro's propensity for indiscriminate Ọgbañje murders. But she could at least ensure that the "human" part of his Ọgbañje spirit-human composition does not totally die, leaving in him only a time-traveling, malevolent, and alien spirit that "has total disregard for human life" other than his (*Mind* 23).

* * *

Wild Seed ends on that note of gendered triumph and delicate truce. Anyanwu, who has now taken the name Emma, relocates in 1861 to pre-modern southern California to escape the impending American Civil War. Narrated mostly by Anyanwu's granddaughter Mary and an omniscient consciousness, *Mind of My Mind* begins in contemporary California and the futuristic city of Forsyth, the Pat-ternists' homestead. It is here, in California, that we again encounter the now four-thousand-year-old Doro who, antedating and literarily anticipating the immortal Dawit in Tananarive Due's *The Living Blood* (2001), was alive at the time of Christ. Masterminding a comeback, Doro is still devoted to his twisted power- and race-building initiative. An inveterate Ọgbañje whom Butler figures appropriately as the ultimate survivor, trickster, schemer, contract breaker, and untrustworthy foe, Doro deceives Anyanwu again. He facilely breaches their pact and continues to kill and transfuse into healthy bodies at whim. We find him, a shape-shifter, obligating Anyanwu to take care of Mary, Rina's child and his and Anyanwu's granddaughter whom he envisions as his "experimental model" of the super telepath.

That Doro's god-schemes, Ọgbañje longevity, and his hold on power always involve children continues to trouble the immortal Anyanwu (Emma). She presently is writing a historiographic trilogy, perhaps her realistic narrative on her centuries' long, gendered encounters with an Ọgbañje. Her spiritual autobiography would record that to date she has borne Doro "through his various incarnations" thirty-seven children. None of them, however, "had proved to be especially long lived. Those who might have been were tortured, unstable people. They committed suicide" *(Mind* 10), extending their ancestress's epic battle against Doro. This irony of fate with regard to Doro's offspring and gene project explains his alarm that all his previous breeding programs have been "Failures. Dangerous failures" *(Mind* 8). Through Mary as his rarest breed yet he hopes to redress those past defeats. And more important, he would surpass himself this time.

As Butler links *Mind of My Mind* and *Wild Seed* through flashbacks, allusions, and other intertextual transitions, she foreshadows that Doro's newest power experiment, which involves assembling his scattered and disharmonious active telepaths, is ill-fated. It would face some setbacks, if not life-threatening, empire-destroying, and epoch-ending opposition for a number of reasons. First, Doro miscalculates, even for an experienced trickster. Just as he, years ago, underestimated Anyanwu's resolve and misread her *ọfọ* and *ogu,* he misjudges reality again by hinging the success of the new research venture on age and gender stereotypes. He hopes that in selecting specifically not only the youngest of his active clairvoyants but a woman as test case he would avail himself of a passive telepath. Second, we are told, against this backdrop, that Mary inherited Anyanwu's Igbo "genes." She looks like "the young version of Emma," except for Mary's green eyes, which she acquired from the eyes of the white man whose body Doro wore when he impregnated Mary's mother Rina, now a prostitute. Third, Mary (a figure connected biblically with messianism and Armageddon through her son Jesus Christ) is positioned as the one who would "complete" her grandmother's legacy of resistance to Doro.

It is not surprising then that from the outset the narrator portrays the physically deceptive and nineteen-year-old Mary as a special and powerful child. Mary is a lawbreaker. She is a "stubborn kid" from infancy, a "not ... good little girl" whom males would be reckless to assault *(Mind* 16–23). It is the fearless Mary that presses Doro on his blackness: Doro admits to being born black. Yet he vacillates on his color because for four thousand years now he has looked white. "But if you were born black, [then] you *are* black," Mary informs him. "Still black, no matter what color you take" (*Mind* 87). As Mary undergoes the seeds' painful and epiphanic transition, her maturing consciousness and psionic powers herald her ability to perceive other people's thoughts and the real threat she poses to Doro.

In a novel, *Mind of My Mind,* in which the past/history/the dead are actually not dead but alive and contemporaneous, Mary reifies a notion prevalent in the 1960s and 1970s that (radical) youth can be a true force for change. Her challenge to Doro's expedient whiteness, his "passing," inserts into the narrative the pre-1960s, 1960s, and post-1970s black racial and identity politics. Mary's seemingly passing correction of Doro is Afrocentric and nationalistic. It writes "multiracial" Egypt back into (black) Africa by way of Doro's admission. Mary thus indirectly counters what had been the (West's) tendency to jettison the pyramidic Egypt from Africa and situate it with the orient, Europe, intelligent design, and everywhere else but black Africa. But then one should be cautious because Mary's emphatic "you *are* black" also sounds absolutist and prescriptive. It recalls the 1960s problematic insistencies on racial homogeneity.

Mary's forced interracial marriage to stranger Karl Larkin is part of Doro's scheme to squash the danger she presents. His plan is to control and thus efface her through implied racial integration. The Mary-Larkin union also allows Butler to comment broadly on the perpetuation of race prejudices and class injustice in contemporary urban America. A rich white man, albeit another of Doro's post-transition telepaths, Karl resents Doro's exploitive power, his "playing God" through "human husbandry" (47, 48). It is ironic, then, that Karl emulates Doro's power complex. He owns his own (ordinary) people whose minds he programs to enforce absolute obedience.

Karl's bitterness that Doro misuses him and other telepaths as puppets heightens the narrative's dramatic tension and forebodes serious conflict. It is in Mary's establishment of the Patternist society and her expanding and moreover shielded psionic powers, however, that the course of apocalypse would be accelerated. Like Karl, Mary feels uneasy with Doro's seeming omniscience. He is so powerful and cavalier, she reflects, "You didn't cheat him. You didn't steal from him or lie to him. You didn't disobey him. He'd find you out, then he'd kill you. How could you fight that?" (26). Doro is so ruthless and unforgiving he kills his own son for stealing from him. As with Anyanwu's insinuation through her son's name Chukwuka that Doro is no almighty, Mary realizes, too, that Doro is indeed flawed by his lack of telepathic capacity. And she can infiltrate his mind. This is a deadly development because Doro summarily kills telepaths that attempt to reach his thoughts. But it is not just Doro that Mary can reach. In what is the genesis of the Patternist cult, Mary also accesses and integrates mentally five of Doro's active, separatist telepaths whom she "calls"/pulls to California. Among them are Seth Dana, the preacher and healer Rachel Davidson, Jesse Bernarr, Ada Dragan, and Jan Sholto. All abandon whatever they are doing and head irresistibly for Forsyth. And because these telepaths are inclined to autonomy, the initial animosities that ensue among them, as well as between them and their captor Mary, compel Mary to see herself portentously as "an experiment going bad before his [Doro's] eyes" (92).

Knowing the enormity of his reliance on them, Doro would rather preserve his valuable telepaths. An unredeemed and calculating double-crosser, he views Mary's newly constituted Patternist society as an excellent opportunity to build his empire and further solidify his power over it through Marian surveillance and intertelepath espionage. In *Wild Seed* Butler contrasts male and female approaches to authority and community by differentiating Doroean despotism from Anyanwu's symbiotic leadership on the Louisiana plantation. In a similar vein, Butler uses the moment of the Pattern formation to distinguish positively Mary's political philosophy from Doro's attitudes to power and to the opposition. It is true that, as the titular mind of the Patternists' minds, Mary wields immense command and leverage over them. It is equally true that she ostensibly detains them against their will, which is why, to Doro, she must now find a way to survive her new authority. Yet like her grandmother's, Mary's ultimate intentions with her subjects are healing rather than malignant. Hers is a "benevolent captivity"[45] and not a dehumanizing, tortuous, and permanent objectification. Mary unites the actives, conciliates their differences, neutralizes their opposition, and is able to get several latents/mutes—non telepathically gifted ordinary people—such as Seth's brother Clay, Mary's cousins Janie and Christine Hanson, and other Doro-discards through transition and into Patternist membership. Doro, on the other hand, pressures her to intimidate and spy on the telepaths.

Mary's growing power is especially threatening to Doro for more reasons than her telepathic advantage. He is unnerved that Mary depletes and consequently undercuts his power base instead of working for his empire's continued expansion and the emperor's health. Mary undermines his project for immortality the more people she assists successfully through transition into Patternism, her network of subversive underground railroads. In other words, the more captives she unchains and delivers from imperial slavery to freedom, from silence to voice, the more she destabilizes the foundation of the institution that Doro sustains and that sustains him. To Emma, to whom Doro complains desperately about Mary's and the Patternists' widening political influence and interferences (they now number 1500), little Mary is a "ruthless, egotistical, [and] power hungry" ingrate (154). But Emma declines to intervene actively in the brewing familial confrontation. She would not intercede beyond her sarcastic complaint that Mary and the Patternists now disrespect Mutes who, to Emma, mean "non-telepaths, us niggers, the whole rest of humanity." When Emma refuses to meddle beyond repudiating the Patternists' disregard of their ancestors (155–56), Doro turns deadly. He decrees Mary's death if she persists in disobedience. Like antebellum planters unsettled by the conspiracy and revolt potential of slave fellowship, an uncompromising Doro orders an immediate end to all Patternist gatherings. His excuse is that Mary is indispensable, when her only successor is her infant son, Karl August Larkin. And because Mary remains insubordinate, the stage is set for a "Civil War," a War of Independence, foreshadowed in America's own slavery-implicated Civil War.

The grueling domestic battle in which Mary commits patricide, backed by her people's mandate, is decisive, revolutionary, and exorcistic. Although in disabling Ọgbañje Doro "[p]atriarchy becomes matriarchy" under Mary,[46] we are persuaded about the need for change. This emancipation from tyranny is imperative even if it costs the Patternist society one hundred and fifty-four of its members. The new dispensation might be complicated, as are political systems, and flawed somewhat, as are human inventions. Yet it is predicated on possibility and a multiracial community rather than on exploitation and monarchical dictatorship. In the Epilogue, we hear that on the day Anyanwu-Emma learns of Doro's passing she wills her own death, like Ozoemena, Ogbuefi Ndulue's wife (*Things* 67–68). "It was just as well," Mary remarks (216). Quadrinitarian Anyanwu, as the sun, sets. She sets, having accompanied Doro from the beginning of his narrated, earthly journey in Igboland to his death. So, Ọgbañje Doro is "[f]inally, thoroughly dead," Mary states, getting *Mind of My Mind*'s last word. "Now we were free to grow again—we, his children" (217).

* * *

I suggested earlier that Butler might have been drawn to the Ọgbañje concept for other reasons than its aesthetic value. As the foregoing discussion expatiates, the spirit child drama ingrains a number of science fiction's thematic, structural, and narrative commonplaces, including "estrangement," "[s]patial and temporal displacement," the existence of "'worlds'" that enable an empowering fabulation, and the tense interplay of "strangeness and familiarity," among others.[47] A look at Butler's familial and personal life, however, would help us see why to her the Ọgbañje experience hits close to home; why the cycle/Doro's power-acts must end. It would also help us appreciate even more the reason Butler reverses literarily familial, filial, and maternal misfortune, as illustrated in Anyanwu's directive to the trinity Ọgbañje/Doro/Death to steer clear of her children.

Although Butler's novels are not autobiographical, she admits to writing herself into her works. She also uses her characters and themes vicariously to manage some aspects of her life.[48] In this case, I postulate, one of such biographical details has to do with her experience with loss and difference. Like *Things Fall Apart's* Ezinma, and also in ways like the child Doro, Butler was literally her mother's only surviving child. Butler lost her father during her infancy. Her four brothers also passed away at birth or shortly after. Butler told John R. Pfeiffer in an interview that these bereavements made her mother "'tiresomely protective'" of her (147–48), reminiscent of Ekwefi's unrelenting determination to preserve Ezinma. In addition, because of Butler's physical appearance, people sometimes misjudged her gender and sexuality.[49] Butler understood full well as does Nwoye the pains and politics of peculiarity, of not being "normal." Through Mary's character, for instance, Butler realizes what she said was her desire "to become a bit forward, not so much to take charge (although sometimes it comes to that) but to take responsibility for what happens to me."[50] It is not inconceivable, then, that by giving Anyanwu at least forty-seven healthy children who survive way into adulthood in Igboland, Butler wanted to "cancel" or disaffirm retroactively her mother's ordeal with loss and infant/child mortality. This was a misfortune her mother shares with many an Igbo and other mother. Butler finds in Anyanwu, then, not just a rebellious voice that helps her "write back" in protest to Death/Doro's power and imperial center. Anyanwu for her is a change-agent as well, an Alpha Quadrinity who through (grand)maternity sets in motion the emperor's ultimate nakedness and demise.

Like Achebe, Octavia Butler is clearly a gifted storyteller. She is truly "that rarity."[51] Her insight into the human condition is as profound as her stories are rich yet lucid, gendered, political, and racially conscious—which makes her untimely death in 2006 an unquantifiable loss. What Butler captures in the two signifyin(g), biblically inflected and contiguous neo-slave texts are, collapsibly, the tension between "slavery" and "freedom" and the Exodus-like journey of an oppressed people—African-descended people—from captivity to emancipation. Butler also thematizes gendered activism and the prospects of that "New World" order often imagined in diasporic black writing.[52] And "[b]y linking familiar scenarios from African-American fiction, including the master's impregnation of female slaves, passing, and escape attempts, with science fiction, Butler highlights similarities," the experiential continuities, between the eighteenth and "nineteenth centur[ies] and the end of the millennium."[53] As stories about bondage and liberation, *Wild Seed* and *Mind of My Mind* can also be read as allusive (post)colonial texts.[54] Both novels together retrace the inseparable historical moments from pre-contact to slavery to imperialism to colonization to the struggles for sovereignty and self-identity by former colonials, the final implosion of empire and the arrival of independence day.

That emperor Doro's imperial might depends largely on his overtaxed overseas settlements makes fellow speculative writer Nalo Hopkinson's observation pertinent. Echoing Frantz Fanon and Walter Rodney,[55] Hopkinson states that it is "pretty clear that for the past 500 years or so, the fortunes of the European nations were built on the backs of black and other racialized bodies." That misuse of blackness continues to have adverse ripples today (in Glave 153). And the 1960s and 1970s social movements cited and extended Fanon, arguing that blacks in America were an internal colony, and that such subjugation must end, as must Doro's reign of terror.

Through her invocations of and dialogue with Achebe, her synthesis of history, myth, folklore, spirituality, genetics, science, and fiction, Butler helps answer some of the entwined questions that students of Igbo world, history, and literature sometimes ask: What was the general Igbo experience with slavery like at least two centuries before the white man, brandishing the Bible, propaganda, and a gun, encountered *Things Fall Apart*'s allegoric Umuofia people in the 1890s? Whatever happened to the Igbo captives brought to North America during the slave trade? And what could be recovered of their trivialized and sometimes forgotten contributions to the Americas? To Butler, the answers are hidden deeply in history, myth, and folklore, and in the epic story of Anyanwu and her African American and black diaspora descendants. The answers are sited in Anyanwu's and her progenies' struggle to forge empowering identities and live decent human lives in the face of protracted adversities over which they continue to triumph.

Chapter 4 Binary Nativity, Subjectivity, and the Wages of (In)Fidelity to "Origins"

The Between

This place [Miami] is too thick with spirits for me, with the Cubans and their *santeros* and the Haitians with their vodun.

Andres
The Between

Like Octavia Butler who found in the religious concept and mythic drama of Ọgbańje the seeds for her characterization of Doro and for her narrativization of the interfaces of power, slavery, race, gender, and resistance, Tananarive Due sees in the synonymic notion of "born-to-die" a trope of considerable creative capital. It enables her to extend Butler's project by exploring the impasse of displacement, belonging, subjectivity, and identity that one of "Anyanwu's" male descendants undergoes decades after Anyanwu's Igbo Landing on the shores of North America.[1] In *The Between,* her semi-autobiographical[2] and first published novel, Due presents the story of Hilton James, an eponymous protagonist that she describes as a man "who dreams himself to different planes of existence"[3] and "does not know which reality he would wake up in from one day to the next."[4]

On the strength of this debut, Due joins the practitioners of Afrofuturism who harness the potentials of speculative mode and African diaspora spirituality and mythologies to represent black people's old and New World experiences. In the arena of speculation,[5] one cannot call Due a "new" voice in the field, given her literary output and popular reception the past twelve years. Though *The Between* has done well commercially, rigorous analysis of its concerns remains scarce.[6] It would not be presumptuous to say that the paucity of scholarship has not helped a critical Due readership appreciate the story more deeply, especially with regard to Hilton's confounded existence as an allegoric living dead, his runnings run-ins with fate, as well as the novel's sub-themes and stylization. Due's recognition of her works' intersections with those by other African American and Western writers situates *The Between* specifically and her imaginative production in general as participants in black texts' system of intertextual repetition, revision, and extension.[7] It is true that, as Due states, the subject of life and death that she explores in *The Between* is universal.[8] In approaching that topic from the mythic paradigm of "born-to-die," however, Due's construction of the theme is by no means elemental. Her treatment of the subject becomes more astute and vivid if valuated not from a universalist or Western perspective but rather in the context of the West African idea of spirit children and the example of a precursor text, Ben Okri's àbíkú story *The Famished Road,* which *The Between* echoes.

Welcome to Miami

This chapter discusses *The Between* as an imprinted narrative. Like *The Famished Road, The Between* intersperses political, cultural, and gendered questions in portraying Hilton as a "born-to-die." In other words, the chapter examines the novel as a story that doubles as a re-mastered "àbíkú" tale with thematic resonances of the neo-slave narrative and with implications for African American-African reunion. The novel unpacks also as Due's thoughts on such interlaced subjects as the place of power in black-white gendered relationship; "home," "house," and black dualistic nativity of America; and the complexity of racism-aware, postmodern black subjectivity in the United States miniaturized in Miami, the novel's setting. The genius of the text lies, however, in how Due cleverly interweaves these issues by exploiting the dialectics of life and death. Due weighs these existential questions against the curtain of Miami, a syncretistic modern city "too thick with spirits," as the character Andres senses (229). In multiethnic and multilingual Miami, Cuban Santería and Haitian vodun, both grounded in Yoruba/African religions transplanted and reshaped by enslaved Africans and their descendents, coexist with Catholicism and Protestantism. They commingle with Spanish, English, Spanglish, patois, pidgin, salsa, reggae, African high-life music, soul, funk, McDonalds, Burger King, sports franchises, "African, Caribbean, and good old soul food," "organized Nigerian I[g]bo community" (140), and Miami's glitzy South Beach.

But to appreciate the impetus for an interpretation of the novel in the context of the spirit child, one should start by looking not just at the text's imprinting of the Anglicization "born-to-die" but the revealing, post-publication introspection Due shares below about her childhood. In *Freedom in the Family: A Mother-Daughter Memoir of the Fight for Civil Rights*—a publication she co-authored with her mother—Due writes, among other things, that growing up in the Due family, which was active politically and imperiled during the 1960s, 1970s, and beyond, she was ever conscious of death. She feared two things deeply. "Loss, for one. And death, for another. . . . I used to lie awake as a child," Due recalls, picturing

> what it would feel like to be nothing. I knew I was only here temporarily, and even as a child, time always passed too quickly for my liking. I hoped there was an after-life, as the Bible taught, but even if the afterlife was waiting, I was not ready to say good bye to this world, and I didn't think I ever would be. For all its problems, I have always loved life. I have always felt blessed, in part because my parents taught us to feel blessed, and in part because plain common sense told me so. My parents loved me. I had a roof over my head. I had my writing. I had two sisters who, for all our bickering, I knew would forever be my best friends. Death was the robber waiting to steal everything I held dear.[9]

In this returning past, Due depicts death as a thief. Her characterization of it evokes the Igbo and Yoruba views, especially Amos Tutuola's excerpted depiction, of the born-and-die as global fetal burglars. Due envisions death as an existential given, a sadist, spoiler of earthly bliss and plunderer of wealth. Most important, Due's remarks leave clues to her attraction to the notion of "born-to-die," which she invokes in-text through Kofi, one of the novel's characters. Her comments suggest as well why Ben Okri's depiction of Azaro as an àbíkú child caught between his love of a complicated earthly life *and* his susceptibility to abduction by Death's mercenaries back to the immortal world of spirits represents an appropriate precursor against which *The Between* attains perhaps its most cultural, critical, and philosophic illumination. For not only does Hilton's ontological dilemma mimic Azaro's "oscillat[ion] between . . . worlds" (*Famished* 8), but the novel's title brings to mind Azaro's statement as to how "It is terrible to forever live in-between" (5). Due wrote *The Between* as her way of confronting her fear of death. By way of Hilton's complicated experience, Due hoped to make sense of the anxieties of youth and her personal dealings with the problems of identity, of belonging [or not] at a de facto segregated college campus.[10] Through those subtleties Due reflects also on the related larger ambiguities of African American identity in America, a nation still troubled by the haunting memory and vestiges of slavery.

Although Due feared death, reckoning, as it were, that everything born dies ultimately, she also understands the counterbalancing power of "life" immanent in human will to rebel and survive even the most inimical of prophecies. The novel situates death as a force that dispatches all kinds of agents, inanimate and animate, including, in this case, the ocean, roadway, motor vehicles, racism, a neo-Nazi, and a letter bomb. Yet it also represents death as a median. In other words, death functions "creatively" as a passport that enables a (spiritual) return and rebirth at "home." In the anthropologic drama of the spirit child, the human baby, body, and world are cast as merely a shell, a temporary housing, for a displaced and alienated soul that yearns for and is at the same time under pressure to return home to kindred and kinship. The most sustained pull is, however, toward that spiritual/ancestral home of the Ọgbañje-àbíkú, with Death as chariot. Contrasting this original "home" to connotative "house," we would consider what the "home" means when racialized.

The Between's evocation of the àbíkú's impasse in Hilton's experience is almost ethnographic. Paralleled in *The Between* are some of the construed key actors in the spirit-child's mortal-versus-immortal dramaturgy, an existential spectacle mimetic of the "soap opera" Hilton finds his adoptive father Carl James (C.J.) watching (247). Among the principal figures in the text's born-to-die display are the spirit agents, whose ubiquitous "presence" and "voices" are assumed in some of the italicized statements externalized in Hilton's subconscious and in narrative space. Then there is the novel's major born-to-die, Hilton. His human and protective parents are Nana and also Carl and Lorraine James. Check, also, the diviner(s)—the Igbo dibia/the Yoruba babaláwo. These Old World "conjurers" are seemingly (re)imagined in New World practitioners of science and exegetes of alternative reality. As a collective, the healers are (1) the voodoo priest houngan that uncovers the Haitian character Marguerite Chatain's identity as a living dead; (2) the unnamed, "real" doctor-son of Kaya's science teacher through whom Kaya, Hilton's daughter, receives a "medical insignia" that she gives Hilton; (3) the Puerto Rican family therapist Raul A. Puerta; and (4) Andres, Raul's brother, who is a University of Miami graduate student conducting research on "death culture and near-death experiences" (229). Consistent with how Western medical practice generally misdiagnoses an Ọgbañje or àbíkú case, Raul mistakes Hilton's crisis as schizophrenia. It is under consultation with Raul, however, that Hilton voices some of the novel's most revealing statements relative to his ascribed born-to-die identity. Hilton talks about "journeys," about being pursued by a "they": construed here as Death's spirit forces. "All of them," he discloses. "The others. The ones who are gone. They are angry" with him because he has "the gift of flight" and "can always find doorways"; so they want him gone because "[n]o one is meant to live in the between." That is "why they've sent [...] Charles Ray. He isn't a traveler, but they talk to him when he sleeps" (208). But it would take the more knowledgeable empiricist, Andres, to correctly interpret Hilton's àbíkú status by way of Andres comparing Hilton's condition to that of Marguerite. As the narrator relates, Marguerite is an "unnatural," cosmically unbound and fugitive dead that "refuse[s] to go" (226–35).

It should be clarified here that in presenting Hilton as the story's "major" spirit child persona, I am simply stressing that he is the most fully developed born-to-die figure in a narrative that features other "living dead." It is not his Ezinma-like, precocious, thirteen-year-old daughter whose placatory Ga female name Kaya means "Stay and don't go back" in Ghana (Julia Stewart 64), in accord with the West African naming of born-to-die children. Neither is it the other in-between, Marguerite, who is hounded to tragic death by her spirit companions. Nor is it Hilton's son, Jamil, whom Dede's Ghanaian mother Kessie suggests is also a possible temporal sojourner. Both Jamil and Kaya were visited at birth by what Kessie calls the "death spirit." As Kessie tries to assure Hilton, "We've managed to trick the spirits. Through prayer? Through resolve? I don't know how or why, but they [Kaya and Jamil] are both still here, and here they'll *stay*" (147, italic added).

Due's reference to the Ghanaian analog of the belief, which occurs the moment Dede's cousin Kofi uses the phrase "born-to-die" while wondering why Dede named her daughter Kaya (143), diverts attention from Hilton as a born-to-die persona. But the allusion does more than that. It speaks to Due's stated knowledge of the belief's spread in West Africa.[11] In addition, Due's depiction of Hilton as a born-to-die who fathers two of his own kind discloses some literary license. It is in line with the Yoruba epistemology of the born-to-die enumerated in chapter 1 and also against the backdrop of Okri's novel, however, that Hilton's strange experience, as well as the novel's title, Prologue, characterizations, plotting, dramatic ironies, juxtapositions, and its other motifs and word plays achieve a strong unity, clarity, and force. Like Azaro's life, which is "full of riddles" (*Famished* 6), Hilton's is also a discontinuous puzzle whose reassembly into a coherent narrative demands a close reading that inevitably would take this analysis back and forth.

Due opens Hilton's life in the earthly terrene and in the 1960s. The story commences in 1963, with a two-sentence, portentous keynote in the Prologue. The narrator relays that "Hilton was seven when his grandmother died and it was a bad time. But it was worse when she died again." The two or "repeated" death-centered events are unmistakable in their unified resonance of the cycle-of-life mythicized in the born-to-die. Inseparable from the text's other signposts, this circularity is reiterated later in Dede's statement to Hilton regarding the "[c]oming and going" of women's menstrual cycles (57)—an assertion reminiscent of Azaro's reflection of his own "coming and going" (*Famished* 6).[12] That theme of orbit recurs also at narrative denouement, moments before Hilton's fatality. Here we are shown, next to Hilton, "[a] woman in sunglasses [who] sat watching her twin sons chasing each other in a circle" (262).

In addition to those introductory motifs of doubling and cycle, which the novel extends with evocative syntax such as traveler, traveling, journeys, migration, exile, roaming, leaving, and staying, Due imbues narration, action, and dialogue with other navigational compasses. She provides the pointers to aid the reader's expedition into a text that demands the full activation and attention of all of our senses for maximum comprehension and impact. There are references to family/(re) union, marriage, spousal (in)fidelity, separation, and divorce. The narrator alludes to team sports (basketball and football) and to the issue of a player's or a playmate's contractual loyalty to and his performance on a team. We hear of "possession of the ball" (80), of dreams, the road, water, boundary, doorways, the house/home binary, song, and sitcom titles. There are also the narrative's multiple moments of mortality: those of Nana; the duck that Jamil finds mysteriously dead at the beach; the funeral procession/hearse incident; the Honda driver, Antoinette, Antonio Guspacci, and Marguerite. Due also employs double entendres. For example, there is a scenario when the narrator says, regarding Hilton's two children, that "Their world was so different from his." This statement refers to Hilton's fears and restlessness. But it alludes also to his membership in another world. At another occasion, Hilton's staffmember Stu jokingly tells him, "Welcome to the world of the living" (192). And in a conversation Jamil remarks casually to Hilton that he, Hilton, posited as a spirit in human body, would be over two centuries old (195).[13]

The foregoing would qualify as what Mikhail Bakhtin calls chronotopes. Bakhtin used that term to describe and explore the conjunctivity of space and time in the novel.[14] In other words, as parts of the novel's structure and its vast network of mnemonics, the above cues collectively enable Due to characterize Hilton especially and also manage the story's integral interest in (dis)placement and temporality. They allow her, in short, to plot Hilton's life as an out-of-place and out-of-time transient late in making his appointment and rejoining the spirit realm.

That the researcher Andres's conclusive determination of Hilton's born-to-die identity occurs much later in the story is not surprising. Performing doubly in the text, its lateness is both strategic and mimetic. On the one hand, while the deferred revelation sustains suspense and helps elevate the story's already crescending "puzzle," it makes the narrative's tragic ending not unanticipated. On the other, the delayed diagnosis, while expressing Due's familiarity with born-to-die ethnography, is consistent with Misty Bastian's observations in chapter 1. Bastian had intimated that although the born-to-die state may leave signs initially, as Hilton's case does, the affliction might not be categorically detected and named early but later in adult life. Azaro declares as much when he affirms that "There are many who are of this [spirit child] condition and do not know it" (*Famished* 487). Moreover, consistent with the human impulse to resist delimitation, Hilton a rational (post) modern man dismisses as antiquated cognition Andres's equation of his state to Marguerite's. He refuses the idea that he is a walking dead. But even before one gets to the moment of Hilton's consultation with Andres, it is already clear, going back to the story's Prologue and then moving critically along from there, that Hilton is a character that since age seven has been close to Death and dying.

Due's hint in the Prologue, reinforced by the "funeral" motif in the epigraphic Emily Dickinson poem and the Abena P. A. Busia piece "Exiles," indicates that what unfolds is a story about identity determination framed within the environment of subjugation, mortality, dislocation, transition, and (spiritual) reunion. Just as Azaro begins his epic tale around his seventh year, *The Between*'s narrator also commences Hilton's at the same age when Nana dies twice. As stated earlier regarding the novel's fronting of the metaphor of (life) cycle inherent in the idea of born-to-die, Nana virtually dies in 1963 in her kitchen. But then she soon comes back to life in a scene that parallels the fiery moment in *Famished Road* when, as does young Hilton, Azaro has a vision of her mother's death in a kitchen and her rebirth. Later that year, Nana dies again, finally, this time as she rescues Hilton from asphyxiating during the Kelly-James's family reunion at Florida's Virginia Key Beach. Trading her life for the near-death Hilton's, she brings him back to life. With death and rebirth situated and subjectified, Due turns attention in the Prologue next to the context of Hilton's double familial ties to both Nana, who alone reared him, and Nana's Belle Glade cousins, the Jameses (C.J. and Auntie), who adopt him upon Nana's death. Due raises into thought the idea of "family reunion."

Furthermore, although it underscores the importance of extended family system in African/African American cultures, Hilton's relocation on separate occasions to the "houses" of relatives—Nana and the Jameses, who are not really his parents but surrogates—suggests his station as an "outsider." He is (a spirit) living away from home. Little wonder Hilton, like Ezinma who does not call Ekwefi "mother" but by her name, "had never grown accustomed to calling [. . . his adoptive parents] Mom and Dad" but instead refers to them as "the Jameses, or C.J. and Auntie." And more provocative, if as H. U. Beier explains in chapter 1, the àbíkú can be seen as a drifting spirit that "'drives'" out/displaces/replaces a mother's real child; then Hilton implicitly came to *stay* with the Jameses in such a manner. For his "adoptive brother, a physician [the Jameses' real child] had moved [out] to New York for college long before Hilton moved in, and Hilton barely knew him" (141). Due also alludes musically to that theme of movement, migration, and displacement when the DJ that Hilton and Dede hire for their party starts playing a Bob Marley title, "Running Away." The song's lyrical refrain states/asks: "Why you can't

find the place where you belong... running away, running away, running away..."
(142). Thus, when Hilton later lodges in Holiday Inn where he takes temporary
refuge from marital quarrels with Dede, the narrator describes him as one who is
exiled. "To be born," Azaro says, "is to come into the world weighed down with
strange gifts of the soul, with enigmas and an inextinguishable sense of exile. So it
was with me" (*Famished* 5).

Like Azaro's, Hilton's "exile"—his change of address and subsequent defection
to another group's "family reunion"—can be construed as an act of rebellion. It
mirrors Doro's delusions of Anyanwu and the àbíkú's breach of pact with kindred
spirits, an intentional contractual violation to which Azaro admits in his description of himself as a renegade. Azaro deems himself "a spirit child rebelling against
spirits, wanting to live the earth's contradictions" (*Famished* 487). Azaro's perfidy
incurs the spirit companions' displeasure and resentment. *The Between* reveals, inextricable from the subject of fate, that what is also at issue here is the critical and
similar question of "allegiances" and "[in]fidelity" (13). Due strategizes that subject
of commitment in Hilton's tardiness to Dede's judicial inauguration. She addresses
it again in his later extramarital affair, real or imagined, with his client Danitra.

To further express the gravity of Hilton's disloyalty to the "home" kin, Due
directs attention to his reactions at a sporting event. Peter Morton-Williams's
explanation of the àbíkú experience helps situate Due's enmeshing of born-to-
die experience in not just the discourse of "family reunion" but the spectacle of
contemporary team sports. In his essay "Yoruba Responses to the Fear of Death,"
Morton-Williams places an àbíkú's actions in the language of group play, with the
àbíkú represented as having "playmates" (35). At a basketball game between the
"home" team the Miami Heat and the "away" team/visitors the Orlando Magic,
Hilton, a Miami resident, paradoxically cheers the Magic's Shaquille O'Neal. He
admits that the Heat are "my boys." Yet he affirms that "Shaq's the man now" (79).
And when Raul, a Magic fan who never forgets to don "his badge of loyalty to his
hometown Mets" (78), playfully calls Hilton a "Fucking traitor," his invective can
be translated as the irate otherworldly company indicting Hilton through Raul's
momentarily "possessed" voice. Nevertheless, given also the idea that the spirit children are generally supposed to die young and on a designated day, the Kelly-James
"family reunion" event is that designated moment, indeed *the* day of "return." The
ceremony transcribes as the festive occasion when Hilton should have died (at age
seven) and reunited with the (spirit)ual fraternity, with oceanic water serving as
his passage, the road, to his homegoing.

Thus, Hilton's encounter after that basketball game with another death
moment—the scene of a fatal car accident on an "empty stretch" of U.S. 1, meta-

phorically a famished road (87)—can be read as the aggravated forces of the spirit world attempting to summon him home to play. The same deduction applies to Hilton's earlier near-fatal encounter with the anthropomorphized ocean. Similarly, not only do Azaro's spirit companions almost get him killed by a car by luring him with his mother's voice to cross a road, but also Okri depicts a body of water as the àbíkú's venue for fraternal meeting. Azaro's spirit kin beckon to him: "Come back to us. . . . We miss you by the river. You have deserted us. If you don't come back we will make your life unbearable" (*Famished* 7). Due comparably pictures the beach as the spirits' rendezvous, their appointed place. Like the basketball court and the road, the ocean is an arena of exciting yet rough and deadly team-play. It should be noted that on the day of the Jameses' family reunion the ocean current is personified as a powerful, deceptive friend that "want[s] to play" with young Hilton. In his exposition of àbíkú experience related in chapter 1, H. U Beier asserted that an àbíkú's spirit mates "will frequently tempt the child to throw itself into the water or to do some dangerous thing that may result in its death" (330). This is fascinating because the ocean's perceptible, original intent is to entice Hilton past "the midway point." There Hilton would be abducted fast by the actively waiting "undertow"— Death's undercover aquatic-operative. The narrator reports that the ocean current turns temperamental abruptly. It becomes irate, mocking and deathly when Hilton disappoints because he tries "to leave so soon" the game and spirit family reunion in progress (5–6).

Acting through the slick ocean current just as it would later use Charles Ray Goode, the inferably upset death/spirit world drowns Nana instead. But as Carl relives the incident to Hilton almost thirty-two years later, it was really Hilton that the ocean craved. Carl tells Hilton, "It's like it wanted you, boy. The water wanted you. That's the only way I can put it. It was like we were fighting all of nature to bring you back" (252). Through its functionary, ocean, Death takes Nana as she attempts to save the drowning Hilton. It takes her presumably because, in the context of àbíkú mythology, she becomes the reparative "substitute" required for sacrifice at the point of the àbíkú's death in atonement for the àbíkú's infraction of pact (Idowu 123). One could adduce that in protecting Hilton and commanding his departing spirit to "*go back*," as he almost drowns (252), Nana becomes a kind of obstruction to his awaited return. In intervening twice in Hilton's death, Nana exemplifies those endearing attributes of the outraged mother in African American letters. She may have saved his life and delayed fate. But she has also unwittingly aided his noncompliance with an ostensibly controlling pact. Nana bequeaths to him what she realizes from the beyond is a kind of "curse" and "not a blessing" (128). Actually, it is both and more.

Nana's "defensive" play, her timely interposition, is indeed a blessing. As the first major parental intervention to prevent her àbíkú grandson's death in infancy, Nana's prompt action obviously sustains Hilton's life. It has helped preserve it long enough for Hilton to complete graduate education and marry Dede, Lionel Campbell's daughter and now a respected county judge. Nana's interference indirectly kept Hilton alive to secure a lucrative employment as a social worker, the director of the suggestively titled Miami New Day Recovery Center. It bought him time to father and raise two children. It implicitly permitted him to purchase in Miami's affluent Coral Gables subdivision a house located denotatively "at the end of a cul-de-sac just east of the boundary" (55), where he lives a middle-class life among white folks (read: "strangers").

These earthly fortunes are, however, made possible by a life that was not supposed to be, had Hilton died in 1963. They are capacitated by a personage, existence, and history Hilton "stole" (214). It adds up, then, why the dead Antoinette would report telepathically that Kaya's and Jamil's names are occluded in the prenatal register of the Unborn. In other words, the two Hilton children would not have been born had fate not been challenged and detoured. Antoinette's disclosure clarifies also why in a dream state Hilton hears voices that advise him to end his repetitive runs. To parrot a popular movie title, he is a dead man walking. But because Hilton has grown attached to and protective of them, the above "material" fortunes—Dede, his children, Nana, his job, house, car, and other worldly possessions—constitute a distraction. They stymie his return to the spirit domain and the elusive peace and freedom he seeks in the human world. But as Azaro also realizes in his case (*Famished* 3–7), earthly life is hardly a utopia, because it brims with racism, hate, chaos, intolerance, and human suffering. Thus, if Hilton is to go "home," the mundane "obstacle" has to be cleared. Or rather, Hilton has to be severed from it by all means possible, hence Charles Ray Goode's role as Death's severer-of-ties. In short, much of the seeming fantastical encounters in the story—Goode's death threats against both Dede and Hilton's children, as well as the telepathic messages, sights, dreams, re-memories, time, and space travels, and other events that burden and complicate Hilton's mortality, marriage, parenthood, sanity, job, social performance, and identity—translate as parts of the physical, spiritual, and psychic hounding that an àbíkú suffers for refusing to repatriate home. And through sporting activity, the novel again illustrates how far the spirit/Death forces have gone and are willing to go to recall forcibly an out-dwelling kin, Hilton.

Just as she does with the metaphor of basketball, Due appropriates another team sport, the National Football League (NFL), to recast and re-enact the born-to-die drama as a tactical, "ball"-centered, offense-versus-defense game with "possibilities of fumbles and interceptions" (30). This motif is, first, such a major unit of the novel's emplotment and its tapestry of tropes it debuts in the Prologue. The theme appears in the narration of Hilton's interaction with the ocean as a game involving playmates. We observed it pointedly also in the notion that the then seven-year-old Hilton *is* a ball "dunked" by oceanic water (5)—a child whom Death played with roughly. Second, the idea allows Due to log not just another of Hilton's many near-death encounters but a moment of missed opportunity. It empowers Due to relay an event at which an offensively dispatched, spirit-agent/player botches a Death assignment to the utter annoyance of the home team's faithful (37). And third, the first major Death-agent, the aquatic undertow's "dunk" is negated because Nana's alert intervention in Hilton's drowning blocks it. The second narrated main effort at Hilton's abduction fails as well because the home team Miami Dolphins' initially celebrated and symbolic "interception" of an Indiana Colts' pass [of Hilton-as-ball] turns out to be "no good because someone was offside" (37). Given these botches, it becomes crucial that Goode, the newest deployed Death enforcer, not stumble.

Due manipulates the ball games and their total win-loss margins as a structural ploy. The games allow her to condense mythic time and historical events relative to Hilton's born-to-die multiple near-fatal encounters to which the novel alludes. They also enable Due to catalogue the necessity for and the implications of Goode's narrative role. What I am suggesting is that Due intimates the number of times Hilton has met and survived Death through the combined differentials in the Home versus Away team's scores. Many times in the story we are presented with what, in the context of the born-to-die, can be seen as the spirit forces asking Hilton: "*how many times . . . do you think you can die?*" (38, original italics). Because the limitations of narrative space and time disallow verisimilar and detailed representation of each and all of those close calls, Due projects them in terms of the total number of points by which the "home"/spirit franchises and their players/agents, the Miami Heat and Miami Dolphins, lose to their "away" opponents.

Consider this: In 1963 at age seven Hilton had his first major, narrated near-death experience. He survives/wins and the forces trying to recall him lose. Shortly later, at age eight presumably, the Jameses adopt him. Now, if this one near-death moment/his eighth (year) is added to the thirty points total by which the home teams Dolphins and the Heat lose their respective games, the sum is thirty-eight (years). That is how long Hilton lives, because he barely makes his thirty-ninth birthday. In other words, not counting the 1963 initial incident with the ocean, Hilton has found the doorway out thirty other times. Having misled, dodged, and thus defied his unrelenting abductors several times, Azaro tells us, "How many times had I come and gone through the dreaded gateway . . . I had no idea" (*Famished* 5). If we concur with the above extrapolation, since 1963 Death made a total of thirty-one annual attempts to snatch Hilton. He has had that many close calls, fortunately evading and surmounting capture, interception, re-possession, and captivity each occasion. This explains the spirits' incredulity as to how much longer Hilton imagines he would keep winning and thus running from putative fate.

In short, each score by which the home team loses marks mythically an instance the home/spirit world's agent "fumbles," hence Hilton's own revealing concession under hypnosis: "I've stolen thirty birthdays from them" (208). It is the apparent intractability of the losses, the triumph of the tenacious "away" team—the (human) club and forces of life—over the "home" team, the conflatable mercenaries of Death, that compels the spirit society to restrategize. It "contracts" this time with a human Death-agent, Goode.

In an interview with Diane Glave, Due speaks revealingly about Goode. She states: "my villain [Goode] is a white supremacist acting as *an* agent of some kind of natural force" (699). Goode's credentials for his performance of banditry are made much more deadly by racial hatred and personal angst. His resume is bolstered by his determined quest for retribution, his agility, and by what the novel infers is his primordial and intimate knowledge of Hilton with whom he shares a common birthday, March 12, 1956. In addition, Goode is ironically named. He, *Goode,* is described as a "bad" enemy, and also as an opponent whom Carl, Hilton's friend and Miami detective, unwittingly confesses to be "bigger than us" (121). Goode was an ROTC and a former Green Beret recruited in 1977 from the Ivy League. He had turned "a munitions advisor" for a Seattle-based neo-Nazi terrorist group called The Order. In Due's fictive oeuvre, this group The Order is reincarnated and strengthened as the Life Brothers and their shadowy enforcers called the Searchers in *My Soul to Keep* and *The Living Blood.* But Goode is also a criminal whom Dede sent to jail for aggravated battery. He is out on probation and intends to avenge his incarceration. Therefore, if agent-water has three times proved incapable of retrieving Hilton as narrativized, if motor vehicle/the hearse is equally ineffective, perhaps Goode can succeed. The shadowy Goode is so sure of victory that when Hilton confronts him with a gun in a neighborhood Circle K, he dares the armed Hilton to shoot him and change (his) fate. But Hilton is unable to do so.

In scripting the story's final moments, Due employs presentiment, pathos, and pun to achieve what readers of this richly imagined novel would agree is a palpable eeriness. The novel's denouement, as if emotively circling and cycling back to the Prologue and its dirges, is gripping, funerary, and funereal. We feel a sense of (a life's) "ending," an impending inevitability signaled in the narrator's solemn tone and Hilton's mood. The visceral calm is also perceptible as Hilton makes what could be seen as his last, goodbye visits. He calls on his adopted/adoptive family the Jameses and his friend Raul. He also gets his son Jamil to promise to always remember his instruction about societal bias against black males. Due achieves this narrative atmosphere through the ominous disappearance of Goode or, rather, what the more nimble Goode, supposedly surveilled by the mighty FBI and Miami PD, sets up as his residential relocation to Pensacola, Florida. In feigning a truce, Goode gives Hilton a false sense of safety, victory, and freedom. Kaya knows intuitively, however, that Goode still lurks somewhere. Kaya's asking Hilton in a somber moment of father-daughter reunion, "How long will you be here, Dad?" is bi-referential. On one hand, it alludes to Hilton's domestic presence. On the other, it points to his imminent "departure," which both Kaya and Dede apparently sense. In what reads as the diviner's performance of ritual to hopefully fetter an àbíkú and block its next death, Kaya gives Hilton her good luck charm, "a winged staff with twin serpents entwined around it" (257). A medical regalia reminiscent of an àbíkú's protective fetish, Kaya's science teacher gave her the pin. But it is said to have come from "a real doctor" (258), a babaláwo. In that instant, Kaya doubles as a saddened daughter turned adult-mother, one trying desperately to save her spirit-child-father and make him *stay*. In what registers as plea, persuasion, prohibition, and sublimated anger, Kaya tells Hilton, "I just don't want you to leave *again*" (258–59). That intervention comes rather late, however.

Hilton's tragic and untimely death by a letter bomb, sent incognito by Goode to his residence on his thirty-ninth birthday, is ironic and strategic. This day, which Hilton had regarded as "a beautiful day, after all" because it dawns brightly (260–71), is also a moment when climatic conditions, indeed inclement weather, forecasts violence in an impending Miami rainstorm. Moreover, character statement and action point toward conclusion, disaster, and (dis)embarkation. Here again Due displays some of her impressive word-plays in the text. Many Christian calendars designate Sunday as a day, in fact *the* day, of rest. According to scripture, God rested on the Sabbath after six days spent creating a complex world that God felt was good. We are told that on waking up this fateful Sunday morning Hilton "*felt* good." That is, he felt great but also premonitorily extra-sensed Goode's/Death's nearness. He "was thirty-nine years old today, in good physical health, in his wife's bed. *So far; so good*" (260).

In its goodness, then, this Sabbath marks a big day of rest for Hilton. It is the occasion of his reprieve from his tiresome time-travels: his earthly, spiritual, and psychological journeys, anxieties and ethereal visitations. The day before, Raul asked Hilton, again forebodingly, "Isn't Sunday the big day?" (255). Preparing for his birthday, ironically his death-day party, Dede told Hilton in a casual conversation, "I've been instructed to send you on a long errand this afternoon" (261). And before the bomb blast that kills Hilton, we would find him browsing "travel" books in the local library. That is, he seems to be seeking directions on how to journey back to a (spirit) home from which he has been absent thirty-eight years. We overhear him intuiting "with agonizing certainty that he would never see his wife again" (263). His life with her, as he sensed earlier at their house party, "wasn't at its beginning; he couldn't help feeling it was near its end" (140). Sunday, as the date of Hilton's passing, has a numerical significance. For as the week's seventh day, it retraces the Prologue's seventh year when Hilton should have first died in 1963 and returned home. The date actuates its original purpose. It indirectly completes the circle and a life journey that began narratively at age seven.

Although it severs him from his human family and loved ones, Hilton's death, transition, and rest from earthly tribulations figure by extension as an act of (re)creation. In other words, his death along with his return in the Epilogue to the spirit realm functions to complete the cycle of life intrinsic to the spirit child experience. But it also succeeds, perhaps more importantly, in saving his family, especially his children. And thus it leads to rebirth as it creates for them a new/another life. Both Jamil and Kaya had come perilously close to death when they toyed with the parcel-bomb, Death's fiery and explosive "message" delivered through Goode as "mail." Ultimately, in willingly surrendering not his family's life but his own (which evokes the idea that the àbíkú die by choice), and thus blocking Goode's intention to "dunk" them or dunk *on* them, Hilton wins part of the primeval human chess game with Life, with Goode and his employer Death, and especially with Fate. That is, he obstinately inserts his hands in and succeeds in tweaking (an overdetermined) destiny, as the Igbo and the Yoruba believe. Just as Nana commands Hilton out of an untimely drowning death and back to life, Hilton also intercedes in what would indubitably have been his children's premature deaths.

Hilton spent much of his childhood torturing himself for his indirect complicity in Nana's drowning. Rekindling Azaro's description of himself as a wearisome àbíkú child overindulged by his parents, Hilton regarded himself retrospectively as "a scrawny eight-year-old kid pampered and nurtured [. . . by the Jameses] for the act of killing his grandmother" (81). His desire was to give back, just as his grandmother Nana sacrificed for him. His death is therefore redemptive. It also reunites him with Nana in spirit land, where he is sustained by fond, futuristic memories of his daughter Kaya as a doctor. And through postmortem telepathy, he hears that Goode is caught and his family is fine.

If the human person is an embodied spirit, and if the material earth is not humanity's true abode, then Hilton's death becomes existentially a requisite, fated return to home and origins. In death, therefore, Hilton finally meets his appointment with destiny. He becomes in essence destiny's child, born anew in (spirit) land, hence his "birthday" celebration. In its enigmatic performative, Death narratively lives out that ultimate spoiler role that Due feared growing up. But death is also transformative in its initiation of Hilton into the colony of immortals—Due's pretext to her figuration of the deathless, timeless, and formerly enslaved character Dawitt/David of *My Soul* and *Living Blood*.

More Than a Born-to-Die Drama

Due's concerns in *The Between* are contemporaneous and overtly political. As a result, it would be analytically reductive to discuss the novel solely as Due's suggested realignment of the epistemes, dramatis personae, stage, directions, and tenor of born-to-die mythic script. For even Ben Okri grafts onto Azaro's àbíkú saga a critique of the tragicomic vicissitudes of Nigeria's postcolonial state. Okri also permeates his novel with sweeping observations on race, Western hegemony, slavery, colonization, oppression, gender, power, and freedom, among other issues. In weaving, similarly, the dialectics of life and death and also the myth of born-to-die children into issues of serious historical and current significance, Due politicizes the text, although she, an NBA and Post Soul writer, understandably quibbles on *The Between*'s politics and social functionality.[15] Of those topics, I would like to consider these three in clusters: (1) the interplay of race, gender, law, power, and white supremacy; (2) the question of origins/ancestry and African American and African reconnections; and (3) the novel's incursions into the discourse of racial subjectivity, identity, and authenticity.

Using Dede's gendered experiences in the story as platform, the novel poses an important question. It wonders: what happens when, for instance, consequential power is vested in those historically excluded from authority? It asks, more specifically, what does it do to a white, male, and racial supremacist's psyche for a woman, a black woman at that, to wield the institutional power of adjudication as the one setting the agenda? What does it mean for the black woman to serve as prosecutor—*the* prosecutor and judge of white character and conduct? Therein lies a charged question that drives the story.

Although the narration shadows Hilton as the titular in-between, his battles against Goode are incited by and tied to Goode's white supremacist resentment of Dede's prosecutorial and gendered power. A cursory look at the text of one of Goode's hate mails (*Between* 60) discloses Goode's perturbation over weighty black success, over (post-1960s black/racial minority) power and empowerment. A perusal uncovers the mail's morphologic and atavistic debt to centuries-old southern caste system, white Negrophobia and minstrelsy, as well as antiblack racial slurs and myths attributed to the Bible. Goode's hate message verbalizies his understanding that race, gender, law, sex, class, *and* power instersect tightly and always have. His sentiments attest to the truth, which Hilton knows rather well (105), that despite racial and social integration race and racism continue to matter in late-twentieth and early twenty-first-century postmodern America. Racism matters precisely because America is a house that "race" built.[16] And for that reason, Aldon L. Nielsen points out, America "has always been a house divided" (26). Nielson remarks that "Africans were forced to come to America as supplements. Africans *were* that which white people, who hold themselves to be wholly self-sufficient, required to undertake their project as white people in America" (26). In a nation where they are presently the numerical majority and are "seldom challenged in daily life," whites hardly think of their whiteness. Not only is the presumption of Caucasian-heteronormativity cavalier, but also it assumes greater relevance only when whites, particularly white men, are challenged or in crisis. The neo-Nazi—"militant white racists"—observes "a world in which almost all positions of power are held by men who are white" and "infer that whites (and men)" are sacrosanct and naturally "superior."[17] A product of the resentful rage of a de-robed white supremacist, a white male invalidated by a 1990s colored woman in authority, Goode's hate letter makes it known, then, that in the United States power is white and masculinized. And its repositioning in favor of those historically shut out of power's inner circle threatens the status quo.

The Between underscores the damage that the white-supremacist Goodes—racism's/Death's operatives—of the world can cause and have inflicted in black life. The novel illustrates that destruction and destructiveness in how Goode unsettles Hilton and Dede's lives once the death threats start. The story shows also the threats' collateral mental injury on innocent black children, Jamil and Kaya, to whom racism, xenophobia, and terrorism are nothing sectarian, scientific, ahistorical, fantastic, futuristic, speculative, geographically distant or comic. Rather, they are a reality close to an oppressive place they miscall "home."

A surviving branch of that post-Reconstruction-era tree of lynching that Stewart E. Tolnay and E. M. Beck call the southern festival of violence (1995), Goode's assault continues the mission of the 1960s antiblack white bombings, shootings, and beatings that targeted not only black churches and black children but also the homes of black civil rights leaders and grassroots workers. His dastardly vengeance leaves in its wake black dreams unrealized again. At its heels are parental promises unkept and what is now ostensibly a single black female-headed household, an urban black family that Moynihan would likely have "studied," statisticized, and pathologized. In the tradition of slave narratives and other precursor black texts, *The Between* witnesses that this earthly/American house could be a dystopia. And that is why, once Hilton got older, he underwent an awakening, as did slaves the first time they met literacy. He switched promptly from the escapist fantasy of young-white-male-orientated comic books to the cauterizing realism of Richard Wright, whose fiction unflatters the United States, condemning it as dehumanizing and coercively deathly for blacks (JanMohamed 2005). Due suggests, therefore, that it is because America could be such an unsheltering place for blacks that Hilton at one point considers seceding. Like the distraught slave girl preparing to inter a fever-killed baby in Wideman's *The Cattle Killing,* he nurses "an overpowering longing to go home, somewhere else" (246). It makes sense then why the near-death AIDS patient Antoinette tells Hilton and Kaya that her favorite song is Luther Vandross's "A House Is Not a Home" (73). Exuding the sorrow but also the reassurances of the Negro spiritual, Luther's song title, prudent as it is, speaks of immanent contradiction, separation, emptiness, loss, mourning, and longing for origins and for a safer place. As Valerie Sweeney Prince writes in *Burnin' Down the House: Home in African American Literature* (2004), for African Americans in the twentieth century, that longing for a better place, a more livable home, translates also as a "search for justice, opportunity, and liberty" (1).

Hilton's dilemma or, to use Toni Morrison's phrase, his "anxieties of belonging"[18] or not belonging completely in the American house uploads the related larger topic of black nativity and racial identity in America. Due could not have chosen a more ideal setting than Miami to enact Hilton's racially symbolic experience with doubling, motion, and de-centering—in short his àbíkú double ties to two antagonistic societies. As an undergraduate at a de facto segregated Northwestern University, Due herself experienced these pressures. Predicting correctly that the politics of the color line would dog the twentieth century, W. E. B. Du Bois had years earlier personally felt and pondered Due's racial tensions. He phrased it variously as "a peculiar sensation," "double consciousness," the sense of "unreconciled strivings," "warring ideals" and internal "strife" that not only typify but sometimes threaten to make things fall apart in black life, save for the toughness of black people's spirit.[19] Due confesses to being distressed "with constantly straddling a racial line . . . during my college years." All she had hoped for during an anxious national period, when with white students she got involved in an Anti-Apartheid Alliance, was to be able to "travel" as does the spirit child "in black and white circles with equal ease." But she was unable to reconcile the sociocultural, political and mental pulls of both worlds. As a consequence, she felt like "an outsider."[20]

It is not surprising, then, that Due locates the story in Miami, a town she knows intimately by residency and profession.[21] But other than the fact that Miami's suffusion with "superstitions," spirits, and the living dead is nurturing for supernatural fiction, the city in its layered diversity and tensions also miniaturizes the United States. Most of all, with its location as an actual geopolitical frontier and a symbolic periphery—evocative of the mythic grill and the arrow-shaped, east-pointing Willow Springs in Gloria Naylor's *Bailey's Cafe* and *Mama Day,* respectively—and with its large foreign-born and African diaspora population, Miami-Dade plays out perennially the nation's recursive immigration debates. Along with related supersites such as Texas, Arizona, and California, Miami remains one of the battlegrounds in which the United States test-runs its decades-old, collapsible, and Ọgbañje-àbíkú-conjuring politics of nativity, nationality, national identity, home and away, boundary, border-crossing, im(migrant)ion, difference, center, and margin. Miami is a province where African-descended people and America's other peoples of color from the Caribbean and Latin America converge, collide, and comprise part of that mixed-race demographic that Suzanne Bost historicizes as the Americas' *mestizaje* population (2003). In Miami, in short, African peoples are simultaneously citizens and aliens, native sons and daughters yet Other, permanent residents yet unsettled foreigners, coming and going, always on a physical, psychic, and spiritual journey. This experience of duplexity that predisposes (contemporary) black life to flux dates back to slavery. It is also a leitmotif in the African American novel.[22]

A defected, earth-dwelling àbíkú's bonding with human family and his love for terrestrial life constitute the major impediment to his return and reconnection with "home" and kindred. Similarly, Hilton's resolve to hold on to the assets of tellurian existence deters his fated journey back to his "roots." It detains his re-induction into an immortal colony and the freedom and timelessness that *that* induction confers. Against those backdrops, one could infer that àbíkú-Hilton is a spirit/spiritual entity under protracted siege in the mundane world, deceived and constrained by its "bondaging" materiality.

Tinged directly and indirectly by the most invisible of slavery's legacies, Hilton's experience of life and death becomes at its base a (neo-slave) narrative of "captivity" and "manumission." *The Between* avers that the wages of forced or uncritical voluntary estrangement from origins is rather serious for blacks. The recompense could be exacerbated with indoctrination into modernity's and postmodernity's dichotomal devaluation of old-fashioned epistemology, as Hilton does with Andres's divination. It could be worsened, even more, with loss of spirituality and a consuming embrasure of the insular individualism and acquisitive materialism of Western culture. In its diaspora implications, Hilton's dilemma of subjectivity alludes to the price of black people's displacement from "ancestry." His conundrum of identity is a complicated and ever contemporaneous subject made more acute with increased black movement into the mainstream. And it has been dramatized in numerous African American/African diaspora texts, sometimes with a tint of sentimentalism, burlesque and pathos.[23] Hilton's life expresses the need for "family union" or a "return." It also resounds Due's emphasis on the dividends of reconnection with ancestry, a linkage she finds to be "rare during an era when we all routinely scatter so far from the places of our roots."[24]

As exemplified in the 1990s nightmarish journeys of Haitians who left home and boated for Miami, however, the powerful yet delusive lure of post–Cold War United States drives a neo-uprooting and dispersal of African-descended people for whom a return "home" ranks second to the pressures of quotidian survival. Furthermore, the ordeals of blacks who in the 1920s and mid-century left the Jim Crow South and headed for the Northeast and the Midwest, the ensnarement of transnational and postcolonial African immigrants in Europe, Canada, Asia, and the Americas, as well as the uncertain futures of evacuee blacks, other ethnic minorities, and poor whites displaced by the 2006 Hurricane Katrina, bear witness to the difficulties of permanent return upon departure from home base. The push-and-pull of U.S. commodity capitalism, its "*dollarism*" as Malcolm X termed it,[25] turns members of the African diaspora into roaming àbíkú in the country. It makes them "homeless" "exiles," "vagabonds," "refugees," "migrants," "aliens," and "strangers" in a nation that entraps, if at all it welcomes, their presence. As Due realized to her dismay, "the hateful words *Go back to Africa!*" could still be hurled at blacks in late-twentieth-century United States.[26]

It was such separatism, rooted deeply in slavery, racism, and white anxiety, that moved black voices of Emigrationism such as Alexander Crummell, Martin Delany, Edward Wilmot Blyden, and later Marcus Garvey to push in the nineteenth and early twentieth centuries for a mass eastward African American exodus "home," to Africa. As Carol V. R. George discloses, the physical removal of blacks from America had actually been the desire of some white churches and politicians including George Washington, Thomas Jefferson, and James Madison as well as the American Colonization Society (A.C.S.) which sought to repatriate "volunteer" black freedmen. But opposition from white abolitionists and, more saliently, the anticolonization protest rallied by northern black clergymen such as Richard Allen thwarted the intended large-scale return and defeated the A.C.S's subliminally racist plot. Its success would have further implanted slavery, fractured a fledgling New World black family, and amounted to African Americans abdicating their centuries-long fight for justice and their rightful claims to U.S. citizenship and its benefits (135–59). When in the 1960s and early 1970s the back-to-Africa call sounded again, intraracially, urged by unremitting racial oppression and black separatists, some African Americans heeded. They excitedly departed for the motherland only to relive Okonkwo's post-exile epiphany: a noteworthy and implicitly parabolic moment whose resonances of African diasporal experience are unmistakable.

Upon returning "home" to Umuofia after his forced exile, Okonkwo—anticipating if not foreboding—his grandson Obi's dilemma, is no longer at ease, as he finds a homeland considerably changed by contact with the British. Once a man of the people, he finds an (un)familiar and inevitably still transitioning people among whom he now feels displaced and unsure. "Seven years was a long time to be away from one's clan," the narrator commiserates. "A man's place was not always there, waiting for him. As soon as he left, someone else rose and filled it. The clan was like a lizard; if it lost its tail it soon grew another" (*Things* 171). Like Okonkwo, some of the African American returnees, "*three centuries removed*" from their ancestry and heritage, as Countee Cullen poetizes (36), were similarly disillusioned. They felt strange at "home," in a developing Africa, where some of their continental cousins regrettably saw and treated them as "Americans" and Westerners.[27]

Given these slavery-implicated intraracial rifts, the ambivalence of some diaspora blacks toward Africa, the financial burden of the journey, and with contemporary mass return difficult if not impossible, Due seems to suggest that it makes sense to find alternative routes home. A more personally tailored emigration, visitation, and/or "family reunion" could be more tenable. In short, as Due proposes, and Craig Werner concurs (290–95), a spiritual, mythic, historiographic, or even literary voyage to homeland, kindred, and forebears as sites of instruction and memory, could be better for African diasporal people long separated from family.

A belated, affirmative response to the 1960s black cultural campaign and its call for a return to origins, *The Between* exemplifies *that* alternative "return" in the individual nature of Hilton's journey(s). It realizes the linkage culturally in its summon of African religious tenets syncretized in the Americas, for example, the àbíkú-related idea of powerful and capricious twins presented through the Haitian character Marguerite. The novel espouses homegoing in conceptual as well as stylistic dialogue with Ben Okri/*Famished Road*. The story achieves it by narrative invocation of Due's literary "ancestors": Toni Morrison, Richard Wright, Alex Haley (whose epic *Roots* Due found inspirational), and Paule Marshall.[28]

Lastly, in depicting Hilton in the milieu of born-to-die with its conceptual resonances of hybridity, Due raises the question of categorization. If, as an àbíkú persona, Hilton signifies a shape-shifting subjectivity, an entity whose life is framed within a narrative that tropes contingency and improvisation, then we can neither type his blackness nor consolidate his racial humanity. Through *The Between,* a project that helped Due revisit and process her own experiences with identity-formation, Due adds her voice to those of African American (women) novelists of the post–Black Power and Black Arts movement era. As stated earlier, these members of New Black Aesthetic engage with the still growing intricacies of contemporary black subjectivity. Using surreal, deviant and sometimes grotesque characters, as well as unsettling themes and postmodernist plot techniques, the authors set out to destabilize both mainstream white and the 1960s and 1970s professions of black racial normative.[29] Their authorial goal is to acknowledge plurality, even as they show racial sympathies, promote African diaspora belief systems, and attack injustice. And what they propose ultimately, as Martin Favor argues in *Authentic Blackness*[30] for instance, is a more complicated understanding of group experience and (gendered) blackness.

It is significant, therefore, that Due elects in *The Between* not the experiences of a black woman but those of a middle-class black male and father as a forum to sieve those matters of black identity and their incursions into the question of late-twentieth-century American multi-ethnic and multicultural heritage. In doing that, Due affirms black men's own dealings with schisms. As Octavia Butler stages in the previous chapter, the African American experience with ontological fragmentation dates back to the abduction, forced translocation, and New World enslavement of the Anyanwus of black diaspora history. Repeating partly ethnographically yet also reconstructing the myth of the born-to-die and (in)directly signifyin(g) on Okri's rendition of Azaro's àbíkú impasse, Due compels us to contemplate the power and transformativity of "iku," the Yoruba force of death, in human life. But she also points attention to the positivist imports of Hilton's will to face, deceive, defy, and defeat "Death" in its shifting shapes and agencies.

Looking back at Achebe's and Okri's texts, it is not accidental that Ezinma and Azaro decide to *stay.* They *stay* because Achebe and Okri want to avouch life and hope. Both writers are interested in the restoration of cosmic balance, despite the trauma exacted by Africa's living-dead encounter with Europe. And although Achebe and Okri appreciate the existence of and also give due credence to the unknown—the supernatural—they still believe in the power of choice. Thus Hilton's self-empowering battle against Goode attests to human resolve. His confrontations with Death directly challenge victimization and threats to "life." Echoing the (black) power and militancy of Claude McKay's Harlem Renaissance poem "If We Must Die" and Silas's self-dignifying martyrdom in Wright's "Long Black Song," Hilton's successful thirty-year outwitting of a destructivist force mediates the truism that the human being under siege dare not yield without a fight.

Chapter 5 Mediating Character, Theme, and Narration

Ọgbañje as Hermeneutics
in The Cattle Killing

[M]aybe there's some kind of taint, or . . . poison, that is part of the
original contact between Europeans and Africans that we have yet
to shed, and it keeps returning in many, many different forms.

John Edgar Wideman
interview with the author

A literary jigsaw, John Edgar Wideman's *The Cattle Killing* further substantiates
Chinua Achebe's and Igbo metaphysics' imprints on contemporary African American fiction. As do Butler's and Due's novels published before it, *The Cattle Killing* evinces the spirit child's idiomatic elasticity. It demonstrates, in this case, the
conceptual plasticity of "Ọgbañje" to foment character and also evoke, edify, and
reconcile African diaspora experience.[1] Wideman is convinced that those traumas
that have haunted collective black humanity for years are linked and traceable to
the initial Africa-Europe encounter. He alludes that they occurred and have been
reborn not just because African-descended people listened to fallacious oracles
but because, putting down their guard and taking a glance away, they fell asleep in
their enemy's dreams.

A speakerly neo-slave narrative whose seething anger, though tonally controlled, remains palpable throughout the text, *The Cattle Killing* serves as a requiem
for many a resilient black dead that return, again and again. Because they died,
sometimes young, violently and in other ways unnaturally, their spirits, not yet
ancestral, (re)appear and agonize the novel's nameless, epileptic and eighteenth-
century preacher-narrator. A man who, like Butler, knows the pains of familial
tragedy,[2] whose works *Sent for You Yesterday* (1983), *Reuben* (1988), *Philadelphia*

Fire (1990), *Brothers and Keepers* (1995), *Two Cities* (1998), *Hoop Roots* (2001:5) and "Weight" (2005) are permuted deliberations on *loss* and mourning: the "loss of children,"[3] community, parent, spouse, sibling, love—Wideman urges us to say no, never again. And so he offers *The Cattle Killing* as a testimony to the power of love and the resiliency of the human spirit. Wideman sees that toughness embodied in his daughter Jamila, whom he describes in Ọgbañje terms. He calls her in the book's dedication one "*who arrived with one of those tough, beautiful old souls that's been here before*" (original italics). In the hands of one of (African) America's finest and challenging writers, a novelist who like Achebe subscribes to the recuperative power of stories, "Ọgbañje" multi-tasks, as it does in Butler's focal texts. It performs as character mythic prototype, thematics, narrative apparatus, and a strainer with which Wideman sifts history and some of life's smallest yet profound questions.

Like other Wideman novels, *The Cattle Killing* is deep in its thematic stretch. Its structural acrobatics remind one of and also affiliate it with the formal trespasses of earlier, African American canonical art and texts, from the modernist innovations of Aaron Douglass's paintings, Jean Toomer's *Cane* (1923), and Ralph Ellison's *Invisible Man* (1952) to the iconoclastic necromancing of Ishmael Reed's *Mumbo Jumbo* (1972) and the linguistic wizardry of Morrison's *Beloved*. The story is intriguing not just because Wideman leaves narratological holes and racially incensing scenes that agitate the reader's emotive response. Nor is its charm simply that Wideman's use of an Ọgbañje protagonist—in whom he re-imagines and overlays the figures and discernible narratives of itinerant, antebellum black preachers—commingles history, literary invention, the traditional memoir form, and "fiction autobiography."[4] The hook really is that *The Cattle Killing* develops a "Third World" cultural principle Ọgbañje into literary postmodernism's tendencies toward hypertextuality, manifest in the novel's metafictionality, its discontinuous plot, and its pastiche of texts: meditation, excerpts, allusions, sermons, biblical verse, letters,[5] diaries, legal depositions, confessionals, and literary criticism. *The Cattle Killing* anachronistically rearranges the fences between beginning and end, past and the present. With its constitutive stories and textualities "layered over one another, interlacing and overlapping, . . . superimposed,"[6] the novel conflates slavery and freedom, the dead, spirits and the living, orality and scriptivity, storyteller-author, and audience-reader. In other words, using the cinematic technique of dissolve[7] and free indirect discourse which Wideman adopted before in *Philadelphia Fire* and his Homewood trilogy—*Hiding Place* (1981), *Sent for You Yesterday,* and *Damballah* (1981)—*The Cattle Killing* dims the boundaries between Wideman as son, father, writer and character/witness in his own novel *and* the in-text performance of his son Daniel Jerome "D.J." Dan makes a cameo in the novel's Epilogue. He interchanges as Wideman's "son" and a "reviewer" of the novel (*The Cattle Killing*) which he supposedly has just finished critiquing during a trip overseas.

The Cattle Killing is a taxing read because its subject matter doesn't allow the reader to rush. Wideman would rather we not graze the book's heavy concerns for which the 1856–57 Xhosa cattle-killing movement in South Africa[8] serves as metaphor, eponym, and caution. Wideman desires then that we confront slowly the reincarnating hurt, the unspeakable things unspoken,[9] that African-descended people have suffered in their forced migration from Africa to North America, particularly during the 1793 Philadelphia yellow fever outbreak. The contagion was so awful it decimated many of the city's inhabitants and forced its government and traumatized survivors into hiding.

Wideman states that he aimed for a sense of dramatic immediacy in writing *The Cattle Killing,* whose theme of "fever" he processes in his 1989 short story of the title. However, his exploration of the black (protagonist's) view of that 1793 Philadelphia catastrophe in "Fever," though somewhat more clinical, intense, and gripping, lacks the present story's mythic pith as well as its degree of historical breadth, racial angst, and diasporic cross-referentiality. In writing *The Cattle Killing* Wideman also wanted readers to see storytelling as an improvised and shared occasion. To him, stories and storytelling are not the teller's private creation and possession. Rather, they are a people's commonwealth, an interactive performance that relies greatly on the audience's active participation and contribution for its fullest completion and unraveling. As a result, Wideman, restyling the genre, intentionally withholds from the novel some of fiction's conventional "hand-holds," for instance time markers and parentheses.[10] This delightfully frustrating absence of brackets is invitational, as in African oral tradition, and hence encourages readerly input. It heightens the audience's challenge to determine and delineate character statements from narration.

Wideman also immediately confronts the reader-audience with a twelve-page stream of consciousness. In this prelude, an introspective Wideman-double named Eye (short for Isaiah) is attending a writers' conference in Pittsburg. He has set out to visit his father to whom he intends to read his new novel (*The Cattle Killing*) in progress. The steep climb to his father's house on Wylie Avenue offers him a moment to reflect portentously on a number of inseparable issues that he exfoliates in the story. He ruminates on the immigrant history and ethnic foundation of Philadelphia, the myth of racial integration with respect to blacks and, evocative of *Sula,* the literal gentrification of Philadelphia's now black Lower Hill neighborhood to make room for the city's Civic Arena, its parking lots, roadways, and other urban infrastructure. Eye/Wideman meditates also on (his) youth, mourning especially the cattle-killing-like loss of black children, marked in the tragedy of young black males shot dead and dying in Philadelphia's dilapidated blocks and anarchic streets. These alleys of the sprawling city of brotherly love, Eye ruminates, are the very paths that his novel's equally young preacher would have traveled two centuries ago, ironically, to save lives and souls for God and America.

It is after the above opener that Wideman drops literally what he has called the novel's most important framework, Ọgbañje. He condenses the Ọgbañje drama in this brilliantly crafted passage worth quoting again:

> Certain passionate African spirits—kin to the ogbanji [*sic*] who hide in a bewitched woman's womb, dooming her infants one after the other to an early death unless the curse is lifted—are so strong and willful they refuse to die. They are not gods but achieve a kind of immortality through serial inhabitation of mortal bodies, passing from one to another, using them up, discarding them, finding a new host. Occasionally, as one of these powerful spirits roams the earth, bodiless, seeking a new home, an unlucky soul will encounter the spirit, fall in love with it, follow the spirit forever, finding it, losing it in the dance of the spirit's trail through other people's lives. (15)

Because of its depth, *The Cattle Killing* has drawn some critical following.[11] As earlier suggested, however, Wideman students have generally disregarded, subordinated, essentialized, and/or outright misread this framework and Ọgbañje proper. As such, they have left unlocked a key aspect of the novel that enables Wideman to merge the "spirits" of the novel's historical and imagined characters. True, the misprint of the word as "ogbanji" does not help matters. For irrespective of *Things Fall Apart*'s worldwide readership, many may still be unfamiliar with the Ọgbañje idea.

Nevertheless, the omniscient narrator's elaboration of the belief should help attenuate the misspelling. Besides, Wideman's published interview comments about the paragraph perhaps should suffice as a primer for anyone curious about the Ọgbañje paradigm and why he leaned on it to help him make some sense of African diaspora experience. But really Wideman's interest in Ọgbañje is hardly surprising. *The Cattle Killing* is not the first or only time that he has reached to the hermeneutic strength of African diaspora cultures and mythologies for artistic and intellectual vision. The indignant provosts of the Black Arts movement might denounce his spotlight on black subjectival fragmentation, doubling, and unconsolidation. They might even dredge up the barb that his pre–Black Power work was shaped not by "the lower frequencies of an African American [and African] tradition, oral and literary," but by white writers such as James Joyce, T. S. Eliot, and Henry Fielding.[12] However, those 1960s and 1970s nationalist aestheticians would quite likely applaud the novel's racial politics, particularly its felt anger, as well as its ancillary and variegated themes of racial vigilance, black power, empowerment, and self-determination. They might even see Wideman's use of Afrocentric mysticism as his positive response to the movement's call to African American writers to mine the reservoir of the black world's cultural cosmology for creative kernels. In earlier works such as the titular short fiction "Damballah" and *Reuben,* for instance, Wideman does just that. He respectively adapts aspects of Haitian pantheon[13] and the Kongo philosophy of doubles.[14] This is fascinating because the latter concept of doubling, which Wideman recycles in *The Cattle Killing* and also thematizes in *Hurry Home* (1970), has counterparts in the Yoruba notion of twins "ibeji." The ibeji experience is associated with the àbíkú cult[15] and, by extension, Ọgbañje.

In any event, Derek McGinty is right to forewarn readers to be very alert because *The Cattle Killing*'s first-person narrator is indeed a shape-shifter. He is "any one of several people," McGinty detects, "and if you skim a paragraph or miss a turn of phrase, you might get lost in one of the [preacher's] transitions" (180). As to who the preacher is, then, Wideman grants that African Methodist Episcopal (AME) Church founder Richard Allen served as a model for the preacher. He adds, however, that Allen is not the novel's protagonist (McGinty 185). Like Absalom Jones and Prince Hall, Allen was a Black Power avant-garde. Allen appears as himself and also witnesses in the story. Allen's self-narrated autobiography *The Life Experience and Gospel Labors of the Rt. Rev. Richard Allen* (1833), parts of which Wideman compresses and re-envisages fluidly in "Fever" and *The Cattle Killing,* documents his birth, family background, enslavement, and purchased manumission. It also addresses Allen's conversion, ministry, sermons, congregant revolt, formation of the Bethel African church, and the Philadelphia fever plague.

Taking a lead from Wideman's statement that he *"sampled"* assorted texts in the novel, including *"passages from various eighteenth-century diaries and sermons"* (front matter; original italics), I would dare to suggest, however, that echoed in the preacher's life and marvelous journeys, the telling of which encrusts the Allen subplot, are scenes from the equally enthralling story of another nomadic, antebellum black evangelist: John Marrant. Readers of Marrant's *Narrative of the Lord's Wonderful Dealings with John Marrant, a Black* (1785) and his *A Journal of The Rev. John Marrant, From August the 18th, 1785, to The 16th of March, 1790* (1790), both of which precede Allen's publication as well as the 1793 Philadelphia fever plague, would recognize the novel's resonances of Marrant's self-relayed and thrilling life of ministry. Trudging through wilderness, snow, storm, and more, Marrant variously encounters and *resurrects* from death—an Ọgbañjeic experience for which Joanna Brooks calls Marrant a black Lazarus. For "[w]hat was life on the black Atlantic,"

Brooks asks pertinently, if not "a series of deaths and [re]births." No wonder death, both literal and metaphoric, is a big issue in Marrant's narrative and journal.[16] In addition, one listening closely to *The Cattle Killing* would hear in the preacher-narrator's tale not just Marrant's and Allen's eighteenth- and nineteenth-century diaries, or the memorable catchphrases/claims in the slave-burglar Johnson Green's 1786 pre-execution and intendedly cautionary confessions. One perceives also certain incidents in the nineteenth-century story of another black ecclesiastic, John Jea, and in the lives of the fugitive slaves Henry Bibb and Harriet Jacobs.[17] Wideman intermingles and echoes these metastories of arduous yet triumphant black life and pioneering black-Atlantic ministry not just to mirror the intertextuality of early spiritual, conversion, confessional, and slave narratives and thus insinuate his neo-slave text in various discursive categories, as Rushdy explained in chapter 2. He analogizes them also to raise and contemporize "the dead." Like Achebe and Morrison, Wideman does not want to obviate the past because history evidently comes back. It is in light of these transmutations—the preacher's embodiment and refraction of many tenacious souls, spirits, and lives, and his smooth shifts into them—that McGinty advises audience attentiveness. Ed Peaco is correct in discerning that Wideman's "mythic reference [Ọgbañje] is a tool for clarifying the seemingly chaotic narrative method" (235).

But what conceptual elements of that mythic device did Wideman diffuse into the story's plot to create a novel that Philip Page calls "spellbinding, provocative— and difficult"?[18] To mull that question, we need to appreciate, again, *Things Fall Apart*. We revisit it because if, as Wideman stated, he discovered the Ọgbañje theme by way of Achebe, then his guidepost is Ezinma and *Things Fall Apart*'s narration. It is crucial then that before analyzing the story we see how the Ezinma-Ekwefi dynamic morphs in *The Cattle Killing*'s characters and reflects also in Wideman's excerpted assertion that the offspring of the original Africa-Europe contact comes back. It returns in different forms, all linked in having as their moment of conception that earliest encounter. Later in the discussion, we shall look also at how the Ezinma-Ekwefi relationship helps reinforce *The Cattle Killing*'s interlaced discourses on love, life, and faith.

* * *

Ezinma's rebirths through Ekwefi resonate in Wideman's remark in the framing passage about the slippages of that passionate African spirit from its unlucky lover. Ezinma's corporealities underpin Wideman's idea of the "trails" of the Ọgbañje spirit (which doubles also as the "spirit," the force, of desire, persistence, rebellion, and survival) in other people's lives, particularly in the variously reincarnated figures in *The Cattle Killing*. They include: the many persons composited in the preacher; the refugee woman who drowns in the lake with a fever-killed baby; the dying spirit-woman whom the preacher hopes to heal through storytelling-as-revivalist-evangelism; the (spirit) woman in blue who helps nurse the preacher during his epiphanic convulsion/anointing outside St. Matthew's one Sunday in October 1792; and Kathryn, Dr. Benjamin Thrush's and his blind wife Elizabeth's slave. In addition, Ekwefi's first meeting with Okonkwo leads later to marriage. It leads again, as it were, to an Ọgbañje offspring, Ezinma—an "entity," "experience," and "idea" whose previous comings and goings doomed Ekwefi's infants and usurp what should be the natural order of things. *The Cattle Killing* posits similarly, and Eric Williams agrees (7), that the meeting of Africa and Europe also produced its own reincarnating and disruptive "child"—slavery and racism. Through the numerous historical events, which for proper critical inventory I have assembled below from various parts of the narrative, the novel suggests that the doom of racism, particularly, does indeed imitate the Ọgbañje pattern.

A changing same, the plague of racism returns and in its multiple (dis)guises has haunted African-descended people. It has come back, for example, as European fallacies about African primitivity, a false and deceptive prophecy that in the story leads to British imperialist extraction of African youths for training as Methodist preachers who would help convert, Christianize, and cleanse their fellow Africans of their purported barbarity. It reincarnates as the white man's, specifically the racist colonial Governor Sir George Grey's opportunistic and ruthless suppression of the Xhosa, who were weakened after their loss of about 400,000 cattle, 50,000 lives, 600,000 acres, and 150,000 displaced people.[19] It journeys back, in the related Igbo case, as white missionary deception of the warlike yet hospitable Umuofia people in *Things Fall Apart,* a contact that leads to imperial settlement, Umuofia's colonization, and Okonkwo's tragic and untimely death.

In the New World, it returned and returns as the institution and injustices of antebellum slavery and African American domestic colonization. It reappears as the racist and unfounded prognosis by the then inchoate science of anatomy regarding the alleged oddity and perverseness of African people's physiology. This conclusion is expressed in the ethnological and freakish display of an African woman's dead body by the group of Resurrectionists at a cadaver auction in New York. The doom survives in white evangelical fabrication about Africans' racial inferiority and second-class citizenship before God. This outcasting manifests in the segregation of Africans in the white-pastored St. Matthew's. It shows also in the then prevailing white doubt about the suitability of the "soulless" and divinely unCalled African for ecclesiastic ordination. The unhealthiness repeats in white Philadelphia's lies, during the fever, about black Haitians as the epidemic's source. It incarnates in the devastating results, on the city's poor black neighborhood, of Matthew Carey's literal, libelous pamphlet that alleged that the trapped, overly exposed, exploited, and criminalized Africans,[20] many of who nursed the sick at home, moved patients to hospitals, and buried the fever-dead, are naturally immune to the pandemic and thus need little or no medical treatment. It re-emerges in the miscegenation laws and sentiments that fuel white mob hate, attack, rape, and murder of their colored neighbors during a night of violence in which the city's interracial couple, the African Liam Stubbs and his English wife, are incinerated in their house. It comes back, shaped as the confinement of surviving black and other children orphaned by the fever, starved, tortured, and sickened, many perishing in the shelter fire. It assumes human form also in Dr. Thrush's repeated rapes and impregnation of Kathryn. Last though not least, it reincarnates in the more contemporary, cyclical urban violence in American cities. There, black boys particularly, the precious "cattle" of black America and the black world, lose their lives.

Like the eighteenth-century Philadelphia fever, roaming violence mimics Ọgbañje. A body snatcher and life-thieving "spirit," violence endangers and robs black America of its "babies": its youth, future, hope, and backbone. For if we see the cattle the Xhosa slaughtered erroneously in response to a phony prophecy of millennial redemption also as a symbol of the people's "center," then racist, institutionalized, and misguided intraracial violence destroys black (America's) "cattle." It steals its most valuable wealth, one integral to its group identity, its generational and genealogical survival, and its continuity in the world.

As imparted in the decisive event of Iyi Uwa excavation in *Things Fall Apart*—a signal moment of triumph paralleled in *The Cattle Killing* in Richard Allen's secession from a white church—Wideman stresses oppositional blackness and counteroffensive institution-building. He suggests that there comes a time when a person, group, or generation must battle head-on that repeating oppression, in this case in its ideological, material, and systemic double, racism. Regardless of the risks involved, such resistance is necessary if one or the group desires full human agency. It is required for the realization of one's earthly calling. It does not matter if—for our narrator-preacher for instance—that calling is a modest career as a pastor. In short, this business of the Word and the Call, that is, the relation of the politics of divine "light," scripture, ministry, soul/spirit conversion, *and* "blackness," which was a racial mountain for early black preachers,[21] is the rugged terrain the narrator traverses. That apostolic vocation, we realize, when the story opens in part 1 and the preacher emerges from the wilderness and soon picks up the telling himself, is really all he a man of color with "modest powers" longs to do (33) in his exilic journeys. And, on duty to help Wideman sort out the preacher's evangelical luggage, itinerary and itinerancy, is the spirit child *as trope.*

* * *

Prepare your baggage as though for exile. . . .
Ezekiel 12:3

Wideman uses this epigraph that begins the novel's part 1 to establish a number of points. A call to duty and service and actually a divine commandment, the racially indiscriminating injunction confirms the Bible and God as the sources of the black preacher's authority to proselytize. But this is not just any kind of ministry. As the immediately adjoining verses and the quoted instruction elaborate, the prophet Ezekiel is charged to succor and help liberate, suggestively, those in captivity. And more telling, like Wideman's antebellum black preacher who lives in a stubbornly oppressive and sinful nation, Ezekiel also dwells in a hardened society that refuses to repent. But terrible punishments await it. On the level of criticism, the epigraphed statement cautions that what lies ahead would be a long, complicated, and potentially inconclusive discursive odyssey. And most significant, the excerpt intimates that the addressee is being readied for more than a separation from roots. He is also asked to prepare for a life, an accounting, that would be marked by the Ǫgbañje-condition of duplicity and mobility.

Various terms with which Wideman associates the preacher reinforce the latter's figuration as Ǫgbañje. Conveyed in the preacher's and the omniscient narrator's vocabularies, the qualifiers include: journey, traveler, visitor, pilgrim, refugee, immigrant, wander[ing], adrift, a passing stranger, vagabond, thief/stealer, spirit, the dead, stay, repeated returns, circles, intruder, trespasser, and house/home invader, among others. At one point the preacher tells his patient that in an old, white man's house he takes several trips, leaving and returning, and is ever moving. Also, the preacher's first appearance is Ǫgbañje-like. As pointed out in chapter 1, the Igbo believe that Ǫgbañje spirits inhabit, depart from and sneak into the human world through two specific entry points: forest/land and river/water. The once-enslaved preacher, having through paid manumission been "cut" or freed from servitude ("cut" as would an Ǫgbañje from the captivity of loyalty to spirit kin), first enters the narrative space from behind some trees around a lake. Moreover, his later identification of himself as "a brightish mulatto" man or a *biracial* persona echoes the Ǫgbañje's dyadic heritage and consciousness as spirit and human. This explains then how the preacher, who is empowered spiritually by his epilepsy and also sees ancestors, humans, and the unborn at the mythical intersection of two roads in a clearing next to St. Matthew's, is able to observe his spirit disengage freely from his physical body. The cleaving occurs in a sick old white man's desolate cabin into which he trespasses in search of lodging, employment, and souls to convert for the Lord.

A major motif in the text, the idea of journey, or rather the Ọgbañje's penchant for fluid back-and-forth movement, enables Wideman to mitigate the spatial and perspectival limitations of first-person, first-person-omniscient, and polyvocal narration. The preacher's evangelistic and revivalist peregrinations are a linking device and thus a critical component of the novel's structure. His physical and spiritual mobility puts him in touch with characters, alive and dead. Continuous movement, like Ọgbañje, puts him in contact—or links him—with people whose stories he tells, or is assisted in telling by the combined voices of an omniscient consciousness and community. It is through traveling that he meets the sick old white man in a desolate cabin, an African spirit woman carrying a fever-killed baby to the lake for burial, Mr. Rowe, Liam Stubbs, Mrs. Stubbs, Elizabeth, Thrush, and Kathryn. It is in his journeys that he learns of the orphanage for black and other children, one of whom as defendant/deponent also self-narrates his ordeal. These characters' testimonies become complementary and *plot sections* of the preacher's grand Slave Narrative. Like Cudjoe in *Philadelphia Fire,* the preacher becomes a witness, an evidence-collector and archivist. Just as his vocation as preacher makes him a vessel of the Lord, his related station as a traveling griot situates him as an authenticating amanuensis for the novel's dispossessed Africans. As Dolan Hubbard explains, the black preacher does not just "recover . . . the community's voice," he also "bind[s] the present to the past" (5). Furthermore, in concert with how a journey-aided reincarnation of an Ọgbañje excavates a buried past in that the Ọgbañje's return to a household pries open (a mother's/parental) anteriorities and also animates all manner of familial responses from vocal to active, the preacher's arrival and presence among the characters is comparably instigative. This compound notion of Ọgbañje as a traveling-excavating-intruder[22] is worth keeping in mind as the story unfolds.

* * *

We quickly realize, once we get past the stream of consciousness moment, that we are not the only or even the first witnesses to what transpires or transpired between the preacher and the inertial white villager whose desolate home he "invades." We discover that the events narrated occurred earlier and thus much of the story is a memorial. It is being told as the preacher's discontinuous remembrances. We recognize as well that someone else, a sick and dying woman undergoing the preacher's alternative healing praxis—storytelling—is listening. She has been listening for she is the person, or part of what James W. Coleman calls the "mysterious collectivity of women" (52) including Kathryn, to whom the preacher is recalling the cabin incident and other stories.

True to his Ọgbañje profile as an enlivening intruder, a mobile vocational Revivalist, if you will, the preacher's presence in his first missionary stop-over, the white widower's cabin, rouses the man from his death-like lethargy. More important, Wideman uses the preacher's encounter with the white man, or rather the man's racist outbursts at the preacher's amenities and entreaties, to comment on two things. The first is general white disinclination at the time to associate blackness with soul, light, liberatory theology, Godliness and Pauline discipleship. For even after the preacher has introduced himself as a man of God, the white man still asks him if he is "the devil." He also calls him "Black Satan," "devil" and "black devil" (25). The white man had earlier "watch[ed] the preacher's approach through an 'eye' in the side of the cabin, fostering unease in the preacher immediately."[23] Inseparable from the first, the second point deals with the racial, cultural, and political weight of the preacher's clarification of what he calls his "thievery," his Ọgbañje act of home burglary.

Though a self-professed honorable man, the preacher admits that he "stole his ax" (28). Wideman here manipulates African American vernacular tradition. He plays cleverly on the homonym "ax" and ["ass"]. This inferably is part of what Wideman's son D.J. calls his father's "off-the-wall-signifying" (210). The preacher's veiled derision of the sick white man resounds the joker's parody of the white missionary to Mbanta as "Your buttocks" (*Things* 147). A figure Du Bois describes as "the most unique personality developed by the Negro on American soil. A leader, a politician, an orator, a 'boss,' an intriguer" (*Souls* 120), indeed "[t]he master of metaphor in the Afro-American community,"[24] a wordsmith whose multipurpose domain "the Negro church may be said to have antedated the Negro family on American soil,"[25] the black preacher "steals" and lays a seditious claim to the white man's ax. He takes it in retaliation for the ax's complicity in shedding his blood and thus hurting him. Besides the hurt of the man's racial insults, his ax hurt him also when, as the preacher voluntarily chops log to build fire and keep the white man warm and alive, a piece of wood that the ax splinters lodges in the preacher's hand.

The preacher confiscates and implicitly castrates the white man's "dangerous," "damag[ing]" and dangling weapon (26). He does this not in gratuitous levity but rather as a symbolic statement of his modest reprisal. Collapsing and condemning the white man and his ax as spillers of (his) black blood, the preacher, now vigilant of that white history and tendency, takes decisive action to forestall its recurrence. His ax, he says, "hurt me once. Perhaps its destiny is to wound me again" (28). In snapping the splinter in two and discarding it, in handling the white man's ax, he refuses to fall asleep in his enemy's dream. Predisposed already to Ǫgbañje deviancy on account of his doctrinal fellowship of the (Protest)ant tradition of historic George Whitefield (ca. 1714–1770), the preacher acts true to his conviction and hauls ax. In classic Ǫgbañje mode, however, his stay at the cabin is both temporary and transitive.

The preacher's personal knowledge of and his distress over the broader, also gendered, injuries that African-descended people have suffered as a result of their contact with whites find more expression in another encounter he shares with his patient. He is still haunted by his meeting, one August day during his migratory ministry, with the African spirit woman carrying a child's cadaver to a lake for burial. The suspenseful incident allows Wideman to remark, as does Due, on how the dystopic house of (antebellum) America is no spiritual "home" for blacks displaced, enslaved, and exiled in it. The experience leaves the preacher morally conflicted and shaken in his faith.

The African woman's washing of the child before its interment is ritualistic. The preacher sees it also as preparation for a return home, to origins, to a paradise not plagued with fever. The spirit woman's damning nakedness, her desecrating urination on American soil, and her ultimate drowning could be viewed as her repudiating cursing of slavery. Her intentional life-taking represents her reclamation of agency and a longing for "home." As noted in the spirituals sung by the preacher's small African congregation that, as he says, Cathedralizes a forested clearing that adjoins St. Matthew's, there is a wide gulf between America and "home." The preacher accedes that the woman's actions alter his impression of the bond between mother and child, especially a child that like an Ǫgbañje was already marked by its caste.

The moment leaves the preacher with more questions than answers. He is curious about the woman herself, her name, aims, and mental wellbeing, as well as the child's gender, race, parentage, and fate. He wonders, among other things, if its father is white or African and if he is the woman's master or her black lover. And because the woman does not reappear from the deep hours after he awaits her reemergence, trusting on possible and promised Divine intervention, he loses faith. He is distraught by his complicity in her demise because, he admits, his vigil was brief. The preacher's continued quest for the African woman, his sightings of her

Ọgbañje trail in others, in short his resolve to heal and rescue his present patient, is a quest for restitution and self-atonement. His steadfast belief on her second coming, that she would return and he would see her, is implicitly redemptive. That belief is his effort to confirm again, to himself, that the God his black self believes in, serves and calls upon not only liveth but is responsive.

Communal responses in Philadelphia to the "strange" story of the African woman and the dead child vary and also compete. Of significance, however, is how those seemingly antagonistic and repeated versions are excavated into the narrative stage by an enabling moment. They are raised to life by the Ọgbañje preacher's contact with an African woman minding her own business on a desolate road. Just as the preacher's chance meeting with the comatose white villager spins a series of events, the present encounter also sets in motion narrative occurrences that lead to our hearing of the story's mutations in the first place. The novel implies that the folk retellings and parodying of the incident are not dissimilar, but are rather unified by their emphasis on two critical points: an African woman and a dead, possibly white or mixed-race child. They are truths about African women's experiences under what Liam dubs slavery's "peculiar arithmetic." No wonder the preacher, who like Ezinma has grown wiser beyond his years in his many life times, readily accepts all the renditions. "My way of reckoning," he asserts, "learned from the old African people, who said all stories are true" (53). Evocative of *Things Fall Apart,* those "old African people" are possibly the Igbo whose homeland, *The Cattle Killing* suggests, is the ancestral birthplace from which one of the characters Liam, alongside nine other African/"Ebo" (103), was snatched by the British for ministerial training. The preacher's belief in the veracity of all stories echoes Okonkwo's maternal uncle Uchendu's declaration that "There is no story that is not true" (*Things* 141). The sagacious Uchendu offers the statement in response to Okonkwo's friend Obierika's remark about Igbo incredulity relative to various and competing tales linking the white man, guns, alcohol, and trans-Atlantic slavery. What the preacher is certain of, though, is that the African spirit woman returns and that, actually, he had seen her before. He had met her following his mythical arrival in Radnor where a snowstorm jettisoned him like the whale offloading biblical Jonah.

Mediated through Wideman's use of the preacher's Ọgbañje propensity to movement and also Ọgbañje's semiotic role as intruder and bridge, this foremost meeting between the preacher and the African spirit woman occurred in the environs of St. Matthew's. It was on an October Sunday in 1792. In the midst of the British export Reverend Doctor Amos Parker's sermon, the preacher had suffered a major fainting fit. His seizure disclosed to him an apocalyptic vision of sinful

America's and St. Matthew's fiery destruction in readiness for Christ's second coming. Certain of his lucidity and of that jeremiadic epiphany despite his brief debilitation during the convulsion, the preacher is convinced that the spirit woman was the woman in a distinctive blue dress. He believes she was one of the Africans that nursed him and also kept a long vigil for what is couched as his rebirth from death. As Ọgbañje figure, however, this present death and rebirth is not his first cycle. He admits that he has "lived uncountable lives" before (69). But what flows in his excited mind now is the African woman's appearance and quick disappearance. What he remembers is her residual scent and allaying calm that day, her youth and undeniable corporeality. He muses on the likelihood that she is a spirit, a kin, perhaps a visitor or a stranger, part of "the world of special seeing," or like himself maybe a "traveler" originally headed another place (66–78). Haunted by her transience, distressed by his inability to find her again but obsessed with doing so, the preacher is a man who has found and just as quickly lost a beloved, like a mother losing a child, an Ọgbañje child, in infancy. His Africa-woman-blues rendered sometimes by Wideman in poetic lyricism, the preacher is a man whose precious cattle have been killed young, leaving him traumatized.

The preacher's mobility-enabled encounter with the African spirit woman in blue dress, along with his weekly fellowship with the African congregation of St. Matthew's, permits Wideman to humanize black Radnor by exhuming the buried stories of its members. As the preacher confesses, it was their lives that forced him, a once enslaved, sheltered, and naïve youth, to rethink his own life, racial sensibility, and pent-up anger at whites. The preacher's celebration of black Radnor becomes even more important because the church's outcast Africans—including Mrs. Lewis, Sister Jones, Cudjo, Old Stevens, Rowe himself, and the rest—are actually already dead, casualties of the awful night when a hateful white mob massacred its black neighbors. By indirectly officiating a literary and liturgical "mass" for them, both preacher and Wideman mark their unsung passing with tombstones. The church's Africans had worshiped under Reverend Parker. Like his British cousin the stern and uncompromising Reverend Smith in *Things Fall Apart,* Parker is strident, intolerant, and insulting to his black parishioners. He preaches piety and obedience but parks and segregates Africans in his church's back seats. He just as coldly denounces Methodist and Baptist egalitarianism, itinerant Negro ministers, and exuberant (African) spirituality. Like Baby Suggs's black followers in Morrison's *Beloved,* however, his church's Africans each Sunday had also had to find freedom, a safe space, in the clearing. And one of them, Mr. Rowe, had drawn the preacher's attention.

Rowe is a deep-voiced, fugitive slave. Reminiscent of the slave autobiographer Henry Bibb, he had lost his wife and children during his daring north-bound flights to freedom. Rowe embodies the blues tenacity and the apocalyptic affect of Radnor's black population. Tortured and scarred/marked, Rowe habitually wears a big smile. But behind his smile is a vengeful rage. Seemingly informed not by New Testament Christ-blanket-amnesty to sinners but rather an Old Testament Mosesian-retributive-justice, Rowe's vision of Armageddon, re-Creation and a New World order inverts black-white power relations and racial entitlements. Rowe's vision transfers power to blacks, with an ancestral black man beheading his Caucasian counterpart. He foresees the white woman, sexually violated with her reproductive ability damaged permanently, serving as a means of white racial extermination. And that, Rowe confides in the preacher, is "what I see sometimes when you see me smiling up at Heaven. Amen" (66). But Rowe, whose *vision* reverses the white enslaver's Ọgbañje-like misuses of the black woman's body, would not live to see if and when his prophecy would be fulfilled. Gaining exposure through the platform created by his encounter with the peripatetic reverend, however, Rowe's voicing of that anguish, that pained intuition, is cathartic. Evidentiary, it puts him on record as having said his peace boldly and "publicly," unlike Liam Stubbs and his English wife. Murdered by the same white mob, the couple had hidden their interracial love and marriage for twenty years, denied by race, law, and custom the chance at full self-actualization.

Perhaps no moment better actualizes the novel's play on the Ọgbañje's conceptual value as a mediator, a traveling excavator of buried memories, than the story of the Stubbs. The familial and especially vocal activity that ensues during the preacher's employment and temporary "stay" with them illuminates that point. As one under their care, a (frigid/dead) intruder whom they symbolically sexually birthed (back) to life, the preacher becomes technically their ward. He shapeshifts, as it were, into their foster "child" (the bi-racial child they would have had) and they, his surrogate "parents." Mrs. Stubbs avows that the preacher's fortuitous arrival in their midst "thaw[s]" (101) or revives her otherwise frozen husband. Verbally and memorially de-frosted, a reticent Liam suddenly becomes loquacious. He says more in a brief period than he had an entire year when his silences made him unfamiliar to his wife. But all he does now is talk and tell stories. As Mrs. Stubbs tells the preacher, upon his arrival, she "lost one stranger, gained two" (101).

We notice, however, that it is not Liam alone but also his wife that is "awakened" by the preacher's presence. Mrs. Liam, too, has a long lost story. But like any and every story, hers needs a listener (insert: the preacher-as-audience) to become. Experiencing Ọgbañje catalysis, Mrs. Stubbs unearths her heart, past, anger, and hurt. She unburdens to the preacher the grief of her sexual abuses in Liverpool, her forced racial "passing" in America, and thus her living a lie in public. She discloses to him the pains of her marriage to a man with whom she shares a history of exploitation, bondage, segregation, and humiliation. Similar to yet anticipating Julia's and her white husband Herman's plight in Alice Childress's provocative drama of early twentieth-century interracial romance *Wedding Band*,[26] Liam and his wife are doomed to a life of hermitage. And like the stigmatized "osu" in *Things Fall Apart,* they are forced to live on the fringes of society. It is no surprise that Mrs. Stubbs subscribes to the Rowean dream of an exacting New World, one where the historical underdog—the allegorical/racialized and gendered "lamb"—triumphs over the long dominant "lion" (99). She has grown rather bitter toward God and what she concludes is God's toying with human beings. Mrs. Stubbs denounces the existence of a hypocritical world that preaches kindness but denies her a modicum of agency, keeping her eternally beholden to God. She declines the conditions of "his bargain" (107). So does her African husband, the son of a powerful magician, shape-shifter and time traveler. Liam, now a farmer in America, was to have succeeded him.

Anticipated in and reinforcing Rowe's picture of a more empowering Afro-centric Genesis, Liam's embedded "autobiography" underscores further the inequities of black people's injury from that bargain with the divine. His story shows how race, gender, and power intermarry. To Liam, whose country (inferably the huge amalgam Nigeria) is size-wise much larger than the enslaving/colonizing England and whose old continent Africa minifies even the expansiveness of the young New World, the problem is essentially matrimonial. To him, the truth is that in his marriage to a white British woman in violation of miscegenation-integration law, he oversteps his boundaries and infringes on white supremacy, power, and purity.

Released/"published" through his contact with an Ọgbañje figure, Liam's captivity narrative takes us back in time and space. It retraces his journeys and reveals his undercut stint in ministry and healing. Liam states that he was uprooted from his homeland by the British for training as a clergyman. We also learn how, arriving in North America from Liverpool by way of Africa, he and his wife had had to contrive a perverse scheme to survive a hostile New World. For all the curious Philadelphia public knows, Mrs. Stubbs is an English gentlewoman and he, her reliable slave companion. But the name Stubbs actually belongs to a wealthy and cunning English merchant George Stubbs senior, who purchased Liam. Like Michael Henry Pascal renaming Olaudah Equiano "Gustavus Vassa," Old Stubbs baptized Liam and inconsiderately (mis)named him Centaur, Othello, Hannibal, and Aesop. He also later propertized Liam as a birthday present to his artist-son, also named George Stubbs (Wideman's figuration of the famous 1724–1806 Liverpool equine painter and anatomist, son of John and Mary Stubbs). Just as the preacher seizes the white man's hurtful ax, however, Liam appropriates Stubbs's surname imposed on him and thus signifies on his master. And through Liam's retaking of the credit for personally toting a horse up the weak stairs of Stubbs's cottage—a stunt George Stubbs claimed in real life—Wideman also signifies on wider European claims to historic feats owed or initiated by "others."

Liam witnesses considerable gore and stench during his indenture as butcher and currier in old Stubbs's butchery. This fictionalized slaughterhouse was literally an "[un]pleasant environment" where "the screams of panic-stricken animals, the blood-stained floors of the abattoir, and the heaps of entrails beneath the suspended carcasses would have presented a scene of terror" (Doherty 1). The horror causes Liam to see the English as cannibals, as does Equiano. Recalling his earlier homophonic signifyin(g) on the white man's ax, Wideman through Liam's disgust suggests that it is the body-snatching Europeans, and not Liam's African people, that needed divine salvation and civilization for their obscene corpse-, carcass-, and blood-fetish. Also, traveling to New York with artist George, whose interest in both anatomy and the cadaver-trafficking Resurrectionists anchors the above point, Liam observes the group's ethnological display, defilement, and auctioning of the body of a pregnant African woman whom Liam sees as his "sister, mother, daughter" (137). As Bernth Lindfors explains in *Africans on Stage: Studies in Ethnological Business* (1999), such dehumanizing, public, pseudo-scientific, and sometimes posthumous exhibitions of Africans have a long history in European and Anglo-American racist imagination. They were staged not for entertainment purposes alone but as evidence of the African's purported racial inferiority (vii–viii). Thus, in his journeys across borders—from Africa to England to New York and now Philadelphia—Liam, exiled like the story's other Africans, has seen enough to convince him of the translucency and falsities of strict racial categories. He has witnessed enough to grasp the insanities of (English) enslavement, as well as the disruptive power of racism.

Like the incarcerated speaker that laments his inability to extend his ancestral bloodline in Etheridge Knight's Black Arts poem "The Idea of Ancestry,"[27] Liam grieves the man-made and encastrative miscegenation that inhibits his procreativity. Power-driven, New World slavery unsettled and unsettles black racial and generational history. It squashed the talents of African-descended people, as evinced in the permanent deferment of Liam's traditional priestly grooming, evangelistic vocation, artistic ambitions, and his yearning for biological parenthood. Liam knows the idea of a New World is a sham, a wily prophecy for blacks. For even with its principle of freshness, hope, and liberty the New World is practically a cemetery for Africans who seem to be consigned to a life of duty and death in it, while other immigrant groups arrive and prosper. Thus, against the outside chaos of a cold world that he expects not to be the final resting place of his beleaguered bones, Liam tries at least to improvise order in domestic rituals. He hopes, as it were, that his "slave" cover would not be blown. But it is, and fatally.

The fiery deaths of Liam and his wife, on the night the preacher drifts off in a dream state that time-travels him back to Liam's Africa and also conjures up the Xhosa cattle-killing, sets the preacher, shocked and outraged, moving, once again, this time to Philadelphia. There he encounters the fleshly ghost of Richard Allen, Absalom Jones's co-pastor, and also opens the novel's part 2: the last if not the beginning stretch of the story's circular journeys. As the preacher reminds his patient, he met or found her when he moved to Philadelphia. It is this meeting that initiates the novel's storytelling-as-revivalist testimony and evangelism. Nonetheless, the preacher had gone to Philadelphia to cleanse his anger at whites and also to help the city fight the fever/racism plague. His fortunate departure from the Stubbs's household just before the fire continues his Ọgbañje role as transient and intruder.

More significant, however, the preacher's dream allows Wideman to represent the two racial tragedies, each of which is augmented by an imposturous prophecy, as sneaky yet systematic white assaults on black life. We note that (the fifteen-year-old child prophetess) Nongqawuse's reimagined self-narration of the cattle-killing event—"the season of death" she calls it (146)—implicates white intrusion and conspiracy in the catastrophic call for expiatory cattle-slaughter (corn-wastage, and cessation of farming). She inculpates white deceit also in the previsions of ancestor resurrection and a paradisic new Xhosa world. Nongqawuse relays that the invading, land-stealing whites succeeded ultimately in their imperial mission partly because they caught the Xhosa at a moment of group vulnerability. For "after the conclusion of the longest, cruelest and most penalizing of all frontier wars," Noël Monsert corroborates, "the frontier Xhosa were in a severe state of spiritual, political, and economic crisis after half a century of progressive land loss, strenuous assault upon their traditions and customs, and military defeat" (1177). Radnor's white criminal gang also slaughtered its black neighbors at night. As in Doro's ambush of Anyanwu, the gang caught them off-guard, at sleep in their enemy's dream (of violence), and with little chance of self-defense. Behind each assault, however, lies the historically protected fantasy of white supremacy.

A thing God condemns through the prophet Ezekiel (152), ersatz vision feeds on vulnerability, self-doubt, humility, and accommodationism. But it cannot in its inherent timidity handle ideological Ọgbañje—the spirit of rebellion. As the novel suggests, spurious prophecy aims ultimately to perpetuate white racial dominance. It seeks to entrench institutional structures that cite the same wrathful God as authority. An instance of this is the white fabrication about biblical Cain and African-descended people. This lie spirals to the outcasting of blacks in Richard Allen's former church, the white-pastored St. George's. Lauded as "the Cradle of American Methodism," St. George's was formerly called "Georg Kirchen" but was renamed "in honor of the [martyred] patron saint of England, St. George."[28]

The preacher's encounter with Allen at his church brings together two Ọgbañje figures: himself and Allen. In identifying the historic Allen as a dissenter, secessionist, blasphemer, liberator of captives, and as the proud, sinful Satan, the story casts Allen as an Ọgbañje: the outlaw. Allen embodies Rowe's and Liam's blues stubbornness. *The Cattle Killing* suggests that the detractor-spirit of doubt tempts Allen to question the audacity of his intent to "forsake" God by leaving the white church with his fellow Africans. Doubt trivializes Allen's credentials to establish and shepherd an alternate religious institution, the Bethel AME church, an edifice whose birth Carol V. R. George charts in *Segregated Sabbaths* (1973). Yet not dissuaded by cost, fear, or white power, Allen plots ahead. Like Ọgbañje or the disloyal Azaro that rejects a bondaging conformity with spirit confederacy and defects to the human world to experience its promises, Allen takes to the street, just to dare.

Allen's need for support brings the preacher-narrator in contact with the Presbyterian physician and crusader Dr. Thrush. A fictional Dr. Benjamin Rush, Rush played a major role during the fever outbreak and also appears in the story "Fever." The preacher's contact with Thrush occurs through Allen's message delivered to the Thrush home by the Ọgbañje-go-between, the preacher. The preacher's errand for Allen—who seeks Thrush's intervention in Matthew Carey's widespread attack on blacks, particularly the black nurses, home caregivers, and undertakers during the fever infestation—also functions as a plot device. It links us with Elizabeth, to her diary, and to the enslaved Kathryn. Wideman remarks that the Kathryn substory is about power and its reifications in issues of race, gender, text, writing, stories, storytelling, and myth.[29]

One notion that Wideman uses the Elizabeth diary to debunk is the then pervasive lie about the African's brain power, creativity and literary aptitude. Wideman also employs the diary's material composition by a racial Other to further denounce how much life and promise slavery robbed from African-descended people. It is therefore ironic that the blind Elizabeth, who depends on Kathryn's eyes and hands to gain voice, would claim ownership of the literary product when in fact it is physically "written" by a slave amanuensis. Moreover, it cannot be lost on us that while what we read on the pages of *The Cattle Killing* is presented by a third-party Wideman as an authentic version of Kathryn's transcription of her mistress's dictations, we do not really see the actual "texts." How does Mrs. Thrush know that Kathryn did not sabotage, as slaves were wont to do, her attempt at autobiography and documentary history? Wideman concurs mischievously: "we don't know what she wrote," he points out. Kathryn "may have written anything she wanted. She does have that power day by day to do it, to draw a map and have that lady over the edge of a cliff, her mistress. So she has tremendous power and she's just learning to use it, and I want certainly the reader to be aware of that."[30] Kathryn's education and attainment of proficiency in her master's tongue despite her bondage speak volumes. Most important, her literacy reminds Elizabeth of Phillis Wheatley's intellectual prowess which eminent citizens of Boston doubted and Phillis had to defend.[31] As Alice Walker has argued,[32] and as Kathryn's life amplifies, one of the gendered evils of slavery is its destruction of the human and "creative" potentials of black women's foremothers.

What slavery murders in Kathryn is much more than a chance at self-expression. It perverts her being and virtue, courtesy of Thrush's nightly power-thrusts into and his markings of her defenseless flesh. Wideman states rightly how like an Ọgbañje, which mediates good and evil, "each one of us carries enough demons . . . to destroy the world, as well as whatever goodness we carry inside."[33] As Elizabeth's diary shares, Thrush is a prominent physician, a powerful and respected man. He is color-blind, a great philanthropist supportive of Bishop Allen's church project, and a tireless advocate for the fever-sick despite peer accusations and skepticism about his bleeding approach to the illness. He is hyped as a friend of all Philadelphia's Africans, their sponsor and guardian, a determiner of their fate, and the father of the black children orphaned by the plague. But Thrush also rapes and impregnates Kathryn in what unravels as the novel's most shocking yet instructive irony. Kathryn's excavated narration of the rapes to the stunned preacher, with whom she forges a strong friendship after their awkward first meeting at the Thrush home, reveals something else. Elizabeth, who sees acutely in the dark, all along sensed but keeps silent about her husband's marital infidelity and the nightly abuses. Like Harriet Jacobs (Linda Brent) in *Incidents in the Life of a Slave Girl*,[34] Kathryn is trapped between the cruel master and his coy mistress—the two powerful allies in the peculiar institution relative to slaves. While the pious, dutiful, loyal, lonely, effaced, and extra-blind Elizabeth harbors her own race prejudice, the master would not let Kathryn go if and when she hollers.

Through Thrush's illicit and violent sexual desire for the forbidden—his black slave—Wideman stresses that what is at stake is much greater than the question of moral frailties. At issue, for him, is the absurdity of America's untenable caste system, puritanic sexual repression, and the legal strictures against blood-mixing.

As Ronald T. Takaki writes, for all their republicanism, intellect, national influence, and abolitionist zeal, Thomas Jefferson and, in this case, Dr. Benjamin Rush were themselves slaveholders and white hegemonists. [It is equally telling the revelation that Jefferson slept with his African slave Sally Hemings and fathered biracial offspring, one of whom William Wells Brown suggests is the tragic mulatto heroine of his *Clotel* (1853).] A member of the Abolition Society and co-signer of the Declaration of Independence, Rush passionately preached against solitary sin (masturbation) and lust. He associated black skin with leprosy and disease. As a consequence, Rush proposed physical and racial segregation in his recommendation that whites avoid interracial sexual liaisons with blacks so as not contract black skin.[35] Wideman intimates that the whole interdiction is utterly insane. Historically occluding black men from the pleasures of occulted white womanhood, pseudo-science and miscegenation law indirectly empower(ed) the white slave holder. They sanctioned the enslaver into a capricious Ọgbañje spirit that misuses the (enslaved black) woman's body. This de jure structure did not just degrade black women, humiliate black men, and embolden white supremacy. It also gave rise to attitudes that culminate in the murder of interracial couples like the Stubbsses, whose unconscionable deaths become, as it were, a kind of cattle-killing—a waste of valuable human life and capital.

Helping a traumatized and dying Kathryn (re)construct and voice her nightmares by offering her a much needed ear every Sunday is a sobering but rehabilitative experience for the preacher. But what incenses him to reject Allen's stoicism, humanism, and steadfast Christian loyalty, what riles him to lose faith in the church, ministry, and even God or in any deity that composes cyclical "horrors for African people" (204), is not just his inability to save Kathryn but another crushing epiphany: In Elizabeth's journal is recorded the horrendous containment, mistreatment, and fiery death of frustrated and resentful black and other children in the tomb-like cellar of Thrush's and Elizabeth's reform orphanage. It baffles the preacher how Allen could calmly sermonize the children's teeming mourners. The preacher cannot understand how Allen could serve as the ambassador of such a deity. Wideman sees those eighteenth-century children reincarnated in twentieth-century black children victimized by the streets. He also *calls* up MOVE member/black survivor Ramona Africa and a Philadelphia Independence Square rally to mourn the Osage Avenue victims of the May 13, 1985 MOVE bombing. This tragedy is collocated with a Capetown march celebrating Nelson Mandela's release from prison after twenty-seven years. Thus, the preacher who morphs into a twentieth-century consciousness, unifies black liberation struggles in Africa and North America. He also interplays death and life.

But by now, however, these analogous stories of black trauma have become so daunting, unbearable, and linguistically ineffable that the preacher finds himself tongue-tied. He starts to "sta-sta-sta-sta-stutter" (205). His sermon, his story, fails. For all along it has been told with an alien tongue, a borrowed (English) language whose descriptors "plague" and "slavery" cannot adequately capture the true luridness of the fever pestilence, represent "the unspeakable hellishness of slavery,"[36] or in fact capably shoulder the painful weight of devastated black lives and landscapes. We recall here that plaintive moment in *Things Fall Apart* when Okika, lamenting the abomination Umuofia has suffered because of its contact with the white man, mourns that Umuofia's ancestors and all their gods are weeping (203). The preacher decries a similar sacrilege in black America and by extension the black world. *The Cattle Killing* declares that blacks are victims of racial injustice and violence not solely in American cities. Black people, implacably, are grieving. They are holding rituals, vigils, rallies, and funerals in the diaspora, each requiem a celebration, each celebration a long, long black song. All are, however, a cautionary tale.

Mother, Behold Thy Child;
Child, Behold Thy Mother: A Love/Life Homily

Wideman concludes *The Cattle Killing* with his son "D.J." helping him fill some of the expository "holes" in the story. Of importance to both father and son is the fate of Allen's African sailor-brother supposedly lost at sea off the Cape of Good Hope. However, that Wideman ends the section on racial mourning with a call and freedom to love is critical. As indicated earlier, *The Cattle Killing* is more than a literary sermon on the black dead who return—generational casualties of the plague of slavery and racism initiated by the earliest Europe-Africa encounter. That first Africa-Europe contact became the single enabling and most consequential event that let the "death spirit" of racism slip into the world, survive, mutate, and journey back successively. But it also provoked in African-descended people a counter-offensive. Wideman suggests that this response should be rooted in an ethic of faith, love, and life. It must be built on resiliency and rebellion—rebellion against the "captivity" and "death" subsumed in an Ọgbañje familial intrusion. Here, again, the Ezinma-Ekwefi experience is enlightening.

Ekwefi's abiding faith and love for Ezinma, her resolve to indulge and connect with Ezinma through reciprocal storytelling echoed in the preacher's antiphonal relationships with both his patient and Liam, relays Wideman's advocacy of transcendent love. Wideman sees this love-abundant, which he preaches emphatically in his works, most recently *God's Gym,* as a counterforce to loss, the loss of the beloved. The love- and life-imperative underneath the Ekwefi bond with Ezinma is inherently disobedient. It is a revolt by a subversive (Igbo) woman, one who we are told is drawn tellingly to wrestling matches. That is, Ekwefi does not shy away from conflicts, contests, and battle sites. Nor does she have any compunction about abandoning her former husband to live with Okonkwo. Thus, with respect to her only child, Ekwefi refuses the implications of the dibia's intrinsically destructivist divination. Like Liam's wife, Ekwefi is a blues avatar who scoffs at the sacred bargain, the "prophecy" that says that because of its "different" subjectivity (read: her Ọgbañjeness, blackness, Otherness), her child is already marked, fated adversely, and thus "born-to-die." A fighter, Ekwefi volitively insists on the alternate destiny. She claims the antithesis "born-to-live": an affirmation that this child, her tenth child, Ezinma, must survive and will, even if it costs her own life.

Wideman circulates that (self) love- and life-principle in *The Cattle Killing*. It resonates, for instance, in Allen and his brother buying not theirs alone but also their mother's freedom from slavery, as does Sethe's husband Halle in *Beloved*. It is exemplified also in the altruism and bravery of the African slave girl/spirit-woman who defies death to attend to a fever-stricken child when her master has hastily bunkered his wife and family in his fortress to hopefully stave off the epidemic. That ethos of love resounds when Liam Stubbs and his English wife rescue "their" child-visitor-stranger from freezing to death by lending their body heat, Liam less consciously, to resuscitate his frigid body. We see it also in the compassion of the segregated Africans of St. Matthew's, particularly the women. Contrastive to Reverend Parker's repulsion and rant, these Africans would not treat one of their own, the preacher, as a pariah because of his "difference," his humiliating public fits. They instead embrace him even with those spasms, just as Medallion's black Bottom community accommodates the aberrant Eva Shadrack, Sula, and the Deweys. The Ekwefi resolve anticipates literarily and amplifies the preacher's devotion to his patient/audience whom he tries desperately to keep alive even against her foreseeable death.

As do Cornel West and Morrison,[37] Wideman emphasizes that this love-, life-, and community-ethic sustained Africans and their descendants during slavery. It is that premium on life—affirmed in Okonkwo's maternal uncle's name "Uchendu" and in Mbanta village's magnanimity and compassion—that refuses to despise but instead shields and hugs even a belligerent "son" and an unlucky daughter's "child," Okonkwo during his forced exile among his mother's people. That ethos is needed even more today as an intervention to protect all black children. It is essential to shelter young black males, especially, from what West laments as *"the nihilistic threat"* to black America.[38] Years earlier, James Baldwin called it the "darkness" prowling inside and outside in America's cities and streets: the shape-shifting darkness of racism, modernity and urbanity that "steals" black children, allowing them little and often no prelapsarian interlude for infancy and adolescence; that in Harlem drives Sonny to rage, drugs, crime, and incarceration in Baldwin's "Sonny's Blues" (1958); and also shadows, entraps, stunts, and destroys Bigger Thomas in Chicago. It is *that* "darkness" that in Pittsburgh literally hunted and haunted Wideman's own brother Robert. Like Wideman's middle son Jacob, Robert is presently serving a life sentence: Jacob, for murdering his roommate at a summer camp and Robby, for his role in a fatal robbery. As Jerry H. Bryant elucidates correctly in *'Born in a Mighty Bad Land'* (2003), Robby's tragedy and the complex familial, racial, historical, social, psychological, and other issues surrounding it are the wheels driving Wideman's *Brothers and Keepers* and his Homewood trilogy.

In short, a community devotion to life is needed to save black children from all other kinds of reincarnating American death-spirits: joblessness, homelessness, guns, police brutality, the justice system, prejudiced media, black-on-black assaults, the AIDS epidemic, and more. To Wideman, that continental Africans were initially seen as originators of HIV and AIDS, just as eighteenth-century white Philadelphians blamed African and black West Indian immigrants as vectors of the fever, shows that like Ọgbañje history *repeats*. History, Wideman states, "is an ogbanje"; it "can be represented by the process of ogbanje."[39] And blacks should stay alert to that reality.

Ekwefi's vigilance and iron will to safeguard Ezinma transcribes then as an act of self-salvation. For in helping save/manumit Ezinma, Ekwefi redeems herself as well. Ekwefi's committed attempts also keep her alive, active, and hopeful. The preacher-storyteller and his stories are similarly rescued and vivified, and above all buoyed through care-giving and narratability to a responsive listener. To Wideman, therefore, African-descended people invariably liberate themselves by promoting intraracially a culture of love, life, and faith. They self-preserve through voicing and vigilance: vigilance against group betrayal, as cautioned in the Tortoise tale (*Things*); against mass inattention and self-injurious hospitality, whose pitfalls reverberate in the Anyanwu entrapment (*Wild*), Abame deracination, and Umuofia pacification (*Things*); and also against other delusory and irreversibly "fatal prophecies"[40] of white *and* black messianism that have historically debilitated Africans and their homelands. That, in the end, is the black diasporal lesson of the Xhosa cattle-killing movement. Noël Mostert calls it "probably the greatest self-inflicted immolation of a people in all history" (1187). It is historically and critically noteworthy that the Xhosa tragedy occurred the very years, 1856–57, that Britain, through its "establishment of a [Church Missionary Society] CMS mission on the Niger really began" its disastrous "civilizing" project in Igboland.[41]

One could argue, even at the risk of pardonable exaggeration, that perhaps only a Wideman can do with Ọgbañje what he achieves with it conceptually, thematically, rhetorically, philosophically and politically in *The Cattle Killing*. It is remarkable how he strategizes the idea's subtexts fairly imperceptibly into various aspects of the story, from the novel's characters and themes to its language and frame. For instance, the chaos that Ọgbañje thrusts into order reflects in the novel's structural fissures. Ọgbañje's comings and goings destabilize linearity. The story's circularity mimics that Ọgbañje cycle. *The Cattle Killing* is a quilt of forms and Ọgbañje is, likewise, an expressive mosaic of interlinked epistemes and codes. Ọgbañje's disruptiveness is filtered fittingly in a text that similarly "disrupt[s] the master narrative."[42]

Wideman dialogizes with Achebe, with his "master" text *Things Fall Apart* and with Igbo world. One of those additional quiet exchanges with Achebe registers in what reads as Wideman's thoughts on pre-colonial Umuofia's "killing" of its own "cattle," its greatest capital: people (the osu, the *efulefu,* mothers of twins, twins, Ikemefuna) pursuant to oracular order. It was the same (African) "man-eating oracles"[43]—for instance the powerful, influential, and widely dreaded "*Chukwu,* the Ibinukpabi oracle" of Aro called "Long Juju" by the Europeans[44]—whose "insatiable taste for human victims"[45] helped condemn thousands of Igbo and other captives and victims to both domestic servitude and trans-Atlantic slavery. This is an issue that also interested Octavia Butler, as *Wild Seed* reveals. If *The Cattle Killing* were any indication, we would expect Wideman to have considered those oracular edicts against Ikemefuna, twin births, and mothers of twins to be an intra-ethnic delusion. Wideman's unease with slavery in general and with that defunct (Igbo) practice is subsumed, or could be said to be absorbed, in the alarmed voice of the young African woman who cries out in *The Cattle Killing:* "No. No . . . Dare not" trade in your fellow human beings, your brothers and sisters, or "destroy your own offspring. Your future. Your hope. You must risk all to save th[ese] helpless, innocent babe[s]," your children, your life, your cattle (50–51).

In February of 1990 Wideman was in South Africa to witness a Life/Live event: the release of Nelson Mandela from prison. The long delayed project that presumably became *The Cattle Killing* had been swirling in his mind at the time. He knew South Africa would feature in it somehow.[46] But then, as was the case in "Damballah" and *Reuben,* he needed an integrative device. Thus, when he found the valence Ọgbañje he knew that he had located the right ligament to unify the project's fragments and the issues he had been processing awhile. That discovery, he says, was "like meeting an old friend." And so he thanks goodness for Igbo language.[47] Wideman is grateful for Ọgbañje also because its metaphoric geometry and density unfetter artistic innovation. The myth allows Wideman to purposely reconstruct, as submitted, John Marrant's and Richard Allen's slave/spiritual autobiographies. He synthesizes them into a neo-slave text that is as tricky interpretively as the shape-shifting Ǫgbañje spirit. That elusiveness makes the novel uncontainable or, one might say, "unenslavable" to the homogenizing and restrictive blueprints of the 1960s and 1970s nationalist aesthetic. It makes the story untotalizeable by white mainstream's stereotyped assumptions about authentic black letters or those not black enough. For black or white readers used to expecting what Wideman calls "a certain something from a black text—an African American text,"[48] *The Cattle Killing* in its postmodern formal aberrances is not the novel for them. It is a story in which "the center" does not hold.

In *Things Fall Apart,* Achebe infuses Igbo philosophy and cultural material with the goal of Igbonizing, Africanizing but more importantly expanding the boundaries of the received Western and realist novel. In the same vein, Wideman weaves the "strange," unsettling and mythic Ǫgbañje into the contemporary politics of slavery by way of *The Cattle Killing.* Wideman also African Americanizes the genre of historical novel whose protocols the white writer William Styron slanted in the heat of the civil rights and Black Power movements. Styron took extreme liberties with the mode to scandalize a former slave, preacher, and black hero, Nat Turner, even after Styron "was advised against the project by his Random House editor."[49] Wideman alters the (historical novel) form to restore the dignity of another white-slighted, antebellum black minister, rebel, and leader, Richard Allen. He also enlists Ǫgbañje to help him sort through the clutter of his New World black experience. But then it could not be otherwise because, as Wideman essays in "The Architectonics of Fiction," "Good stories transport us to those extraordinary diverse regions where individual lives are enacted. . . . People's lives resist a simple telling, cannot be understood safely, reductively, from some static point, some universally acknowledged center around which all other lives orbit. Narrative is a reciprocal process, regressive and progressive, dynamic."[50]

It is fitting to end this chapter with a coda on Allen. In addition to Marrant's ministry, as contended, it as Allen's nomadic yet vigorous and racially uplifting episcopacy that entices Wideman's distillation of Ǫgbañje into *The Cattle Killing*'s architecture. Furthermore, as Clarence E. Walker discusses, Allen's life and career forerun not just Booker T. Washington's and later Marcus Garvey's more publicized advocacies and support of black entrepreneurship. Allen heralds also, particularly, the 1960s and 1970s renewed emphasis on black institution-building: what with Bethel's honor as *the* vanguard black establishment ("the greatest Negro organization in the world," Du Bois lauded it [*Souls* 126]), Allen's inspiration if not instigation of independent black churches, A.M.E's anticolonial initiatives, and the church's pioneering foundation of its own newspaper the *Christian Recorder,* its university Wilberforce, and a publishing outlet.[51] Wideman would concur, therefore, that although Allen's narrative *The Life Experience* is "primarily a work of church history [. . . he, Allen,] is the first historian of and apologist for a black power movement in the Afro-American autobiographical tradition."[52] Most important, Allen's and his fellow black Methodists' adamant rejection of continued white control, segregation, and condescension and their decision to walk out en masse and found their own religious fellowship, as Allen relays (24–36), are a powerful lesson in decolonization, in "self-affirmation, self-determination and self-reliance."[53] In short, their revolt "offers early commentary on the import of self-naming in Afro-American culture."[54] Wideman extends the Allen project aesthetically in *The Cattle Killing* through his keen reconstructions of the Ọgbañje drama. If there is another African American novelist that achieves that feat just as remarkably, it is Nobel Laureate Toni Morrison in whose "twin" imbricated novels *Sula* and *Beloved* we find and follow the child spirit's tropological trails—again.

Chapter 6 Sula, Beloved, and the Constructive Synchrony of Good and Evil

The slaves' idea of the devil appeared strange to . . . whites for the same reason that the idea of so many West Africans would have. Good and evil could not easily be separated in the projection of discrete personalities. However terrifying to the slaves in some of his aspects, the devil could also be a friend in need. . . .

Eugene D. Genovese
Roll, Jordan, Roll

It is a sentimental error . . . to believe that the past is dead. . . .
James Baldwin
"Many Thousands Gone"

Although Toni Morrison's *Sula* and *Beloved* are two separate and seemingly unrelated texts, both pieces are actually interconnected novels. Published before Wideman's *The Cattle Killing* but explicated after it here for category differentiation, *Sula* and *Beloved* are reciprocal stories because they are imbricated neo-slave narratives shaped by the mythic trope of the child spirit. They are complementary also in terms of being works whose eponymous children, concerns, and crafting are sharpened further when explained relative to the "Ọgbańje" concept, the figure *and* idea Ezinma, the Ezinma-Ekwefi dynamic, and *Things Fall Apart* in general.

In these—her second and fifth—novels Morrison mirrors Achebe's cultural, gendered, political, philosophic, and aesthetic applications of the supernatural. In *Sula,* for example, Morrison echoes Achebe's employment of the mystifying, in Ezinma, as site to meditate on the politics of aberration and the paradoxes of good and evil in the frameworks of religious cosmology and the colonial encounter.

European enslavers and later imperialists, seeking to justify their invasion, exploitation, and geographical/"bodily" mapping and markings of Africa, branded Africans as heathens. They historicized Africans as barbaric, peculiar, and diabolic and contrastively authenticated themselves as civilized, normative, and noble. Achebe counters through *Things Fall Apart,* however, that such European claims to "enlightenment" and the West's certainties about "evil" are preposterous if not naïve. He also marshals, among other things, the parabolic Ezinma as a positivist Other, colonial devastations of Igbo/African world, and how the empire precipitously drives Okonkwo to an early grave, as proofs that the opposite might indeed be the case in Europe's good-evil hierarchy and dichotomy. In *Beloved,* Morrison resonates more than Achebe's uses of Ezinma/the diction of "strangeness" to disarticulate the above racialized Order and muddle the semantics of good and evil. She reinforces, most of all, Achebe's supreme belief in black and human survival even in the face of tragedy, loss, and mourning. Thus, Morrison's postmodernist explorations of good and evil in both *Sula* and *Beloved* rekindle Achebe's instructive implication that things are sometimes more indeterminate and interdependent than they seem. Her stories share his extensive uses of irony and, by default, his Igbo culture's elevation of ambiguity, complexity, and complementarity over reductionism, binaries, and absolutes.

Of Morrison's eight novels to date, *Beloved* is arguably the most popular with literary critics, students, and casual readers. In addition to the import of its thematic novelty and formal richness, and its appearance amidst national retrospections on slavery and the surge of academic and scholarly interest in contemporary black women's writings, *Beloved* owes its success to extensive promotion by Oprah Winfrey's influential book club and Oprah's memorable screen adaptation of the story in 1998. In terms of scholarly attention, then, *Beloved* dwarfs even the equally intriguing *Bluest Eye, Song of Solomon,* and *Sula.* As noted earlier, reviewers have discerned Beloved as Morrison's incarnation of the West African myth of spirit child. It should be pointed out, however, that it is the clarity of Beloved's child-spirit ontology that has led critics to associate her character with Ọgbañje, although Morrison does not use any of the words/terms Ọgbañje, àbíkú, or born-to-die in either novel. Critical interest in Beloved as the most obvious born-to-die in Morrison's fiction, along with Morrison's interview statement to Robert Stepto that she had no model for Sula, continues to have an unintended effect. It distracts attention from the fact that, fourteen years earlier in 1973, there was Sula, Morrison's first "Ọgbañje" child-woman and Beloved's precursor.

Natural yet unnatural, powerful, decentered, and baleful, Sula heralds Beloved's surrealism and malevolence, or her demonology, as Trudier Harris qualifies it. For

it is in *Sula,* Harris estimates perceptively, that Morrison initiates her female characters' shape-shiftings, her "transformation of woman from human being to something other than human."[1] Given how subtly and sometimes unambiguously *Sula*
anticipates *Beloved,* one could call them prequel and sequel. In addition, critical
affirmations that Beloved is a New World Ọgbañje and that *Sula* is permeated with
African traditions[2] infer that, like Butler, Due, and Wideman, Morrison returned
foundationally to her West/African ancestry and religious roots in tandem with
the Black Arts movement's cultural campaign and the movement's efforts to decol-
onize black art.

In "Rootedness: The Ancestor as Foundation," Morrison proudly admits to
practicing black art whose attributes she argues persuasively.[3] Morrison had concerns, however, about the "reactionary" manner in which the 1960s racial politics
and art asserted their mission and mandate.[4] Morrison invariably disapproved
of how the period's conservative politics reduced black female subjectivity as an
already-known. By portraying Sula ironically, (non)realistically, grotesquely, and
even through "the poetic freedom and Gothic vision of modern and postmodernist writers" (Bell, *Contemporary* 182), Morrison queries such simplifications of
the black woman. Morrison problematizes also the Black Power and nationalist
aesthetic's assurances about the black community, authentic black identity, and the
idea of a unified human person.[5] As we might remember, consolidating the African
American personality was one of the major aims of the 1960s and 1970s African
American literature, according to Larry Neal.

If *Sula*/Sula overturns authoritative epistemologies and also reveals the ultimate impossibility of human consolidation, *Beloved* traces and also illustrates *that*
futility of containment in antebellum slave revolt. It also brings this study full
circle, historically and critically. Hinting at the possibilities of "closure," *Beloved*
contemplates the prospects of healing from the scars of New World slavery: that
dehumanizing experience begun for blacks from the fictionalized displacement
and despoiling of the Anyanwus of African diaspora history. As does *The Cattle
Killing, Beloved* alludes to the power of human agency. It expresses, especially, the
countervailing weight of Life to check the excesses of Death. Therefore, using as
evidence the Bottom's failure to delimit Sula, Morrison cautions against essentialism. Resounding Achebe in whose *Things Fall Apart* the subject of "evil" is both
pervasive and relative, Morrison stresses that the human being minimized as "evil"
might just be "good" and, ironically, that good relies on evil for differentiability.
Perhaps in no facet of the spirit child mythic drama is that ironic interplay allegorized more acutely than in Ezinma's vitality to her parents and to the integrity of
Things Fall Apart's plot, politics, and philosophy. Like Ezinma, Sula and Beloved

reify the primordial fluidity and coexistence of evil and good. It is through both eponyms' analogous executions of the Ọgbañje's parts of "the diabolical" and "an enabler" that Morrison intermediates her character "frames" of the two women and the dominant themes and structural components of both novels.

Morrison's double-edged sketch of Sula as a "woman who could be used as a classic type of [a constructive] evil force,"[6] and, later, her similar profile of Beloved as demonic, are not derived from Western thought. Like Achebe's culturally grounded vision of evil in *Things Fall Apart,* Morrison's exploration of the subject is also place-specific. Hers emanates largely from an African/African American cosmological orientation and not from—though it is in part critically responsive to— Western world views. The Western mind often depicts good and evil as rivalrous, caught, as it were, in a Zoroastrianianic, Manichaean, and Neo-Manichaean battle and irreconcilability.[7] This sense of the concepts' rigid if not total antagonism is reflected also in Western Christianity's and rationalism's tendency to delineate absolute barriers between God and Devil, heaven and hell, religion and super- stition, the natural and the supernatural (worlds), sin and innocence, the sacred and the profane, and between the chosen and the damned/outcast. The Western propensity to dichotomize resolvable phenomena is fundamentally incongruent with, in this case, African and African American cultural philosophies that gener- ally insist on relativity and an organic universe.

Like the Western world, African societies have ideas about good and evil. Un- like the occident, however, they interpret both principles less as abstractions. African religions construe evil more in the context of the tight interdependence of group-life and "land." That is, "land" as not merely the physical, inherited, and inhabited earth, which is the fountain of life, but as a "sprit," a powerful deity of fer- tility, creativity, justice, and morality, as in the Igbo case. Relatedly, as Jomo Kenyatta explains in *Facing Mount Kenya* (an assertion Kenyan novelist Ngugi wa Thiong'o affirms in *Weep Not, Child* [1964]), the Kikuyu so revere the land that they see it as "the 'mother' of the tribe" and "the most sacred thing above all that dwell in or on it." "Communion with the ancestral spirits," Kenyatta elucidates, "is perpetuated through contact with the soil in which the ancestors of the tribe lie buried" (22).

Undoubtedly, then, Africans value the "land," as do other human groups. But more important, they judge evil in terms of the close relationship between com- munity (survival) and a person's conduct, function, or action within the commu- nity, within the meta-physical "land" whose sanctions and sanctity must be upheld for preservation of cosmic equilibrium. Africans also elevate community over the individual, recognize the intricate and mutual reliance of self and the collective, take ethical behavior seriously, and see God as the ultimate arbiter of righteousness.

Equally significant, African peoples understand and strive to affirm the inherent human and spiritual worth of each member of the community.[8] Enslaved Africans must have taken with them to the New World memories of these commonly shared, cosmological attitudes. Thus, not only are African American notions of the preternatural influenced by African religious thought, as Melville Herskovits observed, but also black America eschews the Western European opinion of good and evil as incompatible.[9]

The foregoing helps explain why African American folklore and fiction tend to recognize differences between "subversive" suicides and escapist self-murders. And in addition, instead of pitting them irreconcilably against each other, black folk thought complicates the figures of "God" and "the oppressor," or "God" and Satan/"the Devil" and invests them with religious, racial, socio-political, gendered, and ethical denotations. The two entities are depicted occasionally as switching performances, as illustrated in Sula's accusation that God participated in Plum's death through divine inaction. Sometimes also, the outmatched "Devil," extended in the willful, "degenerate" and "retrograde" badman or badwoman figure in African American cultural expression, is cast as victor, messiah, hero, celebrant, or "a friend in need," as Genovese explains above.

Almost always subject to our discrete experiences and perspectives, good and evil apply also to other, non-ethical issues. The good-evil tension resides in the contradiction that is life itself, hence Carl Jung's equation of the two "principles," when reduced to their ontological roots, as "aspects of God" and "names for God" (85–86). Good and evil crystallize also in the stress balanced between the material and the immaterial, predictability and mystery, clean and dirty, and significantly, between sameness and difference. The pressure is coded also in the interlacings of life and death. It is expressed in the arbitrariness and performatives of "black" and "white" as stable, racial categories, as Morrison shows in her short story, "Recitatif" (1983). The tightness is felt, more instructively, in the wisdom or objectionability of an antebellum black mother killing her mixed-blood child to both scorn its white father and save it from slavery. The tension resonates just as strongly in the idea of a child or the now fictionalized child, through her "return," subjecting her mother to near-fatal guilt. Yet the same child enables her mother to excavate her horrendous past and in doing so begin the process of self- and by extension racial-healing from the trauma of infanticide. Good and evil prompt questions about nature's occasional aberrancy, as manifested in the Bottom community's tense and deathly encounters with the cosmos.

Much like Achebe's cosmological pictures of Umuofia and *Arrow of God*'s Umuaro as societies whose prominent members Okonkwo and the Chief Priest

Ezeulu, respectively, are ultimately subordinate to the actual protagonist, the people, Morrison paints The Bottom as an organic New World African "village." She makes it "as strong a character" as possible, a black "community" whose strongest feature is its assembly and cohesion of a "fantastic variety of people and things and behavior," which Sula exemplifies (Stepto "'Intimate Things,'" 474–75). But also like Umuofia and Umuaro, The Bottom is imperfect.

The Bottom is, ironically, a community that de-emphasizes its collective human flaws and instead brands its avatar Sula's Ọgbañje atypicality as evil. Sula plays, then, the Ọgbañje's generative and degenerative roles in her overarching eccentricity. It is this eccentricity that subsumes what could be posited as Sula's Ọgbañje traits. They include her birthmark, supernaturality, selfish individualism, intractability, vagrancy, malignancy, ostracizing naming, short life, obvious and implied deaths and (re)births, her burial, and then her equally constitutive but veiled goodness. Just as an Ọgbañje entity is marked sometimes as "evil, threatening, [and] a demon"[9] because of its menacing, repetitive life journeys and its desire to live out that irregular subjectivity, the black community of the Bottom also regards Sula and her idiosyncrasies lopsidedly as "evil." This conflict between the normative and the anomalous creates and is the catalytic tension that permeates, strikingly similarly, the Ọgbañje drama and Sula's experiences with her townspeople.

Up in the Bottom, They Say She Was Laughing at Their God

Morrison circularly plots that tension in the story of women's friendship in the Bottom. Already gentrified when the novel opens, a geographical palimpsest like the equally oxymoronically named black "Lower Hill" in *The Cattle Killing,* the Bottom is an Ohio black community with roots in a plantation economy and antebellum experience in general. Still bearing the scars of slavery, this New World town inhabited by archetypic racial ancestress Anyanwu's other descendants was created out of what was originally intended as a "nigger joke." According to its myth of origin and land settlement, the Bottom traces to a moment of consequential Europe-Africa encounter, indeed to another primal scene of white (oracular) deception that reinforces Achebe's and Wideman's imperativization of untiring racial vigilance. The Bottom dates back to a good white farmer's mocking betrayal of his loyal, former slave to whom he offered a torturous land that he appraised apocryphally as "the best land there is" (5).

The survival of this "outcast" community situated/elevated on the hills (like the irony of "Umuofia": people of the bush), and forged out of the crucible of white dishonesty and false prophecy, is affected by an interaction of natural, human, and inanimate forces. Among the Bottom's "inhabitants" is Hannah's daughter—

the firebrand, Sula Peace. A live wire and life's wire interfused, indeed an "electric seal,"[11] Sula is Nel Wright's childhood friend, spiritual double, and the Bottom's Ọgbañje figure. She is also Morrison's personification of nature's enigma. The Bottom community must find a way to manage this marked child-spirit Sula, who like Ezinma is both a *person* and a *thing*—a characteridea, a force of nature whom/ which the people compress and condemn as evil. But how the Bottom responds to this puzzling and gendered "difference," nature's rough hand, white injustice, and the perceived twilight of racial integration in the mid-1960s would determine ultimately its continued survival as a community.

Like eccentric Ezinma that commands considerable parental and familial interest, Sula draws an immense attention. She is also her community's pulse. And although she dies young as do many an Ọgbañje and much before the story ends, which makes us miss her as Morrison intended, Sula names the novel and integrates its concerns. Her oddity surfaces early and in various ways during her childhood. Sula has been atypical even before, with a smile and a glide, she departs Medallion in 1927 following Nel's marriage to Jude Greene. Evoking the idea that the Ọgbañje are unusual and generally erratic, Sula's (un)naturalness shows in her inconsistent temperament and moodiness. Her (ab)normality is revealed also in her self-mutilation in deterrence of bothersome Irish boys, and in her involvement in Chicken Little's drowning. It is expressed in her "acting up, fretting the deweys and meddling . . . newly married couple." It is communicated as well in her "dropping things," in what the narrator calls her unbearable "sulking and irritation," and more tellingly in her "craziness." Reminding us of Raul's surficial and distractive reading of Hilton's psychosis as mere schizophrenia in *The Between,* the narrator associates Sula's "craziness" with natural and thus normal teen behavior. The narrator's psychosomatic, indeed scientific, evaluation of Sula's startling behavior is understandable, because much of that behavior coincides deceptively with the onset of her puberty (53–75). But biology and psychology alter in Sula, just as her facial birthmark darkens and ambiguates.

It is not until the story's part 2, however, with Sula's catalytic "return" in 1937 to Medallion or what extrapolates as her Ọgbañje re-birth after a ten-year absence (read "death"), that Morrison introduces "evil" in narrative lexicon. Morrison then diffuses the idea in the religious consciousness, communal ethos, gendered politics, and racial survivalism of Medallion's black community. Sula's return or her second coming to the Bottom is presaged by a "plague" of robins (89), an event for which the narrator casts her "reincarnation" in supernatural terms.

Upon her return to the Bottom, Sula conducts her self in ways that "defile" the "land." She subverts the gendered, ethical, and even spiritual codes that permeate the Bottom's spatiotemporal linkage with their "ancestors," both living and dead. Illustrative of Sula's insubordination of the land's customs is her heated exchange with her maverick, mythic, and matriarchal grandmother Eva once she steps into the old woman's spatially liberating house. Recalling the Unoka-Nwoye/grandparent-grandchild ontologic inheritance and connections, the confrontation reveals the two women's shared steeliness and their suspicions and embittered memories. It also unwraps Eva's Okonkwo-like quest to retain her *parental* or grandparental control and Sula's intent, as does Ezinma during the Iyi Uwa-excavation episode, to contest, resist, and usurp that right and power. In this scenario, Morrison dress-rehearses the Ọgbañjeic mother/parent-child edgy relationship repeated in *Beloved*. Sula is also disinterested in those socio-biological activities of marriage, maternity, and/or motherhood that patriarchal black males advocated for and assigned to black women in the 1960s. Sula refuses to create another human being by mandate, a decision that anticipates and also finds support in the blues singer Ursa's rejection of that bequeathed burden of "making generations" and perpetuating the white enslaver's hideous legacy of black female desecration in Gayl Jones's *Corregidora* (1975). For now, however—during *this* (her brief) *stay* in Medallion—Sula's attention is not altruistic. Her concern is with her spirit child intent to experience maximally the earth's and life's contradictions which she, as Ọgbañje, embodies. But her quarrel with her grandmother is significant also for two other reasons. One, it signals the very queerness the Bottom totalizes as evil and evil days. Two, it foreshadows the chaos, the Ọgbañje plague, awaiting the Bottom community, as well as Beloved's plaguing of Sethe.

Eva views Sula's de-colonizing insistence on self-governance, her disenchantment with customary marriage and motherhood, as selfishness. Nel, too, fears that Sula is "act[ing] like a man" because of her rebellious specters of sexuality. Okonkwo expresses similarly a patriarchal displeasure with Ezinma's infraction of Igbo cultural dogma when Ezinma sits like a man, with her legs apart. To the conformist Nel, Sula cannot be so uninhibited and daring because she is not just "a woman" but, even more worrisome, "a colored woman at that" (142). An outlaw like her forebear Anyanwu, a "prime example of a female mind controlled by masculine thought patterns" (Personi 443), Sula disrupts the experimental lifestyle often conceded to men. And like Janie Crawford's and Eva Medina Canada's gendered trespasses in Zora Neale Hurston's *Their Eyes Were Watching God* (1937) and Gayl Jones's *Eva's Man* (1976), respectively, Sula forays into privileged male subjectivity and sexual sites. In addition, like Liam's wife's scoff of the divine bargain, Sula's irreverence becomes almost sacrilegious. For instance, when Eva summons as authority the Bible, God, and God's power to judge and punish, Sula wonders, "Which God? The one watched you burn Plum?" And when Eva warns that "Pride goeth before a fall"—resonating the obstacle of lowered ambition that dominant white power and segregationists threw the way of Richard Allen and the 1960s black sociocultural movements—Sula invokes her near-divine Ọgbañje powers. She threatens to "split" the Bottom "in two and everything in it" should anyone attempt to impede her self-actualization (92–93).

Part of that self-fulfillment is inlayed in hunger for (earthly) life and in travel. Or rather, it is rooted in the desire to come and go, to roam unfettered and recursively. Sula's journeys send her drifting circularly from Medallion, Nashville, Detroit, New Orleans, and New York to Philadelphia, Macon, San Diego, and back to Medallion. As do Doro's time-travels, the unnamed preacher-narrator's physical and spiritual migrations, and Hilton James's subconscious peregrinations, Sula's vagrancy parallels the Ọgbañje's errancy, itinerancy, and mockery of bounded space and linear time. Consistent also with the Ọgbañje's resistance to familial permanency, Sula "has trouble with making a [durable] connection with other people."[12] Her one "relationship" with Ajax, a kindred free spirit of sorts whose real/full name, Albert Jacks, she discovers only later, falters. Then the relationship fails no sooner than it begins, in part because against her Ọgbañje knack for liberating detachment Sula yearns for closeness and constancy. Little wonder that Nel at one point describes Sula, who has just burgled Nel's familial and marital space by sleeping with her husband Jude, as sitting there unperturbed, in Nel's bed, like "*a visitor* from out of town" (106, italics added). In other words, in born-to-die parlance, Sula is like Ọgbañje—a traveling intruder, a sojourning spirit dwelling among another family on a temporary albeit mischievous *stay*.

It should be noted, nonetheless, that if Ezinma *stays* ultimately with (the Okonkwo) family in the human realm and thus becomes a "good," understanding (Ọgbañje) girl as the "Ezi" that prefixes her name suggests, it is mostly because of love and sympathy for her long suffering mother, particularly, that she chooses to break her pact with her spirit companions. Ezinma *stays* or "conforms" not exactly because of the patriarchal Okonkwo's intimidating physical size, his human parentage, commands, verbal threats, and assaults. Nor is it because of the Umuofia community's hopes, curiosity, and doubts during the diviner Okagbue Uyanwa's ritual performance. Ezinma *stays* not in uncontested and thus unqualified submission to Okagbue whom she tricks and evades with delight. She tarries because *she wants to* remain with her parents, especially her mother. In her case, Sula, living as does Ezinma in a still male-dominated society and time, reverses Ezinma's sensitivity. Sula refuses to be a good girl by not ingratiating family, friend, and community through compassion or interpersonal and spatial attachment. She resists boundaries and boundedness because forced stasis, with its meanings of confinement and immobility not elected by the self, is not the Ọgbañje's pattern. Nor does it represent for Sula acceptable prospects. Like enslavement and colonization, fixity contains. Thus, because of Sula's preference of waywardness, the Bottom deems her categorically capricious.

Sula's malice grows and the Bottom vilifies her further as the evil one when she commits two additional *nsọ ala,* the Igbo term for cultural taboo against the land. She places her aging grandmother Eva in a Sunnydale nursing home. Then, as just noted, she sleeps with Nel's husband and rationalizes her adultery as friendship. Sula's Ọgbañje-like repeated breaches of "pact"—that is, her phenomenal violations of those communal, familial, friendship, and ethical values/ties *that bind*—earn her pejorative names. They also evoke spirit child mythology. For in addition to a ritual mutilation of the body of a deceased Ọgbañje, the act of disgracing it nominally and socially is another measure that family and community adopt to eradicate the child's "unusual" behavior. Recall Okonkwo, frustrated by Ezinma's evasive detours during the Iyi Uwa excavation, berating her as "you wicked daughter of Akalogoli" (*Things* 82)—Akalogoli being in Igbo cosmos the roving troublous spirits of wicked men or generally people who died a bad death, "Ajo Onwu" or "Onwu Ekwensu" (Obiego 135).[13] The Bottom similarly despises Sula as a pariah. They call her a "roach," "bitch," and "witch." Also, because she "came to their church suppers without underwear, bought their steaming platters of food and merely picked at it—relishing nothing, exclaiming over no one's ribs or cobbler[, they] believed that she was laughing at their God" (114–15). And worse, the men gossip that Sula sleeps with white men, an allegation also levied against black women during the 1960s civil rights and Black Power movements. This accusation stimulates discussions of issues of rape, miscegenation traceable to slavery, integration, and racial betrayal. Together with Shadrack, the shell-shocked war veteran and inaugurator of the now ritualized National Suicide Day—the Bottom's "prophylaxis against disorder"[14]—Sula is stigmatized as a community outcast and one of the Bottom's "Two [d]evils" (117).

Through the black community's discriminatory treatments of those two "devils" Morrison remarks, as does Butler on Anyanwu's related experience, on the problem of intraracial gender demonization. The Bottomites accommodate Shadrack's (male) quirks summated in his National Suicide Day but cast aspersions at Sula. And to fortify themselves against the presence of that now-gendered devil in their midst, the people resort to conjure: "They laid broomsticks across their doors at night and sprinkled salt on porch steps" (113). Interestingly, West African women and families similarly perform rituals to ward off the wandering spirits or the "threats" of the born-to-die Ọgbañje from infiltrating their wombs and households. However, just as the Okonkwo family and Umuofia village accept Ezinma, the problem child and the "evil" Ọgbañje in their midst, and similar to how Umuofia still makes space for its own "pariahs," including the new Christian converts and the osu, the Bottom—despite its resentment of Sula—leaves her physically untouched. "As always," asserts the narrator, "the black people looked at evil stony-eyed and let it run" its course (113; *Things* 185). The Bottom believes that this gendered evil has had its time when Sula dies suddenly.

Sula's short life and quick death and burial situate her deeper in Ọgbañje mythology. Her passing also compels a re-assessment of someone/something the Bottomites simplify as evil. The narrator describes Sula's death as "the best news folks up in the Bottom had had since the promise of work at the tunnel" (150). Although their translation of her death as a sign of better days ahead is bad enough, it is their refusal to bury her themselves that is indeed the most damning. Their decision is a major slight, an act of contempt that borders on severance of kinship ties. It further buttresses their stance that Sula is indeed evil and her body something not to be touched. Descended from African peoples in whose land proper funeral ritual is imperative, and who generally believe life to be cyclical and that ancestors often are reborn among the living, people of the Bottom seem intent on thwarting Sula's passage to the beyond. They neither want her tarnished ancestorship nor desire that she, a pesky Ọgbañje like that in *Arrow of God* (21), *return*—again. Just as the Okonkwo family and the Umuofia village deny one of Ekwefi's dead Ọgbañje children Onwumbiko a proper burial ceremony, the Bottomites refuse to grieve for Sula. They also abandon her body to "strangers," strikingly like Umuofia men who, pursuant to their custom, decline to bring down and bury Okonkwo. They instead transfer to "strangers," to the white man and his posse, the critical last rites for Okonkwo's dangling body which they deem to be "evil" because he disobliged Ala in taking his own life. The Bottomites, too, delegate Sula's interment to white contractors. The black people who attend the burial come not exactly to mourn but rather to confirm their outliving of the evil that was Sula—a woman enchanted with death.

Sula's intrigue with death, her Ọgbañje laughter at death's power to hurt, extends both her defiance of bondage and her search for thrill. Her final uttered response and casual attitude to death's call are seemingly those of a person used to mortality. And the fact that she outlasts death in her postmortem consciousness further underlines her Ọgbañje supernaturality. The idea that "In death Sula returns to infancy [in her curled, fetal death-position], to the watery womb of the river in which she accidentally killed Chicken Little"[15] helps instantiate deductions of her insinuated reincarnation.

Like spirit-children, generally, Sula lives multiple lives. But like Ezinma more specifically, she implicitly undergoes many beginnings, disappearances, and continuations in narrative space and time. Or rather, she has technically "lived," "died," and been "reborn" in several places (Medallion, Nashville, Detroit, New Orleans, Philadelphia, Macon, San Diego, and Medallion). She has drifted, shape-shifted or time-traveled through them for ten years and more. Thus her death in fetal position is revealing. For in that form she prepares to come back, a readiness that anticipates the crouching near a tree of Beloved's exorcized spirit at the novel's end. In other words, Sula in that birth angle is depicted as a baby, the same spirit/baby/child/woman already in the womb, some womb, viable for and awaiting a new life. The discernible imminence of that (re)birth alludes to the near futility of parental, familial, societal, and/or divinatory efforts to contain Ọgbañje. Such regulative attempts are embedded also in the Bottom's disparaging responses to Sula's death. As the narrative ends, Sula meets Nel near a tree—a vegetated location that recalls the Igbo and Yoruba designation of trees as one of spirit child's entry points into the human world. Though returned home, as Ọgbañje, to the immortal realm of spirits, Sula signals through "mud," "leaves," and "soft ball of fur" (174) her still unfettered access to and presence in the human domain. Thus she ultimately triumphs over captivity and conservation.

If Nel, raised in a conservative albeit controlling house, epitomizes Morrison's vision of conventional goodness, Sula alternates as the evil despised among one's people. The narrator even calls her an independent and experimental artist perplexingly unaffiliated with any aesthetic philosophies. She is a baseless, uncontrollable "artist with no art form," "dangerous" and strange (121). But as earlier intimated, Morrison argues against minimalist interpretation of that corporate evil, given that good and evil ironically complement each other and sometimes inhabit and are refracted in the same entity. In other words, like the Ọgbañje child that is both capricious and enabling, or that in theoretical jargon intermediates construction and deconstruction, Sula converges modalities of both customary and metaphysical evil and good. Ezinma, for instance, exerts a powerful, positive influence that reveals her masculinist father's female element. Her presence and nurturance literally restore Okonkwo to life in the wake of Ikemefuna's death, his forced, seven-year exile in Mbanta, and after his humiliating imprisonment by the District Commissioner. More than that, and as recalled in the previous chapters, Okonkwo finds in Ezinma the son he desperately hopes for but believes he lacks in Nwoye. Thus, in what is an extraordinary "sex-role inversion," to invoke Ifi Amadiume's *Male Daughters, Female Husbands* (15), Ezinma becomes a male daughter in an Umuofia/Igbo world that prioritizes maleness. "Amid pervasive change," Aron Aji and Kirstin Lynne Ellsworth remark, Ezinma "stands out as a symbol of hope, renewal, and continuity for both Okonkwo and Umuofia" (174). Similarly, Sula unsettles her community's master mores, yet she constructs an affirmative presence in the Bottom. The irony is that her people do not fully appreciate her, reminiscent of Anyanwu's experience with her Onitsha people. The Bottomites cannot see the overt and subtle benefits that Sula orchestrates in their lives any more than they can see how their lore conjures their lives under oppressive whites, horrible weather, and failed crops.

Sula "clearly conjures with evil," writes Bonnie Barthold, but as an Ọgbañje she is also an enabler, "a means, however ironic, toward both goodness and truth" (110). Sula challenges Nel's righteous assumption about who or what is good. In that unforgettable conversation with Nel later in the story, Sula in her sick bed queries Nel: "How you know it was you? I mean maybe it wasn't you. Maybe it was me" (146). Eva, too, suggests that Nel with whom Sula shares and interchanges human, spiritual, and conceptual essences might be just as "evil" as Sula. Eva accuses Nel of complicity in Chicken Little's death, telling her knowingly that she and Sula are "Just alike. Both of you. Never no difference between you" (169). A child/woman linked to divinity as is Ezinma, Sula understands her creator/creative powers regardless of how much "dirt" the community accuses her. She knows by experience and clairvoyance what her presence and absence mean for the Bottom.

The narrator highlights Sula's value in terms of her charisma and friendship with Nel. But it is in the broader context of how she, as the enabler, "assists" Ala by *forcing* the Bottom to re-define more positively its parental, familial, marital, sexual, and social life, however, that we can best qualify her positivity, both normative and planetary. Sula's capital for her people is magnified once they indict her. The outcomes of their allegations thrust Sula into cosmic operation. She becomes at once destroyer and rebuilder, life and death, order and chaos, unifier and divider; a free force, knowing, unknowable, inseparable, unbreakable, protean. She is such a catalyst that even her mystifying birthmark is provocative.

A form of Ọgbañje branding that foreshadows the "tree" in Sethe's back, Sula's birthmark, her kaleidoscopic facial stem rose, is polysemous. Just as Ezinma's esoteric Iyi Uwa generates talk in Umuofia, Sula's mysterious stem rose equally instigates speculations. As a grotesque text of history, it insinuates slavery's heinous, physical, and social lacerations of the black body. The mark could also be seen as a sociomythic impression of Sula's racial, gendered, and aesthetic difference. In other words, it reads further as an insignia of her otherworldliness, timelessness, elusiveness, defiance, powers, and survivalism. We are reminded that some of the "really evil" Ọgbañje children "were not deterred by mutilation, but came back with all" their occultic "scars" (*Things* 185). And although it stigmatizes her, striking her triply as *woman, native, other,* to invoke Trinh Min-ha (1989), Sula's inscrutable mark is productive. It is a power-point, an enigma that indirectly expands the Bottom's folk and mythic consciousness. In addition, her body's baffling immunity to natural law at age thirty—a prefiguration of the infant-woman Beloved—also gives the town's women something to pontificate on. In short, like a knotty proverb, Sula's mystifying "difference" animates theory. And expectedly, it has inspired diverse hypotheses even among literary critics to whom the mark signifies various things.

Morrison infers, however, that in an organic yet mystifying universe where a life force permeates all, good and evil or at least their semantic properties are perceptible even in the elements. An understanding of Ọgbañje's ideologic extensions makes that point clearer. Morrison intimates that nature's creative principles, including sun, earth, wind, fire, water, and even fruits such as tomato, are "good" or can and do effect positive outcomes, because of their benefits to life. But the Bottom knows too well adverse encounters with nature. For instance: its relationship with a restive river that takes Chicken Little or a little chicken for pacification in what translates as an appeasement ritual sacrifice; the fire that fatally burns Hannah; the destructive wind; a sun whose appearance sets in motion events that culminate in community catastrophe by the river. These elements that sustain life also take it. They wrest it with a perplexing Ọgbañje-indifference. Like Ala the Igbo earth goddess who destroys while she nourishes,[16] and as in Ọgbañje's life-mortality oscillations, those forces conflate creative and negativist energies. Nature, like Sula, like the Ọgbañje, is bewildering.

* * *

In *Sula* Morrison has told a story steeped in irony anthropomorphized in its eponym. The novel responds to the 1960s and early 1970s formal developments, political tensions, and aesthetic conversations. A neo-slave and postmodernist narrative constructed thematically and formally around the characteridea of spirit child, *Sula* begins by or rather would not go forward without returning to the past of slavery. It instructively opens with the Bottom's myth of land and land occupancy. From *that* past it proceeds with remarkable artistry to narrate the lingering effects of that initial Africa-Europe encounter on the Bottom. *Sula* nicely welds together art and politics, ethics and aesthetics. It dismantles gendered typecasting, advances black feminist/womanist agenda and, concomitantly, refuses to standardize the African American (woman's) personality. A didactic as well as racially and culturally conscious writer, Morrison alters and thus expands the traditional novel form. Like Achebe, Butler, Due, and Wideman, she *blackens* the genre with African American and African/ "Third World" religious beliefs and cultural practices syncretized in the New World. And similar to its predecessor, for instance Ernest J. Gaines's *Of Love and Dust* (1967) whose protagonist Marcus Payne rejects neo-plantation captivity, *Sula* unravels also as a signifyin(g) "protest" novel.[17] Its structural and thematic iconoclasm centers, however, not on a black male quester for liberty and identity, but rather on a female Ọgbañje figure. It focuses on an uncolonizable spirit child that upsets "domestic" norms and rebuffs a life of "slavery" in its twentieth-century incarnations.

Sula traverses issues of early through late twentieth-century African American history. It addresses the politics of war, definitions, naming, love, integration, modernity, and urbanity relative to blacks in the United States. As Winthrop D. Jordan writes in *White Over Black* (1968), the New World has negativized blackness since its colonial-settler days. The U.S., in this case, is a nation that during slavery exploited the black woman's body with impunity. But it belittles if not ignores—ironically, as Sula's experience symbolizes—the many ways African-descended people and their presence continue to humanize the country, *forcing* it to live out its founding democratic principles. Through Sula's Anyanwu-like ordeal with "marking," Morrison stresses the costs of gendered and group branding, and the perils of integration for blacks.

Morrison posits also that what we sometimes hastily embrace as "progress" could be dis-abling. For even with its potential to empower blacks, racial integration concurrently gentrified and dispossessed them, and thus is ambiguously "good" and "evil." Morrison emphasizes, however, that a (black) community that invalidates its members' Chi, their individualities and potentials, prolongates slavery's intent. Yet as Okonkwo's conflicts with Umuofia's codes of temperance amplify, and as Ezeulu the powerful chief priest realizes in his own quarrels with his people in *Arrow of God,* no single person is or can be so mighty that he or she would displace a people's collective wisdom or impede their group survival. Nevertheless, after the forty-six years covered in *Sula's* "linear" time, after over forty-six years of waiting and hoping and enduring, what do blacks steered intentionally toward American society's bottom have to show for those years, except failed promises, dreams deferred, pervasive suffering, and senseless, "cyclic" deaths.

In apprehending the semantics of death in born-to-die mythology, we apprehend *Sula* better. We make greater sense of Morrison's sustained meditation on the immanence and repetitiousness of suffering and death. Morrison's inauguration of death as character and leitmotif in *Sula*/Sula anticipates the Dead family of *Song of Solomon,* the dead and undead of *Paradise,* but especially the Ọgbañje of *Beloved*. Consistent with Ọgbañje's mediation of diabolism and construction, which Sharon Patricia Holland also notes correctly here, the child-spirit Beloved is "a blessing to those who wish to know her and a promoter of chaos to those who do not" (51). Morrison suggests, however, that "Death" can be challenged, if construed in the Bottom's case as white power and antebellum slavery's (re)incarnations in twentieth-century Jim Crow segregation and more contemporary acts of (gendered) subjugation. Ekwefi confronts Death illustratively in her seditious naming of one of her children "Death may please himself." She dares death also the night Agbala's priestess Chielo consecrates the sick Ezinma before the oracle. "Death" can also be endured, as reified in Ekwefi's overcoming of the trauma of repeated infant mortality and in Umuofia's collective survival and surpassing of slavery's extensions: imperialism and colonization.

Comparably, that not all black Medallions perish in the Bottom bridge tragedy testifies to the above points. For even as Sula leaves her best friend Nel in "circles and circles of sorrow" as the novel ends, Nel is alive. Nel lives past the immediate horror of a Medallion black community that loses its gendered center, falls apart, and is uprooted and gentrified subsequently from its homestead, as though by the Middle Passage and New World slavery proper. And in Nel's and the other Bottomites' "escape" of the catastrophe is a message of hope, one that heralds the positivity of Sethe's racialized survival of slavery's haunting and her start of healing as *Beloved*'s narration closes.

Excavating a Horrid and Haunting Past, Imagining a Healing Closure: Beloved

In one of the most indelible racial encounters in *Beloved*—the scene of "life"/ Denver's birth, featuring two fugitives: a pregnant slave Sethe escaping a traumatizing Kentucky plantation Sweet Home and a white girl Amy Denver on her way to Boston for velvet—Amy reminds Sethe that "Anything dead coming back to life hurts" (35). Amy's statement is dense, despite its appearance pages into a polyvocal novel in which Morrison keeps alive the long disremembered but true story of Margaret Garner. As Steven Weisenburger historicizes the event in captivating detail, Garner was a twenty-two-year-old Kentucky slave and mother of four. During a bold but failed escape in 1856, Garner preemptively murdered her illicitly begotten, mulatto infant Mary (44–49) not just in rejection of Mary's assured life of bondage but as a reprisal of her white master Archibald Kinkead Gaines's sexual and other abuses. The Garner case would be "the longest, most expensive and dramatic fugitive slave trial in United States history" (5).

Amy's remark addresses also and connects the novel's major themes. For instance, it alludes to the physical pain that Sethe suffers from Amy's reviving massage of her swollen (read: "dead") legs. The almost fantastical Sethe-Amy meeting actually precedes Sethe's murder of Beloved. As such, Amy's reminder equally forebodes the persecuting siege of Beloved's spiritual and subsequently bravado "physical" return, her second coming to and haunting of 124 Bluestone Road, "an arena for cosmic and terrestrial interrelations" (Washington, *Our Mothers* 227). Beloved returns after Paul D fails to exorcize her completely in what resembles Okonkwo's confrontational shouts and threats at Ezinma during the Iyi Uwa excavation. Sethe's mother-in-law Baby Suggs's Cincinnati home would become Sethe's residence for about twenty years. And most important, Amy's assertion houses the story's unifying concern with the generational burden and emancipative potential of memory, especially those "memories within," which Morrison calls "the subsoil" of her work.[18] Reminiscent of Wideman's epigraph "Prepare your luggage as though for exile" that also alerts readers to the long, zigzagging, and taxing narration ahead in *The Cattle Killing,* Morrison forewarns that the buried stories that *Beloved*/Beloved exhumes would be long and painful. Morrison demonstrates through Sethe's experiences, however, that it is by recognizing and facing that awful past, rather than by avoiding it, that we can have some "closure." This is not to say, though, that the story *and* the semantics of Beloved "close" totally. As Martha Cutter postulates, Morrison continues the Beloved saga in *Jazz.*[19]

In any case, that truth-telling is critical. It is needed because, as Morrison has noted, the United States, in its quest to suppress or camouflage the ugliest and without question the most embarrassing chapter in its democratic history, has tended to downplay the severity of New World slavery. Such an amnesic misrepresentation, which slavery-apologist Ulrich B. Phillips championed in his *Life and Labor in the Old South* (1929), trivializes the degree to which the trans-Atlantic slavery's aftershocks continue, like Ọgbañje, to time-travel and interpose cyclically and malevolently in the nation's and African diaspora's collective memory and sociopsychic health.

Morrison dedicates *Beloved* to the "Sixty Million and more" victims and survivors of that history-shaping calamity. These are human beings whose stories are often forgotten, falsified, or untaught in discussions of both the slavery experience and African-descended people's mammoth albeit minimized contributions to the United States. For instance, the building of America's greatest megalopolis, New York City, is often mostly conceded to European and Anglo-American ingenuity, Michael L. Blakey writes. In 1991, just four years after the publication of *Beloved,* however, Americans were shocked at the discovery of a colonial cemetery, an "African Burial Ground," in one of the city's construction sites. More than four hundred interments of slaves were unearthed at the location. And it was possible that "twenty thousand original burials" took place "in the total 5.5-acre burial ground" (222–31). New Yorkers were astounded and outraged once again, fourteen years later. In 2005, Felicia R. Lee reports, the New-York Historical Society opened the "Slavery in New York" exhibition, a stunning display that "illustrates the centrality of 200 years of slavery to the growth of New York City."[20] The above events, coupled with the recent disclosures that the founders of some of America's Ivy League and other prestigious institutions traded in and/or held slaves,[21] argue three things, at least. They lampoon the white-ingenuity thesis, testify to the aliveness of captivity and the past, and powerfully justify Morrison's election of dedicatees in *Beloved.*

Morrison thus poses the following related questions in the novel. How can Americans—as a people made "kindred" by that scourge, as Butler inculcates—not repeat anything that internecine as a new millennium dawns? How can African-descended people, particularly, continue to stay vigilant, however, without letting that still ravenous holocaust and its rebirths "consume" them into a literal and symbolic deadly emaciation and insanity? How can black people unpack, sort through, and re-assemble into a coherent narrative the constitutive shards of their disrupted histories? Put simply, how can they, like Anyanwu, Allen, Okonkwo, Azaro, Hilton, and Sula, take control of their own self-definitions and destinies individually, collectively, and aesthetically instead of surrendering them to their oppressors?

Linden Peach is right in observing that "[i]n some respects *Beloved* draws upon [and responds to] the black aesthetic discourse of the 1960s." That discourse's chief aims included "self-reconstruction and re-definition through deconstructing Western assumptions about blackness." The aesthetic was preoccupied also with an issue central to *Beloved,* namely, the "unearthing [of] narratives which have been hidden by or buried within other narratives" (94). In *Beloved,* Morrison uncovers Garner's story. More important, the Garner slave revolt offers Morrison a legendary ancestor *as foundation,* an inspiriting superstructure upon which she can initiate a re-visioning of blackness and the racial self in an exercise of literary archaeology. Morrison also found expressions of maternal strength and women's nobility captured just as powerfully in the graphic pictures of the dead, especially one of a deceased girl, collected in James Van Der Zee's *Harlem Book of the Dead* (1978), the foreword to which Morrison penned. In evaluating the compilation as "neither sentimental nor reactionary" but rather "stunning" in the pictures'/stories' "narrative quality ... intimacy ... [and] humanity," and in celebrating the work as a "remarkable concert of Black subject, Black poet [Owen Dodson], Black photographer and Black artist," Morrison at once alludes to and signifies on the nationalist aesthetic's literary conceit, emotionalism, and propagandism. She also insinuates *Harlem* as an exemplary black art. And most important, Morrison uses the occasion of her preamble to reflect on that *Beloved*-anticipating theme of "nostalgia: a love affair with the past." This yearning to unbury and memorialize *the dead* is "made more loving," Morrison opines, "because the beloved is no longer with us and able to assert itself." Noting correctly that the dead portrayed in *Harlem* are "So living, so 'undead,'" Morrison concludes that Van Der Zee's collaborative visual text confirms "what Africans say: 'The Ancestor lives as long as there are those who remember'" ("Foreword").

Even with the above memorable germs in hand, Morrison still needed an implement to navigate the historical digging. She required an apparatus with which to knit the other formal, political and philosophical dimensions of the novel, including her continued authorial fascination with good and evil. To help her meet those challenges of narrativization, to undertake literarily that task of historical reassembly that requires "journeys"/migrations back to and from Garner's past, Morrison returns to the trope of child spirit. We have earlier granted that the narrator does not qualify either Sula or Beloved specifically as "Ọgbañje." Actually, Beloved functions pluralistically in the story. To "superstitious" Sethe, for example, Beloved is her dead child come back to life. Denver is certain that Beloved is her sister. Beloved is also a cryptograph of the many thousands gone, the casualties of the Middle Passage, those Africans who were involuntarily expropriated to "this place from the other (livable) place" (198). Beloved functions additionally as part of the supernatural, a wayfaring spirit from the nether world. And, critics that view her as an externalization of history and (Sethe's) traumatized memory have a point and thus should not be dismissed.

Ostensibly, that indistinct identification of Beloved opens up many interpretive interstices. Also, Morrison is reputed to be prodigiously familiar with African diaspora and Western mythologies whose subtleties she loops into her works. As a result of the aforementioned indistinction and Morrison's deft intertextuality, the fullest unveiling of which requires a "knowledge of the multiplicity of literary and cultural confluences that constitute American identity" (Stave 1), critics have understandably tracked Morrison's source for Beloved's character to various quarries. They include the genii, the succubus, and the Zairean bakulu. Others are the Sierra Leonean Mende spirit myth, Haitian/Afro-Caribbean religion, Yoruba *Àjẹ́* and Obatala, Greek Persephone, the Biblical myth of Cain, and the repressed (un)conscious of psychoanalysis.[22] These reviews of the novel are important, for they help magnify the semantic depth and cultural contours of a story that is as arresting as it is solicitous of audience input.

The present illumination of *Beloved*/Beloved against the template of Ọgbañje mythology, Ezinma, and the Ezinma-Ekwefi matrix complements the above insights. It deviates from them, however, in redirecting attention to a potential albeit critically ignored Achebean imprint on the text. My interrogation departs also from and yet complements Ogunyemi's "An Abiku-Ogbanje Atlas" and Angelyn Mitchell's reading of Beloved in *The Freedom to Remember* (2002). Although Ogunyemi also inevitably mentions Ezinma and Achebe, she nonetheless accentuates *Beloved*'s resonances of the "àbíkú" dynamic in Soyinka's autobiography *Aké: The Years of Childhood*. Mitchell, on the other hand, identifies Harriet Jacobs's *Incidents in the Life of a Slave Girl* as the major, antecedent black woman's text to which *Beloved* responds. In their stresses, "Atlas" and *Freedom* de-emphasize *Things Fall Apart,* Ezinma, and the Ezinma-Ekwefi experience. They also overlook Morrison's expressed aesthetic and philosophic debt to Achebe. The Achebe impact includes Morrison's appreciation of Achebe's stylistic and quite possibly cultural legitimization of her own work—the "doors" she acknowledged he opened for her. Achebe's influence might be registered also in Morrison's interest in Igbo world and philosophy, and how facets of Igbo cosmology have probably been extracted into or compare with the subtlest details of antebellum and contemporary African American culture and consciousness.

Nevertheless, *Beloved*'s manifestations of Ọgbañje epistemes suggest therefore the extent to which, as in *Things Fall Apart,* the ideological extensions of the born-to-die trope shape the novel's eponym. Those idiomatic tributaries also inflect the story's various concerns, particularly its critically under-studied interest in good and evil, as well as its insistence on salvific rememory. A look at the Ọgbañje conceptual estuaries, composited below, can help us better put the rest of this chapter's argument into perspective.

One of the most obvious ontological parallels between Beloved and Ezinma is Beloved's death and "rebirth," along with her station as spirit and matter. But the similarities are deeper than that. Like Ezinma, Beloved is suggestively and prayerfully named. And not only is the reincarnated, older Beloved drawn to stories and call-and-response storytelling sessions with Sethe as Ezinma is with Ekwefi, but she does not call Sethe "mother," referring to her rather by name. Allusive in ways to Ezinma but mostly to the other conceptual branches of the born-to-die, Morrison figures Beloved as "homeless" and a time traveler. Beloved is invasive, evasive, cunning, tyrannical, erratic, de-centered, shape-shifting, and clairvoyant. To the thirty Cincinnati colored women on course to confront the physically marked

Beloved, to unearth her Iyi Uwa sort of, she is "[t]he devil-child." Reminiscent also of Ezinma, the narrator describes Beloved as precocious, "clever," "beautiful," and with a "dazzling smile" (261). In addition, Beloved's spiritual ingress and egress into the human realm are associated with water, trees, and woods, recalling both Sula and the Igbo deities Nne Mmiri's and Onabuluwa's cosmic checkpoints. Mimicking also Ezinma's cyclic, back-and-forth trips into Ekwefi's life, Beloved is an in-between, a transient, migrant, and border-crosser that bridges space and time, as well as the abodes of the dead, the living, and the unborn. For at the end of the narrative Beloved becomes an-unborn-in-waiting, a depiction Morrison initiated earlier in Sula's death in fetal position. That is, after the women's ritualistic opposition of Beloved, we are told with a cautious timbre that Beloved is finally gone. To Paul D, the re-emergence of the ancient and spirit-sensing dog Here Boy confirms her exit. But Ella knows that "people who die bad," what the Igbo call *ajọ ọnwụ* or *ọnwụ ekwensu,* "don't stay in the ground" (188). Thus whether divined as an Ọgbañje spirit or as guilt, memory, history, the dead, and the brutal past, Beloved lives on. And as the narrator warns, she/it could just be concealed in the "trees," expecting another opportunity to return (263), like the fetal Sula.

In addition, Morrison's variation on the spirit-child drama recalls *Things Fall Apart* in terms of *Beloved's* rendition of an Ezinma-Ekwefi dynamic in the Beloved-Sethe tense relationship rehearsed in the Sula-Eva intense debacle. Like Achebe, and indeed like Butler and Wideman, Morrison treats the born-and-die myth and the Sethe-Beloved kinship in the context of tough love and (child) deliverance. Or more precisely, she navigates it as a love story, the love between mother and child, in this case a powerful and otherworldly child whose uncertain earthly *stay* keeps the bereaved mother Sethe distressed, aggrieved, and vigilant. Similar to Ekwefi's situation, Sethe's encounter with an Ọgbañje, in Beloved, complicates her mothering and motherhood. For in obliging the tyrannical Beloved, Sethe is forced to adjust to the reversals of the power dynamic between parent and child. And just as Ekwefi over-indulges Ezinma, who must be placated, with adult delicacies such as eggs as part of her counter-offensive to make Ezinma *stay,* Sethe also goes to length to satiate Beloved's inquisitions, tantrums, and appetites. She lures Beloved with scarce "eggs" and other "fancy food" (240). We note, remembering Sula's filial impermanency, that part of Sethe's anxiety, the reason she so entices and propitiates Beloved, is her knowing or suspecting that the reincarnated Beloved might not *stay* but would "leave," again, thus adding to her child "losses." Her two boys, Burglar and Howard, had already disappeared, petrified by Beloved's spiritual and physical haunting of 124 Bluestone Road. Little wonder the narrator earlier calls Beloved a "sweet, if peculiar, guest" (57). And when Denver discusses Beloved with the Bodwins' black housekeeper Janey Wagon, the narrator qualifies Beloved as a "visit[or]" (255). Interestingly, Nel and *Sula*'s narrator describe Sula in related terms also.

Returning now to the rest of this chapter's focus, Morrison echoes Achebe also in how for her the child-spirit myth, as played out in the Sethe-Beloved mother-daughter experience and in Beloved's ontology, uploads the topical issue of good and evil. Morrison revisits that philosophical subject, which she marinated in *Sula/* Sula, in the two major enigmas that *Beloved* raises. One, we are called upon to join the novel's internal jury in responding to the question of whether it is ethically defensible or unconscionable for an enslaved mother to substitute one abomination, slavery, with another, child-murder (see Botste in "Things Fall Together"). Trudier Harris has also noted Morrison's effort to get the audience involved in the storytelling act and in addressing the novel's ultimate moral question (144). Paradox number two is Beloved's Ọgbañje duality. On one hand is her malevolence and, on the other, her positivist situation as an agitator, a trigger, a kind of change agent that helps set in motion Sethe's as well as Paul D's healing rememories of their repressed pasts.

Morrison positions the Cincinnati black community as a jury, the "in-house" jury of Sethe's peers. Their informal/unofficial adjudications of Sethe's infanticide, in contrast to the antebellum white law's predictable verdict on it, constitute an intratextual, racialized deliberation of the "crime" and, concordantly, on the question of evil. As with the Medallion black community's reactions to Sula's misdemeanors, or perhaps anticipating those reactions, antebellum black Cincinnati is characterized as having shrewd, complicated but ultimately land-based views on evil. As though asking "Why did [s/]he do it?"—that rhetorical question Okonkwo overhears when he kills the white man's messenger and fails to rouse Umuofia to war (*Things* 205)—Sethe's townsfolk disapprove of her chosen course of action. They respond to it with a sense of disdain and survivalist outrage. They also see Sethe as proud, selfish, and deserving of her domestic tribulations. Identifying "good" in Baby Suggs (the "unchurched" and venerated evangelist, transcendentalist, and mender of impaired soles/souls) and "evil" in the child-killer's act and comportment, they ostracize Sethe. We hear that even the incorruptible and compassionate Stamp Paid who ferried Sethe and her children to "Canaan," across the Ohio River, now worries that he has been tainted by the town's harsh judgment of Sethe. That perhaps clarifies his hasty and inconsiderate disclosure of the newspaper clipping about Sethe's crime to Paul D.

Paul D responds emotionally and subjectively to the question of the crime. He initially is unable to see the "tree," the grotesque scars, on Sethe's back. His skepticism of Stamp Paid's revelation, his incredulity that Sethe has "shape"-shifted from her husband Halle's Sweet Home girl to a fearless and complex woman and his judging of her decision to kill her child all suggest that to him her "crime" is horrifying and unjustified. In addition, Paul D considers Sethe's mother-love to be "too thick." He concludes that death (her killing her baby) is worse than Sweet Home and School Teacher, and then suggests that she should have run away instead. He would later regret his rashness and certainties and try to make amends by vouching to put her story next to his as they attempt to forge a family together. Yet his abandonment of her after assuming a righteous stance is just as condemning as the community's virtuous indignation. Without saying so, he makes her a bad mother and a sinful woman. Like Sula, Sethe is outcast by her people, for eighteen years. And still like Sula, she refuses to succumb to the townspeople's conjure, their aspersions, or sense of moral superiority. Sethe is hurt, however, that the blessed Paul D who awakens her past and unloads on her his sufferings in Alfred, Georgia could not bear her own burdensome news.

Conversely, Baby Suggs, yet another juror, cannot bring herself to either endorse or damn Sethe's choice. A mother of eight children, all lost to slavery, Baby Suggs, like Sethe, has known the nastiness of life and the cruelty of whites. Her decision is to dedicate the remainder of her life, her freed life, to existential oneness. Baby Suggs intends to contemplate color in a country whose residences are all haunted, each house "packed to its rafters with some dead Negro's grief" (4–5). However, it is Ella—*Beloved*'s version of an Obierika, Okonkwo's greatest friend, foil, and *Things Fall Apart*'s intellectual, philosopher, and cultural critic—through whom Morrison espouses what stands as her "balancing" perspective on the matter.

As does Baby Suggs, Ella construes Sethe's crime and hence her "evil" as situational and relative. Much more like Obierika, however, Ella carries *Beloved*'s unifying moral philosophy. Therefore, a comparativist understanding of the Ọgbañje myth, pre-colonial Igbo religion, Umuofia view on crime, criminality and redemption, as well as Obierika's specific intervention would help us contextualize better black Cincinnati's verdicts on Sethe's bloody act. The illustrative Igbo backdrop would assist us in answering these interlocking questions: "Why ostracism?" and "What has 'land'/'Ala' got to do with it?" Furthermore, that Igbo response tightens our agreement with Ella's counseling of moderation in the black community's dealings with Sethe.

Readers of *Things Fall Apart* may recall the moment of unforeseen tragedy and criminalization in the novel, the funeral of Ogbuefi Ezeudu, when Okonkwo's gun explodes accidentally, killing Ezeudu's sixteen-year-old son. In Umuofia, the narrator reveals, "It was a crime against the earth goddess to kill a clansman, and a man who committed it must flee from the land." The offense has two levels: "male" and "female." That is, first-degree, premeditated murder and second-degree, accidental killing or manslaughter, respectively. Because Okonkwo's violation is the "female" kind, he and his family are banished for seven years after which they can and do return and reintegrate fully with the village. Upon Okonkwo's exile, Umuofia men destroy his property. They are merely executing the Earth goddess Ala's justice and seeking to "cleans[e] the land" that Okonkwo has contaminated with a clansman's blood. But after Ala's decree has been implemented, Obierika agonizes over Okonkwo's misfortune. He wonders why his friend should pay so dearly for an unintentional homicide. But even though Obierika mulls the issue with characteristic rigor and earnestness, deepened into poignancy because he too has lost twins upon Ala's mandate, he discovers no controlling explanation. In his pre-postmodernist thought, he encounters instead "greater complexities" in thinking about the power of the land, the inscrutability and sometimes problematic arbitrariness of deital jurisprudence, and the frightening inseparability of one and all. It is this consequential interdependence of self and community that Igbo/Umuofia elders coded in the proverb: "if one finger brought oil it soiled the others" (124–25).

Morrison echoes, revises, and extends Achebe here. She seemingly signifies on the above powerful moment by gendering her own "Obierika" as female. Supposing that antebellum black Cincinnati had syncretized its African cosmological precepts on the crime-land dialectic into its Protestant Christianity, then that community's ostracism of Sethe might have another cultural explanation. It could be interpreted also from a religious, ritualistic, and spiritual standpoint and not simply as an expression of the community's abhorrence of Sethe's pride and self-sufficiency. Understood from such a metaphysical angle, then, Sethe's implicit banishment untangles as a cosmic imperative. It unpacks, in short, as the people's stoic attempt to purify the land of Sethe's "desecration" with the blood of a clanswoman, a female child. Comparable to the pacificatory understones of Chicken Little's implicitly sacrificial death in *Sula,* the broader goal of the Sethe sentence is to reconcile Sethe with community, and also Sethe with the transgressed earth, *Ala,* whose foreseeable wrath on the collective must be avoided at all cost. And just as there must be an end to Okonkwo's penalty for his "female" wrongdoing, however, Sethe's punishment for her crime of passion, her equally unpremeditated and circumstantial abomination, ought to be attenuated also.

Thus, although some Mosesian-law or retributionist black Cincinnatians insist that Sethe "had it coming"—referring to Beloved's battering of her—Ella knows full well, as does Obierika in Okonkwo's case, that "What's fair ain't necessarily right." And while it is true that "You can't just up and kill your children," to Ella "the children can't just up and kill the mama" (256). Things evidently are not that infallible, especially not in an abstruse world where, Ella opines, nothing is totally dependable, a universe in which "solution" and "problem" are indistinguishable (256). As their divergent responses to the murder indicate, and as Ella's adroit convictions relay, the jurors' apparent deadlock on Sethe's crime—reminiscent of the protracted "public opinion battle [that] raged" over the Garner case[23]— demonstrates a point that the trope of spirit child enables Morrison to translocate from *Sula,* namely, the quicksands of reductive universalism.

In addition, just as Ezinma and Sula make excellent case studies on good and evil, Ekwefi's and Sethe's mothering lends more tonnage to Ella's idea regarding the ambiguities of "fair" and "right," "problem" and "solution." Underlying both Ekwefi's fierce sheltering of Ezinma and Sethe's defensive, offensive, and spiteful infanticide is the quest for Emancipation. Both women's acts are clearly well-meaning. Their unthinkable activisms, like Anyanwu's suicidal option, are driven by their motherly intents to keep their children safe by any means possible. Ekwefi and Sethe desire to liberate their progenies from two interrelated kinds of forced "abduction" and "captivity" that translate life/living and death/dying as functionally equivalent. Seethed and steeled by life, Ekwefi battles Death to affirm life, Ezinma's life, and manumit her beloved and only begotten child from (spirit) bondage. She fights to humanize Ezinma and save her from capture by and allegiance to a subjugating preternatural Ọgbañje cult/colony *ndi otu* explained in chapter 1. Beset and toughened, similarly, by a life of slavery and sexual abuse, Sethe murders Beloved. She is pressured by that emotional state that bell hooks, seconding James Baldwin,[24] aptly calls "the killing rage." At some point in their encounter with whites and racism, hooks guarantees, many a black person would feel that eruption of fury (1–20). And thus incensed, Sethe kills her already crawling baby—Beloved's best thing—to avouch Beloved's right to life.

To some, Sethe's infanticide, her antebellum black power performance, may seem irrational, extreme, reactive, and contradictory. But really her seeming implausible choice is not without literary and historical precedents, as discussed in chapter 3. Sethe's aim is to rescue Beloved from abduction into slavery and propertization by the New World version of the *ndi otu.* In *Beloved,* this antebellum pedigree of the metaphoric spirits of death and misery, the "soul stealers,"[25] is structured and embodied in the collectivity of Sweet Home, School Teacher, his nephew that suckles Sethe, slave raiders, catchers, drivers, the white sheriff, and the Fugitive Slave Act of 1850. The "cult" comprises the novel's Mr. and Mrs. Garner, slave auctions, Slave Codes, whippings, lynchings, fatal maimings, arsons, rapes, castrations, jails, and chain gangs. It subsumes white naming and animalizing of black human beings, as well as every other clandestine Southern hospitality that hoisted many a black body into "strange fruit,"[26] and thus aided the peculiar institution in its Ọgbañje-like early, violent, unnatural, and repeated thefts of the black body, black children and black life. The cult encapsulates, most of all, the peculiar institution's diabolical intent to despoil the black woman's womb, her somatic space, as a vessel for ideological immortality and white power. The narrator makes it clear: slavery sought to perpetuate black women as free and self-reproducing chattel.

Through Sethe's Ekwefi-like tough, oppositional, and sacrificial mothering Morrison extends *Things Fall Apart*. But she also puns, on gendered lines, on one of the most sacred and canonical of Western Christian letters, the *Bible* as master text. Herbert Aptheker has noted how antebellum planters and clergymen consciously misquoted the Bible as part of slavocracy's "complex and thorough systems of control" (53). By adulterating scripture and even the American constitution as their "strategies of containment,"[27] slaveholders attempted to keep slaves ignorant, humble, pious, docile, and immobile. As erstwhile slave Henry Bibb avers, it is because the religion-professing slaveholders hypocritically denied their chattel meaningful awakening and enlightenment but instead had them "educated in the school of adversity, whips, and chains," and also because they "preach[ed] a pro-slavery doctrine," that slaves distrusted the master's brand of religious pedagogy and moral responsibility (12, 17). And some slaves, like Bibb himself, had to philosophically and practically redefine the then-prevailing notions of ethics, slave love, slave marriage, fidelity, black parenthood, family, virtue, authority, slave community, freedom and social agency.[28]

In that vein, Morrison suggests through *Beloved* that historically enslaved and colonized blacks generally, and black women specifically, have learned to "clarify" scripture heretically, as Bibb intimates. African-descended people have re-read, adopted and adapted God's apparently ironic example—His creation of life/good in death/evil. For God so loved the world, the scripture states, that He gave His only begotten and beloved son, Jesus, whose death God arguably practically masterminded, authorized and "permitted" in order to subvert an oppressive Order: sin. God's revolutionary life-taking has long been elaborated in black liberation struggle and creative writing. As discussed previously, the repetition-and-extension has sometimes taken the shape of black Jacobins like Sethe and the eponymous Dessa Rose willing to pay or in fact paying the ultimate measure for freedom and for an end to racism and the irreversible destruction of white supremacy. It also takes the shape of that second philosophic riddle that Morrison poses through the spirit child. That is, Beloved's malevolence but then her facilitation of both Sethe's rememory and her start of healing.

That Beloved, seen as a wicked Ọgbañje, "plague[s]" and "bedevil[s]" her mother Sethe is an understatement (254, 255). Beloved's acerbity toward Sethe is such that she circumvents the mother-child power differential. She warps a guilt-consumed Sethe into an obedient, subdued, and helpless child. Beloved almost strangles her. She assaults and emaciates Sethe to the point that Denver is forced to seek outside intervention. Even Denver herself, whose filial claim of Beloved is just as possessive as Sethe's and for whom Beloved's domestic companionship breaks 124 Bluestone Road's isolation and solitude, does not escape Beloved's admonition and fury. We remember also how the powerful and retributive Beloved vengefully, sexually, and spatially "fixes" the pseudo-dibia/exorcist Paul D, who had deemed her an "evil" presence and, worse, interfered in the Sethe-Denver-Beloved trinity and Beloved's malicious "plans" for Sethe.

Similar to how Ezinma and Sula cause their parents and the community at large grief and anxiety and yet are positive influences, Beloved with all her "evil" stands as a cardinal "force" among the characters *and* in the novel's composition and emotive power. As a "characteridea" with capacity to time-travel, it is the child spirit Beloved through whom Morrison achieves the novel's space-time interpositions, its fragmented floorplan and discontinuous historicity. Linden Peach asserts: "The sense of fracture which is at the heart of the book—together with a concomitant sense of healing—is maintained, if not actually initiated, by the slippage of the signifier [the shape-shiftings of] 'Beloved' throughout the novel" (102). In addition, Beloved's presence awakens a recognition of her ethereality, Karla F. C. Holloway argues. And it is she Beloved, Holloway states, that mediates the story's "historical, contemporary, and spiritual spaces" (*Moorings* 168). Beloved, as Ọgbañje, effectuates the novel's aesthetic postmodernism. She empowers Morrison conceptually to make the story simultaneously oral and aural through Morrison's use of a felt audience and Beloved-related anthropomorphic keynotes such as "124 WAS SPITEFUL. Full of a baby's venom," "124 WAS LOUD," and "124 WAS QUIET." Beloved lures Sethe to unfetter "the 'ghosts' that are harbored by memory and that hold their 'hosts' in thrall, tyrannically dictating thought, emotion, and action."[29] In short, Beloved "challenges others to face the pain and shame of the past."[30]

I stated in chapter 1 that, in the spirit child mythic drama, the spirit's return to and rebirth in the same household amounts to something dead—a past, the past, and its polyvalent significations—that comes back to life and cognition. The return of the dead, in an Ọgbañje's reincarnation, stirs all manner of vigil and parental responses from vocal and nominal to visceral and performative. In *Things Fall Apart,* for instance, that activation is clearest in Ekwefi's child-naming rituals. It is expressed in her brooding attentiveness, her instinctive, frenetic reactions each time Ezinma's life is or seems to be threatened by god, man, and fever. That catalysis is noted also in *The Cattle Killing* in how the preacher's meeting with Liam and his wife thaws the couple's frozen and unvoiced pasts. Sethe, too, undergoes a similar catharsis, courtesy of her encounters with Beloved, in Beloved's incarnations as spirit, ghost, flesh, guilt, memory, history, ancestor, and/or "pilot."

In *Song of Solomon,* Pilate guides her "blind" nephew Milkman Dead on his flight toward *life* masked as his ancestral legacy. Similarly, Beloved as pilot maneuvers Sethe through those sore, concealed, and yet empowering spaces of our collective (black) history. And equally, in August Wilson's neo-slave drama *Joe Turner's Come and Gone* (1988), Herald Loomis cannot proceed with his post-Reconstruction quest for a new beginning in the north until he has done a sankofa: an Akan word that stresses the significance of retrospection. That is, like the sankofa bird, Herald must look back and recover his forgotten "song" by acknowledging and bidding farewell to his Southern past figured as his estranged wife Bertha Holly. Morrison suggests invariably that those sites and stories of pain, those splintered and buried texts of blackness, must be unpacked, unbound, and re-read. They must be retrieved and shared as a corrective to the lethality of silence and the interstices and distortions of black life in occlusive, totalizing master narratives. To Sethe, "the future was a matter of keeping the past at bay" (42). But as the positivist enabler, Beloved assists in Sethe's "rememory." Just as the Ọgbañje-preacher as a defogger instigates a needed revival of Liam's and his wife's stories, and how in Morrison's "Recitatif" the haunting question of Maggie's fall forces the two women Roberta and Twyla to rememory their days at the orphanage St. Bonny's, Beloved ensures that Sethe returns to that anteriority that stores the stories of the Middle Passage. For in that determinative past rest the suspended epics of Sethe's marked, raped, hung, and unnamed African mother; her black father after whom she is named, and her other-mothers, particularly Nan. In *it* lives the stories of Sixo and other black Sweet Home men, women, and children. From her earliest "spiritual" visitations to 124 Bluestone Road and her instigative prodding about Sethe's diamond wedding earrings to her use of other physical prompts, Beloved gets Sethe to self-empower through narration. Beloved nudges Sethe to feel, talk, confess, justify, and (re)order her experience. But most of all, Sethe attempts restitution. She tries to atone for those past errors, such as her love-motivated infanticide, for which Beloved torments her and with which she must make peace.

Morrison is concerned, however, that an obsessive self-flagellation and a mollification of that capriciously insatiable past, symbolized in Beloved's increasingly avaricious stomach, could be quite expensive for black humanity. In the same way that attending to a sickle-cell sufferer's or an Ọgbañje's incessant health crises, needs and demands could drain parents financially and emotionally, as Ezinma's and Azaro's cases show, a devouring requital could be retardive. It could derail black people's quest to move forward toward a more affirmative life in the post-bellum and postcolonial world. In short, an unmitigated attendance to guilt, to a slavery-sickened United States, could be physically, psychically, and spiritually debilitating, as Sethe's near-fatal dementia illustrates. That Sethe, as the story closes, goes after "the wrong enemy"—the abolitionist Edward Bodwin—with an ice pick to save the torturous Beloved reveals how much mental damage the montage of slavery, trauma, and endless penance has caused and still can cause. If the notorious, allegoric "Joe Turner" is come and gone, as August Wilson suggests and if, as Trudier Harris observes, "Slavery has ended; the man [Edward] approaching is a rescuer rather than an enslaver," then "Sethe needs rescue *from* Beloved [and every malignancy she rarefies] rather than rescuing her from someone else." Harris adds, significantly, "one thing is clear: Sethe and Beloved cannot exist on the same plane. If Sethe is to live, Beloved must depart. If Beloved stays, Sethe can only die" (137–38). Which brings us back to Ella.

It takes us to the gendered community's self-redeeming resolve to confront Ọgbañje Beloved. It returns us to the women's will to ritually exorcize that troublous presence, whose "evil" the community has allowed to run its course, as the Bottom does with Sula's. Whatever Sethe's crime,

> Ella didn't like the idea of past errors taking possession of the present. Sethe's crime was staggering and her pride outstripped even that; but she could not countenance the possibility of sin moving on in the house, unleashed and sassy. Daily life took as much as she had. The future was sunset; the past something to leave behind. And if it didn't stay behind, well, you might have to stomp it out. Slave life; freed life—every day was a test and a trial. Nothing could be counted on in a world where even when you were a solution you were a problem. 'Sufficient unto the day is the evil thereof,' and nobody needed more; nobody needed a grown-up evil sitting at the table with a grudge. As long as the ghost showed out from its ghostly place—shaking stuff, crying, smashing and such—Ella respected it. But if it took flesh and came in her world, well, the shoe was on the other foot. She didn't mind a little communication between the two worlds, but this was an invasion. (256–57)

With that said, the women, led by Ella, get on fearlessly with the crucial business of rescuing one of their own and thus themselves. It "was not a story to pass on" (275).

For African-descended people whose ancestral homelands were invaded and burgled by alien Europeans, who like the fictional Anyanwu and her descendants were subjected to new languages, nativities, names, and cultures in the New World, the collective expurgation of Beloved's malevolent spirit stands as a testimony of hope. The same can be said of Sethe's and Denver's ultimate survival. It applies, too, to the intimated end to Paul D's nomadism, his Ọgbañje/Sula-like vagrancy symbolic of the dislocated, unsettled, and unrested black soul and spirit in America. Promise-portentous, even more, is the initiated reconstruction of the Beloved-/slavery-disrupted black family as implied in Paul D's and Sethe's reunion at the novel's end. Like Ekwefi's perseverance and Ezinma's *staying,* those triumphs are panegyric. They are praisesongs of collective black history, life, tenacity, and survival. Those fictionalized, incremental victories foretell sustainable healing from and transcendence of the blues of captivity.

Comparable with Butler, Due, and Wideman, who re-imagine the born-to-die myth to treat a wide range of racial, gendered, historical, cultural, political, philosophical, and aesthetic issues raised by the neo-slave narrative and the 1960s and 1970s socioliterary movements, Morrison also refines the trope of spirit child to explore the interfaces of good and evil. As complementary novels that respond to the volatile politics of the 1960s through the 1980s, *Sula* and *Beloved* demand that we rethink essentialist notions of race, gender, the black family, art, community, authenticity, identity, and more. Echoing *Things Fall Apart,* both stories insist on irony, relativities, and the revision of stable centers. For centers are often as shape-shifting and thus as slippery as the mythic spirit child itself. But of this one can be certain: those epic tales of black life, history, and survival that Chinua Achebe, Ben Okri, Octavia Butler, Tananarive Due, John Edgar Wideman, and Toni Morrison render in haunting details, scenes and blues language are not stories to disremember, but to pass on.

Epilogue This Blues Called Ọgbañje

The putative increase in African American novelists' explorations of the Ọgbañje, born-to-die, child spirit mythic principle, as marked by Butler, Due, Wideman, and Morrison's cultural and aesthetic (re)incarnations of the idea, is noteworthy. That quantitative and qualitative spike is enough grounds for a designation of the proliferation as a significant development in late twentieth-century African American literary production. Like Morrison's Paul D, who patiently "contains" his "blues" story of grievous itinerancy in a tobacco tin, or like Ezeulu who habitually though prudently restrains the onset of sudden emotional excitement in clenched fist in Achebe's *Arrow of God,* we should wait. It makes sense to wait for more African American works that reconstruct Ọgbañje/born-to-die mythologies before declaring that felicitous development "a trend." For as an Igbo proverb states, a "snake" seen by only one person could be exaggerated into a "python."

Needless to say, one would be hard pressed to disregard this modest beginning. We should not trivialize the significance of Butler, Due, Wideman, and Morrison's interpretations of the spirit child encounter as an ephemeral love affair with a concept that is demonstrably so archetypic, connotative, and generative. Even its casual adjectival usage for Tupac startles in its appositeness. Such is the belief's magnifying power. Such, too, is myth's affective potential. And even more so is Ọgbañje's conceptual capacity to yield to the concerns and structures, the content and the form, of works in various genres, from science, speculative, supernatural, and historical fiction to postmodern, magical realist, and realistic texts. Chinua Achebe and Ben Okri understood, as do other Nigerian writers, *that* considerable prospect of the spirit child idea to serve as a sign of significations or what Jonathan Culler calls a "figure of figures, a figure for figurality."[1] The same is true for Butler, Due, Wideman, and Morrison—Achebe's and Okri's New World and African diaspora cousins and admirers—in whose storytelling Ọgbañje, born-to-die, spirit child continues its shape-shifting and timeless travels.

Once upon a time someone insisted that epilogues, conclusions, postscripts, afterwords, and other such signifiers of project completion should not be topical. Rather, they ought to be short, recapitulative, and polemical. Disregarding that good-intentioned advice in part, I have chosen instead to swim against the current. I find in the deep, titular keyword "blues" or, rather, "matrix" and "blues" two germane articles with which to sort through some closing remarks relative to this book's goals and its broader implications for African American, African, and really African diaspora cultural and literary studies. As signaled in my introductory supplication of the blues idea and in this epilogic play on Ọgbanje as both a *matrix* and a *blues experience,* I have since this book's gestation several years ago been struck by certain affinities between (experiential and conceptual) Ọgbanje and blues. And thus I have wondered about the possibility of ending the study on a strong blues note.

Those correlations I owe in part to Houston A. Baker Jr.'s transcription of the blues as a trope. An African American musical, experiential, social, epistemological, and aesthetic register, the blues roots its emotive force and purposive beginnings firmly in slavery days and, before that, in Africa and African work songs, as LeRoi Jones (Amiri Baraka) explains insightfully in *Blues People* (1963). For Baker, however, blues is, like Ọgbanje, "the symbolically anthropological." Also comparable with the "constellar"[2] spirit child, blues for Baker is a "matrix," an "*enabling* script," a juncture and junction, a "code" and a "force," the site of interchanging roadbeds and discourses, the railway "X" crossing marked by ceaseless energy, motion, and voices, all calling and responding, as it were, in what are at their marrow dialogues on the hard facts of life, on the complex yet peculiar experience of blackness—particularly in the United States.[3]

Burrowing in the depths of that bluesy black experience from its dawn in Africa through its continuance in slavery times and on to our moment of postmodern indeterminacies has been the project of the novels discussed closely in this book. In the foregoing chapters, I have ventured to argue the lexical presence of that matrix—Ọgbanje, born-to-die, spirit child—in Butler, Due, Wideman, and Morrison's explicit and implicit neo-slave narratives. I have equally attempted to contextualize and theorize Ọgbanje and àbíkú, and to propose the historical, formal, political, ideological, and gendered climates that occasioned the four authors' adoptions and subjections of the myth to fresh uses. The preceding signifyin(g) interrogations of *Wild Seed, Mind of My Mind, The Between, The Cattle Killing, Sula,* and *Beloved* relative to Achebe's and Okri's renderings of the mythotrope have revealed the myth's efficiency, as experience and matrix, to link and dialogize African American and West/African fiction.

The exchanges between *Things Fall Apart, The Famished Road,* and the six neo-slave texts have been mapped in the analysis. How the spirit child premise and its semantic estuaries interconnect *Wild Seed* and *The Cattle Killing, The Cattle Killing, Sula* and *Beloved,* and *The Between* and *Wild Seed,* however, is less so point-edly delineated. Let the following suffice as a sketch of those polydirectional yet converging relationships.

Responding to Derek McGinty's interview question about whether he was familiar with Butler's depiction of Doro as an immortal Ǫgbañje in *Wild Seed* and if both he and Butler were exploring the same legend, Wideman implicitly agrees. He states, "Well, we all draw from the same pots when you get right down to it."[4] The Ǫgbañje experience unifies *Wild Seed* and *The Cattle Killing* in, among other ways, both stories' emphasis on the Igbo, the mystical, slavery, displacement, loss, mother-child relationship, mother love, reincarnation, immortality, resistance, and diaspora. Further, critics often say that Wideman's and Morrison's novels converse. That is true. In this case, Ǫgbañje helps harmonize *Beloved* and *The Cattle Killing.* It enables both Morrison and Wideman to speak about their expressed shared interests in "the unspeakable," including the nature- and state-involved destruction and displacement of once-thriving black neighborhoods mourned in both *Sula* and *The Cattle Killing.* Like Beloved, a figure that represents the many thousands gone, the preacher-narrator in *The Cattle Killing* embodies also the black evangeli-cal and radical dead. The spirit child paradigm also empowers both writers to real-ize the subjects of African cosmological retentions, loss, trauma, mother-child rela-tionship and bond, mother love, space-time travel, postmodern characterization, and textuality. *The Cattle Killing* and *Beloved* are also connected by Wideman's and Morrison's corresponding "interest in making overt the crisis of language that trauma entails" (Lynch 794). Furthermore, Due has asserted that she read Butler only after completing *My Soul to Keep*—her second novel which, as posited, elabo-rates on the Hilton James figure and saga in *The Between.* Due admits, however, to recognizing the semblances between the deathless former slave David/Dawitt of *My Soul* and Ǫgbañje Doro, the immortal African in *Wild Seed.*[5] These layers of conjunctivity further ground Ǫgbañje/born-to-die's station as Baker's "crossroad" sign, or as Julia Kristeva's "ideologeme."[6] The interfaces translate the belief as a platform where black authors and texts "meet" and "talk" to each other about issues that are at once racial, diasporic, spiritual, gendered, personal, political, artistic, philosophic, and theoretic.

In addition, it is instructive that Butler, Due, Wideman, and Morrison are not just in dialogue with each other, with Achebe and Okri, but also with the 1970s, 1960s, and beyond. These writers' communications indicate how strongly those turbulent decades in world and United States history and the Black Aesthetic smithed out of their flames continue to affect black life and literary imagination. But more significant, Butler, Due, Wideman, and Morrison's postmodernist transpositions of the Ọgbañje/born-to-die mythotrope portend that they were also looking for a framework appropriate for their goal of preserving and extending their enslaved forebears' cultural, literary, and political legacies. They desired a periscopic fount that would enable them to go back in time, to see far, widely, and clearly and then give voice and meaning to the black experience. In the course of their stellar careers, Butler, Due, Wideman, and Morrison have drawn inspiration from European and Anglo-American authors, texts, themes, metaphors, symbols, myths, and artistic conventions. That is not surprising. As Ishmael Reed rightly notes in an assertion that Jacqueline de Weever (1–32) shares, African American literary history is replete with "examples of writers using other people's literary machinery and mythology in their work."[7]

However, the focal writers' choice of the West African born-to-die myth as an alternative path to insight on form, reality, and the incubus of slavery bears eloquent witness to a certain truism. It testifies that there still are aspects of black racial humanity and experience that Western scientific and cosmological precepts cannot adequately lay bare. The blues as subterfuge conceals from dehumanizing white gaze the deepest reasons black people code-shift and switch, why they tend to shout and dissemble, sometimes don the mask, and also laugh to keep from crying. The blues transfers back to blacks knowledge and ownership of those very interiorities of their being. As both code, force, and concealed Africanism, Ọgbañje/born-to-die does something similar for the African and African American writers, works, topics, and experiences "gathered" here in *A Spirit of Dialogue*.

The question then becomes: are there ways that the mythic drama of Ọgbañje/born-to-die, with the heteroglossic epistemes, character profiles, and plot structures it assimilates, can help illuminate other African American and African diaspora texts not treated in this book? In other words, what are the broader heuristic promises of this study? The answer to *how* the Ọgbañje/born-to-die notion can augment expositions of other African American and African diaspora cultural works should be preceded, I think, by a word or two on why, in addition to the points made above on "creative" usage, a wider theoretic and critical adaptation of the idea might be necessary.

Worried that post-1960s and 1970s African American fiction was at risk of thematic atrophy, the novelist Charles Johnson called for a more phenomenon-based and penetrating treatment of the black experience. "Because all conception—philosophy—is grounded in perception," Johnson asserts in "Philosophy and Black Fiction" (1980), "there is no reason, in principle, that we cannot work through the particulars of Black life from *within* and discover there not only phenomenon worthy of philosophical treatment in fiction, but also . . . significant new perceptions."[8] Still pressing the issue eight years later in *Being and Race: Black Writing since 1970,* Johnson contends that African American writers need not "plow the same racial and social [and, one might add, tropological] ground over and over when an entire universe of phenomena lay waiting for investigation."[9] The degree to which one such ground, Esu Elegbara for instance, has been troped, plowed, invoked, distillated, and ubiquitized in African diaspora religious vision, creative writing, and critical-theoretical studies for decades lends greater weight and sense of urgency to Johnson's misgivings. Laced in Johnson's emphasis on indigenity, on the *within,* however, is a concern with the *without:* a conviction, as it were, that binaristic Western thinking has historically proved to be pernicious for black racial humanity and survival.

It is in recognition of how that relationship between the West and the rest of us[10] disaffirms one's black life that the late Richard Barksdale drew a rather tough line in the sand. As we build the still emerging African American [*and* African diaspora] literary canon[s], Barksdale advises in *Praisesong of Survival* (1992), black critics should ignore if not banish altogether the now over-influential French school, from Derrida and Paul de Man to Lacan. Barksdale was concerned, and not without good reason, that "African American literature cannot effectively survive critical approaches that stress authorial depersonalization and the essential unimportance of racial history, racial community, and racial tradition." As a result, he urges black critics to "remain ever mindful of the need to utilize the politics of survival. This," he argues, "is something to be found in the text of our racial history that ahistorical theorists like Derrida, a Gramsci, or a Lacan would not begin to understand."[11] This is why Baker, for whom the vernacular idiom of blues represents one such site of ideological resistance, affirms Johnson and Barksdale.

The "task of present-day scholars," Baker enjoins, "is to situate themselves inventively and daringly at the crossing sign in order to materialize vernacular faces." Scholars should entify the faces of America's blues people, the nation's Others whose conceptions of the sublime and "literary-critical discourse in the United States have been powerfully arrested for generations among (and by) New England male Brahmins." Baker adds, "If scholars are successful, their responses to literature, criticism, and culture in the Unites States will be wonderfully energetic and engrossing."[12] Although issued some years ago, and though a number of culturally informed studies published in the recent past indicate that such calls as Johnson's, Baker's, and Barksdale's have not gone unheeded and uncomplicated, a realization of those unpublicized vernacular faces *and* tropes remains and should stay a priority. It should not be a generation-specific exercise but rather a sustained intellectual, interdisciplinary, and pragmatic engagement to which (West) African cosmologies would continue to make an important contribution. Cheryl A. Wall affirms that. She notes, and I concur, that European thought could be illuminating in certain things. (For instance, "The critique of essentialism encouraged by post-modernist thought is useful for African-Americans concerned with reformulating outmoded notions of identity."[13]) Much could be gained, however, Wall continues, from interpreting black women's [and men's] novels in terms of "African . . . philosophical and religious systems" and from "more relational readings that put individual [black] texts in dialogue."[14]

In addition to how the Ọgbañje/born-to-die matrix relativizes and amplifies the primary texts and the other works with which they are cross-referenced, Wideman and Maureen Warner-Lewis illustrate further the concept's other capacity to provoke and accentuate. For instance, it would not readily occur to most people to associate the 1960s civil rights leader Dr. Martin Luther King Jr. with Ọgbañje. Because the words Ọgbañje and àbíkú do not generally conjure positive images and experiences but rather the opposite, as posited in the introduction, some might find any such association of King and Ọgbañje to be inappropriate, offensive, or outright scandalous—but not Wideman. To Wideman, who (un) names the "negative" Ọgbañje, repositions it within the discourse of transcendent love, and also sees in it not only a fertile gem for a theory of character but a certain "ferocious energy [that is] . . . beyond good and evil, beyond appetite,"[15] King possessed the Ọgbañje energy. The Ọgbañje, Wideman proposes, are those people "whose spirits are so strong that, even when the person dies, they continue to have an effect."[16]

Wideman hypothesizes also that one can even see [the societally negativized] gangsta rappers as embodying Ọgbañje force in terms of the rappers' toughness, hunger, and survivalist spirit. He adds, still provocatively, that if viewed as the energy and prototype of "the strong, quiet men," the "troubadour who always moves on," "the gambler, the outlaw, the blues singer," then Ọgbañje has long had counterparts in African American society, culture and thought.[17] In that case, one could argue that "Ọgbañje," along with àbíkú, projects back to antebellum black world, folklore and explanatory mythic imagination. The mythic force, discontent, and elusiveness that Ọgbañje exudes find ontological complementation then in those lawless subversives that comprise the black "pantheon of heroes," from the fugitive and ungovernable slave figure and the tricksters Signifying Monkey and Bre'r Rabbit to the uncontainable Wild Negro Bill, John Henry, (Morris Slater) Railroad Bill, and

Stackolee.[18] It is quite fascinating and in fact theologically inciting that in Trinidadian folk and mythic consciousness the Christian Savior is seen as an àbíkú—as He, Christ, is one born-to-die.[19] Like the blues, which "express[es] a black perspective on the incongruity of life and the attempt to achieve meaning in a situation fraught with contradiction,"[20] Ọgbañje/born-to-die mediates the crisscrossing patterns of and the resolvable tensions between the sacred and the secular.

E. M. Herd has stated that "a mythical pattern can emerge within the structure of a novel without conscious development by the author." The critic's task, then, Herd declares, is to show "that this pattern forms a coherent and meaningful whole within the overall structure of the work" (175). If that were true, then the illustrative "unusual" figures, enumerated below, can be discussed comparatively and illuminated alongside the totality of Ọgbañje and àbíkú's metaphysical, empirical, conceptual, and philosophical expressivity.

The first persona is the young boy Abiku Waddell, nicknamed "Snail" by his school friend Renaldo in Alden Reimonenq's "Snail." "Snail" evokes the àbíkú speaker-protagonist in Soyinka's poem "Abiku." The story also introspects on such 1960s issues as school busing, segregation, and (student) protest. In portraying Abiku as an àbíkú figure, Reimonenq weaves into Waddell's character the àbíkú's various metaphoric attributes. As the self-declared son of a Nigerian Yoruba mother and an American father, Abiku has a dual parentage. As a non-Catholic in a New Orleans Catholic school class tutored by a crucifix-wielding, prayer-enforcing sister, as a non-believer in prayer and dogma, Abiku is depicted as a non-conformist. He disbelieves, suggestively, that Jesus died for him. Reimonenq's àbíkú is different and startlingly precocious. A problem student/child to whom bedevilment is ascribed in the story, Abiku is elusive, stubborn, rebellious, defiant of exorcistic rituals, given to mischief and, above all, drawn to "Amandla," to freedom. In other words, he does not want to be fettered (237–42).

Other characters, works and references include, in no particular order: Deidre L. Badejo's brief adaptation of the dualities, restlessness, paradox, and malice of the àbíkú in her captivating piece, "Tokunbo: A Divination Poem." In this poem, Badejo addresses the subjects of slavery and rebellion, among other things. Furthermore, by having her fictionalized Chinua Achebe character, Albert, call and describe *Tunneling*'s white, time-traveling, and androgynous protagonist Rachel Finch as Ọgbañje, Beth Bosworth[21] suggests the possibilities of comparing the space- and time-traversing figures of Western time-travel narratives and the Ọgbañje. There are also those "profane" blues (women) singers of the twenties, from Ma Rainey and Bessie Smith to Clara Smith and Billie Holiday; Lil Augie the blues character born with a caul in Arna Bontemps's *God Sends Sunday* (1931);

Janie Crawford and the blues figure Teacake in Hurston's *Their Eyes Were Watching God;* the blues pianist/singer in Langston Hughes's "The Weary Blues"; Ajax in *Sula;* Avatara (Avey) Johnson as an incarnate of her maternal grandmother in Paule Marshall's *Praisesong for the Widow;* and the severally reincarnated Lissie Lyles in Alice Walker's *The Temple of My Familiar* (1989). Add to the list the Unborn Child in Julie Dash's *Daughters of the Dust* (1992 and 1997); Joe Trace in Morrison's *Jazz* (1992), Lena McPherson, a child born with a caul in Tina McElroy's Ansa's *Baby of the Family* (1989) and its sequel *The Hand I Fan With* (1996), and the ungovernable child LaShawndra Pines, also born with a caul in Ansa's *You Know Better* (2002); the character that experiences mysterious stigmata, Elizabeth Joyce DuBose, in Phyllis Alesia Perry's *Stigmata* (1998). Others are the Ọgbañje-like in-between and immortal David/Dawitt in Due's *My Soul to Keep* and *Living Blood;* Fana, the powerful demon-child, born after the death of the mother Jessica-Jacob Wolde's first daughter Kiya, in Due's *Living Blood;* and the child Armstrong rein-carnated as the precocious W.T. in Bebe Moore Campbell's *Your Blues Ain't Like Mine* (1992). Campbell is right.

Black people's blues stories are not exact. Were our blues the same, we would be talking problematically about monolithic blackness. What is undisputed, however, is that those seemingly discordant stories are reconcilable. They are harmonized by their being incited and shadowed, in one way or another, by that blues-inducing, historic, haunting, and yet survivable act of Africa's encounter with Europe.

In *Shadow and Act* Ralph Ellison offers a sobering view of the blues that should stand as this book's ultimate benediction. He defines the blues as that "impulse to keep the painful details and episodes of a brutal experience alive in one's aching consciousness, to finger its jagged grain, and to transcend it, not by consolation of philosophy but by squeezing from it a near-tragic, near-comic lyricism."[22] Ellison might as well have been describing the experiences of African-descended people in toto. But more specifically, he could just have been depicting *Things Fall Apart*'s Okonkwo, whose adamant refusal to surrender to gripping serial adversity, con-spired against him by the sacred and the secular is nothing but the blues made immanent. It is unfortunate, therefore, that Ellison had a tepid personal meeting with the visiting Achebe in the 1960s and also rejected inheriting an "African" cultural and artistic influence.[23] For in explicating the Africa-originated blues, he could easily have been talking about Ekwefi and her encounter with and attitude to Ọgbañje. For what, really, animates Ekwefi's response to her almost rhythmi-cally repeated, antiphonal, death-and-life chess game with a seemingly intractable grief if not a "blues" impulse. Ekwefi sings the blues. It is the blues impulse that recharges her insistence on a life imperative. It is *it* that saturates her intent to document nominally (in "Onwumbiko," "Ozoemena" and "Onwuma") the agonizing episodes and details of a brutal life. It is that stimulus that emboldens her to finger, stomp, contend with, contest, and outlast life's jagged grains thrust at her as successive losses of children. For nobody but her companion Chi knows the trouble she has seen. Touched, tested, and toughened by the Ǫgbañje blues, with her eyes still watching God, Ekwefi, a black woman and mother drawn to "wrestling" matches, neither concedes turf and fight to god, man, or fever. Nor does she cease to believe in tomorrow's promises even in the face of "Death." She stays resolute and faithful even while confronted, as she is, by yesterdays' hurts and traumas that have yet to fully heal, memories, desires and dreams betrayed and deferred yet again by her Ǫgbañje babies' tragicomic refusal to *stay* (alive)—until "Ezinma," her beloved, her blessing, whose lovely name says, Enough tears, earth mother.

Achebe, Okri, Butler, Due, Wideman, and Morrison nod "Ise!" "Ashe!" and "Amen" to that. Through their collective talking books, and toasting to *Things Fall Apart*'s fiftieth birth/life-day, thanking God that the manuscript/story ultimately did not get lost in England,[24] and celebrating Achebe's enormous accomplishments, they join the incantatory chorus in Sterling Brown's blues poem "Strong Men."[25] They chant along, "The strong men [and women] keep a-comin' on / The strong [women and] men git stronger...." And by his use of ellipsis in the speaker's performative last utterance "Stronger...," Brown proposes that this indomitable blackness, this perplexing continuance of black life against incredible, deathly odds that peaked in the enslavement of Africans and their descendants in the New World through colonization, as well as institutionalized racism further weakened by African diaspora liberation struggles and, in this case, the civil rights, Black Power and Black Arts movements, is an unfinished blues epic, an ongoing journey of (Black) Life.

Notes

Introduction: An Aesthetic (Re)Mark on the Spirit Child

1. I am playing on John F. Mbiti's discussion of the idea of the living-dead as those long departed but who are in what he calls "the state of personal immortality . . . and their process of dying is not yet complete." These living-dead are affiliated with both the spirit and human realms, and they exert a powerful influence on the living. The posthumous following that Tupac maintains compels my suggestion that, though dead, he lives on, like the Ọgbañje-àbíkú. For more on the subject of the living-dead, see Mbiti, *African Religions and Philosophy*, 83.

2. In works such as *Holler If You Hear Me, Passed On,* and *Raising the Dead,* critics Michael Eric Dyson, Karla F. C. Holloway, and Sharon Patricia Holland, respectively, shed important light on Tupac's obsession with death and dying as well as on his tattooed black body. Tupac's marked body, like that of the Ọgbañje-àbíkú, is semiotic: it encodes, among other things, memory, pain, and atypical subjectivity. See Armon White, *Rebel for the Hell of It: The Life of Tupac Shakur;* Darrin Keith Bastfield, *Back in the Day: My Life and Times with Tupac Shakur;* and Angela Ardis, *Inside a Thug's Heart: With Original Poems and Letters by Tupac Shakur* for more on Tupac's life, works and career. Carol E. Henderson's *Scarring the Black Body: Race and Representation in African American Literature* also offers an insightful reading of the politics of the mutilated black body in black letters.

3. Ọgbañje and àbíkú have been described using all the terms which together capture the various dimensions of the concepts. Though born-and-die and born-to-die appear to be semantically different, one implying ontology, the other implying fate, both descriptions intimate death as a given.

4. I owe my use of the phrase to Stuart J. Edelstein's *The Sickled Cell: From Myths to Molecule,* 21.

5. Baker is convinced of the enunciative potential of the symbolic, especially the "symbolically anthropological" in "the comprehension of Afro-American expressive culture in its plenitude." See his *Blues, Ideology, and Afro-American Literature: A Vernacular Theory,* 1.

6. See Jacqueline de Weever, *Mythmaking and Metaphor in Black Women's Fiction,* 4, and Walter Mosley, "Black to the Future," 405.

7. See John Vickery, "Literature and Myth," 296.

8. In *The Archeology of Knowledge* Michel Foucault discusses "an optimum" as "the meeting-place of different discourses"; it resolves "the greatest possible number of contradictions" (149) and contradiction "constitutes the very law of existence" (151).

9. Bonnie Barthold alludes to the "*ogbanje* cycle of destruction" in her exploration of issues of temporality in Gayl Jones's *Eva's Man,* Richard Wright's *Native Son* and Orlando Patterson's *Children of Sisyphus.* See Barthold, *Black Time: Fiction of Africa, the Caribbean, and the United States,* 131.

10. Ogunyemi comparatively discusses Wole Soyinka's *Aké: The Years of Childhood* and *Beloved* in the context of Ọgbañje-àbíkú's evocation of mother-daughter relationship/parent-child struggle. Her exploration revisits some of her conceptualizations of and arguments on Ọgbañje and àbíkú earlier in her brilliant study *Africa Wo/Man Palava: The Nigerian Novel by Women.* "An Abiku-Ogbanje Atlas" is certainly a perceptive essay that hints at some parallels between Ọgbañje-àbíkú as figure, idea, characters, and themes in African American literature. But it is also somewhat elliptical if not conscripted particularly in its attempt in one essay article to situate the trope *also* in Pan-African political exchanges, experience, subjectivities, texts, and textual production.

11. I have in mind such works as Carol Boyce Davies, *Black Women, Writing, and Identity: Migrations of the Subject* (1994); Arlene R. Keizer, "*Beloved:* Ideologies in Conflict, Improvised Subjects"; Nancy Jesser, "Violence, Home, and Community in Toni Morrison's *Beloved*"; O. R. Dathorne, *Worlds Apart: Race in the Modern Period* (2001); Sharon Holland, *Raising the Dead: Readings of Death and (Black) Subjectivity;* and Amy K. Levin, *Africanisms and Authenticity in African American Women's Novels.*

12. Tananarive Due has published the following novels, among other single-authored and collaborative projects: *The Between; My Soul to Keep; The Black Rose,* the sequel to *My Soul, The Living Blood; The Good House;* and *Joplin's Ghost* (2005). In 2003, she and her legendary mother Patricia Stephens Due together published *Freedom in the Family: A Mother-Daughter Memoir of the Fight for Civil Rights.* With reference to Due's novels, there truly is little of serious critical weight available, unless one wants to count online publishers' and fan reviews of the works. Furthermore, the theme of the April 18–21, 2007, College Language Association (CLA) convention held in Miami is "Religion and Spirituality in Literature." That none of the dozens of papers given at this professional meeting focuses on Due or any of her works to date is noteworthy. It seems as though it is Due herself who has furnished much of the insight into the works, as indicated in *Freedom* and the recently published interview she had with Dianne Glave, "'My Characters are Teaching Me to be Strong': An Interview with Tananarive Due." Sandra M. Grayson's recent study *Visions of the Third Millennium: Black Science Fiction Writers Write the Future* is to my knowledge the one book-length project that allocates some discursive space to Due's novels. However, given what I see as the importance of *Between* as a founding text to Due's fictive oeuvre, it is surprising to say the least that Grayson totally ignores *Between* and instead focuses, in six brief and cursory paragraphs that amount to plot summaries, on *My Soul to Keep* and *The Living Blood.*

13. Northrop Frye, *Anatomy of Criticism: Four Essays,* 161.

14. Benston proposes that we can actually see "All of Afro-American literature . . . as one vast genealogical poem that attempts to restore continuity to the ruptures or disconti-

nuities imposed by a history of the black presence in America." Benston notes that while whites had named blacks and called them derogatory names as a weapon of enslavement and control, black people have had to un-name to thereby rename themselves. According to Benston, this concern with self-naming reached its zenith in the 1960s. See Benston's "I yam what I yam: the topos of (un)naming in Afro-American literature." In his *Understanding the New Black Poetry: Black Speech and Black Music as Poetic References,* Stephen Henderson terms this praxis of (un)naming "this tradition of saying things beautifully even if they are ugly things. We say them in a way which takes language down to the deepest common level of our experience while hinting still at things to come," 33.

15. Bakhtin, *The Dialogic Imagination: The Dialogic Imagination: Four Essays,* 294.

16. I agree with Ralph Ellison that the novel is "basically a form of communication," and that it "communicat[es] its vision of experience." The novel's "medium of communication consists in a 'familiar' experience occurring among a particular people, within a particular society or nation." Ellison adds that "the novel is rhetorical. For whatever else it tries to do, it must do so by persuading us to accept the novelist's projection of an experience. . . ." Throughout its history the novel has been tied to society, and as a social text its interest since centuries ago has been the articulation of "the impact of change on personality." For more, see Ellison's "Society, Morality, and the Novel," 241–46.

17. In *The Afro-American Novel and Its Tradition,* Bernard W. Bell writes that "From its inception . . . the Afro-American novel has been concerned with illuminating the meaning of the black American experience and the complex double-consciousness, socialized ambivalence, and double vision which is the special burden *and* blessing of Afro-American identity," 35.

18. I am here playing on Gates's conception of "The Trope of the Talking Book." In discussing African American slave narratives, Gates notes how some of the slave autobiographers, in quest of literacy, describe their encounters with books and also their longing to have books/texts speak to them, as they did to their masters. If the (black) text talks, then it is anthropomorphized; it achieves "conscious" vocality. *The Signifying Monkey: A Theory of African-American Literary Criticism,* 127–32.

19. W. D. Wright, *Black Intellectuals, Black Cognition and a Black Aesthetic,* 114.

20. The idea of displacing the author, which W. D. Wright rejects relative to black authors and texts, found support in Roland Barthes. Barthes suggests that the author dies at the point writing begins. He argues that the author is a modern figure and that has come to loom large as source, as creator, the knower of what she or he creates, tyrannical, etc. For Barthes, the removal of the author "utterly transforms the modern text." For more, see Barthes, "The Death of the Author" in *Image.Music.Text,* 142–48.

21. See, for instance, Robert Elliot Fox, *Conscientious Sorcerers,* 8–10; Bernard W. Bell, *The Contemporary African American Novel: Its Folk Roots and Modern Literary Branches,* 193; and Madhu Dubey, *Signs and Cities: Black Literary Postmodernism,* 10.

22. Todd L. Savitt, *Medicine and Slavery: The Diseases and Health Care of Blacks in Antebellum Virginia,* 27–34; Dick Campbell, "Sickle Cell Anemia and Its Effect on Black People," 7–9; and Doris Y. Wilkinson, "For Whose Benefit?: Politics and Sickle Cell," 26–31.

23. There is a surplus of scholarship on this subject. Robert Farris Thompson's *Flash of the Spirit: African and Afro-American Art and Philosophy* is one of the most important and cited of such studies. However, in addition to the works noted below, these, too, are enlightening: Elsie Clews Parsons, *Folk-lore of the Sea Islands, South Carolina;* Newbell Niles Puckett, *Folk Beliefs of the Southern Negro,* 100, 112 (see also Talbot, *Women's Mysteries of a Primitive People,* 221, for a complementary view on Puckett); Georgia Writer's Project, *Drums and Shadows: Survival Studies among the Georgia Coastal Negroes.* Also informative are Barbara Frankel, *Childhood in the Ghetto: Folk Beliefs of Negro Women in a North Philadelphia Hospital Ward;* Melville J. Herskovits, *The Myth of the Negro Past,* 189–90; Eugene D. Genovese, *Roll, Jordan, Roll: The World the Slaves Made,* 212–25; Lawrence W. Levine, *Black Culture and Black Consciousness: Afro-American Folk Thought From Slavery to Freedom,* 66, 74; George Eaton Simpson, *Black Religions in the New World,* 217; Albert J. Raboteau, *Slave Religion: The "Invisible Institution" in the Antebellum South,* 24, 32, 45, 86; Mechal Sobel, *Trabelin' On: The Slave Journey to an Afro-Baptist Faith,* 33–41; Patricia Jones-Jackson, *When Roots Die: Endangered Traditions on the Sea Islands,* xix, 26, 37–46. Additional sources are Joseph E. Holloway, ed. *Africanisms in American Culture* (1990) and its second edition (2005); Margaret Washington Creel, "Gullah Attitudes toward Life and Death" in *Africanisms* (1990), 89; Mary A. Twining and Keith E. Baird, eds. *Sea Island Roots: African Presence in the Carolinas and Georgia;* and Pattern M. Drake, "African-American Spiritual Beliefs: An Archeological Testimony from the Slave Quarter" in Peter Benes, ed. *Wonders of the Invisible World: 1600–1900* (1995), 44–52. I address the subject of sickle cell anemia relative to slavery and Ọgbañje more in Chapter 3 and in my analysis proper and endnotes to Butler's *Wild Seed* and *Mind of My Mind.* For a copious insight into African American folklore, see Anand Prahlad's recent and edited three-volume anthology, *The Greenwood Encyclopedia of African American Folklore.*

24. Table 2.8, "Decadal British Export Trade by Region, 1700–1807," shows the Bight of Biafra with 1,155,590 slaves exported. Source is David Richardson's "Slave Exports from West and West-Central Africa, 1700–1810: New Estimates of Volume and Distribution." In Michael A. Gomez, *Exchanging Our Country Marks* (1998), 30. For more on this subject, see, for instance, Herskovits, *Myth of the Negro Past* (1941), Philip D. Curtin, *The Atlantic Slave Trade: A Census;* Sterling Stuckey, *Slave Culture: Nationalist Theory and the Foundations of Black America;* Twining and Baird, eds. *Sea Island Roots;* Lorena S. Walsh, *From Calabar to Carter's Grove;* Mary Cuthrell Curry, *Making the Gods in the New World: The Yoruba Religion in the African American Community;* William S. Pollitzer, *The Gullah People and Their African Heritage;* and Douglas B. Chambers, *Murder at Montpelier: Igbo Africans in Virginia.* See also Genovese, Levine, Raboteau, and Jones-Jackson.

25. Michael A. Gomez, *Exchanging Our Country Marks: The Transformation of African Identities in the Colonial and Antebellum South,* 30.

26. Afigbo, *Ropes of Sand: Studies in Igbo History and Culture,* x–xi.

27. Gomez, *Exchanging,* 114.

28. Christopher N. Okonkwo, "'It Was Like Meeting an Old Friend': An Interview with John Edgar Wideman," 349.

29. See Henry H. Mitchell, *Black Belief: Folk Beliefs of Blacks in America and West Africa,* 9.
30. The list is too long, but I will mention a few here. In addition to the works mentioned above (in notes 23 and 24), I build upon these studies also: Charles T. Davis and Henry Louis Gates Jr., eds. *The Slave's Narrative;* Ashraf H. A. Rushdy, *Neo-slave Narratives: Studies in the Social Logic of a Literary Form;* Robert B. Stepto, *From Behind the Veil: A Study of Afro-American Narrative;* Henry Louis Gates Jr., *Black Literature and Literary Theory* and *The Signifying Monkey;* Madelyn Jablon, *Black Metafiction: Self Consciousness in African American Literature;* and Keith E. Byerman, *Fingering the Jagged Grain: Tradition and Form in Recent Black Fiction.* Others are Lawrence Hogue, *Discourse and the Other: The Production of the Afro-American Text;* John F. Callahan, *In the African-American Grain: The Pursuit of Voice in Twentieth-Century Black Fiction;* Michael Awkward, *Inspiriting Influences: Tradition, Revision, and Afro-American Women's Novels;* Aldon L. Nielsen, *Writing Between the Lines, Race and Intertextuality;* and Deborah E. McDowell, *"The Changing Same": Black Women's Literature, Criticism, and Theory.* Please see Bibliography for the rest.
31. Deserving of mention here is Ogunyemi's earlier cited *African American Review* essay, "An Abiku-Ogbanje Atlas," a piece whose interest to strategize the idea into African American poetics is one of this study's points of continuation. Another study worthy of note is Douglass McCabe's unpublished dissertation, "'Born-to-Die': The History and Politics of Ogbanje and Abiku in Nigerian Literature." McCabe discusses *Things Fall Apart* and *Famished Road,* and other oral and written Ọgbañje and àbíkú texts. McCabe considers the concepts from an historical, and also analytical perspective. My book differs from his thesis in several ways; the most glaring of which is my focus on African American literature, theoretical underpinning and trajectory, as well as contextualization and text selection. Though some of McCabe's inferences and conclusions are quite problematic if not contestable, the study offers readers an extensive bibliography on the concept of born-to-die.
32. Cartwright's study is quite enlightening in terms of the unexplored cultural, linguistic, and literary crosscurrents it locates between the corpus of Senegambia oral narratives and African American texts and thematics. His interest to draw attention to the neglected African sources of American literature is one I share. See Cartwright, *Reading Africa into American Literature,* 2–3. See also Gay Wilentz's "'What Is Africa To Me?': Reading the African Cultural Base of (African) American Literary History" for an interrogative review of Cartwright's book.
33. Houston A. Baker Jr., *Blues, Ideology, and Afro-American Literature: A Vernacular Theory,* 9–10.
34. Larry McCaffery, "An Interview with Octavia E. Butler," 65. See also Stephen W. Potts, "'We Keep Playing the Same Record': A Conversation with Octavia E. Butler," 331–38.
35. Shinn, *Worlds Within Women: Myth and Mythmaking in Fantastic Literature by Women,* 5.

Chapter 1. *Ọgbañje and Àbíkú: Contexts, Conceptualizations, and Two West African Literary Archetypes*

1. See Stephen C. Ausband, *Myth and Meaning, Myth and Order*, 2.

2. Kofi Asare Opoku relays this view in his essay "Death and Immortality in the African Religious Heritage," 9–21.

3. Wole Soyinka uses this phrase in *Myth, Literature and the African World* (2d edition) to talk about humankind's inseparability from and location in the cosmic whole that includes, among other things, gods and other mythic powers from antiquity. In addition, Soyinka reminds us that myths themselves "arise from man's attempt to externalize and communicate his inner intuitions," 3. Soyinka sees ritual drama, or what he calls the "drama of the gods," in the Yoruba metaphysics. Human beings perform alongside Yoruba orisha as an arena of myth reification.

4. Northrop Frye places "the mythical mode," the "stories about gods, which characters have the greatest possible power of action" as "the most abstract and conventionalized of all literary modes. . . ." He adduces that "the structural principles of literature are as closely related to mythology and comparative religion as those of painting are to geometry." *Anatomy of Criticism: Four Essays*, 134. See also Jane Campbell, *Mythic Black Fiction: The Transformation of History*, ix–xv.

5. Chidi Okonkwo, *Decolonization Agonistics in Postcolonial Fiction*, 54.

6. In *Where Reincarnation and Biology Intersect*, Ian Stevenson writes that "Children who claim to remember a previous life have been found in most countries where they have been sought. Reports of such children occur frequently in countries and cultures in which the belief in reincarnation is strong: the Hindu and Buddhist countries of South Asia, the Shiite peoples of Lebanon and Turkey, the tribes of West Africa, and the tribes of northwestern North America. We also have many (but fewer) reports of cases from Europe, North America, and elsewhere," 1. While research in the above cultures will certainly yield valuable insight into the idea of reincarnation and rebirth, I am inclined to remark on variants of Igbo and Yoruba notions of Ọgbañje and àbíkú concepts in Asia, some Caribbean nations, Amerindian, European, and Australian cultures.

The Hindu and Buddhist ideas of reincarnation stress the precept of karma. The principle of karma supposes, among other things, that one's ethical behavior (ill or good) in the present life will directly influence one's fortunes in the next incarnation. Trinidadian folklore, for instance, features the idea of Douennes (Dwen). Sharing with Ọgbañje and àbíkú an association with both forests and rivers, and having a Kalabari (Efik Ibibio and thus Nigerian) origin, the Dwen are said to be the eternally vagrant, sometimes mischievous and abode-seeking spirits of children who died prior to baptism, generally in infancy (see Warner-Lewis's *Guinea's Other Suns: The African Dynamic in Trinidad Culture* 1991). Unlike Ọgbañje and àbíkú, however, the Dwen are not said to be reborn to the same mother. Relatedly, the cosmic relationship that has been drawn between àbíkú etiology and ontology *and* twins ("ibeji") as special categories of powerful, mischievous, and disruptive children in Yoruba cosmos relativizes àbíkú and the Haitian cult of twins. For more on this, see Harold Courlander, *A Treasury of African Folklore,* 233–37; Alfred Metraux, *Voodoo in Haiti* (1972); and Taiwo Oruene, "Magical Powers of Twins in the Socio-Religious Beliefs of the Yoruba," 208–16. See also Maya Deren's discussion of "the Marassa," the venerated Divine Twins in Haitian worldview. Comparable to the Ọgbañje and àbíkú, the marassa are seen not only as "half matter, half metaphysical; half mortal, half immortal; half human, half divine" but the "origin of all loa." See Deren's *Divine Horseman: The Living Gods of Haiti,* 38–41.

The different essays collected in the seminal edited volume by Antonia Mills and Richard Slobodin, *Amerindian Rebirth: Reincarnation Belief among North American Indians and Inuit,* focus attention on the various forms of reincarnation beliefs among native peoples. As in the Ọgbañje and àbíkú cases, the Amerindian types, specifically that of the Tha, involve use of birthmarks and naming rituals to identify the entity that is reincarnating into the same family. A special category of mystifying children, those "born with a deformity, or a physical or mental handicap" noticeable soon after birth were called "the changeling" in Europe of the Middle Ages through the Enlightenment. Like Ọgbañje and àbíkú, these "abnormal child[ren]" excite all kinds of emotions in the parents and elicit varying societal responses to their mothers. The "child of nature demons of semi-human form," indeed "a subhuman . . . not borne by the mother but surreptitiously substituted for the real child shortly after birth," the changeling was seen as the product of the "powers of the underworld: they must be propitiated, outwitted or rendered docile by brutal methods." See Carl Haffter, "The Changeling: History and Psychodynamics of Attitudes to Handicapped Children in European Folklore," 55–58. The Aboriginal peoples of Australia maintain a "pre-conception paradigm" that focuses on the supplemental necessity of a "spirit child" to enter a woman's womb during sex to complete the process of human conception. See Elizabeth Carman and Neil Carman, "Spirit-Child: The Aboriginal Experience of Pre-Birth Communication," and Francesca Merlan, "Australian Aboriginal Conception Beliefs Revisited," *Man* 21.3 (Sept., 1986): 474–93. Among the people of Western Papua, New Guinea, the embryo, called the Birumbir, is seen as a "spirit child" in that it is from the material body that grows in the uterus. See A. P. Lyons, "Paternity Beliefs and Customs in Western Papua," *Man* 24 (April 1924): 58–59. See also Simon Bockie's *Death and the Invisible Powers: The World of Kongo Belief* (1993) for a discussion of funeral rites involved in deaths of children taken/attacked by malevolent death spirits, bandoki, among the Kongo people of Central Africa (123–24).

7. Rev. Samuel Crowther and Rev. John Christopher Taylor, *The Gospel on the Banks of the Niger: Journals and Notices of the Native Missionaries Accompanying the Niger Expedition of 1857–1859,* 308-310. See also Edelstein, *The Sickled Cell,* 19.

8. In my interview with him in Nigeria (Monday, 24 May 2004), the Reverend Dr. Anthony Ekwunife—a professor of African Traditional Religion and the Sociology of Religions at the University of Nigeria Nsukka and also a specialist in Ọgbañje—affirms that Ọgbañje children are "a reality," because he has encountered many of them as patients. He adds that belief in and attitudes toward the phenomenon remain strong

among the Igbo today. But any investigation of the subject, he emphasizes, must start from a contextual recognition of and respect for the legitimacy of Igbo belief system.

He stressed that Occidental skepticism about the reality of Ǫgbañje should be viewed in light of the Western world's historical campaign to denigrate African epistemology. Suggesting that the idea of Ǫgbañje is dynamic, Father Ekwunife remarked that the current, adverse socio-economic and political situation in Nigeria, especially in Igboland, has led to popular identification of "newer" categories of Ǫgbañje. For instance, he states, babies born with "dreadlocks" are sometimes seen as Ǫgbañje. The gravity of this situation has prompted the church—especially the Pentecostal and the charismatic wings of Catholicism—to get intensely involved in the business of delivering the afflicted from the menaces of Ǫgbañje. Father Ekwunife remarked that the church sees Ǫgbañje spirit as an evil paranormal that causes deaths of children in a family. Chinua Achebe hints at the church's response to the belief in *Things Fall Apart*, 185. See also Esther Nzewi, "The Abiku/Ogbanje syndrome: A dimension of pathology of childhood," 106.

One recalls also Nobel Laureate Wole Soyinka who, speaking with Jane Wilkinson some time ago, not only sees àbíkú as "real" and as the "very physical expression of the link between the living, the unborn, [and] the ancestral world," but also admits to having siblings who were àbíkú. See Jane Wilkinson, ed., *Talking With African Writers: Interviews with African Poets, Playwrights and Novelists*, 108.

9. Douglas McCabe has sounded a similar note of caution to readers and critics not to confuse literary Ǫgbañje and àbíkú with those in anthropologic studies. For more on McCabe's thoughts on this, see the introductory chapter to his dissertation, "'Born-to-Die': The History and Politics of *Abiku* and *Ogbanje* in Nigerian Literature."

10. See Sanya Dojo Onabamiro, *Why Our Children Die: the Causes, and Suggestions for Prevention, of Infant Mortality in West Africa* (1949).

11. See Ekwunife, *Meaning and Function of 'Ino Uwa' (Reincarnation) in Igbo Traditional Religious Culture*, 32–33.

12. Ester Nzewi, "Malevolent Ogbanje: recurrent reincarnation or sickle cell disease?" 1404.

13. See Illogu, *Christianity and Igbo Culture: A Study of the Interaction of Christianity and Igbo Culture*, 42.

14. The listing here is barely a survey of the extant research on the subject. However, see, for instance, John A. Noon, "A Preliminary Examination of the Death Concepts of the Ibo"; D. Amaury Talbot, *Woman's Mysteries of A Primitive People: The Ibibios of Southern Nigeria;* Simon Ottenberg, *Double Descent in an African Society: The Afikpo Village-Group,* 67–68; Elizabeth Isichei, "Ibo and Christian Beliefs: Some Aspects of a Theological Encounter"; M. Ogbolu Okonji, "Ogbanje: (An African Conception of Predestination)"; Edwin Sidney Hartland, *Primitive Paternity: The Myth of the Supernatural Birth in Relation to the History of the Family;* Richard N. Henderson, *The King in Every Man: Evolutionary Trends in Onitsha Ibo Society and Culture;* Edmund Ilogu, *Christianity and Igbo Culture;* Mazi Elechukwu Nnadibuagha Njaka, *Igbo Political Culture;* Isichei, *A History of the Igbo People;* James K. Onwubalili, "Sickle

cell anemia: an exploration for the ancient myth of reincarnation in Nigeria"; Cosmas Okechukwu Obiego, *African Image of the Ultimate Reality: An Analysis of Igbo Ideas of Life and Death in Relation to Chukwu-God,* 190–94; Ian Stevenson, "The Belief in Reincarnation Among the Igbo of Nigeria" and "Characteristics of Cases of the Reincarnation Type among the Igbo of Nigeria"; Edelstein, *The Sickled Cell;* [Christie] Chinwe Achebe, *The World of the Ogbanje;* Peter O. Ebigbo and B. Anyaegbuna, "The Problem of Student Involvement in the Mermaid Cult—a variety of belief in Reincarnation (Ogbañje) in a Nigerian Secondary School"; Misty Bastian, "Married in the Water: Spirit Kin and Other Afflictions of Modernity in Southern Nigeria"; Ekwunife, *Meaning and Function of "Ino Uwa" (Reincarnation) in Igbo Traditional Religion;* and Esther Nzewi, "Malevolent Ogbanje: recurrent reincarnation or sickle cell disease?" The above list excludes creative and critical interpretations of the Ọgbañje. However, for a near-comprehensive bibliography on Ọgbañje and àbíkú, see Douglas McCabe's unpublished dissertation, "'Born-to-Die': The History and Politics of Abiku and Ogbanje in Nigerian Literature."

15. Chinwe Achebe's discussion follows her exploration of the concept among Afa diviners from select communities in Anambra State, a section of Igboland.

16. Igbo scholars and scholars of the Igbo world have debated the semantics of Chukwu, Chineke, and "Chi" in Igbo metaphysics. This study does not intend to rehash, nor does it presume to be able to settle, that debate. However, in addition to the sources enumerated above, these are a few additional enlightening discussions of the subject: C. K. Meek, *Law and Authority in a Nigerian Tribe;* Victor Uchendu, *The Igbo of Southeast Nigeria;* Francis Arinze, *Sacrifice in Ibo Religion;* Chinua Achebe, "Chi in Igbo Cosmology"; I. Chukwukere, "Chi in Igbo Religion and Thought: The God in Every Man"; Obiego, *African Image of the Ultimate Reality;* and Donatus Nwoga, *The Supreme God as Stranger in Igbo Religious Thought.*

17. For more on this water divinity, see, for instance, Kathleen O'Brien Wicker, "Mami Water in African Religion and Spirituality"; Herbert M. Cole, *Mbari: Art and Life among the Owerri Igbo,* 64–65; Christie Chinwe Achebe's discussion of the deity "Nne Mmiri" in *World of the Ogbanje;* Flora Nwapa's novel *Efuru;* and Sabine Jell-Bahlsen, *The Water Goddess in Igbo Cosmology.*

18. Chinwe [Christie] Achebe, *The World of the Ogbanje,* 15–28.

19. Achebe, *World,* 19, 30.

20. Achebe, *World,* 32.

21. Achebe, *World,* 29.

22. Misty Bastian, "Married in the Water," 119–23.

23. Achebe, *World,* 37–57.

24. S. N. Nwabara, *Iboland: A Century of Contact with Britain, 1860–1960,* 17.

25. I thank Dr. Chika Okeke-Agulu of the University of Pennsylvania for sharing this important information with me.

26. Christie C[hinwe] Achebe, "Literary Insights into the *Ogbanje* Phenomenon," 33.

27. Esther Nzewi notes that many Ọgbañje names are generally prefixed by "'onwu' ('death') and express a wish that the new born is not a reincarnating deceased child

as well as an appeal for good health." Here are examples: Onwubiko—Death please; Onwuamaegbu or Onwuegbu—Death will spare the child; Onwuchekwa—Death, please wait; Onwurah—Death, leave the child, among other such names. See Nzewi, "Malevolent Ogbanje," 1405.

28. Samuel Johnson, *The History of the Yoruba: From the Earliest Times to the Beginning of the British Protectorate,* 82–84.

29. See H. U. Beier, "Spirit Children Among the Yoruba," 329–30. See also Jonathan Wright's racism-inflected essay, "Demonology and Bacteriology in Medicine," 449–500.

30. Beier, "Spirit Children Among the Yoruba," 330.

31. Timothy Mobolade, "The Concept of Abiku," 62.

32. See McCabe, " 'Born-to-Die.'"

33. Mobolade, "The Concept of Abiku," 62–63.

34. From Mobolade's listing and translation we have such names as: Durojaiye: "Wait and enjoy life"; Pakuti: "Shun death and stop dying"; Rotimi: "Stay and put up with me"; and Omolelebe: "The child should be appeased." Others are Igbekoyi: "Bush . . . has rejected this"; Kokumoa: "It does not die again"; Ajeigbe: "Monetary expenses are never a waste"; Kosoko: "No more hoe is available"; Aja: "A common dog"; and Tepontan: "No longer feared, respected and cherished" ("The Concept" 63). We have also Jekiniyin: "Let me have a bit of rest"; and Apara: "One who comes and goes," In Johnson, *The History of the Yorubas,* 84. Other African societies dealing with the problem of infant mortality also have related names and naming practices. The Akan of Ghana have the names Bagyina: "May this one stay"; Kronhia: "If you choose to go to Hell, we don't need you here on earth"; Kuntu: "Stick for trapping animal, a worthless object"; Umurezi: "Death, I am tired." The Bassa of Cameroon have Sohna: "Anxiety (that the child will not live)"; and the Kikuyu of Kenya have Kimondo, meaning big/ ugly bag (Source: Rebecca Gilbert, "Another Kind of Unfortunate." In http://rjg42. tripod.com/Anotherkind.html. 30 March 2006.) In the funeral rites of the Fanti of Ghana, writes James Boyd Christensen, "A child who has not lived for eight days will receive rather summary treatment, for the body is known as kukuba (pot child), is placed in a clay vessel and buried in a trash heap, and the ritual of purification for the parents of such a child is held to a minimum. Moreover, it is deemed unwise to mourn over such a death, for one should not show sympathy or sorrow over a person who was so inconsiderate as not to remain in this world." In Christiansen, *Double Descent among the Fanti,* 68. Among the Akamba people of East Central Kenya, John S. Mbiti's name "Mbiti," which means "child vowed to God," is "commonly given to a child born into a family who have suffered several infant death." Jacob K. Olupona, "A biographical sketch," in *Religious Plurality in Africa: Essays in Honor of John S. Mbiti,* ed. Jacob K. Olupona et al. (1993), 3.

35. Mobolade, "The Concept of Abiku," 63.

36. The poem "Abiku" was first published in Soyinka's collection, *Idanre and Other Poems* (1967). Elucidating it from various angles, critics altogether characterize the poem's àbíkú protagonist similarly. They call him, in paraphrase: marked, powerful, force-

ful, mocking, boastful, self-centered, an iconoclast, carefree, defiant, unknowable, uncontrollable, timeless, errant, spaceless, aberrant, heartless, brash—all to capture the àbíkú's wanderings, vagrancy, irreducibility, intransigence, lawlessness, and heroism, in short his *difference*. Further, critics such as Chidi Okonkwo, *Decolonization Agonistics in Postcolonial Literature,* 54–58 and Ato Quayson, *Strategic Transformations in Nigerian Writing,* 121–22, have commented on Ben Okri's debt to Soyinka and Amos Tutuola. Okri's mother is Igbo.

37. Neil Ten Kortenaar, "Fictive Stories and the State of Fiction in Africa," 241–42. See also Douglas McCabe, "'Higher Realities': New Age Spirituality in Ben Okri's *The Famished Road*" for McCabe's suggestion that Okri draws also from New Age spiritualism, and not just from Yoruba religion and folklore (2005).

Chapter 2. Chinua Achebe, the Neo-Slave Narrative, the Nationalist Aesthetic, and African American (Re)Visions of the Spirit Child

1. One reading Gates's description of Esu's attributes in *Signifying Monkey* would find those qualities quite similar to the metaphoric properties of Ọgbañje and àbíkú, as enumerated in chapter 1. Not only does Gates establish Esu as a trickster, which the spirit child idiomatically is, but he also associates Esu with "individuality . . . irony, magic, indeterminacy, open-endedness, ambiguity . . . chance, uncertainty, disruption and reconciliation, betrayal and loyalty, closure and disclosure, encasement and rupture. But it is a mistake," Gates adds, as one would say of àbíkú and Ọgbañje, "to focus on one of these qualities as predominant," 6.

Further, I am familiar with the controversy surrounding Olaudah Equiano's Igbo birth, identity, and memory—a heritage that Vincent Carretta, most prominently, puts in doubt in his recent book, *Equiano the African: Biography of a Self-Made Man* (2005). It should be pointed out, however, that other Equiano scholars advance an alternative reading that, though antithetical to Carretta's suggestion that Equiano "may have invented rather than reclaimed an African identity" (xiv), reaffirms the complexity of Equiano's life and autobiography. See, for instance, the chapter "Through a Glass Darkly" in A[diele]. E. Afigbo's *Ropes of Sand: Studies in Igbo History and Culture* , 145–86, and April Langley's *The Black Aesthetic Unbound: Theorizing the Dilemma of Eighteenth-Century African American Literature* (Ohio State UP, 2008).

2. I apply the term "magical realism" to Morrison's *Beloved* cautiously, knowing that it is a loaded term. I'm also aware of Morrison's statement in an interview with Gail Caldwell that she discovered the Latin American novelist Gabriel García Márquez well after *Beloved* and into her writing of *Song of Solomon.* As Chidi Okonkwo has argued in *Decolonization Agonistics in Postcolonial Fiction,* "the tradition of realism-fantasy fusion [was] inaugurated in West African europhone writing by Amos Tutuola with *The Palm-Wine Drinkard* in 1952." He adds that "Theorists and critics who seek to root it [meaning Ben Okri's *The Famished Road,* to which I would add Morrison's

Beloved] in the Latin American so-called magical realism are in error," 57. *Beloved* merits the designation, however, because of Morrison's superlative, seamless mediation of the supernatural and the earthly.

3. See Houston A. Baker Jr., "There is No More Beautiful Way: Theory and the Poetics of Afro-American Women's Writings," 135 and "Belief, Theory, and Blues," 6–7). See also Henry Louis Gates Jr., *Figures in Black: Words, Signs, and the "Racial" Self,* xix–xxii.

4. In "Signifying" (1973) Claudia Mitchell-Kernan discusses the permutations of this culturally specific act of ironic word play in African American culture and sociolinguists. See Alan Dundes, ed., *Motherwit from the Laughing Barrel* (1973), 311. Geneva Smitherman also illuminates the idea in *Black Talk: Words and Phrases from the Hood to the Amen Corner* and in *Talkin and Testifyin: The Language of Black America.*

5. Ralph Ellison makes a related argument in *Shadow and Act,* 131.

6. Mary Helen Washington, *Black-Eyed Susans, Midnight Birds: Stories by and about Black Women,* 7.

7. In her landmark work *In Search of Our Mothers' Gardens* (1983), and more specifically in the collection's title essay, Alice Walker addresses the issue of black women's lives, as well as their intergenerational connections and legacies. Most important, she recovers her mother's unsung gift of unorthodox artistry. Walker extends this quest for literary matrilineage by not only marking the hitherto unidentified gravesite of Zora Neale Hurston, but also in her essays on Hurston's ancestral role in contemporary black women's writing. See also Walker's "Foreword" in Robert E. Hemenway, *Zora Neale Hurston: A Literary Biography* (1977). Michael Awkward, in *Inspiriting Influences,* and Barbara Christian, in *Black Women Novelists: The Development of a Tradition,* address this issue of black women writers' intertextual productions. For more on the subject, see Hazel Carby, *Reconstructing Womanhood: The Emergence of the Afro-American Woman Novelist* (1987), Frances Smith Foster, *Written By Herself: Literary Production by African American Women 1746–1892* (1993), and Deborah E. McDowell "*The Changing Same*": *Black Women's Literature, Criticism, and Theory.* Also, Karla F. C. Holloway's *Moorings and Metaphors* provides an enlightening, intertextual discussion of West African and African American women's works.

8. Hogue, *Discourse and the Other,* 6.

9. The list includes Nkem Nwankwo, John Munonye, Chukwuemeka Ike, T. M. Aluko, Elechi Amadi, Ngugi wa Thiong'o, Mariama Bâ, Flora Nwapa, Nurrudin Farrah, Ayi Kwei Armah, Buchi Emecheta, Tsitsi Dangaremgba, Okey Ndibe, Chris Abani, and of course Chimamanda Ngozi Adichie, who in her novels *Purple Hibiscus* (2003) and *Half of a Yellow Sun* (2006) expressly acknowledges her debt to Achebe. See also Innes, *Chinua Achebe* [1990] 19–20, and Emenyonu, "Preface" xi.

10. Emenyonu, "Preface," xii.

11. Gikandi, *Reading Chinua Achebe: Language and Ideology in Fiction,* 3, 5.

12. The Man Booker International Prize is given bi-annually to a living novelist whose canon is determined to have contributed immensely to global fiction. It is worth £60,000. Achebe's award came just a few days after Chimamanda Ngozi Adichie beat out other formidable nominees to become the youngest writer ever to capture the prestigious Orange Prize for fiction for her Nigeria-Biafra war epic *Half of a Yellow Sun.*

13. R. Victoria Arana, "Introduction: The Chinua Achebe Special Edition," 497–501.
14. See Akin Adesokan, "The Tribe Gathers . . . Celebrating Achebe at 70." See also Eisa Davis, "Lucille Clifton and Sonia Sanchez: a conversation," 1047–49, for Sanchez's letter to Chinua Achebe on his 70th birthday anniversary.
15. Innes's interview statement is quoted in Ezenwa-Ohaeto's *Chinua Achebe: A Biography*, 149. The histopolitical significance of the students' sentiment cannot be understated. As Ezenwa-Ohaeto writes, Innes's meeting with Achebe occurred in 1969 during Achebe's "30-campus, two-week journey in North America during which the three writers [Achebe, Cyprian Ekwensi, and Gabriel Okara] lectured at various universities and talked to many people officially and unofficially" about Biafra and its secessionist cause, and thus about "war" and the writer's roles in it. See Ezenwa-Ohaeto, *Chinua Achebe*, 148–49.

It certainly made for a powerful moment in Igbo-Nigeria/black-America experience and history that the Nigeria-Biafra civil war (1967–70)—ignited by various events the most wrenching of which was Igbo genocide, the traumatizing massacre and material dispossession of thousands of Igbos resident in northern Nigeria—coincided with African America's own "war" of freedom and self-determination in the United States. With their leaders Medgar Evers, Malcolm X, Martin Luther King Jr., and others killed in quick succession, their children, like Biafra's babies, viciously violated, terrorized, and murdered while the world watched, and with anti-black southerners like Igbo/Biafra-hating northern Nigerians making the country unlivable for black Americans, it was no surprise that some African American militant political activists called for their people's secession from a hostile nation. Just as African Americans identified with Ethiopians when fascist Italy under Mussolini invaded it in 1935, some of Achebe's African American audience during the campus tours must have similarly seen themselves as the oppressed, numerical minority Igbo/Biafrans of North America. Thus, although an artist, Achebe's 1960s unconditional commitment to his community, to his people Biafra's political/human rights struggle and their group survival—a cause to which Achebe's good friend and another Igbo artist/pioneering African modernist poet Christopher Okigbo gave his life in 1967—must have resonated with the 1960s and 1970s African American writers and aestheticians. For not only did the writers and aestheticians variously thematize "war," guns, and other weapons, but African Americans in general lived in a crisis and Civil War mode. They lived in a state of siege, insomnia, and of vigilance against—to invoke the title of one of Achebe's "war" poems—the "Air Raids" of neo-slavery, racism, bomb-making, gun-toting, baton-brandishing, fire-hosing, and dog-unleashing white supremacists, and death. See Achebe, *Beware Soul Brother and Other Poems* (1971), reprinted as *Christmas in Biafra and Other Poems* (1973).

16. Emenyonu, "Introduction," xv.
17. In 1974, during the movement, *that* Achebe acuity of which Emenyonu writes had prompted Ihechukwu Madubuike to wager in his essay "Achebe's Ideas on Literature" that "Achebe's ideas will be invaluable when finally we come to define what Black Aesthetics are" (70). See also Chestyn Everett, "'Tradition' in Afro-American Literature" (1975).

The late 1950s, as well as the mid-1960s and early 1970s could be seen as important moments in the concurrent evolutions of Black Aesthetic on both sides of the Atlantic. The periods witnessed various personal meetings and exchanges of intellectual ideas between African American and African political activists, creative artists, and literary critics. The First Conference of Negro Writers in 1959 and, particularly, the First World Festival of Negro Arts, which took place in Dakar, Senegal, in 1966, brought together African, African American, and Caribbean thinkers and artists. Just as the journals *Presence Africaine* and *Black Orpheus* published works by African American writers, the First American Festival of Negro Art (AFNA, 1965) and the Second AFNA (1969) printed African works in African American periodicals. (See Patricia Liggins Hill, ed., *Call and Response* [1998], 1354–55.)

Contemporaneous with the Black Arts movement in the United States were efforts by three U.S.-educated, Nigerian, equally Afrocentric and nationalist scholars Chinweizu, Onwuchekwa Jemie, and Ihechukwu Madubuike to declare "war" on the pervasive Eurocentrism of African literature and its criticism in their landmark study *Toward a Decolonization of African Literature* (1980). Like the self-styled revolutionary aestheticians and artists of the Black Arts movement, the African troika named themselves "*bolekaja* critics" and their informing school "*bolekaja* criticism" after a Yoruba term meaning "Come down let's fight!" (See "Preface" and dedication, *Toward a Decolonization of African Literature*.) In "The Black Aesthetic and African *Bolekaja* Criticism" (1989), Chidi T. Maduka comparatively examines the two movements. See also Abraham Chapman, "The Black Aesthetic and African Continuum (1991)," for an internationalist look at the subject.

18. Achebe, *Home and Exile*, 35, 79.

19. Quoted in Emenyonu, "Preface," xi.

20. Christina Davis, "An Interview with Toni Morrison," 228–29. Original italics.

21. Michael Silverblatt, "Interview with John Edgar Wideman about *Fatheralong*," 160.

22. It is only fair to point out that in *Home and Exile*'s preface, Achebe expresses his gratitude to Gates and his colleagues at Harvard's W. E. B Du Bois Institute not only for requesting that he give the lectures that would become *Home and Exile* but for their hospitality as well.

23. In both my personal interview with him and in his "Acknowledgements," Okey Ndibe (*Arrows of Rain* 2000), for instance, recognizes John Edgar Wideman's inspiration. Tsitsi Dangaremgba also admits the additional influence of African American women novelists in her works, especially *Nervous Conditions* (1988). During his appearance on C-SPAN 2 Book TV program "Writers in Exile" (23 April 2005), Chris Abani, one of the more well known of this new generation of Nigerian/African novelists, acknowledges the influence of Ralph Ellison and James Baldwin, especially Baldwin's *Another Country,* in his growth as a writer. Chimamanda Ngozi Adichie completed her M.F.A. at Johns Hopkins and also studied at Drexel, Princeton, and Yale; and Uzodinma Iweala also writes from the United States. And, in his preface to his still provocative study *The West and the Rest of Us: White Predators, Black Slavers, and the African Elite* (1975), Chinweizu acknowledges that the book, which Toni

Morrison edited at Random House, was partly "instigated by several events of the 1960s," including "the Afro-American rebellion against their suffering under a systematized racism . . ." (xxi).

24. Achebe, "Postscript: James Baldwin (1924–1987)," 171–76.

25. Achebe, "Postscript," 173.

26. See Lilyan Kesteloot, *Black Writers in French: A Literary History of Negritude,* 56–74.

27. John Gruesser makes these valid points in his studies, *Black on Black: Twentieth-Century African American Writing about Africa* and *Confluences: Postcolonialism, African American Literary Studies, and the Black Atlantic.*

28. Adélékè Adéékó's makes a similar observation in *The Slave's Rebellion: Literature, History, Orature,* 123. In his meditation on Equiano and in the documentaries, *Africans in America (Part I): The Terrible Transformation* (1998) and *Chinua Achebe: The Importance of Stories* (1996), Achebe speaks more on slavery. And at the conference marking his seventieth birthday, Achebe identifies Morrison's *Beloved* as the one book that he could see himself bringing to the anecdotal deserted island. Morrison, he affirms, is the one writer grappling with the African quandary through her exploration of slavery, especially the haunting aftermaths of Sethe's infanticide. To Achebe, continental Africans would have to deal with the question of their participation in the slave trade, regardless of Europe's complicity in that horror. (For more, see Akin Adesokan, "The Tribe Gathers," and Somini Sengupta, "Chinua Achebe.")

That *Things Fall Apart* does not thematically probe the trans-Atlantic slave trade should not be misconstrued to mean, however, that Achebe did not have slavery centrally in mind while writing the novel. The author biography in the back of the (American) 1959 edition of the novel, which appends the phrase "The story of a strong man" to the title, includes the following pertinent remark by Achebe regarding the story's setting and time: "My main interest," declares Achebe, "is in the life of I[g]bo communities in the past. I have chosen a hinterland community far from the coastal peoples who have been debased by their participation in the cruelties of the slave trade." Thus, one can technically call *Things Fall Apart* a slavery-implicated novel; a "post" (trans-Atlantic) slavery story "almost," in the sense that, although the 1890s Umuofia is unaffected directly by the trade, as narrated, Adiele Afigbo argues that domestic abductions and slavery persisted in Igboland in various forms during that period and way into the twentieth century. (See Afigbo, *The Abolition of the Slave Trade in Southeastern Nigeria, 1885–1950.*)

29. See, for example, Nwana, *Omenuko* (1933); Aidoo, *Anowa* (1970); Ouloguem, *Bound to Violence* (1971); Head, *Maru* (1971); Armah, *Two Thousand Seasons* (1973); Awoonor, *Comes the Voyager: A Tale of Return to Africa* (1992); Echewa, *I Saw the Sky Catch Fire* (1992); and Okpewho, *Call Me by My Rightful Name* (2004).

30. The character Ojebeta in Emecheta's *The Slave Girl* is an Ọgbañje figure merchandised into slavery, hence Emecheta's linkage of the Ọgbañje experience with politics of property acquisition and exploitation.

31. I have in mind here such works as J. P. Clark, "Abiku" (1965), Elechi Amadi, *The Concubine* (1966), Buchi Emecheta, *The Bride Price* (1976), Nathan Nkala, *Mezie,*

The Ogbanje Boy (1981), Gracy Nma Osifo, *Dizzy Angel* (1985), and Sam Chekwas, *Ogbanje: "Son of the gods."*

32. Quoted in Sandra Y. Govan. "Connections, Links, and Extended Networks: Patterns in Octavia Butler's Science Fiction," 87.

33. *Things Fall Apart,* 77.

34. Personal email communication (12 June 2005). See also Dianne Glave, "'My Characters are Teaching Me to be Strong': An Interview with Tananarive Due," 695–705.

35. The part-spirit, part-human, time-traveling and seemingly ageless character David/Dawitt in Due's *My Soul to Keep* was a slave, had died multiple times, but lives in the present. To discern traces of àbíkú trope in the novel, readers should pay attention to these aspects of the novel: like the àbíkú, David is a killer. He is scarred/marked, an exile, displaced from his home. He is associated with the Life Brothers, which Due equates to the "Yorubas' immortal orishas." Like an Ọgbañje-àbíkú, David made a "pact" with this immortal/spirit club or kin but his allegiance is tellingly fickle. His dilemma, which echoes and is anticipated in Hilton James's in *The Between,* is the classic Ọgbañje-àbíkú impasse: David/Dawitt wants to stay alive in the human realm and with his wife Jessica and his human family but is shadowed and drawn by his spirit kin, the Life Brothers, and their contract/death-enforcer.

36. Okonkwo, "'It Was Like Meeting an Old Friend,'" 348.

37. *The Cattle Killing,* 15.

38. Diane Matza, "Zora Neale Hurston's *Their Eyes Were Watching God* and Toni Morrison's *Sula:* A Comparison." See also Gloria Naylor's "A Conversation: Gloria Naylor and Toni Morrison," 213–14.

39. See Patterson, *Freedom in the Making of Western Culture* (1991).

40. *Playing in the Dark,* 38, 52.

41. William L. Andrews uses this titular phrase to qualify the aims of the first century of African American autobiography in *To Tell a Free Story: The First Century of Afro-American Autobiography,* 1760–1865, xi.

42. Morrison, "The Site of Memory," 109.

43. Jahn, *Neo-African Literature: A History of Black Writing,* 121–27.

44. I borrowed this phrase from Margaret I. Jordan's *African American Servitude and Historical Imaginings,* 3.

45. I am paraphrasing Angelyn Mitchell's idea that the neo-slave narratives she studies in *The Freedom to Remember: Narrative, Slavery, and Gender in Contemporary Black Women's Fiction* are ultimately liberation stories, 3–6.

46. In his well-regarded study *The Historical Novel* (1937), George Lukács observes that "It was the French Revolution, the revolutionary wars and the rise and fall of Napoleon, which for the first time made history a *mass experience,* and moreover on a European scale. During the decades between 1789 and 1814 each nation of Europe underwent more upheavals than they had previously experienced in centuries. And the quick succession of these upheavals gives them a qualitatively distinct character, it makes their historical character far more visible than would be the case in isolated, individual instances: the masses no longer have the impression of a 'natural occurrence,'"

23. Missing in Lukács's historiography of the historical novel, however, is how the trans-Atlantic slave trade, imperialism, and European colonization of non-Caucasian peoples contributed to those upheavals in Europe. Perhaps nothing could be as *"mass experience,"* man-made, and as enlightening on a trans-continental scale as the four centuries of trade in human beings that still interlocks and haunts Europe, Africa, the Caribbean, and the Americas.

47. Ishmael Reed, *19 Necromancers,* 16.

48. John W. Blassingame, "Black Autobiographies as History and Literature," 2–4.

49. Bell, *The Afro-American Novel and Its Tradition,* 289.

50. Rushdy, "Neo-Slave Narrative," 353–535.

51. See, for instance, Paul D. Escott, "The Art and Science of Reading WPA Slave Narratives"; C. Vann Woodward, "History from Slave Sources"; and John W. Blassingame, "Using the Testimony of Ex-Slaves: Approaches and Problems." All in Charles T. Davis and Henry Louis Gates Jr., eds., *The Slave's Narrative.*

52. Frances Smith Foster, *Witnessing Slavery: The Development of Ante-Bellum Slave Narratives,* 14–17.

53. Charles Johnson, "Foreword," In *I Was Born a Slave: An Anthology of Classic Slave Narratives,* x.

54. Rushdy is right in observing that the publication of Styron's *The Confessions of Nat Turner* in the middle of a turbulent decade in African American and American history galvanized African American writers' creative responses. Black writers and intellectuals challenged Styron's work through their counterdiscourses. Styron assumes an autobiographical tone to ostensibly tarnish the antebellum slave rebel Nat Turner. Rushdy insightfully intimates that if the 1960s marked a new way of perceiving the racial self, grassroots insurgency, and the subaltern, if the civil rights movement, especially the Black Power movement, drew inspiration from Nat Turner's rebellion, then Styron's *Confessions* told the movements that their iconic hero, Nat Turner, was emasculated and overrated. Styron indirectly undermined the idea of Black Power. Citing Styron's novel as an additional impetus for writing *Dessa Rose* (1986), Sherley Anne Williams admits to "being outraged" by Styron's work. Thus, the neo-slave narratives written by black writers engaged with not only Styron but the period's intellectual contestations. For excellent treatment of the controversies sparked by Styron, see, for instance, John Henrik Clarke, ed., *William Styron's Nat Turner: Ten Black Writers Respond* (1968), Albert E. Stone, *The Return of Nat Turner: History, Literature, and Cultural Politics of Sixties America* (1992) and Naomi Jacobs, *The Character of Truth: Historical Figures in Contemporary Fiction,* 32–41.

55. *Neo-slave Narratives,* 22.

56. *Neo-slave Narratives,* 22.

57. Madhu Dubey, *Signs and Cities: Black Literary Postmodernism,* 19–31.

58. In *The Poetics of Postmodernism: History, Theory, Fiction,* Linda Hutcheon sees the postmodern difference as untotalizeable, 12. H. Lawrence Hogue uses the term "polycentric" to suggest the integrity and interactivity of the various subject locations occupied by African Americans. For more, see Hogue's "Introduction" to *The African*

American Male, Writing, and Difference: A Polycentric Approach to African American Literature, Criticism, and History (2003).

59. bell hooks, "Postmodern Blackness," *Yearning,* 29.

60. In Gloria Naylor's *Linden Hills* (1985), generations of the Nedeed men use their black wives as vehicles to copy the fathers. But the abnormal birth by one of the women, Willa Prescott Nedeed, thwarts the men's quest for immortality.

61. Elizabeth Ann Beaulieu, *Black Women Writers and the American Neo-Slave Narrative: Femininity Unfettered,* xiv–27.

62. I am playing on the title of David Gasper and Darlene Clark Hine's study, *More Than Chattel: Black Women and Slavery in the Americas* (1996).

63. Cheryl Clarke *"After Mecca": Women Poets of the Black Arts Movement,* 19.

64. Darryl Dickson-Carr and Bernard W. Bell agree with this claim. See Dickson-Carr, *The Columbia Guide to Contemporary African American Fiction* (2005), and Bell, *The Contemporary African American Novel: Its Folk Roots and Modern Literary Branches,* 250–382.

65. See Terry McMillan's "Introduction" to *Breaking Ice: An anthology of Contemporary African-American Fiction,* xx–xxiv.

66. In the provocative essay "Naming the Problem That Led to the Question 'Who Shall Teach African American Literature'?," McKay recalls the ordeal of white doubt and black proof that the young African girl and poet Phillis Wheatley had to suffer before eminent citizens of Boston adjudged her the rightful creator of her poems. I am suggesting that the 1960s exponents of Black Arts were actually fighting not to have black humanity and intellect undergo Wheatley's experience two centuries later. But to McKay, the Wheatley court actually has yet to dismiss and disband because white academic and publishing institutions still question black intellectual capacities. See Lisa A. Long, ed., *White Scholars, African American Texts,* 17–26.

67. Jeffrey O. G. Ogbar, *Black Power: Radical Politics and African American Identity,* 222.

68. Malcolm X, "The Ballot or the Bullet," in *Norton Anthology of African American Literature,* CD-ROM *Audio Companion,* ed. Robert G. O'Meally (W.W. Norton and Co., 1996). The part of the speech cited here exactly does not appear in the George Breitman edited collection *Malcolm X Speaks.* Perhaps, as Breitman suggests, the actual taped recording of the speech was not available when he completed the book.

69. Stephen Henderson, *Understanding the New Black Poetry: Black Speech and Black Music as Poetic References,* xiii.

70. Larry Neal, *Visions of a Liberated Future: Black Arts Movement Writings,* 15.

71. Jeffrey O. G. Ogbar, *Black Power,* 222.

72. In *Connecting Times: The Sixties in Afro-American Fiction,* Norman Harris provides interesting insight on this subject, 92–93. Also, in the documentary *Black Is . . . Black Ain't* (1994), the late Marlon Riggs focuses his cameras on the inherent flaws and dangers of such racial absolutism.

73. William M. Banks, *Black Intellectuals: Race and Responsibility in American Life,* 160–72.

74. Larry Neal, "The Black Arts Movement," 272.

75. For the complete text of Du Bois's earlier and much examined position on the inseparability of art and lived black experience, see his "Criteria of Negro Art" in *Call and Response: The Riverside Anthology of African American Literature,* ed. Patricia Liggins Hill et al. (1998), 850–55. In *Race Matters* (1993), Cornel West addresses this issue of black duality with reference to Malcolm X's notion of psychic conversion. West writes that "Malcolm X's notion of psychic conversion is an implicit critique of Du Bois's idea of 'double consciousness.' . . . For Malcolm X this 'double consciousness' pertains more to those black people who live 'betwixt and between' the black and white worlds—traversing the borders yet never settled in either. . . . For Malcolm X," West continues, "this 'double consciousness' is less a description of a necessary black mode of being in America than a particular kind of colonized mind-set of a special group in black America," 97. For more, see "Malcolm X and Black Rage," chapter 8 of *Race Matters.* See also Locke, "Art or Propaganda?" in Nathan Irvin Huggins, ed., *Voices from the Harlem Renaissance,* 312–13.

76. Addison Gayle, "Introduction," *The Black Aesthetic,* xxi.

77. Alain Locke's and particularly Richard Wright's caustic reviews of Hurston's *Their Eyes Were Watching God,* a novel permeated with black folkways, remain memorable.

78. James T. Stewart, "The Development of the Black Revolutionary Artist," 8.

79. Peter Bruck. "Protest, Universality, Blackness: Patterns of Argumentation in the Criticism of the Contemporary Afro-American Novel," 19.

80. Malcolm X, "The Ballot or the Bullet," *Malcolm X Speaks: Selected Speeches and Statements,* ed. George Breitman, 25–26.

81. Cheryl Clarke, "*After Mecca,*" 1.

82. Audre Lorde notes how "In the 60s, white America—racist and liberal alike—was more than pleased to sit back as spectator while Black militant fought Black Muslim, Black Nationalist badmouthed the non-violent, and Black women were told that our only useful position in the Black Power movement was prone. . . . We know in the 1980s, from documents gained through the Freedom of Information Act, that the FBI and CIA used our intolerance of difference to foment confusion and tragedy in segment after segment of Black communities of the 60s." (See Lorde, "Learning from the 60s," 137.)

83. Paula Giddings, *When and Where I Enter: The Impact of Black Women on Race and Sex in America,* 299–324.

84. See Smethurst, *The Black Arts Movement: Literary Nationalism in the 1960s and 1970s* (2005), 84–89; Kimberly Springer, "Black Feminists Respond to Black Power Masculinism," 111; and Audre Lorde, *Sister Outsider,* 134–44.

85. I am using this biblical expression "Speaking in tongues," as Mae Gwendolyn Henderson uses it in her essay of the same title, to address black women's experience of engaging inevitably and simultaneously with multiple audiences: black, white, gendered, and other. In the highly controversial *Black Macho and the Myth of the Superwoman* (1979) and, earlier, in the short story "Like a Winding Sheet" (1945), for instance, Michelle Wallace and Ann Petry respectively draw attention to the issues of black male-female relationship and how it is affected by an encounter with the white

world, especially with white women. See Eldridge Cleaver, *Soul on Ice,* 155–75. In "Africa-Centered Womanism," however, Joyce A. Joyce takes issue with black women writers' literary glorification of the black female at the expense of the black male.

86. Paula Giddings, *When and Where I Enter,* 301.

87. For recent and rigorous discussions of the movements, see, for instance, Peniel E. Joseph, *The Black Power Movement: Rethinking the Civil Rights–Black Power Era* (2006); James Edward Smethurst, *The Black Arts Movement: Literary Nationalism in the 1960s and 1970s* (2005); and Jeffrey O. G. Ogbar, *Black Power: Radical Politics and African American Identity* (2004).

88. Frances M. Beal, a *Black Scholar* interview with Octavia Butler, "Black Women and the Science Fiction Genre," 16.

89. Frances Smith Foster, "Octavia Butler's Black Female Future Fiction," 38.

90. Elyce Rae Helford. "(E)raced Visions: Women of Color and Science Fiction in the United States," 127.

91. Helfrord, "(E)raced Visions," 127–29.

92. Beal, "Black Women and the Science Fiction Genre," 18.

93. Patricia Melzer, *Alien Constructions: Science Fiction and Feminist Thought* (2006), 45.

94. Melzer, *Alien Constructions,* 36, 32.

95. Amiri Baraka, "Myth of a Negro Literature," 105.

96. Nathan Irvin Huggins emphasizes this point in his "Introduction" to his edited volume *Voices from the Harlem Renaissance,* 3-11.

97. Stephen Henderson, *Understanding the New Black Poetry,* 17.

98. Gayl Jones, *Liberating Voices: Oral Tradition in African American Literature,* 191.

99. Henderson, *Understanding,* 24.

100. Awkward, *Inspiriting Influences,* 8–11.

Chapter 3. Of Power, Protest and Revolution: Wild Seed *and* Mind of My Mind

1. Randall Kenan, "An Interview with Octavia E. Butler," 496.

2. Although *Things Fall Apart* merely includes a passing comment on trans-Atlantic slavery (140–41), Achebe addresses the subject in more detail in the documentary, *Chinua Achebe: The Importance of Stories.* See also chapter 2, endnote 28.

3. Esther Nzewi, "'Malevolent Ogbanje: recurrent reincarnation or sickle cell disease?" 1405.

4. G. T. Basden's *Niger Ibos,* chapter 17, for instance, provides an informative discussion of the issue of *osu* in Igboland. In addition, Achebe revisits the subject in his *No Longer at Ease.*

5. While S. N. Nwabara, in *Iboland: A Century of Contact with Britain, 1860–1960,* implies that such contact between the Igbo and Egyptians might have occurred (17), Adiele Afigbo rejects such supposition. He asserts that "the revolution which has taken place in African studies since the 1950s has providentially freed us from the shackles of the Hamitic hypothesis. We are thus in a position to take leave of Dr. M. D. W. Jeffreys

and his like with their easy explanation of Igbo culture history in terms of Egyptian impact and look at the old material in new light. This means, *inter alia,* that we can treat the Nri and the Aro as Igbo clans rather than as colonies of conquering Hamites and use their rich oral traditions to gain some insight into the Igbo past," *Ropes of Sand,* 2–7.

6. Information on sickle cell anemia is available in published research and online. The present citation is taken from the entry "Genetic Disease Profile: Sickle Cell Anemia" in http://www.ornl.gov/sci/techresources/Human_Genome/posters/chromosome/sca.shtml. See also Stuart J. Edelstein, *The Sickled Cell* (1986) and the sources cited in Esther Nzewi, "Malevolent Ogbanje."

7. "Genetic Disease Profile: Sickle Cell Anemia." See also Elizabeth Anionwu and Carl Atkin, *The Politics of Sickle Cell and Thalassaemia,* 9–44.

8. See also Frank B. Livingstone, "Anthropological Implications of Sickle Cell Gene Distribution in West Africa," and Todd L. Savitt, *Medicine and Slavery,* 17–35.

9. See Peter H. Wood, *Black Majority: Negroes in Colonial South Carolina from 1670 through the Stono Rebellion,* 86–91.

10. The following works provide useful insight on the subject: Philip D. Curtin, "Epidemiology and the Slave Trade"; Walter A. Schroeder et al., "Sickle Cell Anemia, Genetic Variations, and the Slave Trade to the United States"; Christian Warren, "Northern Chills, Southern Fevers: Race-Specific Mortality in American Cities, 1730–1900"; Livingstone, "Anthropological Implications of Sickle Cell Gene Distribution in West Africa"; Kenneth F. Kiple and Virginia H. Kiple, "Slave Child Mortality: Some Nutritional Answers to a Perennial Puzzle"; Todd L. Savitt, "Smothering and Overlaying of Virginia Slave Children: A Suggested Explanation"; Richard H. Steckel, "A Dreadful Childhood: The Excess Mortality of American Slaves"; and Wilma King, *Stolen Childhood: Slave Youth in Nineteenth-Century America,* 10–11.

11. Stacy Alaimo, "'Skin Dreaming': The Bodily Transgressions of Fielding Burke, Octavia Butler, and Linda Hogan," 127.

12. See for instance Simon Ottenberg, "Ibo Receptivity to Change."

13. Larry McCaffery, "An Interview with Octavia Butler," 66–67.

14. Henderson, *The King in Every Man,* 311.

15. Henderson, *The King,* 45, 106–17, 109, 129, 192.

16. In "The Future of Female: Octavia Butler's Mother Lode," Dorothy Allison takes the position that although Butler's women are depicted as strong and rebellious, they make wrong choices when it comes to the place of family and children in one's life (470–71).

17. Achebe, *Girls at War and Other Stories,* 43–44.

18. Henderson, *The King,* 311.

19. Anthonia Kalu, "Achebe and Duality in Igbo Thought," 142.

20. See Achebe, *The World of Ogbanje,* 38, 66; Ekechi, *Missionary Enterprise and Rivalry in Igboland 1857–1914,* 117; and Ogbu Kalu, "Gods as Policemen: Religion and Social Control in Igboland," 113.

21. Elochukwu E. Uzukwu, *Worship as Body Language: Introduction to Christian Worship: An African Orientation,* 101.

22. Thelma J. Shinn, "The Wise Witches: Black Women Mentors in the Fiction of Octavia E. Butler," 212.

23. John Anenechukwu Umeh, *After God is Dibia: Igbo Cosmology, Healing, Divination and Sacred Science in Nigeria,* 19. See also Obiego, *African Image of the Ultimate Reality,* 121–25; S. N. Ezeanya, "The Place of the Supreme God in the Traditional religion of the Igbo," 1; Elizabeth Isichei, *A History of Igbo People,* 25; Uchendu, *The Igbo of Southeast Nigeria,* 96–97; and John Anenechukwu Umeh, *After God is Dibia,* 1–59, 72.

24. Victor Uchendu, *The Igbo of Southeast Nigeria,* 74.

25. See Melville J. Herskovits, *The Myth of the Negro Past,* 36–37, and his *Life in a Haitian Valley,* 20–21; Alfred Metraux, *Voodoo in Haiti,* 44; Philip D. Curtin, *The Atlantic Slave Trade: A Census,* 161; and Maya Deren, *Divine Horseman: The Living Gods of Haiti,* 58. For another fictionalization of the idea of Igbo unorthodox resistance to slavery, see Paule Marshall's *Praisesong for the Widow.*

26. Nkiru Uwechia Nzegwu, *Family Matters: Feminist Concepts in African Philosophy of Culture,* 23–62.

27. Herbert M. Cole, *Mbari: Art and Life among the Owerri Igbo,* 216–20.

28. Elizabeth Isichei, *The Ibo People and the Europeans: The Genesis of a Relationship—to 1906,* 17–60.

29. Alan Rice, "'Who's Eating Whom': The Discourse of Cannibalism in the Literature of the Black Atlantic from Equiano's *Travels* to Toni Morrison's *Beloved,*" 106–16.

30. Rice, "'Who's Eating Whom,'" 106.

31. Samuel Crowther and John C. Taylor, qtd. in F. K. Ekechi, *Missionary Enterprise and Rivalry in Igboland 1857–1914* (1971), 6.

32. Gates and Andrews, *Pioneers of the Black Atlantic: Five Slave Narratives from the Enlightenment, 1772–1815* (1998), 218.

33. Sandra Y. Govan, "Homage," 86.

34. Bernard W. Bell, *The Contemporary African American Novel,* 346.

35. See Donatus Nwoga, *The Supreme God as Stranger in Igbo Religious Thought.*

36. Anthonia Kalu, "Those Left Out in the Rain," 83.

37. U. I. Ukwu, "Markets in Iboland," 127–29.

38. Adiele Afigbo, *Ropes,* 137–43.

39. Elochukwu E. Uzukwu, *Worship as Body Language,* 106–7.

40. Holloway, "Africanisms in African American Names in the United States," 85.

41. Teresa N. Washington, *Our Mothers, Our Powers, Our Texts* (2005), 195.

42. A footnote in *Drums and Shadows: Survival Studies among the Georgia Coastal Negroes* describes the incident as follows: "A group of slaves from the Ibo tribe refused to submit to slavery. Led by their chief and singing tribal songs, they walked into the water and were drowned at a point on Dunbar Creek later named Ebo (Ibo) Landing," 150. See also Gomez, *Exchanging Our Country Marks,* 114–53; Gay Wilentz, "If You Surrender to the Air: Folk Legends of Flight and Resistance in African American Literature," 21–32; Wendy W. Walters, "'One of Dese Mornings, Bright and Fair,/Take My Wings and Cleave De Air': The Legend of the Flying Africans and Diasporic Consciousness," 3–29; and William D. Piersen, "White Cannibals, Black Martyrs: Fear,

Depression, and Religious Faith as Causes of Suicide Among New Slaves," 147–59. The "Ibo landing" forms part of the thematic, cultural, structural, and political core of such works as Paule Marshall's *Praisesong for the Widow* and Julie Dash's *Daughters of the Dust*. Marshall traces her knowledge of the legend to *Drums and Shadows*. In the eponymous short story "Flying Home" and in *Song of Solomon,* Ralph Ellison and Toni Morrison respectively explore that theme of flight.

    Furthermore, Chinua Achebe would for the first time learn about this story of the Igbo slaves during his 1969 speaking tour of the United States. As he recalls: "The story of the Igbo slaves who walked into the sea was told at a meeting which I addressed in the south, in the United States, during the [Nigeria-Biafra civil] war. I was traveling there to explain what was going on; and at the end of my lectures this old man, this old black man, got up and told the story of the Igbo landing. It was a very strange feeling! Nobody knew what to say after that! He didn't say: 'Your people have done that before or anything like that!' He just told the story and sat down!" (Quoted in Ezenwa-Ohaeto, *Chinua Achebe,* 150.)

43. Quoted in Eric Sundquist, *To Wake the Nations: Race in the Making of American Literature,* 13.

44. In the course of his speech, "The Significance of Emancipation in the West Indies: An Address Delivered in Canandaigua, New York, on 3 August 1857," Douglass, in assertions quite germane to Anyanwu's unorthodox resistance to Doro's oppressive power, reminds his listeners that "Power concedes nothing without a demand. It never did and it never will. Find out just what any people will quietly submit to and you have found out the exact measure of injustice and wrong which will be imposed upon them, and these will continue till they are resisted with either words or blows." A few sentences later, Douglass edifies the courage of fugitive slave Margaret Garner who, just the year before, Douglass writes, "plunge[d] a knife into the bosom of her infant to save it from the hell of our Christian Slavery." *The Frederick Douglass Papers* 3, 1855–1863 (1985): 204.

45. John R. Pfeiffer, "Octavia Estelle Butler," 151.

46. Ruth Salvaggio, "Octavia E. Butler," 14.

47. Patricia Melzer, *Alien Constructions,* 1–3.

48. Randall Kenan, "Interview," 58; see also Octavia Butler's *Bloodchild,* 31.

49. Larry McCaffery, "An Interview with Octavia E. Butler," 58.

50. McCaffery, "An Interview with Octavia E. Butler," 58.

51. Janice Antczak, *Science Fiction: The Mythos of a New Romance,* 3.

52. See, for instance, Houston A. Baker Jr.'s *Long Black Song,* 42–57 and Maxine Lavon Montgomery's *The Apocalypse in African American Fiction* for fascinating discussions of the idea of the end of the world in African American fiction.

53. Suzanne Bost, *Mulattas and Mestizas: Representing Mixed Identities in the Americas, 1850–2000,* 184.

54. See also Patricia Melzer's discussion of the themes of colonization in Butler's works in *Alien Constructions,* 35–66.

55. Fanon, *The Wretched of the Earth* and Howard Rodney, *How Europe Underdeveloped Africa.*

Chapter 4. Binary Nativity, Subjectivity, and the Wages of (In)Fidelity to 'Origins': The Between

1. Given that Anyanwu is an Igbo woman, I am playing on "Igbo Landing" just to suggest her arrival in America.

2. Due told Dianne Glave in an interview that there are traces of her experience in Miami in *The Between*. Refer to "'My Characters are Teaching Me to be Strong,'" 698.

3. Due characterizes Hilton this way in *Freedom in the Family: A Mother: A Mother-Daughter Memoir of the Fight for Civil Rights,* 331.

4. Glave, "'My Characters,'" 701.

5. In his essay, "Racism and Science Fiction," Samuel R. Delany addresses this issue in greater detail. For more, see Delany's essay "Racism" in *Dark Matter: A Century of Speculative Fiction from the African Diaspora.*

6. Sandra M. Grayson's recent study *Visions of the Third Millennium: Black Science Fiction Writers Write the Future* is the one monograph-length project that discusses Due's novels. It is surprising that though she pays attention to Due's as well as Butler's appropriations of West African religious precepts and especially Butler's invocation of Agbala's powerful priestess Chielo in *Things Fall Apart,* she ignores *Between*. In six brief and cursory paragraphs that amount to plot summaries, Grayson focuses instead on Due's subsequent novels, including *My Soul to Keep* and its sequel, the award winning epic *The Living Blood*.

7. Glave, "'My Characters,'" 696; Due, *Freedom,* 126–27, 331.

8. Glave, "'My Characters,'" 701.

9. Due, *Freedom,* 349–50.

10. Due, *Freedom,* 25, 109.

11. In a private email communication with me, Due states that she became familiar with the idea of born-to-die and its spread in West Africa while a graduate student at the University of Leeds.

12. People familiar with the Nigerian writer J. P. Clark's poem, "Abiku," will find Due's use of the phrase "coming and going" interesting. Clark's work begins with the line "Coming and going these several seasons" in reference to the àbíkú cycle. For more, see Clark's *A Reed in the Tide* (1965), 5.

13. In *Famished Road,* the bar owner Madame Koto tells Azaro, "I am two hundred years old and unless I get your young blood I will die soon" (496).

14. Bakhtin describes chronotope as "(literally, 'time space') . . . the intrinsic connectedness of temporal and spatial relationships that are artistically expressed in literature." See Bakhtin's *The Dialogic Imagination,* 84.

15. For a work that is so politically charged, one might find it interesting that Due hedges on *The Between's* political value and strength. Due states that some of her calculations in writing the novel were political. But again, she cautions, *Between* "is not a political book." One understands Due's desire that her book not be treated as militant or as a blueprint for some political action, as were many works of the 1960s and 1970s nationalist aesthetic. But it's not as though we were about to confuse a novel with *The Communist*

Manifesto. The idea that the novel is not a political piece rings of false dichotomy because, as Octavia Butler reminds us, "[t]o be human is to be political. . . . Everything is political in one way or another." (Marilyn Mehaffy and AnaLouise Keating, "'Radio Imagination': Octavia Butler on the Poetics of Narrative Embodiment," 65). For Due's additional remarks on this subject, see *Freedom,* 352–53.

16. I borrowed the phrase from the title of Wahneema Lubiano's edited collection, *The House that Race Built.*

17. Raphael S. Ezekiel, *The Racist Mind: Portraits of American Neo-Nazis and Klansmen,* xviii.

18. Morrison, "Home," 10.

19. Du Bois, "Of Our Spiritual Strivings," in *The Souls of Black Folk.* Reference is to the Norton Critical edition, 10–11.

20. Due, *Freedom,* 109.

21. Due was also a journalist with the *Miami Herald* for a number of years.

22. See, for instance, Lawrence R. Rogers, *Canaan Bound: The African American Great Migration Novel,* 3–4; Robert Butler, *Contemporary African American Fiction: The Open Journey,* 11; and Philip Page, *Reclaiming Community in Contemporary African American Fiction,* 1–2.

23. The list is quite extensive, but let these examples suffice: James Weldon Johnson, *The Autobiography of an Ex-Colored Man;* Jessie Redmond Fauset, *Plum Bun: A Novel Without a Moral* (1928); Nella Larsen, *Quicksand* (1928) and *Passing* (1929); George Schuyler, *Black No More* (1931); Claude McKay, *Banana Bottom* (1933); Paule Marshall, *Brown Girl, Brownstones* (1951); Chinua Achebe, *No Longer at Ease;* Ayi Kwei Armah, *The Beautyful Ones Are Not Yet Born* (1968); Toni Morrison, *Song of Solomon;* Toni Cade Bambara's *The Salt Eaters* (1980); Marshall, *Praisesong for the Widow;* Gloria Naylor, *Linden Hills* (1985); August Wilson, *Joe Turner's Come and Gone* and *The Piano Lesson* (1987); Tsitsi Dangaremgba, *Nervous Conditions* (1988); and Tina McElroy Ansa, *Baby of the Family.*

24. Due, *Freedom,* 126.

25. Malcolm X used the word "*dollarism*" in reference to the contagious power of American capitalist economy in his July 17, 1964 address to the Organization of African Unity (OAU). See Breitman, ed., *Malcolm X Speaks: Selected Speeches and Statements,* 75.

26. Due, *Freedom,* 91.

27. See, for instance, Ron Finney, "'We Are All Babylonians': Afro-Americans in Africa"; Reginald McKnight's novel, *I Get on the Bus;* and Tunde Adeleke, "Black Americans and Africa: The Racial Hermeneutics of Popular Response to Keith Richburg." Widely criticized and equally debated on both sides of the Atlantic, Henry Louis Gates's video-taped pilgrimage to Africa, *Wonders of the African Continent,* in which he suggests among other things that the continent might be cursed because of its participation in the slave trade, has not helped heal the rift and wound between Africans and some of their New World cousins. Thankfully, though, Richburg's and Gates's sentiments are not shared by all their African American and African diaspora brothers and sisters.

28. Due, *Freedom,* 125–26.

29. See Madhu Dubey's "Introduction" to her study, *Black Women Writers and the Nationalist Aesthetics.*

30. See Favor's incisive exploration of how the intersections of race, culture, gender, and class shape literary constructions of black subjectivity. As Favor infers, the vocabulary of such constructions sometimes becomes exclusionary and veers, as it were, on the politics of authenticity.

Chapter 5. Mediating Character, Theme and Narration: Ǫgbañje as Hermeneutics in The Cattle Killing

1. Wideman made this remark during my interview with him on Monday, 5 July 2004. A transcript of the conversation appears in *Callaloo* 29.2 (2006): 347–60. Subsequent references to this interview in this chapter shall be designated "Personal Interview."

2. See Patricia Smith's interview with Wideman, "Getting Under Our Skin" in *Conversations with John Edgar Wideman*, 142.

3. Smith, "Getting Under," 143

4. In *The Character of Truth: Historical Figures in Contemporary Fiction,* Naomi Jacobs says this about the genre: "Instead of conveying the pill of historical fact in a sugar coating of fiction," writers of fiction autobiography " . . . openly ignore, revise, or contradict accepted facts; instead of simply filling in the gaps in the historical record—coloring in the rigid outline of a historical persona—they may transform the persona into a three-dimensional sculpture or, alternately, exaggerate and exploit its cartoon qualities. They offer not a rational reconstruction or recreation of history but a new creation in which historical figures may, like any other fictional material, be altered to suit the purposes of the work," p. xvi.

    In addition, in his interview with Derek McGinty and Bonnie TuSmith, Wideman talks about his coalescing of historical figures and events and people still living. For instance, the character George Stubbs is based on the self-taught English painter, George Stubbs (1724–1806), who was renowned for his paintings of horses, portraits, and landscapes. Wideman's evangelist George Whitefield is modeled after the great revivalist George Whitefield (1714–1770), identified with the Great Awakening in England. See McGinty's "John Edgar Wideman" and TuSmith's "Benefit of the Doubt: A Conversation with John Edgar Wideman." See also Lisa Lynch, "The Fever Next Time: The Race of Disease and the Disease of Racism in John Edgar Wideman."

5. The letter dated "Philadelphia, 22 August 1793" in *The Cattle Killing* (164–65) is Benjamin Rush's letter to his wife Julia Stockton Rush. But Wideman excludes the last two paragraphs of the letter. See *Letters of Benjamin Rush* 2: 1793–1813, ed. L. H. Butterfield, 639–40. Furthermore, parts of the letter dated "Philadelphia, 18 January 1793" in the novel appear in Rush's letter to Elizabeth Graeme Ferguson, dated "Philadelphia, January 18th, 1793." In *Letters of Benjamin Rush* 1: 627–28.

6. Jennifer D. Douglas, "'Ill Seen, Ill Said': Tropes of Vision and the Articulation of Race Relations in *The Cattle Killing*," 212.

7. Bonnie TuSmith, "Optical Tricksterism: Dissolving and Shapeshifting in the Works of John Edgar Wideman," 250–53.

8. For more on this still controversial historical incident in which the Xhosa people of South Africa slaughtered their cattle reportedly on what turned out to be a fallacious white proposition of redemption, see, for instance Noël Mostert, *Frontiers: The Epic of South Africa's Creation and the Tragedy of the Xhosa People,* Timothy J. Stapleton, "'They No Longer Care for their Chiefs': Another Look at the Xhosa Cattle-Killing of 1856–1857," and J. B. Peiers, *The Dead Will Rise: Nongqawuse and the Great Xhosa Cattle-Killing Movement of 1856–7.*

9. I appropriated this phrase from the title of Toni Morrison's essay "Unspeakable Things Unspoken: The Afro-American Presence in American Literature." However, in his interview with Bonnie TuSmith (*Conversations*), Wideman says that in his works he also engages with the "unspeakable" (214).

10. McGinty, "John Edgar Wideman," 188.

11. For such studies, see, for instance, Fritz Gysin, "'Do Not Fall Asleep in Your Enemy's Dream': John Edgar Wideman and the Predicament of Prophecy"; Kathie Birat, "'All Stories are True': Prophecy, History and Story in *The Cattle Killing*"; James W. Coleman, *Black Male Fiction and the Legacy of Caliban;* Sheri I. Hoem, "'Shifting Spirits': Ancestral Constructs in the Postmodern Writing of John Edgar Wideman"; and Lisa Lynch, "The Fever Next Time."

12. Bernard W. Bell, *The Contemporary African American Novel,* 217.

13. Wideman acknowledges Maya Deren's *Divine Horseman: The Voodoo Gods of Haiti* for insight on Haitian metaphysics he employs in the short fiction "Damballah."

14. Wideman recognizes also Robert Farris's *Flash of the Spirit* for his use of Kongo worldview.

15. For some insight on the àbíkú-ibeji connection, see, for instance, Harold Courlander, "The Worship of Twins Among the Yoruba."

16. Joanna Brooks, *American Lazarus: Religion and the Rise of African-American and Native American Literatures,* 98, 103.

17. Versions of the following events and statements, addressed in *The Cattle Killing,* are recorded in Marrant's narrative and journal, as well as in John Jea's and Henry Bibb's narratives collectively: In Marrant's 1785 *Narrative* (anthologized in Gates and Andrews, eds. *Pioneers of the Black Atlantic*) and his 1790 *Journal* (included in Joanna Brooks and John Saillant, *"Face Zion Forward": First Writers of the Black Atlantic, 1785–1798*), the words/tropes of traveling, journey, moving/movement recur. Marrant talks about waking up one morning and emerging from a tree, his usual lodging (*Pioneers* 69), and about dying and being reborn a number of times. He encounters a serious storm and likens himself to Jonah saved miraculously in the bible (79). The event in which (Marrant's) the preacher-narrator's blood is spilled/shed for Christ in *The Cattle Killing* occurs also in the *Journal* (*"Face"* 112–13). Like the preacher in *The Cattle Killing,* Marrant attends to a terminally sick woman/patient (*"Face"* 113). An Armanian, part of Mr. Wesley's society, calls Marrant "a devil" (*"Face"* 126). Like the preacher-narrator, Marrant feels "a great desire and eagerness to leave this body"

("*Face*" 133); he encounters "two women on the road, one was lying down and just expiring, and the other stood over her weeping" ("*Face*" 133). Marrant, drowsy, falls asleep in the grass, is touched by a supernatural presence, and hears a voice ("*Face*" 136). Marrant also stammers, "Reader, I am at a loss for words"; he acknowledges his "stammering tongue" ("*Face*" 147). John Jea talks about slave holders likening slaves to the devil and commonly miscalling them "*black devils*" (*Pioneers* 373)—an indignity that Wideman's preacher suffers also. Jea was angry at God initially. He says, "I had such malice against God and his people" (*Pioneers* 374). Jea also sees his conversion as being "born again."

In his August 17, 1786 pre-execution public admission or rather cataloging of his numerous crimes, the most recurrent of which were burglary, robbery, and illicit and miscegenetic sexual liaisons with both black and white women, married and single, Johnson Green prefaces several claims with "I broke into . . ." and/or "I stole . . ." this or that. (See Green's testimony in Dorothy Porter, ed., *Early Negro Writing, 1760–1837* [1971].) In a statement indirectly supportive of Wideman's intent to memorialize the black dead in the novel, Arthur P. Davis notes in his untitled review of Porter's collection that "In his crooked and abortive way Johnson Green was 'heroic' and achieved through this confession and the broadside poem written on it a kind of attenuated immortality" (see *The Journal of Negro Education* 41.1 [Winter 1972]: 92–93). (See also Richard Slotkin, "Narratives of Negro Crime in New England, 1650–1800" [1973].) Henry Bibb, who without remorse steals a horse, also stutters and loses words with which to describe slavery's cruelties (See *I Was Born a Slave: An Anthology of Classic Slave Narratives.* Vol. 2. Ed. Yuval Taylor (1999), 14, 26). I address the parallels between *The Cattle Killing*'s Kathryn and Harriet Jacobs (Linda Brent) in the chapter proper.

18. Philip Page, review of "*The Cattle Killing.*"
19. J. B. Peires, *The Dead Will Rise: Nongqawuse and the Great Cattle-Killing Movement of 1856–7* (1989), 315–21.
20. In *A Narrative of the Proceedings of the Black People, During the Late Awful Calamity in Philadelphia, in the Year 1793: and A Refutation of Some Censures, Thrown Upon Them in Some Late Publications,* Allen and Absalom Jones present black people's side of the story and also contest inflammatory accusations that Matthew Carey made against the black nurses and undertakers during the emergency.
21. See, Chanta M. Haywood, *The Prophesying Daughters: Black Women Preachers and the Word, 1823–1913,* and Joycelyn Moody, *Sentimental Confessions.*
22. Samar Attar provides a fascinating conceptualization of the intruder figure in *The Intruder in Modern Drama,* 9–10.
23. Douglas, "Ill Seen, Ill Said," 215.
24. Houston A. Baker Jr. "Belief, Theory, Blues: Notes for a Poststructuralist Criticism of Afro-American Literature," 7.
25. W. E. B. Du Bois, *The Philadelphia Negro,* 142
26. See Childress, *Wedding Band: A Love/Hate Story in Black and White* (1973).
27. Knight, in *Call and Response,* 1483–84.

28. Rev. Bishop Fred Pierce Corson, "St. George's Church: The Cradle of American Methodism," 230, 232.

29. Personal interview.

30. Personal interview.

31. In "In Her Own Write," his foreword to Pauline E. Hopkins's *Contending Forces,* Henry Louis Gates Jr. discusses this issue.

32. See Walker's "In Search of Our Mothers' Gardens" in her book of the same title.

33. Personal interview.

34. In Harriet Jacobs's *Incidents in the Life of Slave Girl,* the enslaved black girl Linda Brent is caught between her abusive mistress Mrs. Flint and the sexual advances of her master Dr. Flint.

35. Takaki, *Iron Cages: Race and Culture in Nineteenth-Century America,* 3–35.

36. William L. Andrews, *To Tell a Free Story,* 10.

37. West writes: "The genius of our black foremothers and forefathers was to create powerful buffers to ward off the nihilistic threat, to equip black folk with cultural armor to beat back the demons of hopelessness, meaninglessness, and lovelessness. These buffers consisted of cultural structures of meaning and feeling that created and sustained communities; this armor constituted ways of life and struggle that embodied values of service and sacrifice, love and care, discipline and excellence" (*Race Matters,* 15). Morrison shared the same sentiment about the black community of her youth with Robert Stepto in their interview "'Intimate Things in Place,'" 474–75.

38. West, *Race Matters,* 12 (original italics).

39. Okonkwo, "'It Was Like Meeting an Old Friend,'" 358.

40. J. B. Peires, *The Dead Will Rise,* 311.

41. F. K. Ekechi, *Missionary Enterprise and Rivalry in Igboland 1857–1914,* 4.

42. Sheri I. Hoem, "'Shifting Spirits': Ancestral Constructs in the Postmodern Writing of John Edgar Wideman," 260.

43. Adiele Afigbo, *The Abolition of the Slave Trade in Southeastern Nigeria, 1885–1950,* 56.

44. Kenneth Onwuka Dike and Felicia Ekejiuba, *The Aro of South-eastern Nigeria, 1650–1980,* 44.

45. Innocent I. Asouzu, *The Method and Principles of Complementary Reflection In and Beyond African Philosophy,* 246.

46. Rebekah Presson, "John Edgar Wideman," 12.

47. Personal interview.

48. Bonnie TuSmith, "Benefit of the Doubt," 210.

49. Naomi Jacobs, *The Character of Truth: Historical Figures in Contemporary Fiction,* 34.

50. Wideman, "Architectonics," 43.

51. Walker, *A Rock in a Weary Land,* 4–29.

52. Andrews, *To Tell a Free Story,* 68.

53. Alexander E. Curtis, *Richard Allen: The First Exemplar of African American Education,* 85.

54. Andrews, *To Tell a Free Story,* 69.

Chapter 6. Sula, Beloved, *and the Constructive Synchrony of Good and Evil*

1. Trudier Harris makes this observation in her essay "Beloved: Woman, Thy name is Demon," 129.

2. Gay Wilentz, in "An African-Based Reading of *Sula,*" and Vashti C. Lewis, in "African Traditions in Toni Morison's *Sula,*" make such affirmations.

3. See Toni Morrison's "Rootedness," 339–45.

4. Morrison, "Behind the Making of *The Black Book,*" 86–90. See also Robert B. Stepto, "Intimate Things in Place,'" 474.

5. Madhu Dubey, *Black Women Novelists and the Nationalist Aesthetic,* 1–32.

6. Stepto, "'Intimate Things in Place,'" 12.

7. Paul S. J. Siwek, *The Philosophy of Evil,* v.

8. Mbiti, *African Religions and Philosophy,* 177–79.

9. Gay Wilentz makes this point in her essay "An African-Based Reading of *Sula,*" 132.

10. Christie C. Achebe, "Literary Insights," 33.

11. Vashti C. Lewis, "African Tradition in Toni Morrison's *Sula,*" 91.

12. Morrison describes Sula this way in her interview with Robert Stepto, "'Intimate Things in Place,'" 477.

13. Cosmas Okechukwu Obiego, *African Image of the Ultimate Reality,* 135.

14. Houston Baker, *Workings of the Spirit,* 139.

15. Biman Basu, "Hybridity and the Dialogic in Black Women's Fiction," Ph.D. diss., U of Minnesota (1992), 189. See also Jacqueline de Weever, *Mythmaking and Metaphor in Black Women's Fiction,* 170.

16. Alexis Brooks De Vita, *Mythatypes,* 55.

17. See Joseph H. Wessling, "Narcissism in Toni Morrison's *Sula,*" 283.

18. Morrison, "Site," 111.

19. Martha J. Cutter, "The Story Must Go On and On," 61–75.

20. Lee, "The Anger and Shock of a City's Slave Past," online.

21. See Thomas Bartlett, "After Brown University's Report on Slavery, Silence (So Far)," A32–35.

22. See Kathleen Marks, *Toni Morrison's Beloved and the Apotropaic Imagination,* 1–25; Therese E. Higgins, *Religiosity, Cosmology and Folklore: The African Influence in the Novels of Toni Morrison,* 20–32; Sharon Patricia Holland, *Raising the Dead: Readings of Death and (Black) Subjectivity,* 41–67; Carolyn M. Jones, "*Sula* and *Beloved:* Images of Cain in the Novels of Toni Morrison," 615–16; Trudier Harris, "Beloved: Woman, Thy Name is Demon," 129; A. Timothy Spaulding, *Reforming the Past,* 61–76; and Washington's *Our Mothers, Our Powers, Our Texts,* 226–44.

23. Steven Weisenburger, *Modern Medea,* 6.

24. Baldwin recounts his painful experiences with Jim Crow in New Jersey in 1942, the year before his father died. Humiliated and maddened, he states that "There is not a Negro alive who does not have this rage in his blood—one has the choice, merely, of living with it consciously or surrendering to it." For more, see "Notes of a Native Son," 93–98.

25. John A. Noon, "A Preliminary Examination of the Death Concepts of the Ibo," 639.
26. In "Strange Fruit," her lyrically haunting song about, yet a blistering attack on, lynching in the south, Billie Holiday bemoans that "Southern trees bear a strange fruit, / Blood on the leaves and blood at the root, / Black bodies swaying in the Southern breeze, / Strange fruit hanging from the poplar trees." For the full text of the song, see John White, *Billie Holiday: Her Life and Times* (1987), 50.
27. Fredric Jameson, *The Political Unconscious*, 10.
28. See also Charles J. Heglar, *Rethinking the Slave Narrative: Slave Marriage and the Narratives of Henry Bibb and William and Ellen Craft* (2001).
29. David Lawrence, "Fleshly Ghosts and Ghostly Flesh," 231.
30. Angelyn Mitchell, *The Freedom to Remember*, 19.

Epilogue: This Blues Called Ọgbañje

1. Jonathan D. Culler, *The Pursuit of Signs: Semiotics, Literature, Deconstruction*, 189.
2. Quayson calls Ọgbañje and àbíkú "a 'constellar concept'" that "embraces various beliefs about predestination, reincarnation, and the relationship between the real world and that of spirits." *Strategic Transformations in Nigerian Writing*, 123.
3. See Baker's introduction to *Blues, Ideology*, 1–14.
4. McGinty, "John Edgar Wideman" in *Conversations with John Edgar Wideman*, 192.
5. Diane Glave, "'My Characters,'" 696–97.
6. I am playing on Julia Kristeva's notion of "ideologeme" which Kristeva describes as "the intersection of a given textual arrangement (a semiotic practice) with the utterances (sequences) that it either assimilates into it sown space or to which it refers in the space of the exterior texts (semiotic practices)." See Kristeva, "The Bounded Text" in *Desire in Language: A Semiotic Approach to Literature and Art* (1980), 36.
7. Reed, *19 Necromancers*, 12.
8. Johnson, "Philosophy and Black Fiction," 57.
9. Johnson, *Being and Race*, 119.
10. I borrowed the phrase "the West and the rest of us" from Chinweizu et al.'s book of the same title.
11. See *Praisesong of Survival: Lectures and Essays 1957–89*, 37–38.
12. Baker, *Blues, Ideology*, 202–3.
13. bell hooks, "Postmodern Blackness," *Yearning*, 28.
14. See Cheryl A. Wall, "Taking Positions and Changing Words" in *Changing Our Own Words: Essays on Criticism, Theory, and Writing by Black Women*, 9.
15. Personal interview with Wideman, as cited above.
16. See Derek McGinty's interview, "John Edgar Wideman," 192.
17. Personal interview with Wideman.
18. The phrase "pantheon of heroes" is Lawrence W. Levine's. See his *Black Culture and Black Consciousness*, 367, and John W. Roberts's *From Trickster to Badman: The Black Folk Hero in Slavery and Freedom* for stimulating discussions of the subject.
19. Maureen Warner-Lewis, *Guinea's Other Suns*, 135.

20. James H. Cone, *The Spirituals and the Blues,* 103.
21. What starts out in chapter 5 of *Tunneling* as Rachel Finch's encounter with a Professor Achebe in 2003, and her recalled, chance meeting with the young Achebe many years ago in Igboland, quickly becomes Bosworth's interesting re-imaginings of Achebe's life and literary career. The section on Achebe, who is one of the novel's besieged world-famous authors along with Shakespeare and Kafka whom Rachel endeavors to rescue, touches on various people, subjects and events, including Wole Soyinka, Conrad, Christopher Okigbo, the Nigeria-Biafra civil war, and the country's post-independence history. Bosworth acknowledges Ezenwa-Ohaeto's biography of Chinua Achebe as source for the material on Achebe.
22. Ellison, *Shadow and Act,* 78.
23. Ellison, "A Very Stern Discipline," *Going to the Territory,* 302–3.
24. In his 1994 *Paris Review* interview with Jerome Brooks, Achebe recounts in detail how his handwritten manuscript of *Things Fall Apart,* which he had sent to a London typing agency, almost got lost. For more, see Brooks, "Chinua Achebe," 8–10. See the interview also at http://www.theparisreview.org/viewinterview.php/prmMID/1720.
25. For full text of the poem, see for instance Patricia Liggins Hill, ed., *Call and Response: The Riverside Anthology of African American Literary Tradition,* 1004–5.

Bibliography

Achebe, Chinua. *Things Fall Apart*. 1958. New York: Doubleday, 1994.

———. "The Sacrificial Egg." 1959. *Girls at War and other Stories*. New York: Anchor Books, 1991.

———. *No Longer at Ease*. 1960. New York: Doubleday, 1994.

———. *Arrow of God*. 1964. New York: Anchor Books, 1989.

———. *A Man of the People*. 1966. New York: Anchor Books, 1989.

———. "Uncle Ben's Choice." 1966. *Girls at War*. 75–81.

———. *Beware Soul Brother and Other Poems*. Enugu: Nwankwo-Ifejika, 1971. Rev. ed. London: Heinemann 1972. Rpt. *Christmas in Biafra and Other Poems*. Garden City, NY: Anchor/Doubleday, 1973.

———. "The Madman." 1971. *Girls at War*. 3–12.

———. "Chi in Igbo Cosmology." *Morning Yet on Creation Day: Essays*. New York: Anchor Books, 1975. 131–45.

———. "An Image of Africa: Racism in Conrad's *Heart of Darkness*." 1975. *Hopes and Impediments: Selected Essays*. New York: Anchor Books, 1988. 1–20.

———. "The Writer and His Community." *Hopes and Impediments*. 47–61

———. "The Igbo World and Its Art." *Hopes and Impediments*. 62–67.

———. *Anthills of the Savannah*. 1987. New York: Anchor Books, 1988.

———. "Postscript: James Baldwin (1924–1987)." *Hopes and Impediments*. 171–76.

———. *Home and Exile*. Oxford: Oxford UP, 2000.

———. "The Day I Finally Met Baldwin." *Callaloo* 25.2 (2002): 502–4.

Achebe, Christie C[hinwe]. "Literary Insights into the *Ogbanje* Phenomenon." *Journal of African Studies* 7.1 (Spring 1980): 31–38.

———. *The World of the Ogbanje*. Enugu: Fourth Dimension Publishing Co., 1986.

———. "The Ogbanje Phenomenon—A Tentative Interpretation." Paper presented at a Workshop on Igbo World View. Institute of African Studies and the Faculty of Arts, University of Nigeria, Nsukka. N.d.: 1–23.

Acholonu, Catherine. "Ogbanje: A Motif and a Theme in the Poetry of Christopher Okigbo." *African Literature Today* 16 (1988): 103–11.

Adéékó, Adélékè. *The Slave's Rebellion: Literature, History, Orature*. Bloomington: Indiana UP, 2005.

Adeleke, Tunde. "Black Americans and Africa: The Racial Hermeneutics of Popular Response to Keith Richburg." *Ufahamu: Journal of African Activist Association* 25.3 (Fall 1997): 86–109.

Adesokan, Akin. "The Tribe Gathers . . . Celebrating Achebe at 70." *Nigerians in America.* <http://www.nigeriasinamerica.com/artiscle/21/1>, 28 May, 2005.

Afigbo, A[diele] E[berechukwu]. *Ropes of Sand: Studies in Igbo History and Culture.* Ibadan: UP Limited, 1981.

———. *The Abolition of the Slave Trade in Southeastern Nigeria, 1885-1950.* New York: U of Rochester P, 2006.

Aidoo, Ama Ata. *Anowa.* Harlow: Longmans, 1970.

Aji, Aron, and Kirstin Lynne Ellsworth. "Ezinma: The Ogbanje Child in Achebe's *Things Fall Apart.*" *College Literature* (double issue) 19.3 (Oct. 1992) and 20.1 (Feb. 1993): 170–75.

Alaimo, Stacy. "'Skin Dreaming': The Bodily Transgressions of Fielding Burke, Octavia Butler, and Linda Hogan." *Ecofeminist Literary Criticism: Theory, Interpretation, Pedagogy.* Ed. Greta Gaard and Patrick D. Murphy. Urbana: U of Illinois P, 1998. 123–38.

Alexander, E. Curtis. *Richard Allen: The First Exemplar of African American Education.* New York, ECA P, 1985.

Allen, Graham. *Intertextuality.* New York: Routledge, 2000.

Allen, Rt. Rev. Richard. *The Life Experience and Gospel Labors of the Rt. Rev. Richard Allen.* 1833. Nashville: Abingdon P, 1960. Bicentennial edition 1983.

Allison, Dorothy. "The Future of Female: Octavia Butler's Mother Lode." *Reading Black, Reading Feminist: A Critical Anthology.* Ed. Henry Louis Gates Jr. New York: Meridian, 1990. 471–78.

Amadi, Elechi. *The Concubine.* Oxford: Heinemann Educational Publishers, 1966.

Amadiume, Ifi. *Male Daughters, Female Husbands: Gender and Sex in an African Society.* London: Zed Books, 1987.

Andrews, William L. *To Tell a Free Story: The First Century of Afro-American Auto-biography, 1760–1865.* Urbana: U of Illinois P, 1988.

Anionwu, Elizabeth N., and Karl Atkin. *The Politics of Sickle Cell and Thalassaemia.* Philadelphia: Open UP, 2001.

Ansa, Tina McElroy. *Baby of the Family.* San Diego: Harcourt, Brace and Co., 1989.

———. *The Hand I Fan With.* New York: Anchor Books, 1998

———. *You Know Better.* New York: William Marrow, 2002.

Antczak, Janice. *Science Fiction: The Mythos of a New Romance.* New York: Neal-Schuman P, 1985.

Appiah, Kwame Anthony. *Cosmopolitanism: Ethics in a World of Strangers.* New York: W. W. Norton and Company, 2006.

Aptheker, Herbert. *American Negro Slave Revolts.* 1943. New York: International Publishers, 1983.

Arana, R. Victoria. "Introduction: The Chinua Achebe Special Edition." *Callaloo* 25.2 (2002): 497–501.

Ardis, Angela. *Inside a Thug's Heart: With Original Poems and Letters by Tupac Shakur.* New York: Dafina Books, 2004.

Arinze, Francis A. *Sacrifice in Ibo Religion.* Ibadan: Ibadan UP, 1970.

Armah, Ayi Kwei. *Two Thousand Seasons.* Nairobi : East African Publishing House, 1973.

Asouzu, Innocent I. *The Method and Principles of Complementary Reflection In and Beyond African Philosophy.* Calabar, Nigeria: U of Calabar P, 2004.

Attar, Samar. *The Intruder in Modern Drama.* Frankfurt am Main: Lang, 1980.

Ausband, Stephen C. *Myth and Meaning, Myth and Order.* Macon, Ga.: Mercer UP, 1983.

Awkward, Michael. *Inspiriting Influences: Tradition, Revision, and Afro-American Women's Novels.* New York: Columbia UP, 1989.

Awoonor, Kofi. *Comes the Voyager at Last.* Trenton, NJ: Africa World P, 1992.

Babalola, E. O. "Traditional Therapeutics and Its Application to the Abiku Phenomenon in Owo Yoruba Community." *Africana Marburgensia* 16 (1996): 60–69.

Badejo, Deidre L. "Tokunbo: A Divination Poem." *Black American Literature Forum* 23.3 (Fall 1989): 486–89.

Baker, Houston A. Jr. "Freedom and Apocalypse: A Thematic Approach to Black Experience." *Long Black Song: Essays in Black American Literature.* Charlottesville: The UP of Virginia, 1972. 42–57.

———. *Blues, Ideology, and Afro-American Literature: A Vernacular Theory.* Chicago: U of Chicago P, 1984.

———. "Belief, Theory, Blues: Notes for a Poststructuralist Criticism of Afro-American Literature." *Belief vs. Theory in Black American Literary Criticism.* Ed. Joe Weixlmann and Chester J. Fontenot. Greenwood: Penkevill Publishing Co., 1986. 5–30.

———. *Modernism and the Harlem Renaissance.* Chicago: U of Chicago P, 1987.

———. "There is No More Beautiful Way: Theory and the Poetics of Afro-American Women's Writing." *Afro-American Literary Study in the 1990s.* Ed. Houston A. Baker Jr. and Patricia Redmond. Chicago: The U of Chicago P, 1989. 135–63.

———. *Workings of the Spirit: The Poetics of Afro-American Women's Writing.* Chicago: U of Chicago P, 1991.

Baker, Lisa. "Storytelling and Democracy (in the Radical Sense): A Conversation with John Edgar Wideman." *African American Review* 34.2 (2000): 263–72.

Bakhtin, Mikhail M. "Discourse in the Novel." *The Dialogic Imagination: Four Essays.* Ed. Michael Holquist. Trans. Caryl Emerson and Michael Holquist. Austin: U of Texas P, 1981. 259–422.

Baldwin, James. "Many Thousands Gone." *Notes of a Native Son.* 1955. Boston: Beacon P, 1984. 24–45.

———. "Notes of a Native Son." *Notes of a Native Son.* 85–114.

———. "Sonny's Blues." *Going to Meet the Man.* New York: Dial P, 1965. 103–41.

Banks, William M. *Black Intellectuals: Race and Responsibility in American Life.* New York: W. W. Norton and Co., 1996.

Banyiwa-Horne, Naana. "The Scary Face of the Self: An Analysis of the Character of Sula in Toni Morrison's *Sula.*" *SAGE* 2.1 (Spring 1985): 28–31.

Baraka, Amiri (LeRoi Jones). *Blues People: The Negro Experience in White America and the Music that Developed from It.* New York: Morrow Quill Paperback, 1963.

———. "Myth of a Negro Literature." *Home: Social Essays.* Hopewell, NJ: Ecco Press, 1998. 105–15.

Barksdale, Richard. "Critical Theory and Problems of Canonicity in African American Literature." *Praisesong of Survival: Lectures and Essays 1957–89.* Urbana: U of Illinois P, 1992. 33–38.

Barthes, Roland. *The Pleasure of the Text.* 1973. Trans. Richard Miller. New York: Hill and Wang, 1975.

———. *Image.Music.Text.* Ed. and trans. Stephen Heath. New York: Hill and Wang, 1977.

Barthold, Bonnie J. *Black Time: Fiction of Africa, the Caribbean, and the United States.* New Haven: Yale UP, 1981.

Bartlett, Thomas. "After Brown University's Report on Slavery, Silence (So Far)." *The Chronicle of Higher Education,* Nov. 24, 2006: A32–35.

Bascom, William. *Ifa Divination: Communication Between Gods and Men in West Africa.* Bloomington: Indiana UP, 1969.

———. *The Yoruba of Southwestern Nigeria.* New York: Holt, Rinehart and Winston, 1969.

———. "Gulla Folk Beliefs Concerning Childbirth." *Sea Island Roots: African Presence in the Carolinas and Georgia.* Ed. Mary A Twining and Keith E. Baird. Trenton, NJ: Africa World P, 1991. 27–36.

Basden, G. T. *Niger Ibos: A Description of the Primitive Life, Customs and Animistic Beliefs, Etc. of the Ibo People of Nigeria By One Who, For Thirty-Five Years, Enjoyed the Privilege of their Intimate Confidence and Friendship.* 1938. New York: Barnes and Noble, 1966.

Bastfield, Darrin Keith. *Back in the Day: My Life and Times with Tupac Shakur.* New York: Ballantine Books, 2002.

Bastian, Misty L. "Irregular Visitors: Narratives About Ogbaanje [*sic*] (Spirit Children) in Southern Nigerian Popular Writing." *Readings in African Popular Fiction.* Ed. Stephanie Newell. Bloomington: Indiana UP, 2002. 59–67.

———. "Married in the Water: Spirit Kin and Other Affliction of Modernity in South-eastern Nigeria." *Journal of Religion in Africa.* 27.2 (1997): 116–34.

Bastide, Roger. *The African Religions of Brazil: Toward a Sociology of the Interpretation of Civilizations.* Trans. Helen Sebba. 1960. Baltimore: Johns Hopkins UP, 1978.

Basu, Biman. *Hybridity and the Dialogic in Black Women's Fiction.* Ph.D. diss. U of Minnesota, 1992.

Beal, Frances M. "Interview with Octavia Butler: Black Women and the Science Fiction Genre." *Black Scholar* 17. 2 (Mar.–Apr. 1986): 14–18.

Beaulieu, Elizabeth Ann. *Black Women Writers and the American Neo-Slave Narrative: Femininity Unfettered.* Westport, CT: Greenwood P, 1999.

Beier, H. U. "Spirit Children Among the Yoruba." *African Affairs* 53.213 (Oct. 1954): 328–31.

Bell, Bernard W. *The Afro-American Novel and Its Tradition.* Amherst: U of Massachusetts P, 1987.

———. *The Contemporary African American Novel: Its Folk Roots and Modern Literary Branches.* Amherst: U of Massachusetts P, 2004.

Benes, Peter, ed. *Wonders of the Invisible World, 1600–1900.* Boston: Boston UP, 1995.

Benston, Kimberly W. "I yam what I yam: the topos of (un)naming in Afro-American literature," *Black Literature and Literary Theory*. Ed. Henry Louis Gates Jr. New York: Methuen, 1984. 151–72.

———. *Performing Blackness: Enactments of African-American Modernism*. London: Routledge, 2000.

Berger, James. "Ghosts of Liberalism: Morrison's Beloved and the Moynihan Report." *PMLA* 111.3 (May 1996): 408–20.

Bibb, Henry. *Narrative of the Life and Adventures of Henry Bibb, An American Slave, Written By Himself.* 1849. In *I Was Born a Slave: An Anthology* of *Classic Slave Narratives*. Volume 2: 1849–1866. Ed. Yuval Taylor. Chicago: Lawrence Hill Books, 1999. 4–101.

Bigsby, C. W. E. *The Second Black Renaissance: Essays in Black Literature*. Westport, CT: Greenwood P, 1980.

Birat, Kathie. "'All Stories are True': Prophecy, History and Story in *The Cattle Killing*." *Callaloo* 22. 3 (1999): 629–43.

Blakey, Michael L. "The Study of New York's African Burial Ground: Biocultural and Engaged." *African Roots/American Cultures: Africa in the Creation of the Americas*. Ed. Sheila S. Walker. Lanham, MD: Rowman and Littlefield Publishers, 2001. 222–31.

Blassingame, John W. *The Slave Community: Plantation Life in the Antebellum South*. New York: Oxford UP, 1972.

———. "Black Autobiographies as History and Literature." *Black Scholar: Journal of Black Studies and Research* 5. 4 (Dec. 1973–Jan. 1974): 2–9.

———. "Using the Testimony of Ex-Slaves: Approaches and Problems." *The Slave's Narrative*. Ed. Charles T. Davis and Henry Louis Gates Jr. New York: Oxford UP, 1985. 78–98.

Bontemps, Arna. *Black Thunder*. 1936. Boston: Beacon P, 1992.

Bost, Suzanne. *Mulattas and Mestizas: Representing Mixed Identities in the Americas, 1850–2000*. Athens: The U of Georgia P, 2003.

Bosworth, Beth. *Tunneling*. New York: Shaye Areheart Books, 2003. 111–52.

Botstein, Leon. "Things Fall Together: A Conversation with Chinua Achebe and Toni Morrison." *Transition* (Kampala Uganda) 89 (2001): 150–65.

Bowers, Maggie Ann. *Magic(al) Realism: the New Critical Idiom*. London: Routledge, 2004.

Bradley, David. *The Chaneysville Incident*. New York: Harper and Row, P, 1981.

Brogan, Kathleen. *Cultural Haunting: Ghosts and Ethnicity in Recent American Fiction*. Charlottesville: UP of Virginia, 1998.

Brooks De Vita, Alexis. *Mythatypes: Signatures and Signs of African/African Diaspora Goddesses*. Westport, Connecticut: Greenwood P, 2000.

Brooks De Vita. "Not Passing on Beloved: The Sacrificial Child and the Circle of Redemption." *Griot: Official Journal of the Southern Conference on Afro-American Studies* 19.1 (2002): 1–12.

Brooks, Jerome. "Chinua Achebe." (Interview.) The Art of Fiction No. 139. *The Paris Review* 133 (Winter 1994): 1–25.

Brooks, Joanna. *American Lazarus: Religion and the Rise of African-American and Native American Literatures.* Oxford: Oxford UP, 2003.

Bruck, Peter. "Protest, Universality, Blackness: Patterns of Argumentation in the Criticism of the Contemporary Afro-American Novel." *The Afro-American Novel Since 1960.* Ed. Peter Bruck and Wolfgang Karrer. Amsterdam: B. R. Grüner Publishing Co., 1982. 1–27.

Bryant, Jerry H. *'Born in a Mighty Bad Land': The Violent Man in African American Folklore and Fiction.* Bloomington: Indiana UP, 2003. 166–78.

Butler, Octavia E. *Patternmaster.* 1976. New York: Warner Books, 1995.

———. *Mind of My Mind.* 1977. New York: Warner Books, 1994.

———. *Survivor.* New York: Doubleday, 1978.

———. *Kindred.* 1979. Boston: Beacon P, 1988.

———. *Wild Seed.* 1980. New York: Warner Books, 1999.

———. *Clay's Ark.* New York: St. Martin's P, 1984.

———. *Dawn.* New York: Warner, 1987.

———. *Adulthood Rites.* New York: Warner, 1988.

———. *Imago.* New York: Warner, 1989.

———. "The Evening and the Morning and the Night." 1987. *Bloodchild and Other Stories.* New York, NY: Seven Stories P, 2005. 33–70.

Butler, Robert. *Contemporary African American Fiction: The Open Journey.* Cranberry, NJ: Associated UP, 1998.

Butterfield, L.H, ed. *Letters of Benjamin Rush.* Vol. 1. 1761–1792. Princeton UP, 1974. 627–28.

———, ed. *The Letters of Benjamin Rush.* Vol. 2: 1793–1813. Princeton: Princeton UP, 1951. 639–40

Butterfield, Stephen. *Black Autobiography in America.* Amherst: U of Massachusetts P, 1974.

Byerman, Keith E. *Fingering the Jagged Grain: Tradition and Form in Recent Black Fiction.* Athens: U of Georgia P, 1985.

Caldwell, Gail. "Author Toni Morrison Discusses Her Latest Novel *Beloved.*" *Conversations with Toni Morrison.* Ed. Danielle Taylor-Guthrie. Jackson: UP of Mississippi, 1994. 239–45.

Callahan, John F. *In the African-American Grain: The Pursuit of Voice in Twentieth-Century Black Fiction.* Urbana: U of Illinois P, 1988.

Campbell, Dick. "Sickle Cell Anemia and Its Effect on Black People." *Crisis* 78.1 (Jan.–Feb. 1971): 7–9.

Campbell, Jane. *Mythic Black Fiction: The Transformation of History.* Knoxville: U of Tennessee P, 1986.

Carby, Hazel V. *Reconstructing Womanhood: The Emergence of the Afro-American Woman Novelist.* New York: Oxford UP, 1987.

Cardinal, A. W. *The Natives of the Northern Territories of the Gold Coast: Their Customs, Religion and Folklore.* New York: Negro UP, 1969.

Carman, Elizabeth, and Neil Carman. "Spirit-Child: The Aboriginal Experience of Pre-Birth Communication." <http://www.birthpsychology.com/lifebefore/concept10.html>. 24 March, 2006.

Carmichael, Stokely, and Charles V. Hamilton. *Black Power: The Politics of Liberation in America.* New York: Vintage, 1967.

Cary, Joyce. *The African Witch.* New York: W. Morrow and Co., 1936.

———. *Mister Johnson.* 1939. New York: New Directions, 1989.

Cartwright, Keith. *Reading Africa into American Literature: Epics, Fables, and Gothic Tales.* Lexington : UP of Kentucky, 2002.

Chambers, Douglas B. *Murder at Montpelier: Igbo Africans in Virginia.* Jackson: UP of Mississippi, 2005.

Chapman, Abraham. "The Black Aesthetic and the African Continuum." *Pan-African Journal* 4.4 (Fall 1991): 397–406.

Chekwas, Sam. *Ogbanje: "Son of the gods."* New York: Seaburn, 1994.

Childress, Alice. *Wedding Band: A Love/Hate Story in Black and White.* New York: Samuel French, Inc., 1973.

Chinweizu. *The West and the Rest of Us: White Predators, Black Slavers, and the African Elite.* Lagos: Pero P, 1987.

———, Onwuchekwa Jemie, and Ihechukwu Madubuike. *Toward a Decolonization of African Literature.* Vol. 1. *African Fiction and Poetry and Their Critics.* Enugu: Fourth Dimension Publishing Co., 1980.

Christian, Barbara. *Black Women Novelists: The Development of a Tradition, 1892–1976.* Westport: Greenwood P, 1980.

Christensen, Boyd James. *Double Descent among the Fanti.* New Haven: Human Relations Area Files, 1954.

Chukwukere, I. "Chi in Igbo Religion and Thought: The God in Every Man." *Anthropos: International Review of Ethnology and Linguistics.* 78.3–4 (1983): 519–34.

Clark, J. P. "Abiku." *The Penguin Book of Modern African Poetry.* Ed. Gerald Moore and Ulli Beier. London: Penguin Books, 1998. 260.

Clarke, Cheryl. *"After Mecca": Women Poets and the Black Arts Movement.* New Brunswick, NJ: Rutgers UP, 2005.

Clasby, Nancy Tenfelde. "Sula the Trickster." *LIT* 6 (1995): 21–34.

Cleaver, Eldridge. *Soul on Ice.* New York: McGraw-Hill Book Company, 1968.

Cole, Herbert M. *Mbari: Art and Life among the Owerri Igbo.* Bloomington: Indiana UP, 1982.

Coleman, James W. *Black Male Fiction and the Legacy of Caliban.* Lexington: U of Kentucky P, 2001.

———. *Faithful Vision: Treatments of the Sacred, Spiritual, and Supernatural in Twentieth-Century African American Fiction.* Baton Rouge: Louisiana State UP, 2006.

Collomb, M. "The Child Who Leaves and Returns or the Death of the Same Child." *The Child in His Family: The Impact of Disease and Death.* Vol. 2. Ed. E. James Anthony and Cyrille Koupernik. New York: John Wiley and Sons, 1973. 439–52.

Cooper, J. California. *Family.* New York: Double Day, 1991.

Cone, James H. *The Spirituals and the Blues: An Interpretation.* Maryknoll, NY: Orbis Books, 2000.

Connor, Kimberly Rae. *Imagining Grace: Liberating Theologies in the Slave Narrative Tradition.* Urbana: U of Illinois P, 2000.

Conrad, Joseph. *Heart of Darkness*. 1902. New York: Penguin Books, 1983.

Corson, Rev. Bishop Fred Pierce. "St. George's Church: The Cradle of American Methodism." *Transactions of the American Philosophical Society, Held At Philadelphia for Promoting Useful Knowledge*. Independence Square, Philadelphia: The American Philosophical Society, 1953. 230–36.

Courlander, Harold. "The Worship of Twins Among the Yoruba." *A Treasury of African Folklore: The Oral Literature, Traditions, Myths, Legends, Epics, Tales, Recollections, Wisdom, Sayings, and Humor of Africa*. New York: Marlowe and Co., 1996. 233–38.

Creel, Margaret Washington. "Gullah Attitudes toward Life and Death." *Africanisms in American Culture*. Ed. Joseph E. Holloway. Bloomington: Indiana UP, 1990. 69–97.

Crowther, Rev. Samuel, and Rev. John Christopher Taylor. *The Gospel on the Banks of the Niger: Journals and Notices of the Native Missionaries Accompanying the Niger Expedition of 1857–1859*. London: Dawsons of Pall Mall, 1968.

Cullen, Countee. "Heritage." *Color*. 1925. New York: Arno Press and New York Times, 1969. 36–41.

Culler, Jonathan D. *The Pursuit of Signs: Semiotics, Literature, Deconstruction*. Ithaca, NY: Cornell UP, 1981.

Curry, Mary Cuthrell. *Making the Gods in New York : the Yoruba Religion in the African American Community*. New York: Garland Publishers, 1997.

Curtin, Philip D. *The Atlantic Slave Trade: A Census*. Madison: U of Wisconsin P, 1969.

———. "Epidemiology and the Slave Trade." *Political Science Quarterly* 83.2 (June 1968): 190–216.

Cutter, Martha J. "The Story Must Go On and On: The Fantastic, Narration, and Intertextuality in Toni Morrison's *Beloved* and *Jazz*." *African American Review* 34.1 (Spring 2000): 61–75.

Dash, Julie. *Daughters of the Dust*. New York: Dutton, 1997.

———. *Daughters of the Dust: The Making of an African American Woman's Film*. New York City: The New Press, 1992.

Davis, Angela. "Reflections on the Black Woman's Role in the Community of Slaves." Black *Scholar: Journal of Black Studies and Research* 3.4 (Dec. 1971): 2–15.

Davis, Arthur P. Untitled Review. *Early Negro Writing, 1760–1837*. Ed. Dorothy Porter. Boston: Beacon P, 1971.

Davis, Charles T., and Henry Louis Gates Jr., eds. *The Slave's Narrative*. New York: Oxford UP, 1985.

Davis, Christina. "An Interview with Toni Morrison." *Conversations with Toni Morrison*. Ed. Danielle Taylor-Guthrie. Jackson: UP of Mississippi, 1994. 223–33.

Davis, Eisa. "Lucille Clifton and Sonia Sanchez: a conversation." *Callaloo* 25.4 (Fall 2002): 1038–74.

Delaney, Samuel R. "Racism." *Dark Matter: A Century of Speculative Fiction from the African Diaspora*. Ed. Sheree R. Thomas. New York: Warner Books, 2000. 383–97.

Deren, Maya. *Divine Horsemen: The Living Gods of Haiti*. London: Thames and Hudson, 1953.

De Weever, Jacqueline. *Mythmaking and Metaphor in Black Women's Fiction*. New York: St. Martin's P, 1991.

Dickson-Carr, Darryl. *The Columbia Guide to Contemporary African American Fiction.* New York: Columbia UP, 2005.

Dike, Kenneth Onwuka and Felicia Ekejiuba. *The Aro of South-eastern Nigeria, 1650– 1980.* Ibadan: UP Limited, 1990.

Doherty, Terence. *The Anatomical Works of George Stubbs.* Boston: David R. Godine, 1974.

Douglas, Frederick. *Narrative of the Life of Frederick Douglas, an American Slave, Written by Himself.* 1845. In *I Was Born a Slave: An Anthology of Classic Slave Narratives.* Vol. 1, 1772–1849. Ed. Yuval Taylor. 1999. 523–99.

———. "The Significance of Emancipation in the West Indies: An Address Delivered in Canandaigua, New York, on 3 August 1857." *The Frederick Douglass Papers. Series One: Speeches, Debates, and Interviews.* Vol. 3: 1855–63. Ed. John W. Blassingame. New Haven: Yale UP, 1985. 183–208.

Douglas, Jennifer D. "'Ill Seen Ill Said': Tropes of Vision and the Articulation of Race Relations in *The Cattle Killing.*" *Critical Essays on John Edgar Wideman.* Ed. Bonnie TuSmith and Keith E. Byerman. Knoxville: The U of Tennessee P, 2006. 205–20.

Drewal, Margaret Thompson. *Yoruba Ritual: Performers, Play, Agency.* Bloomington: Indiana UP, 1992

Dubey, Madhu. *Black Women Novelists and the Nationalist Aesthetic.* Indiana: Indiana UP, 1994.

———. "Contemporary African American Fiction and the Politics of Postmodernism." *Novel* 35.2/3 (Spring 2002): 151–68.

———. *Signs and Cities: Black Literary Postmodernism.* Chicago: U of Chicago P, 2003.

Du Bois, W. E. B. "Of Our Spiritual Strivings." *The Souls of Black Folk: Essays and Sketches.* 1903. A Norton Critical Edition. Ed. Henry Louis Gates Jr. and Terri Hume Oliver. New York: W. W. Norton and Co., 1999. 9–16.

———. "Criteria of Negro Art." *Call and Response: The Riverside Anthology of African American Literature.* Ed. Patricia Liggins Hill, et al. Boston: Houghton Mifflin Company, 1998. 850–55.

———. *The Philadelphia Negro: A Social Study.* 1899. Oxford: Oxford UP, 2007.

Due, Tananarive. *The Between.* New York: HarperCollins, 1995.

———. *My Soul to Keep.* New York: HarperPrism, 1997.

———. *The Black Rose.* New York: Ballantine, 2000.

———. *The Living Blood.* New York: Pocket Books, 2001.

———, and Patricia Stephens Due. *Freedom in the Family: A Mother-Daughter Memoir of the Fight for Civil Rights.* New York: Ballantine Books, 2003.

———. *The Good House.* New York: Atria Books, 2003.

———. Private Email Correspondence. June 12, 2005.

Dyson, Michael Eric. *Holler If You Hear Me: Searching For Tupac Shakur.* New York: Basic Civitas Books, 2001.

Ebigbo, Peter O., and B. Anyaegbuna. "The Problem of Student Involvement in the Mermaid Cult—A Variety of Belief in Reincarnation (OgbaNje) in a Nigerian Secondary School." *Journal of African Psychology* 1.1 (1988): 1–14.

Edelstein, Stuart J. *The Sickled Cell: From Myths to Molecule.* Cambridge, MA: Harvard UP, 1986.

Ekechi, F. K. *Missionary Enterprise and Rivalry in Igboland 1857–1914*. London: Frank Cass and Co., 1972.

Ekwunife, Anthony Nwoye Okechukwu. *Meaning and Function of 'Ino Uwa' (Reincarnation) in Igbo Traditional Religious Culture*. Onitsha, Nigeria: Spiritan Publications, 1999.

——. Personal interview. Monday, May 24, 2004.

Ellis, A[lfred] B[urdon]. *The Yoruba-Speaking Peoples of the Slave Coast of West Africa. Their Religion, Manners, Customs, Laws, Language, Etc*. London: Chapmen and Hall, 1894.

Ellis, Trey. "The New Black Aesthetic." *Callaloo* 38 (Winter 1989): 233–43.

Ellison, Ralph. *Invisible Man*. New York: Vintage Books, 1952.

——. "Society, Morality, and the Novel." *Going to the Territory*. 1986. New York: Vintage International, 1995. 239–74.

——. "'A Very Stern Discipline.'" *Going to the Territory*. 275–307.

——. *Shadow and Act*. New York: Vintage New York, 1995.

——. "Flying Home." *Flying Home and Other Stories*. New York: Vintage International, 1996. 147–73.

Emecheta, Buchi. *The Slave Girl*. New York: George Braziller, 1977.

——. *The Joys of Motherhood*. New York: George Braziller, 1979.

Emenyonu, Ernest N., ed. *Emerging Perspectives on Chinua Achebe, Vol. I. OMENKA: The Master Artist*. Trenton, NJ: African World P, 2004. xi–xiv.

——. "Introduction" and ed., with Iniobong I. Uko. *Emerging Perspectives on Chinua Achebe, Vol. II. ISINKA: The Artistic Purpose: Chinua Achebe and the Theory of African Literature*. Trenton, NJ: African World P, 2004. xv–xix.

Equiano, Olaudah. *The Interesting Narrative of the Life of Olaudah Equiano, or Gustavus Vassa, the African, Written by Himself*. 1794. In *Pioneers of the Black Atlantic: Five Slave Narratives from the Enlightenment, 1772–1815*. Ed. Henry Louis Gates Jr. and William L. Andrews. Washington, DC.: Civitas, 1998. 183–366.

Escott, Paul D. "The Art and Science of Reading WPA Slave Narratives." *The Slave's Narrative*. Ed. Charles T. Davis and Henry Louis Gates Jr. 40–48.

Everett, Chestyn. "'Tradition' in Afro-American Literature." *Black World* 25.2 (Dec. 1975): 20–35.

Eze, Emmanuel Chukwudi, ed. *Race and the Enlightenment: A Reader*. Oxford: Blackwell, 1997.

Ezeanya, S. N. "The Place of the Supreme God in the Traditional Religion of the Igbo." *West African Religion* 3 (1963): 1–4.

Ezekiel, Raphael S. *The Racist Mind: Portraits of American Neo-Nazis and Klansmen*. New York: Viking, 1995.

Ezenwa-Ohaeto. *Chinua Achebe: A Biography*. Oxford: James Currey, 1997.

Fanon, Frantz. *The Wretched of the Earth*. Trans. Constance Farrington. New York: Grove, 1963.

Favor, J. Martin. *Authentic Blackness: The Folk in the New Negro Renaissance*. Durham, NC: Duke UP, 1999.

Feyisetan, Bamikale J., Sola Asa, and Joshua A. Ebigbola. "Mothers' Management of Childhood Diseases in Yorubaland: the Influence of Cultural Beliefs." *Health Transition Review* 7 (1997): 221–34.

Field, M. J. *Religion and Medicine of the Gā People.* 1937. London: Oxford UP, 1961.

Finney, Ron. "'We Are All Babylonians': Afro-Americans in Africa." *Black Scholar: Journal of Black Studies and Research* 4.5 (Feb. 1973): 45–48.

Foster, Frances Smith. *Witnessing Slavery: The Development of Ante-bellum Slave Narratives.* Westport, CT: Greenwood P, 1979.

———. "Octavia Butler's Black Female Future Fiction." *Extrapolation* 23.1 (Spring 1982): 37–49.

———. *Written By Herself: Literary Production by African American Women, 1746–1892.* Bloomington: Indiana UP, 1993.

Foucault, Michel. *The Archeology of Knowledge.* Trans. A.M. Sheridan Smith. New York: Pantheon Books, 1972.

Fox, Robert Elliott. *Conscientious Sorcerers: The Black Postmodernist Fiction of LeRoi Jones/Amiri Baraka, Ishmael Reed, and Samuel R. Delany.* New York: Greenwood P, 1987.

Frankel, Barbara. *Childbirth in the Ghetto: Folk Beliefs of Negro Women in a North Philadelphia Hospital Ward.* San Francisco: R & E Research Associates, 1977.

Franklin, John Hope, and Alfred A. Moss Jr. *From Slavery to Freedom: A History of Negro Americas.* 1947. 6th ed. New York: McGraw-Hill Publishing Company, 1988.

Frazier, Franklin E. *The Negro Church in America.* 1963. New York: Schocken Books, 1974.

Frye, Northrop. *Anatomy of Criticism: Four Essays.* Princeton: Princeton UP, 1957.

Gaines, Ernest J. *Of Love and Dust.* New York: Vintage Contemporaries, 1967.

———. *The Autobiography of Miss Jane Pittman.* New York: Dial P, 1971.

Gaines, Kevin K. *Uplifting the Race: Black Leadership, Politics, and Culture in the Twentieth Century.* Chapel Hill: The U of North Carolina P, 1996.

Gasper, David Barry, and Darlene Clark Hine, eds. *More than Chattel: Black Women and Slavery in the Americas.* Bloomington : Indiana UP, 1996.

Gates, Henry Louis Jr., and William L. Andrews, eds. *Pioneers of the Black Atlantic: Five Slave Narratives from the Enlightenment, 1772–1815.* Washington, D.C.: Civitas, 1998.

Gates, Henry Louis, Jr. *Figures in Black: Words, Signs, and the "Racial" Self.* New York: Oxford UP, 1987.

———. *The Signifying Monkey: A Theory of African-American Literary Criticism.* New York: Oxford UP, 1988.

———. "In Her Own Write." Foreword. Hopkins, Pauline E. *Contending Forces: A Romance Illustrative of Negro Life North and South.* New York: Oxford UP, 1988. vii–xxii.

———. *Black Literature and Literary Theory.* New York: Methuen, 1984.

Gayle, Addison Jr., ed. and "Introduction." *The Black Aesthetic.* Garden City, NY: Doubleday, 1971. xv–xxiv.

———. "The Function of Black Literature at the Present Time." *The Black Aesthetic.* 1971. 407–19.

————. *The Way of the New World: The Black Novel in America*. Garden City, New York: Anchor Press/Doubleday, 1975.

"Genetic Disease Profile: Sickle Cell Anemia." <http://www.ornl.gov/sci/techresources/Human_Genome/posters/chromosome/sca.shtml> 28 May, 2006.

Genovese, Eugene D. *Roll, Jordan, Roll: The World the Slaves Made*. New York: Vintage Books, 1976.

George, Carol V. R. *Segregated Sabbaths: Richard Allen and the Emergence of Independent Black Churches 1760–1840*. New York: Oxford UP, 1973.

Georgia Writers' Project, Savannah Unit. *Drums and Shadows: Survival Studies among the Georgia Coastal Negroes*. 1940. New York: New York UP, 1988.

Giddings, Paula. *When and Where I Enter: The Impact of Black Women on Race and Sex in America*. New York: William Morrow Co., 1984.

Gikandi, Simon. *Reading Chinua Achebe: Language and Ideology in Fiction*. London: James Currey, 1991.

Gilroy, Paul. *The Black Atlantic: Modernity and Double Consciousness*. Cambridge, Massachusetts: Harvard UP, 1993.

Githae-Mugo, Micere M. "The Relationship between African and African-American Literatures as Utilitarian Art: A Theoretical Formulation." *Global Dimensions of the African Diaspora*. Ed. Joseph E. Harris. Washington, DC: Howard UP, 1982. 85–93.

Glave, Dianne. "An Interview with Nalo Hopkinson." *Callaloo* 26.1 (Winter 2003): 146–59.

————. "'My Characters are Teaching Me to be Strong': An Interview with Tananarive Due." *African American Review* 38.4 (Winter 2004): 695–705.

Gomez, Michael A. *Exchanging Our Country Marks: The Transformation of African Identities in the Colonial and Antebellum South*. Chapel Hill: U of North Carolina P, 1998.

Gorn, Elliot J. "Black Spirits: The Ghostlore of Afro-American Slaves." *American Quarterly* 36.4 (Fall 1984): 549–65.

Govan, Sandra Y. "Homage to Tradition: Octavia Butler Renovates the Historical Novel." *MELUS* 13.1/2 (Spring–Summer 1986): 79–96.

————. "Connections, Links, and Extended Networks: Patterns in Octavia Butler's Science Fiction." *Black American Literature Forum* 18.2 Science Fiction Issue (Summer 1984): 82–87.

Grayson, Sandra M. *Visions of the Third Millennium: Black Science Fiction Novelists Write the Future*. Trenton, NJ: Africa World P, 2003.

Green, Johnson. *The Life and Confession of Johnson Green, Who is to be Executed this Day, August 17th, 1786, for the Atrocious Crime of Burglary; Together with His Last and Dying Words*. In *Early Negro Writing, 1760–1837*. Ed. Dorothy Porter. Boston: Beacon P, 1971. 405–13.

Gruesser, John Cullen. *Black on Black: Twentieth-Century African American Writing about Africa*. Lexington: The UP of Kentucky, 2000.

————. *Confluences: Postcolonialism, African American Literary Studies, and the Black Atlantic*. Athens: The U of Georgia P, 2005.

Gutman, Herbert G. *The Black Family in Slavery and Freedom, 1750–1925*. New York: Vintage Books, 1977.

Gysin, Fritz. "'Do Not Fall Asleep in Your Enemy's Dream': John Edgar Wideman and the Predicament of Prophecy." *Callaloo* 22.3 (1999): 623–28.

Haffter, Carl. "The Changeling: History and Psychodynamics of Attitudes to Handicapped Children in European Folklore." *Journal of the History of Behavioral Sciences* 4.1 (1968): 55–61.

Harris, Norman. *Connecting Times: The Sixties in Afro-American Fiction.* Jackson: UP of Mississippi, 1988.

Harris, Trudier. "Beloved: Woman, Thy Name is Demon." *Toni Morrison's* Beloved*: A Casebook.* Ed. William L. Andrews and Nellie Y. McKay. New York: Oxford UP, 1999. 127–57.

Hartland, Edwin Sidney. *Primitive Paternity: The Myth of Supernatural Birth in Relation to the History of the Family.* New York: Benjamin Blom, 1971.

Haywood, Chanta M. *The Prophesying Daughters: Black Women Preachers and the Word, 1823–1913.* Columbia: U of Missouri P, 2003.

Head, Bessie. *Maru.* London: Heinemann Educational Publishers, 1971.

Heglar, Charles J. *Rethinking the Slave Narrative: Slave Marriage and the Narratives of Henry Bibb and William and Ellen Craft.* Westport, CT: Greenwood P, 2001.

Helford, Elyce Rae. "(E)raced Visions: Women of Color and Science Fiction in the United States." *Science Fiction, Canonization, Marginalization,* and the *Academy.* Ed. Gary Westfahl and George Slusser. Westport, CT: Greenwood P, 2002. 127–38.

Henderson, Carol E. *Scarring the Black Body: Race and Representation in African American Literature.* Columbia: U of Missouri P, 2002.

Henderson, Mae Gwendolyn. "Speaking in Tongues: Dialogics, Dialectics, and the Black Woman Writer's Literary Tradition." *Changing Our Own Words: Essays on Criticism, Theory, and Writing by Black Women.* Ed. Cheryl A. Wall. New Brunswick: Rutgers UP, 1989. 16–37.

Henderson, Richard N. *The King in Every Man: Evolutionary Trends in Onitsha Ibo Society and Culture.* New Haven: Yale UP, 1972.

Henderson, Stephen. *Understanding the New Black Poetry: Black Speech and Black Music as Poetic References.* New York: William Morrow and Co., 1973.

Herd, E. M. "Myth Criticism: Limitations and Possibilities." *Literary Criticism and Myth.* Ed. Robert A. Segal. New York: Garland Publishing, 1996: 173–81.

Herskovits, Melville J. "The Cult of Twins and of the Dead." *Life in a Haitian Valley.* New York: Alfred A. Knopf, 1937. 199–218.

———. *Dahomey: An Ancient West African Kingdom.* Vol. 1. New York: J. J. Augustin, Publisher, 1938.

———. *The Myth of the Negro Past.* 1941. Boston: Beacon P, 1958.

Higgins, Therese E. *Religiosity, Cosmology, and Folklore: The African Influence in the Novels of Toni Morrison.* New York: Routledge, 2001.

Hirsch, Jerrold. *Portrait of America: A Cultural History of the Federal Writers' Project.* Chapel Hill: The U of North Carolina P, 2003.

Hoem, Sheri. "'Shifting Spirits': Ancestral Constructs in the Postmodern Writing of John Edgar Wideman." *African American Review* 34.2 (Summer 2002): 249–62.

Hogue, Lawrence. *Discourse and the Other: The Production of the Afro-American Text.* Durham: Duke UP, 1986.

———. *Race, Modernity, Postmodernity: A Look at the History and the Literatures of People of Color Since the 1960s.* Albany: State U of New York P, 1996.

————. *The African American Male, Writing, and Difference: A Polycentric Approach to African American Literature, Criticism, and History.* Albany: State U of New York P, 2003.

Holiday, Billie. "Strange Fruit." In John White, *Billie Holiday: Her Life and Times.* Tunbridge Wells: Spellmount Ltd., 1987. 50.

Holland, Sharon Patricia. *Raising the Dead: Readings of Death and (Black) Subjectivity.* Durham, NC: Duke UP, 2000.

Holloway, Joseph E, ed. *Africanisms in American Culture.* 1990. 2d ed. Bloomington: Indiana UP, 2005.

————. "Africanisms in African American Names in the United States." *Africanisms in American Culture.* Ed. Holloway. 82-110.

Holloway, Karla F. C. *Moorings and Metaphors: Figures of Culture and Gender in Black Women's Literature.* New Brunswick, NJ: Rutgers UP, 1992.

————. *Passed On. African American Mourning Stories: A Memorial.* Durham, NC: Duke UP, 2002.

hooks, bell. "Postmodern Blackness." *Yearning: Race, Gender, and Cultural Politics.* Boston, MA: South End Press, 1990. 23–31.

————. *Killing Rage: Ending Racism.* New York: Henry Holt and Co., 1995.

Hubbard, Dolan. *The Sermon and the African American Literary Imagination.* Columbia: U of Missouri P, 1994.

Huggins, Nathan Irvin. *Harlem Renaissance.* New York: Oxford UP, 1971.

————. "Introduction," ed. *Voices from the Harlem Renaissance.* New York: Oxford UP, 1996. 3–11.

Hurston, Zora. *Mules and Men.* 1935. New York: Harper Perennial, 1990.

————. *Their Eyes Were Watching God.* 1937. New York: Perennial Classics, 1990.

Hutcheon, Linda. *The Poetics of Postmodernism: History, Theory, Fiction.* New York: Routledge, 1988.

Hutchinson, George. *The Harlem Renaissance in Black and White.* Cambridge, Massachusetts: The Belknap P of Harvard UP, 1995.

Idowu, E. Bolaji. *Olòdùmarè: God in Yoruba Belief.* New York: Praeger, 1963.

Ilogu, Edmund. *Christianity and Igbo Culture: A Study of the Interaction of Christianity and Igbo Culture.* New York: NOK Publishers, 1974.

Innes, Catherine Lynnette. *Chinua Achebe.* Cambridge: U of Cambridge P, 1990.

Inyama, N[nadozie]. F. "'Beloved Pawns': The Childhood Experience in the Novels of Chinua Achebe and Mongo Beti." *African Literature Today* 21 "Childhood in African Literature" (1998): 36–42.

Irele, F. Abiola. "The Crisis of Cultural Memory in Chinua Achebe's *Things Fall Apart.*" *The African Imagination: Literature in Africa and the Black Diaspora.* Oxford UP, 2001. 115–153.

Irele, F. Abiola, and Simon Gikandi, eds. *The Cambridge History of African and Caribbean Literature.* 2 vols. Cambridge: Cambridge UP, 2004.

Isichei, Elizabeth. "Ibo and Christian Beliefs: Some Aspects of a Teleological Encounter." *African Affairs* 68.271 (April 1969): 121–34.

———. *The Ibo People and the Europeans: The Genesis of a Relationship—to 1906.* New York: St. Martin's P, 1973.

———. *A History of Igbo People.* New York: St. Martin's P, 1976.

Jabbi, Bu-Buakei. *West African Poems (Fifteen Analyses).* Outline Hints in African Literature 2. May 1974.

Jablon, Madelyn. *Black Metafiction: Self Consciousness in African American Literature.* Iowa City: U of Iowa P, 1997.

Jacobs, Harriet A. *Incidents in the Life of a Slave Girl, Written by Herself.* 1861. Miami, Florida: Mnemosyne Publishing Co., 1969.

Jacobs, Naomi. *The Character of Truth: Historical Figures in Contemporary Fiction.* Carbondale: Southern Illinois UP, 1990.

Jahn, Janheinz. *Muntu: An Outline of the New African Culture.* 1958. Trans. Marjorie Grene. New York: Grove P, 1961.

———. *Neo-African Literature: A History of Black Writing.* Trans. Oliver Cobwin and Ursula Lehrburger. New York: Grove P, 1968.

Jameson, Fredric. *The Political Unconscious: Narrative as a Socially Symbolic Act.* Ithaca, NY: Cornell UP, 1981.

JanMohamed, Abdul R. *The Death-Bound Subject: Richard Wright's Archeology of Death.* Durham: Duke UP, 2005.

Jea, John. *The Life, History, and Unparalleled Sufferings of John Jea, the African Preacher, Compiled and Written by Himself.* 1815. In *Pioneers of the Black Atlantic: Five Slave Narratives from the Enlightenment, 1772–1815.* 366–439.

Jell-Bahlsen, Sabine. *The Water Goddess in Igbo Cosmology: Ogbuide of Oguta Lake.* Trenton, New Jersey: Africa World P, 2007.

Jesser, Nancy. "Violence, Home, and Community in Toni Morrison's *Beloved.*" *African American Review* 33.2 (1999): 325–45.

Johnson, Charles. "Philosophy and Black Fiction." *Obsidian* 6.1–2 (1980): 55–61.

———. *Oxherding Tale.* Bloomington: Indiana UP, 1982.

———. *Being and Race: Black Writing since 1970.* Bloomington: Indiana UP, 1988.

———. *Middle Passage.* 1990. New York: Plume, 1991.

———. "Foreword." *I Was Born a Slave: An Anthology of Classic Slave Narratives.* Ed. Yuval Taylor. Chicago: Lawrence Hill Books, 1999. ix–xiii.

Johnson, James Weldon. *The Autobiography of an Ex-Colored Man.* 1912. New York: Vintage P, 1989.

Johnson, Rev. Samuel. *The History of the Yorubas: From the Earliest Times to the Beginning of the British Protectorate.* 1921. Lagos: C.M.S Bookshops, 1956.

J[ones], A[bsalom] and R[ichard] A[llen]. *A Narrative of the Proceedings of the Black People, During the Late Awful Calamity in Philadelphia, in the Year 1793: and A Refutation of Some Censures, Thrown Upon Them in Some Late Publications.* Philadelphia: William W. Woodward, 1794.

Jones, Carolyn M. "*Sula* and *Beloved:* Images of Cain in the Novels of Toni Morrison." *African American Review* 27.4 (Winter 1993): 615–26.

Jones, Eldred D. "Childhood Before and After Birth." Editorial Essay. *African Literature Today.* 21. Oxford: James Curry, 1998. 1–8.

Jones, Gayl. *Corregidora.* 1975. Boston: Beacon P, 1986.

———. *Eva's Man.* 1976. Boston: Beacon P, 1987.

———. *Liberating Voices: Oral Tradition in African American Literature.* Cambridge, MA: Harvard UP, 1991.

Jones-Jackson, Patricia. *When Roots Die: Endangered Traditions on the Sea Islands.* Athens: U of Georgia P, 1987.

Jordan, Jennifer. "Cultural Nationalism in the 1960s: Politics and Poetry." *Race, Politics, and Culture: Critical Essays on the Radicalism of the 1960s.* Ed. Adolph Reed, Jr. New York: Greenwood P, 1986. 29–60.

Jordan, Margaret I. *African American Servitude and Historical Imaginings: Retrospective Fiction and Representation.* New York: Palgrave, 2004.

Joseph, Peniel E., ed. *The Black Power Movement: Rethinking the Civil Rights–Black Power Era.* New York: Routledge, 2006.

Jordan, Winthrop D. *White Over Black: American Attitudes Toward the Negro 1550–1812.* Chapel Hill: U of North Carolina P, 1968.

Joyce, Joyce A. "Africa-Centered Womanism: Connecting Africa to the Diaspora." *The African Diaspora: African Origins and New World Identities.* Ed. Isidore Okpewho, Carole Boyce Davies, and Ali Mazrui. Bloomington: Indiana UP, 1999. 538–54.

Jung, Carl. "Good and Evil in Analytical Psychology." *Encountering Jung: On Evil.* Ed. Murray Stein. Princeton: Princeton UP, 1995. 84–94.

Kalu, Anthonia C. "Those Left out in the Rain: African Literary Theory and the Re-Invention of the African Woman." *African Studies Review* 37.2 (September 1994): 77–95.

———. "Achebe and Duality in Igbo Thought." *Emerging Perspectives on Chinua Achebe, Vol. 2. ISINKA: The Artistic Purpose: Chinua Achebe and the Theory of African Literature.* 2004. 137–50.

Kalu, Ogbu U. "Gods as Policemen: Religion and Social Control in Igboland." *Religious Plurality in Africa: Essays in Honor of John S. Mbiti.* Ed. Jacob K. Olupona and Sulayman S. Nyang. Berlin: Mouton de Gruyer, 1993. 109–31.

Karenga, Ron. "Black Cultural Nationalism." *The Black Aesthetic.* Ed. Addison Gayle. 32–38.

Keizer, Arlene R. "*Beloved:* Ideologies in Conflict, Improvised Subjects." *African American Review* 33.1 (1999): 105–23.

Kenan, Randall. "An Interview with Octavia Butler." *Callaloo* 14.2 (Spring 1991): 495–504.

Kenyatta, Jomo. *Facing Mount Kenya: The Tribal Life of the Gikuyu.* New York: Vintage Books, 1962.

Kesteloot, Lilyan. *Black Writers in French: A Literary History of Negritude.* Trans. Ellen Conroy Kennedy. Washington, D.C.: Howard UP, 1991.

King, Wilma. *Stolen Childhood: Slave Youth in Nineteenth-Century America.* Bloomington: Indiana UP, 1995.

Kiple, Kenneth F., and Virginia H. Kiple. "Slave Child Mortality: Some Nutritional Answers to a Perennial Puzzle." *Journal of Social History* 10.3 (March 1977): 284–309.

Kipling, Rudyard. *Kim*. 1901. Penguin Books, 1989.

Knight, Etheridge. "The Idea of Ancestry." *Call and Response: The Riverside Anthology of the African American Literary Tradition*. Ed. Patricia Liggins Hill et al. Boston: Houghton Mifflin Co., 1998. 1483–84.

Kortenaar, Neil Ten. "Fictive Stories and the State of Fiction in Africa." *Comparative Literature* 52.3 (Summer 2000): 228–45.

Kraft, Marion. *The African Continuum and Contemporary African American Women Writers: Their Literary Presence and Ancestral Past*. Europäischer Verlag der Wissenschaften: Peter Lang, 1995.

Kubitschek, Missy Dehn. *Claiming the Heritage: African American Women Novelists and History*. Jackson: UP of Mississippi, 1991.

Kubik, Gerhard. *Africa and the Blues*. Jackson: UP of Mississippi P, 1999.

Lawrence, David. "Fleshly Ghosts and Ghostly Flesh: The World and the Body in *Beloved*." *Toni Morrison's Fiction: Contemporary Criticism*. Ed. David D. Middleton. New York: Garland Publishing Co., 1997. 231–46.

Lazin, Lauren, director. *Tupac: Resurrection*. Distributed by Paramount Pictures, 2003.

Lee, Debbie. *Slavery and the Romantic Imagination*. Philadelphia: U of Pennsylvania P, 2002.

Lee, Felicia R. "The Anger and Shock of a City's Slave Past." *New York Times* 26 Nov. 2005 (online).

Lee, Valerie. *Granny Midwives and Black Women Writers*. New York: Routledge, 1996.

Leighton, Alexander H., T. Adeoye Lambo, et al. *Psychiatric Disorder among the Yoruba*. Ithaca: Cornell UP, 1963.

Leis, Nancy B. "The Not-So-Supernatural Power of Ijaw Children." *African Religious Groups and Beliefs: Papers in Honor of William R. Bascom*. Ed. Simon Ottenberg. Folklore Institute, 1982. 151–69.

Leonard, Maj. Arthur Glyn. *The Lower Niger and Its Tribes*. London: Macmillan and Co., Ltd., 1906.

Lévi-Strauss, Claude. "The Structural Study of Myth." *Myth: A Symposium*. Ed. Thomas A. Sebeok. Philadelphia: American Folklore Society, 1955. 50–60.

Levin, Amy K. *Africanism and Authenticity in African American Women's Novels*. Gainesville: U of Florida P, 2003.

Levine, Lawrence W. *Black Culture and Black Consciousness: Afro-American Folk Thought from Slavery to Freedom*. Oxford: Oxford UP, 1977.

Lewis, Vashti C. "African Tradition in Toni Morrison's *Sula*." *Phylon* 47.1 (1987): 91–97.

Lindfors, Bernth, ed. "Introduction" and *Africans On Stage: Studies in Ethnological Show Business*. Bloomington: Indiana UP, 1999. vii–xiii.

Livingstone, Frank B. "Anthropological Implications of Sickle Cell Gene Distribution in West Africa." *American Anthropologist,* New Series, 60.3 (June 1958). 533–62.

Locke, Alain. "Art or Propaganda?" *Voices from the Harlem Renaissance*. Ed. Nathan Irvin Huggins. 1976. 312–13.

———. Untitled review of *Their Eyes Were Watching God*. 1938. *Zora Neale Hurston: Critical Perspectives Past and Present*. Ed. Henry Louis Gates Jr. and K. A. Appiah. New York: Amistad, 1993. 18.

Lorde, Audre. "Learning from the 60s." *Sister Outsider: Essays and Speeches by Audre Lorde.* Trumansburg, NY: Crossing P, 1984. 134–44.

Lubiano, Wahneema, ed. *The House that Race Built.* 1997. New York: Vintage Books, 1998.

Lukács, Georg. *The Historical Novel.* 1937. Trans. Hannah and Stanley Mitchell. Boston: Beacon P, 1963.

Lynch, Lisa. "The Fever Next Time: The Race of Disease and the Disease of Racism in John Edgar Wideman." *American Literary History* 14.4 (Winter 2002): 776–804.

Lyotard, Jean-François. *The Postmodern Condition: A Report on Knowledge.* Trans. Geoff Bennington and Brian Massumi. Minneapolis: U of Minnesota P, 1993.

Madubuike, Ihechukwu. "Achebe's Ideas on Literature." *Black World* 24.2 (Dec. 1974): 60–70.

Maduka, Chidi T. "African Religious Beliefs in Literary Imagination: Ogbanje and Abiku in Chinua Achebe, J. P. Clark and Wole Soyinka." *Journal of Commonwealth Literature* 22.1 (1987): 17–30.

———. "The Black Aesthetic and African *Bolekaja* Criticism." *Neohelicon* 16.1 (1989): 209–28.

Malcolm X. "The Ballot or the Bullet." *Malcolm X Speaks: Selected Speeches and Statements.* 1965. Ed. George Breitman. New York: Pathfinder, 1989. 23–44.

———. "Appeal to African Heads of State." *Malcolm X Speaks.* 72–87.

Marks, Kathleen. *Toni Morrison's Beloved and the Apotropaic Imagination.* Columbia: U of Missouri P, 2002.

Marrant, John. *A Journal of the Rev. John Marrant, From August the 18th, 1785, to The 16th of March, 1790.* 1790. In *"Face Zion Forward": First Writers of the Black Atlantic, 1785–1798.* Ed. Joanna Brooks and John Salient. Boston: Northeastern UP, 2002. 93–160.

———. *Narrative of the Lord's Wonderful Dealings with John Marrant, a Black, (Now Going to Preach the Gospel in Nova Scotia), Born in New York.* 1785. In *Pioneers of the Black Atlantic.* Ed. Gates Jr. and Andrews. 60–80.

Marshall, Paule. *Praisesong for the Widow.* New York: Putnam's, 1983.

Matza, Diane. "Zora Neale Hurston's *Their Eyes Were Watching God* and Toni Morrison's *Sula*: A Comparison." *MELUS* 12.3. Ethnic Women Writers IV. (Autumn 1985): 43–54.

Mbiti, John S. *African Religions and Philosophy.* London: Heinemann, 1990.

McCabe, Douglas. "Histories of Errancy: Oral Yoruba Abiku Texts and Soyinka's 'Abiku.'" *Research in African Literatures* 33.1 (Spring 2002): 44–74.

———. "'Born-to-Die': The History and Politics of *Abiku* and *Ogbanje* in Nigerian Literature." Ph.D. diss. Cambridge U, 2002.

———. "'Higher Realities': New Age Spirituality in Ben Okri's *The Famished Road.*" *Research in African Literatures* 36. 4 (Winter 2005): 1-21.

McCaffery, Larry. "An Interview with Octavia E. Butler." *Across the Wounded Galaxies: Interviews with Contemporary American Science Fiction Writers.* Ed. Larry McCaffery. Urbana: U of Illinois P, 1990. 54–70.

McDowell, Deborah E. *"The Changing Same": Black Women's Literature, Criticism, and Theory.* Bloomington: Indiana UP, 1995.

McGinty, Derek. "John Edgar Wideman." *Conversations with John Edgar Wideman.* Ed. Bonnie TuSmith. Jackson: UP of Mississippi, 1998. 180–94.

McKay, Claude. "If We Must Die." *The Norton Anthology of African American Literature.* Ed. Henry Louis Gates Jr. and Nellie Y. McKay. New York: W. W. Norton & Company 1997. 984.

McKay, Nellie Y. "Naming the Problem That Led to the Question 'Who Shall Teach African American Literature'?" *White Scholars, African American Texts.* Ed. Lisa A. Long. New Brunswick, NJ: Rutgers UP, 2005. 17–26.

McKnight, Reginald. *I Get on the Bus.* Little, Brown and Company, 1990.

McMillan, Terry, ed. *Breaking Ice: An Anthology of Contemporary African-American Fiction.* New York: Penguin Books, 1990. xv–xxiv.

Meek, C. K. *Law and Authority in a Nigerian Tribe: A Study in Indirect Rule.* London: Oxford UP, 1937.

Mehaffy, Marilyn, and AnaLouise Keating, "'Radio Imagination': Octavia Butler on the Poetics of Narrative Embodiment." *MELUS* 26.1 (Spring 2001): 45–76.

Merlo, Christian. "Statuettes of the Abiku Cult." *African Arts* 8.4 (Summer 1975): 30–35.

Metraux, Alfred. "The Cult of Twins." *Voodoo in Haiti.* Trans. Hugo Charteris. New York: Schocken Books, 1972. 146–52.

Melzer, Patricia. *Alien Constructions: Science Fiction and Feminist Thought.* Austin: U of Texas P, 2006.

Mezu, Rose Ure. *Chinua Achebe: The Man and His Works.* London: Adonis and Abbey P, 2006.

Mills, Antonia, and Richard Slobodin, eds. *Amerindian Rebirth: Reincarnation Belief among North American Indians and Inuit.* Toronto: U of Toronto P, 1994.

Mitchell, Angelyn. *The Freedom to Remember: Narrative, Slavery, and Gender in Contemporary Black Women's Fiction.* New Brunswick, New Jersey: Rutgers UP, 2002.

Mitchell, Henry H. *Black Belief: Folk Beliefs of Blacks in America and West Africa.* New York: Harper & Row, 1975.

Mitchell-Kernan, Claudia. "Signifying." *Mother Wit From the Laughing Barrel: Readings in the Interpretation of Afro-American Folklore.* Ed. Alan Dundes. Englewood Cliffs, NJ: Prentice-Hall, 1973. 310–28.

Mobolade, Timothy. "The Concept of Abiku." *African Arts* 7.1 (Autumn 1973): 62–64.

Moody, Joycelyn. *Sentimental Confessions: Spiritual Narratives of Nineteenth-Century African American Women.* Athens: U of Georgia P, 2001.

Montgomery, Maxine Lavon. *The Apocalypse in African-American Fiction.* Gainesville: UP of Florida, 1996.

Morrison, Toni. *Sula.* New York: Alfred. A. Knopf, 1973.

——. "Behind the Making of *The Black Book.*" *Black World* 23.4 (Feb. 1974): 86–90.

——. "Foreword." James Van Der Zee. *The Harlem Book of the Dead.* Dobbs Ferry, NY: Morgan & Morgan, 1978.

——. "City Limits, Village Values: Concepts of the Neighborhood in Black Fiction." *Literature and the Urban Experience: Essays on the City and Literature.* Ed. Michael C. Jaye and Ann Chalmers Watts. New Brunswick: Rutgers UP, 1981. 35–44.

——. "Rootedness: The Ancestor as Foundation." *Black Women Writers (1950–1980): A Critical Evaluation*. Ed. Mari Evans. New York: Anchor Books, 1984. 339–45.

——. "Recitatif." 1983. *Call and Response: The Riverside Anthology of the African American Literary Tradition*. Ed. Patricia Liggins Hill et al. 1776–1786.

——. "The Site of Memory." *Inventing the Truth: The Art and Craft of Memoir*. Ed. William Zinsser. Boston: Houghton Mifflin Company, 1987. 101–24

——. *Beloved*. New York: Alfred. A. Knopf, 1987.

——. *Playing in the Dark: Whiteness and the Literary Imagination*. 1992. New York: Vintage Books, 1993.

——. *Song of Solomon*. New York: Alfred. A. Knopf, 1993.

——. "Home." *The House that Race Built*. Ed. Wahneema Lubiano. New York: Vintage Books, 1997. 3–12.

——. *Paradise*. New York: Alfred A. Knopf, 1998.

——. "'On The Radiance of the King.'" *The New York Review* (9 Aug. 2001): 18–20.

Mosley, Walter. "Black to the Future." *Dark Matter: A Century of Speculative Fiction from the African Diaspora*. Ed. Sheree R. Thomas. New York: Warner Books, 2000. 405–7.

Mostert, Noël. *Frontiers: The Epic of South Africa's Creation and the Tragedy of the Xhosa People*. New York: Knopf, 1992.

Moynihan, Daniel Patrick. *The Negro Family: The Case for National Action*. Washington, D.C.: Office of Policy Planning and Research, United States Department of Labor, 1965.

Mudimbe, V.Y. *The Invention of Africa: Gnosis, Philosophy, and the Order of Knowledge*. Bloomington: Indiana UP, 1988.

Murphy, Laura. "Into the Bush of Ghosts: Specters of the Slave Trade in West African Fiction." *Research in African Literatures* 38.4 (Winter 2007): 141–52.

Murray, Rolland. *Our Living Manhood: Literature, Black Power, and Masculine Ideology*. Philadelphia: U of Pennsylvania P, 2007.

Naylor, Gloria. "A Conversation: Gloria Naylor and Toni Morrison." *Conversations with Toni Morrison*. Ed. Danielle Taylor-Guthrie. Jackson: UP of Mississippi, 1985. 188–217.

——. *Mama Day*. New York: Vintage Contemporaries, 1989.

——. *Bailey's Cafe*. New York: Vintage Contemporaries, 1992.

Neal, Larry. "The Black Arts Movement." *The Black Aesthetic*. Ed. Addison Gayle Jr. Garden City, NY: Doubleday, 1971. 272–90.

——. *Visions of a Liberated Future: Black Arts Movement Writings*. New York: Thunder's Mouth P, 1989.

Nielsen, Aldon L. *Writing Between the Lines: Race and Intertextuality*. Athens: U of Georgia P, 1994.

Njaka, Mazi Elechukwu Nnadibuagha. *Igbo Political Culture*. Evanston: Northwestern UP, 1974.

Nkala, Nathan. *Mezie, the ogbanje boy*. Lagos: Macmillan Nigeria, 1981.

Noon, John A. "A Preliminary Examination of the Death Concepts of the Ibo." *American Anthropologist* 44.4 (Oct.–Dec.1942). 638–54.

Nwabara, S. N. *Iboland: A Century of Contact with Britain, 1860–1960*. Atlantic Highlands, NJ: Humanities P, 1978.

Nwapa, Flora. *Efuru*. London: Heinemann, 1966.

Nwana, Pita. *Omenuko*. London: Longmans Publishers, 1933.

Nwoga, Donatus I. *The Supreme God as Stranger in Igbo Religious Thought*. Ahiazu Mbaise: Hawk P, 1984.

Nzegwu, Nkiru Uwechia. *Family Matters: Feminist Concepts in African Philosophy of Culture*. New York: State U of New York P, 2006.

Nzewi, Esther. "The Abiku/Ogbanje syndrome: A dimension of pathology of childhood." *Child Health in Nigeria: The Impact of A Depressed Economy*. Ed. Tola Olu Pearce and Toyin Falola. Aldershot: Avebury P, 1994. 103–16.

———. "Malevolent Ogbanje: recurrent reincarnation or sickle cell disease?" *Social Science & Medicine* 52 (2001): 1403–16.

Obiechina, Emmanuel N. *Language and Theme: Essays on African Literature*. Washington: Howard UP, 1990.

Obiego, Cosmas Okechukwu. *African Image of the Ultimate Reality: An Analysis of Igbo Ideas of Life and Death in Relation to Chukwu-God*. New York: Peter Lang, 1984.

Odinga, Sobukwe. "Chinua Achebe Interviewed." *Black Renaissance* 6. 2 (Spring 2005): 32-46.

Ogbar, Jeffrey O. G. *Black Power: Radical Politics and African American Identity*. Baltimore: The Johns Hopkins UP, 2004.

———. "Rainbow Radicalism: The Rise of the Radical Ethnic Nationalism." *The Black Power Movement: Rethinking the Civil Rights–Black Power Era*. Ed. Peniel E. Joseph. New York: Routledge, 2006. 193–228.

Ogunjuyigbe, Peter O. "Under-Five Mortality in Nigeria: Perception and Attitudes of the Yorubas towards the Existence of 'Abiku.'" *Demographic Research* 11.2 (Aug. 1994): 42–56.

Ogunyemi, Chikwenye Okonjo. "An Abiku-Ogbanje Atlas: A Pre-Text for Rereading Soyinka's *Aké* and Morrison's *Beloved*." *African American Review* 36.4 (2002): 663–78.

———. *Africa Wo/Man Palava: The Nigerian Novel by Women*. Chicago: U of Chicago P, 1996.

Ojo-Ade, Femi, ed. *Of Dreams Deferred, Dead or Alive: African Perspectives on African American Writers*. Westport, Connecticut: Greenwood , 1996.

Okonji, M Ogbolu. "Ogbanje: (An African Conception of Predestination)." *African Scholar* 1.4 (1970): 1–2.

Okonkwo, Chidi. *Decolonization Agonistics in Postcolonial African Fiction*. New York: St. Martin's P, 1999.

Okonkwo, Christopher N. "The Spirit-Child as Idiom: Reading *Ogbanje* Dialogic as a Platform of Conversation among Four Black Women's Novels." Ph.D. diss. Florida State University, 2001.

———. "A Critical Divination: Reading *Sula* as Ogbanje-Abiku." *African American Review*. 38.4 (Winter 2004): 651–68.

———. "Of Caul and Response: *Baby of the Family,* Ansa's Neglected Metafiction of the Veil of Blackness." *CLA Journal* 49.2 (Dec. 2005): 144–67.

———. "'It Was Like Meeting an Old Friend': An Interview with John Edgar Wideman." *Callaloo* 29.2 (2006): 347–60.

Okri, Ben. *The Famished Road.* 1991. New York: Anchor Books, 1993.

———. *Songs of Enchantment.* 1993. New York: Anchor Books, 1994.

———. *Infinite Riches.* London: Phoenix House, 1998.

Onabamiro, Sanya Dojo. *Why Our Children Die: the Causes, and Suggestions for Prevention, of Infant Mortality in West Africa.* London: Methuen, 1949.

Onwubalili, James K. "Sickle cell anemia: an exploration for the ancient myth of reincarnation in Nigeria." *The Lancet.* 8348 (August 1983): 503–5.

Onwuka, Chegwe, Austin. "Re-Incarnation: A Socio-religious Phenomenon among the Ibo-Speaking Riverines of the Lower Niger." *Cashiers des Religions Africaines* 7.13 (1973): 113–37.

Opoku, Kofi Asare. "Death and Immortality in the African Religious Heritage." *Death and Immortality in the Religions of the World.* Ed. Paula and Linda Badham. New York: Paragon House, 1987. 9–21.

Oruene, Taiwo. "Magical Powers of Twins in the Socio-Religious Beliefs of the Yoruba." *Folklore* 96.2 (1985): 208–16.

Osundare, Niyi. "The Poem as a Mytho-linguistic Event: A Study of Soyinka's 'Abiku.'" *Oral and Written Poetry in African Literature Today.* Ed. Eldred Jones et al. 16. London: James Currey, 1989. 90–102.

Ottenberg, Simon. "Ibo Receptivity to Change." *Continuity and Change in African Cultures.* Ed. William R. Bascom and Melville J. Herskovits. Chicago: U of Chicago P, 1959. 130–43.

———. *Double Descent in an African Society: The Afikpo Village-Group.* Seattle: U of Washington P, 1968.

Ouloguem, Yambo. *Bound to Violence.* 1968. Oxford: Heinemann Educational Publishers, 1971.

Oyedale, E. O. "Evil in Yoruba Religion and Culture." *Evil and the Response of World Religion.* Ed. William Cenkner. St. Paul: Paragon House, 1997. 157–69.

Page, Philip. "John Edgar Wideman. *The Cattle Killing.*" Review. *African American Review* 32.2 (Summer 1998): 362–63.

———. *Reclaiming Community in Contemporary African American Fiction.* Jackson: UP of Mississippi, 1999.

Parrinder, Geoffrey D. D. *West African Religion: A Study of the Beliefs and Practices of Akan, Ewe, Yoruba, Ibo, and Kindred Peoples.* London: The Epworth P, 1961.

Parry, Benita. "The Presence of the Past in Peripheral Modernities." *Beyond the Black Atlantic: Relocating Modernization and Technology.* Ed. Walter Goebel and Saskia Schabio. London: Routledge, 2006. 13–28.

Parsons, Elsie Clews. *Folk-lore of the Sea Islands, South Carolina.* Cambridge: The American Folk-Lore Society, 1923.

Paton, Huey P. *Revolutionary Suicide.* New York: Ballantine Books, 1973.

Pattern, M. Drake. "African-American Spiritual Beliefs: An Archeological Testimony from the Slave Quarter." *Wonders of the Invisible World.* Ed. Peter Benes. 44–52.

Patterson, Orlando. *Slavery and Social Death: A Comparative Study.* Cambridge, Massachusetts: Harvard UP, 1982.

———. *Freedom in the Making of Western Culture.* New York: Basic Books, 1991.

Peach, Linden. *Toni Morrison.* New York: St. Martin's P, 1995.

Peaco, Ed. "*The Cattle Killing.*" Review. *Antioch Review* 55.2 (Spring 1997): 235–36.

Peires, J. B. *The Dead Will Rise: Nongqawuse and the Great Cattle-Killing Movement of 1856–7.* Johannesburg: Ravan P, 1989.

Pelton, Robert D. *The Trickster in West Africa: A Study of Mythic Irony and Sacred Delight.* Berkeley: U of California P, 1980.

Perry, Phyllis Alesia. *Stigmata.* New York: Hyperion, 1998.

Personi, Michele. "'She was laughing at their God': Discovering the Goddess Within *Sula.*" *African American Review* 29.3 (1995): 439–51.

Petry, Ann. "Like a Winding Sheet." *Call and Response: The Riverside Anthology of the African American Literary Tradition.* Ed. Patricia Hill Collins et al. Boston: Houghton Mifflin Co., 1998. 1031–37.

Pfeiffer, John R. "Octavia Estelle Butler." *Science Fiction Writers (Second Ed.): Critical Studies of the Major Authors from the Early Nineteenth Century to the Present Day.* Ed. Richard Bleiler. New York: Macmillan Publishing USA, 1999. 147–58.

Phillips, Ulrich B. *Life and Labor in the Old South.* Boston: Little, Brown and Co., 1929.

Piersen, William D. "White Cannibals, Black Martyrs: Fear, Depression, and Religious Faith as Causes of Suicide Among New Slaves." *The Journal of Negro History* 62.2 (Apr. 1977): 147–59.

Pollitzer, William S. *The Gullah People and their African Heritage.* Athens: U of Georgia P, 1999.

Popoola, Solagbade S. "Abiku—The Recurring Birth-Mortality Syndrome." *Orunmila* 2 (9 June 1986): 22–25.

Potts, Stephen W. "'We Keep Playing the Same Record': A Conversation with Octavia E. Butler." *Science Fiction Studies* 23.3 (Nov. 1996): 331–38.

Prahlad, Anand. *The Greenwood Encyclopedia of African American Folklore.* 3 vols. Westport, Connecticut: Greenwood P, 2006.

Presson, Rebekah. "John Edgar Wideman." *Conversations with John Edgar Wideman.* 1998. 105–12.

Prince, Valerie Sweeney. *Burnin' Down the House: Home in African American Literature.* New York: Columbia UP, 2004.

Puckett, Newbell Niles. *Folk Beliefs of the Southern Negro.* Chapel Hill: The U of North Carolina P, 1926.

Quayson, Ato. *Strategic Transformations in Nigerian Writing.* Oxford: James Currey, 1997.

———. "Modernism and Postmodernism in African Literature." *The Cambridge History of African and Caribbean Literature.* Vol. 2. Ed. F. Abiola Irele and Simon Gikandi. 2004. 824–54.

Raboteau, Albert J. *Slave Religion: The "Invisible Institution" in the Antebellum South.* Oxford: Oxford UP, 1978.

Reed, Ishmael. "Introduction" and ed. *19 Necromancers from Now.* New York: Doubleday and Co. 1970. 12–27.

———. *Mumbo Jumbo.* New York: Atheneum, 1972.

———. *Flight to Canada.* New York: Random House, 1976.

Reimonenq, Alden. "Snail." *African American Review* 27.2 (Summer 1993): 237–42.

Renne, Elisha P. *Cloth that Does Not Die: The Meaning of Cloth in Bùnú Social Life.* Seattle: U of Washington P, 1995.

Rice, Alan. "'Who's Eating Whom': The Discourse of Cannibalism in the Literature of the Black Atlantic from Equiano's *Travels* to Toni Morrison's *Beloved.*" *Research in African Literatures* 29.4 (Winter 1998): 106–21.

Roberts, John W. *From Trickster to Badman: The Black Folk Hero in Slavery and Freedom.* Philadelphia: U of Pennsylvania P, 1989.

Rodgers, Lawrence R. *Canaan Bound: The African American Great Migration Novel.* Chicago: U of Illinois P, 1997.

Rodney, Walter. *How Europe Underdeveloped Africa.* Washington, DC: Howard UP, 1981.

Rosenthal, Judy. "Foreign Tongues and Domestic Bodies: Gendered Cultural Regions and Regionalized Scared Flows." *Gendered Encounters: Challenging Cultural Boundaries and Social Hierarchies in Africa.* Ed. Maria Grosz-Ngate and Omari H. Kokole. New York: Routledge, 1997. 183–203.

Rowell, Charles H. "An Interview with Octavia E. Butler." *Callaloo* 20.1 (1997): 47–66.

Rushdy, Ashraf H. A. *Neo-Slave Narratives: Studies in the Social Logic of a Literary Form.* New York: Oxford UP, 1999.

———. "Neo-Slave Narrative." *The Oxford Companion to African American Literature.* Ed. William L. Andrews et al. New York: Oxford UP, 1997. 533–35.

Rutledge, Gregory E. "Science Fiction and the Black Power/Arts Movements: The Transpositional Cosmology of Samuel R. Delany Jr." *Extrapolation* 41.2 (Summer 2000): 127–42.

Salvaggio, Ruth. "Octavia Butler and the Black Science-Fiction Heroine." *Black American Literature Forum* 18.2 Science Fiction Issue (Summer 1984): 78–81.

———. "Octavia E. Butler." *Suzy McKee Charnas. Octavia Butler. Joan D. Vinge.* Ed. Marleen S. Barr et al. Mercer Island, Washington: Starmont House, 1986. 1–43.

Saunders, Charles R. "Why Blacks Should Read (and Write) Science Fiction." *Dark Matter: A Century of Speculative Fiction from the African Diaspora.* Ed. Sheree R. Thomas. New York: Warner Books, 2000. 398–404.

Savitt, Todd L. "Smothering and Overlaying of Virginia Slave Children: A Suggested Explanation." *Bulletin of the History of Medicine* 49.3 (Fall 1975): 400–404.

———. *Medicine and Slavery: The Diseases and Health Care of Blacks in Antebellum Virginia.* Urbana: U of Illinois P, 1978.

Schroeder, Walter A., et al. "Sickle Cell Anaemia, Genetic Variations, and the Slave Trade to the United States." *The Journal of African History* 31.2 (1990): 163–80.

Senanu, K. E., and Theo Vincent, eds. *A Selection of African Poetry*. 2nd ed. London: Longman, 1988.

Sengupta, Somini. "Chinua Achebe: A Literary Diaspora Toasts One of Its Own." *USAfrica* online. <http://www.usafricaonline.com/achebe70.html> 28 May, 2005

Shinn, Thelma J. "The Wise Witches: Black Women Mentors in the Fiction of Octavia E. Butler." *Conjuring: Black Women, Fiction, and Literary Tradition*. Ed. Marjorie Pryse and Hortense J. Spillers. Bloomington: Indiana UP, 1985. 203–15.

———. *Worlds Within Women: Myth and Mythmaking in Fantastic Literature by Women*. New York: Greenwood P, 1986.

Silverblatt, Michael. "Interview with John Edgar Wideman about *Fatheralong*." *Conversations with John Edgar Wideman*. Ed. Bonnie TuSmith. Jackson: UP of Mississippi, 1998. 158–64.

Simpson, George Eaton. *Black Religions in the New World*. New York: Columbia UP, 1978.

Siwek, Paul S. J. *The Philosophy of Evil*. New York: The Ronald P Co., 1951.

Slotkin, Richard. "Narratives of Negro Crime in New England, 1650–1800." *American Quarterly* 25.1 (Mar. 1973): 3–31.

Smethurst, James Edward. *The Black Arts Movement: Literary Nationalism in the 1960s and 1970s*. Chapel Hill: The U of North Carolina P, 2005.

Smith, Patricia. "Getting Under Our Skin." *Conversations with John Edgar Wideman*. Ed. Bonnie TuSmith. Jackson: UP of Mississippi, 1998. 139–44.

Smitherman, Geneva. *Talkin and Testifyin: The Language of Black America*. Boston: Houghton Mifflin Co., 1977.

———. *Black Talk: Words and Phrases from the Hood to the Amen Corner*. Boston: Houghton Mifflin, 1994.

Snead, James A. "Repetition as a Figure of Black Culture." *African American Literary Criticism, 1773 to 2000*. Ed. Hazel Arnett Ervin. New York: Twayne P, 1999. 206–22.

Sobel, Mechal. *Trabelin' On: The Slave Journey to an Afro-Baptist Faith*. Westport, CT: Greenwood P, 1979.

Soyinka, Wole. *A Dance of the Forests*. 1960. In *Collected Plays 1*. Oxford: Oxford UP, 1973

———. *Idanre and Other Poems*. London: Methuen, 1967.

———. *Myth, Literature and the African World*. Cambridge: Cambridge UP, 1976.

———. *Aké: The Years of Childhood*. New York: Aventura, 1981.

———. "Abiku." *The Penguin Book of Modern African Poetry*. Ed. Gerald Moore and Ulli Beier. London: Penguin Books, 1998. 251–52.

Spaulding, A. Timothy. *Re-Forming the Past: History, the Fantastic, and the Postmodern Slave Narrative*. Columbus: The Ohio State UP, 2005.

Springer, Kimberly. "Black Feminists Respond to Black Power Masculinism." *The Black Power Movement: Rethinking the Civil-Rights-Black Power Era*. Ed. Peniel E. Joseph. New York: Routledge, 2006. 105–18.

Stapleton, Timothy J. " 'They No Longer Care for Their Chiefs': Another Look at the Xhosa Cattle-Killing of 1856–1857." *International Journal of African Historical Studies* 24.2 (1991): 383–92.

Starling, Marion Wilson. *The Slave Narrative: Its Place in American History.* Second Edition. Washington: Howard UP, 1988.

Stave, Shirley A. "Introduction" and ed. *Toni Morrison and the Bible: Contested Intertextualities.* New York: Peter Lang, 2006. 1–7.

Steckel, Richard H. "A Dreadful Childhood: The Excess Mortality of American Slaves." *Social Science History* 10.4 (Winter 1986): 427–65.

Stepto, Robert B. "'Intimate Things in Place': A Conversation with Toni Morrison." *The Massachusetts Review* 3 (Autumn 1977): 473–89.

——. *From Behind the Veil : A Study of Afro-American Narrative.* 1979. Second ed. Urbana: U of Illinois P, 1991.

Stevenson, Ian. "The Belief in Reincarnation Among the Igbo of Nigeria." *Journal of Asian and African Studies* 20.1–2 (1985): 13–30.

——. "Characteristics of Cases of the Reincarnation Type among the Igbo of Nigeria." *Journal of Asian and African Studies* 21.3–4 (1986): 205–16.

——. *Children Who Remember Previous Lives: A Question of Reincarnation.* Charlottesville: UP of Virginia, 1987.

——. *Where Reincarnation and Biology Intersect.* Westport, CT: Praeger, 1997.

Stewart, Dianne M. *Three Eyes for the Journey: African Dimensions of Jamaican Religious Experience.* New York: Oxford UP, 2005.

Stewart, James T. "The Development of the Black Revolutionary Artist." *Black Fire: An Anthology of Afro-American Writing.* Ed. LeRoi Jones and Larry Neal. New York: William Morrow and Co., 1968. 3–10.

Stewart Julia. *African Names: Names from the African Continent for Children and Adults.* New York: Citadel Press, 1993.

Stuckey, Sterling. *Slave Culture: Nationalist Theory and the Foundations of Black America.* New York : Oxford UP, 1987.

Styron, William. *The Confessions of Nat Turner.* 1966. New York: Vintage International, 1993.

Sullivan III, C. W. "Folklore and Fantastic Fiction." *Western Folklore* 60.4 (Fall 2000): 279–96.

Sundquist, Eric J. *To Wake the Nations: Race in the Making of American Literature.* Cambridge: The Belknap P of Harvard UP, 1993.

Taiwo, Oladele. "Two Incantations to 'Abiku.'" *Nigeria Magazine* 106 (1970): 219–24.

Takaki, Ronald T. *Iron Cages: Race and Culture in Nineteenth-Century America.* New York: Alfred A. Knopf, 1979.

Talbot, D. Amaury. *Women's Mysteries of a Primitive People: The Ibibios of Southern Nigeria.* London: Cass and Co., 1968.

Talbot, Percy Amaury. *Tribes of the Niger Delta: Their Religions and Customs.* New York: Barnes and Noble, 1967.

Tate, Claudia, ed. and "Toni Morrison." *Black Women Writers at Work.* New York: Continuum, 1983. 117–131.

ten Kortenaar, Neil. "Oedipus, Ogbanje, and the Sons of Independence." *Research in African Literatures* 38.2 (Summer 2007): 181–205.

Thompson, Robert Farris. *Flash of the Spirit: African and Afro-American Art and Philosophy.* New York: Vintage Books, 1983.

Tolnay, Stewart E., and E. M. Beck. *A Festival of Violence: An Analysis of Southern Lynchings, 1882–1930.* Urbana: U of Illinois P, 1995.

Toomer, Jean. *Cane.* New York: Liveright, 1923.

Trinh T. Min-ha. *Woman, Native, Other: Writing Postcoloniality and Feminism.* Bloomington: Indiana UP, 1989.

TuSmith, Bonnie. "Benefit of the Doubt" and ed. *Conversations with John Edgar Wideman.* 1998. 195–220.

———. "Optical Tricksterism: Dissolving and Shapeshifting in the Works of John Edgar Wideman." *Critical Essays on John Edgar Wideman.* Ed. Bonnie TuSmith and Keith E. Byerman. Knoxville: U of Tennessee P, 2006. 243–58.

Tutuola, Amos. *The Palm-Wine Drinkard* and *My Life in the Bush of Ghosts.* New York: Grove P, 1994.

Twining, Mary A., and Keith E. Baird, eds. *Sea Island Roots: African Presence in the Carolinas and Georgia.* Trenton, NJ : Africa World P, 1991.

Ubahakwe, Ebo. *Igbo Names: Their Structure and Their Meanings.* Ibadan: Daystar P, 1981.

Uchendu, Victor. *The Igbo of Southeast Nigeria.* New York: Holt, Rinehart and Winston, 1965.

Ukwu, U. I. "Markets in Iboland." B. W. Hodder and U. I. Ukwu. *Markets in West Africa: Studies of Markets and Trade among the Yoruba and Ibo.* Ibadan: Ibadan UP, 1969. 111–41.

Umeh, John Anenechukwu. *After God is Dibia: Igbo Cosmology, Healing, Divination and Sacred Science in Nigeria* (vol. 2). London: Karnak House, 1997–1999.

Una Mclean, Catherine M. "Traditional Healers and Their Female Clients: An Aspect of Nigerian Sickness Behavior." *Journal of Health and Social Behavior* 10.3 (Sept. 1969): 172–86.

Uzukwu, Elochukwu E. *Worship as Body Language: Introduction to Christian Worship: An African Orientation.* Collegeville, Minn.: The Liturgical P, 1997.

Van Deburg, William L. *New Day in Babylon: The Black Power Movement and American Culture, 1965–1975.* Chicago: The U of Chicago P, 1992.

Vickery, John B. "Literature and Myth." *Literary Criticism and Myth.* Ed. Robert A. Segal. New York: Garland Publishing, 1996. 283–305.

Vickory, Laurie. "The Force Outside/The Force Inside: Mother Love and Regenerative Spaces in *Sula* and *Beloved.*" *Obsidian II: Black Literature in Review* 8.2 (Fall–Winter 1993): 28–45.

Wall, Cheryl A. "Introduction: Taking Positions and and Changing Words" and ed. *Changing Our Own Words: Essays on Criticism, Theory, and Writing by Black Women.* 1989. New Brunswick: Rutgers UP, 1991. 1–15.

Wallace, Michelle. *Black Macho and the Myth of the Superwoman.* New York: Dial P, 1979.

Walker, Alice. *In Search of Our Mothers' Gardens: Womanist Prose.* San Diego: Harcourt Brace Jovanovich, 1983.

———. *Meridian.* New York: Washington Square Press, 1976.

Walker, Clarence E. *A Rock in a Weary Land: The African Methodist Episcopal Church During the Civil War and Reconstruction.* Baton Rouge: Louisiana UP, 1982.

Walker, Margaret. *Jubilee.* 1966. Boston: A Bantam Book, 1967.

Walsh, Lorena S. *From Calabar to Carter's Grove: the History of a Virginia Slave Community.* Charlottesville: UP of Virginia, 1997.

Walters, Wendy W. "'One of Dese Mornings, Bright and Fair,/Take My Wings and Cleave De Air': The Legend of the Flying Africans and Diasporic Consciousness." *MELUS* 22.3. Varieties of Ethnic Criticism (Autumn 1997): 3–29.

Warner-Lewis, Maureen. *Guinea's Other Suns: The African Dynamic in Trinidad Culture.* Dover, MA: Majority P, 1991.

Warren, Christian. "Northern Chills, Southern Fevers: Race-Specific Mortality in American Cities, 1730–1900." *The Journal of Southern History* 63.1 (February 1997): 23–56.

Washington, Mary Helen. "Re(Visions): Black Women Writers—Their Texts, Their Readers, Their Critics," ed. *Black-Eyed Susan/Midnight Birds: Stories By and About Black Women.* New York: Anchor Books, 1990. 3–15.

Washington, Teresa N. *Our Mothers, Our Powers, Our Texts: Manifestations of Àjé in Africana Literature.* Bloomington: Indiana UP, 2005.

———. "The Mother-Daughter Àjé Relationship in Toni Morrison's *Beloved.*" *African American Review* 39.1–2 (2005): 171–88.

Weisenburger, Steven. *Modern Medea: A Family Story of Slavery and Child-Murder from the Old South.* New York: Hill and Wang, 1998.

Werner, Craig Hansen. *Playing the Changes: From Afro-Modernism to the Jazz Impulse.* Urbana: U of Illinois P, 1994.

Wessling, Joseph H. "Narcissism in Toni Morrison's *Sula.*" *College Language Association Journal* 31.3 (March 1988): 281–98.

West, Cornel. *Race Matters.* Boston: Beacon P, 2003.

White, Armon. *Rebel For the Hell of It: The Life of Tupac Shakur.* New York: Thunder's Mouth P, 1997.

Wicker, Kathleen O'Brien. "Mami Water in African Religion and Spirituality." *African Spirituality: Forms, Meanings, and Expressions.* Ed. Jacob K. Olupona. New York: A Herder and Herder Book, 2000. 198–222.

Wideman, John Edgar. *Hurry Home.* New York: Harcourt Brace Jovanovich, 1970.

———. "Charles Chesnutt and the WPA Narratives: The Oral and Literate Roots of Afro- American Literature." *The Slave's Narrative.* Ed. Charles Davis and Henry Louis Gates Jr. New York: Oxford UP, 1985. 59–77.

———. *Brothers and Keepers.* New York: Vintage Books, 1995.

———. "Damballah." *Damballah.* 1981. New York: Vintage Books, 1988. 15–26.

———. *Hiding Place.* 1981. New York: Vintage Books, 1988.

———. *Sent for You Yesterday.* 1983. New York: Vintage Books, 1988.

———. *Reuben.* New York: Penguin Books, 1988.

———. "Fever." *Fever: Twelve Stories.* New York: H. Holt, 1989. 127–61.

———. *Philadelphia Fire.* New York: Holt, 1990.

———. "Preface." *Breaking Ice: An Anthology of Contemporary African-American Fiction.* Ed. Terry McMillan. 1990. v–x.

———. "The Architectonics of Fiction." *Callaloo* 13.1 (Winter 1990): 42–46.

———. *All Stories are True.* 1992. New York: Vintage Contemporaries, 1993.

———. *The Cattle Killing.* Boston: Houghton Mifflin Co., 1996.

———. *Two Cities.* Boston: Houghton Mifflin Co., 1998.

———. *Hoop Roots.* Boston: Houghton Mifflin Co., 2001.

———. Private Interview: Monday, July 5, 2004.

———. "Weight." *God's Gym.* Boston: Houghton Mifflin Co., 2005. 1–16.

Wilentz, Gay. "If You Surrender to the Air: Folk Legends of Flight and Resistance in African American Literature." *MELUS* 16.1. Folklore and Orature (Spring 1989–Spring 1990): 21–32.

———. *Binding Cultures: Black Women Writers in Africa and the Diaspora.* Bloomington: Indiana UP, 1992.

———. "An African-Based Reading of *Sula.*" *Approaches to Teaching the Novels of Toni Morrison.* Ed. Nellie McKay and Earle Kathryn. New York: Modern Language Association of America, 1997. 127–34.

———. "'What Is Africa to Me?': Reading the African Cultural Base of (African) American Literary History." *American Literary History* 15.3 (2003): 639–53.

Wilkinson, Jane. "Wole Soyinka." *Talking with African Writers: Interviews with African Poets, Playwrights and Novelists.* London: James Currey, 1992. 91–108.

Williams, Eric. *Capitalism and Slavery.* 1944. London: Andre Deutsch, 1964.

Williams, Sherley Anne. *Dessa Rose.* 1986. New York: Berkley Books, 1987.

Wilson, August. *Joe Turner's Come and Gone.* New York: New American Library, 1988.

Wood, Peter H. *Black Majority: Negroes in Colonial South Carolina from 1670 through the Stono Rebellion.* New York: Alfred A. Knopf, 1974.

Woodward, C. Vann. "History from Slave Sources." *The Slave's Narrative.* Ed. Charles T. Davis and Henry Louis Gates Jr. New York: Oxford UP, 1985. 78–98.

Wright, Jonathan. "Demonology and Medicine." *The Scientific Monthly* 4.6 (June 1917): 494–508.

Wright, Richard. [Review of *Their Eyes Were Watching God.*] 1937. *Zora Neale Hurston: Critical Perspectives Past and Present.* Ed. Gates and Appiah. New York: Amistad, 1993. 16–17.

———. "Long Black Song." *Uncle Tom's Children.* 1936. New York: Harper Perennial, 1989. 125–56.

———. *Native Son.* New York: Harper, 1940.

Wright, W. D. "The Modernity and Postmodernity Deceptions." *Black Intellectuals, Black Cognition and a Black Aesthetic.* Westport, Connecticut: Praeger, 1997. 81–128.

Index

A Spirit of Dialogue was designed and typeset on a Macintosh OS computer system using InDesign software. The body text is set in 10/13.5 Garamond Premier Pro and display type is set in Garamond Premier Pro. This book was designed and typeset by Kelly Gray and manufactured by Thomson-Shore, Inc.